T0265410

BLOCKCHAIN TECHNOLOGY FOR EMERGING APPLICATIONS

Hybrid Computational
Intelligence for Pattern Analysis
and Understanding Series

BLOCKCHAIN TECHNOLOGY FOR EMERGING APPLICATIONS

A Comprehensive Approach

Series Editors

SIDDHARTHA BHATTACHARYYA

NILANJAN DEY

Edited by

SK HAFIZUL ISLAM

Department of Computer Science and Engineering,
Indian Institute of Information Technology Kalyani,
Kalyani, West Bengal, India

ARUP KUMAR PAL

Department of Computer Science and Engineering,
Indian Institute of Technology (Indian School of Mines) Dhanbad,
Jharkhand, India

DEBABRATA SAMANTA

Department of Computer Science,
CHRIST University, Bangalore, Karnataka, India

SIDDHARTHA BHATTACHARYYA

Rajnagar Mahavidyalaya, Birbhum, West Bengal, India

ACADEMIC PRESS

An imprint of Elsevier

Academic Press is an imprint of Elsevier
125 London Wall, London EC2Y 5AS, United Kingdom
525 B Street, Suite 1650, San Diego, CA 92101, United States
50 Hampshire Street, 5th Floor, Cambridge, MA 02139, United States
The Boulevard, Langford Lane, Kidlington, Oxford OX5 1GB, United Kingdom

Notices
Knowledge and best practice in this field are constantly changing. As new research
and experience broaden our understanding, changes in research methods, professional
practices, or medical treatment may become necessary.

Practitioners and researchers must always rely on their own experience and knowledge
in evaluating and using any information, methods, compounds, or experiments
described herein. In using such information or methods they should be mindful of
their own safety and the safety of others, including parties for whom they have a
professional responsibility.

To the fullest extent of the law, neither the Publisher nor the authors, contributors, or
editors, assume any liability for any injury and/or damage to persons or property as a
matter of products liability, negligence or otherwise, or from any use or operation of
any methods, products, instructions, or ideas contained in the material herein.

ISBN: 978-0-323-90193-2

For information on all Academic Press publications visit our website
at https://www.elsevier.com/books-and-journals

Publisher: Mara Conner
Editorial Project Manager: Franchezca A. Cabural
Production Project Manager: Maria Bernard
Cover Designer: Christian J Bilbow

Working together
to grow libraries in
developing countries

www.elsevier.com • www.bookaid.org

Typeset by TNQ Technologies

Dr. SK Hafizul Islam would like to dedicate this volume to his Son, Mr. Enayat Rabbi, and his Wife, Mrs. Sabina Yasmin.

Dr. Arup Kumar Pal would like dedicate this volume to his daughters Deeptika, and Oyshee.

Dr. Debabrata Samanta would like to dedicate this volume to his parents, Mr. Dulal Chandra Samanta, Mrs. Ambujini Samanta, elder sister, Mrs. Tanusree Samanta, and daughter, Ms. Aditri Samanta.

Dr. Siddhartha Bhattacharyya would like to dedicate this volume to his teaching and non-teaching colleagues at Rajnagar Mahavidyalaya, Birbhum, India.

Contents

Contributors   xiii

Preface   xvii

1. Blockchain architecture, taxonomy, challenges, and applications   1

Nisanth Reddy Kasi, Ramani S and Marimuthu Karuppiah

  1. Introduction to blockchain   1
  2. History of blockchain   5
  3. Benefits over traditional technologies   6
  4. Blockchain architecture   8
  5. Evolution of blockchain in fields other than cryptocurrency   18
  6. Challenges of blockchain   19
  7. Applications of blockchain   22
  8. Conclusion and future scope   28
  References   29

2. Blockchain: a new perspective in cyber technology   33

T. Venkat Narayana Rao, Purva Pravin Likhar, Muralidhar Kurni
and K. Saritha

  1. Introduction   33
  2. Blockchain architecture   35
  3. Blockchain concepts   38
  4. Consensus algorithms   43
  5. Blockchain validity   50
  6. Blockchain attacks   51
  7. Merkle trees   52
  8. How secure is blockchain?   53
  9. Challenges and recent advances   54
 10. Emerging applications of blockchain   56
 11. Conclusion and future scope   64
  References   65

3. Characteristics, advances, and challenges in blockchain-enabled cyber-physical systems   **67**

Manohar Sai Burra and Soumyadev Maity

1. Introduction   67
2. Background of CPS   69
3. Background of blockchain   73
4. Blockchain-enabled cyber-physical systems   75
5. Characteristics of blockchain-enabled CPS systems   80
6. Challenges in blockchain-enabled CPS systems   83
7. Conclusion and future scope   85
References   85

4. A novel secured ledger platform for real-time transactions   **91**

Debarka Mukhopadhyay, Tanmay Chakraborty, Anirban Saha and Ritam Mukherjee

1. Introduction   91
2. Proposed work   95
3. Result and discussion   100
4. Use cases   100
5. Conclusion   103
References   103

5. Blockchain for intrusion detection systems   **107**

Tanmay Shetty, Saloni Negi, Anushka Kulshrestha, Shaifali Choudhary, Ramani S and Marimuthu Karuppiah

1. Introduction   107
2. Intrusion detection system   109
3. About blockchain   112
4. Host-based intrusion detection system   119
5. Blockchain-based intrusion detection   120
6. Collaborative intrusion detection system   122
7. Applications of IDS: Snort   125
8. Limitations   130
9. Comparison with firewalls   134
10. Conclusion and future scope   134
References   134

6. Blockchain for IoT-based medical delivery drones: state of the art, issues, and future prospects   **137**

Partha Pratim Ray and Dinesh Dash

Nomenclature   137
1. Introduction   137
2. Related works   140
3. Drone suppliers for medical delivery   145
4. Blockchain-IoT aware drone-based medical delivery   149
5. Key issues and future direction   162
6. Conclusion   168
References   169

7. Blockchain for digital rights management   **177**

Ramani S, Sri Vishva E, Lakshit Dua, Arya Abrol and
Marimuthu Karuppiah

1. Introduction   177
2. Illustrations   179
3. DRM requirement   180
4. Parts of a traditional DRM   182
5. Compatibility of blockchain for DRM   185
6. Various cryptographic hash functions in blockchain   186
7. Methodologies and technology in use   188
8. Effects and applications of using blockchain in DRM   190
9. Methodologies for coupling DRM with blockchain   194
10. Advantages of integrating blockchain with digital content   198
11. Limitation of blockchain in DRM   201
12. Conclusion and future research   202
References   203

8. Blockchain technology in biomanufacturing: Current perspective and future challenges   **207**

Muskan Pandey and Barkha Singhal

Abbreviations   207
1. Introduction   208
2. Conception and functionality of blockchain   210
3. Why blockchain is needed in biomanufacturing   212

    4. Key elements of blockchain that are required in biomanufacturing   213

    5. Various avenues of utility of blockchain technology in biomanufacturing   216

    6. Applications of blockchain technology in biomanufacturing (case studies)   221

    7. Blockchain technology as a prospective tool for bioeconomy   226

    8. Current progress   227

    9. Proposed model of biomanufacturing through "FabRec" platform   228

    10. Current challenges   230

    11. Future prospects   231

    12. Conclusion   232

    Acknowledgment   233

    References   233

9. Blockchain-based e-voting protocols   239

Srijanee Mookherji, Odelu Vanga and Rajendra Prasath

    1. Introduction   239

    2. Electronic voting   242

    3. Distributed e-voting   250

    4. Conclusion   261

    References   261

10. Influence of blockchain technology in pharmaceutical industries   267

T. Poongodi, S. Sudhakar Ilango, Vaishali Gupta and Sanjeev Kumar Prasad

    1. Introduction   267

    2. Drug supply chain management in the smart pharmaceutical industry   278

    3. Blockchain technology to prevent counterfeit drugs   283

    4. Blockchain use cases and its applications in the pharmaceutical industry   290

    5. Open Challenges related to blockchain in the pharmaceutical industry   291

    6. Future direction   293

    7. Conclusion   293

    References   294

11. A forefront insight into the integration of AI and blockchain technologies   **297**

Muralidhar Kurni, K. Saritha, D. Nagadevi and K. Somasena Reddy

  1. The rise of blockchain technology   297
  2. Artificial intelligence   299
  3. The arrival of AI in blockchain   301
  4. The possibilities of AI integrated with blockchain   305
  5. Applications of AI and blockchain   308
  6. Challenges of merging AI and blockchain   310
  7. The integration of AI and blockchain for industry 4.0   311
  8. How the app development industry is using blockchain and AI integration to innovate   312
  9. Blockchain and AI building a powerful match   313
10. Conclusion   319
References   319

Index   321

Contributors

Arya Abrol
School of Computer Science and Engineering, Vellore Institute of Technology, Vellore, Tamil Nadu, India

Manohar Sai Burra
Department of Information Technology, Indian Institute of Information Technology Allahabad, Prayagraj, Uttar Pradesh, India

Tanmay Chakraborty
Department of Electronics and Communication Engineering, School of Engineering and Technology, Adamas University, Kolkata, West Bengal, India

Shaifali Choudhary
School of Computer Science and Engineering, Vellore Institute of Technology, Vellore, Tamil Nadu, India

Dinesh Dash
Department of Computer Science and Engineering, National Institute of Technology Patna, Patna, Bihar, India

Lakshit Dua
School of Computer Science and Engineering, Vellore Institute of Technology, Vellore, Tamil Nadu, India

Vaishali Gupta
School of Computing Science and Engineering, Galgotias University, Greater Noida, Delhi-NCR, India

S. Sudhakar Ilango
School of Computer Science and Engineering, VIT-AP University, Amaravati, Andhra Pradesh, India

Marimuthu Karuppiah
Department of Computer Science and Engineering, SRM Institute of Science and Technology, Delhi-NCR Campus, Ghaziabad, Uttar Pradesh, India

Nisanth Reddy Kasi
School of Computer Science and Engineering, Vellore Institute of Technology, Vellore, Tamil Nadu, India

Anushka Kulshrestha
School of Computer Science and Engineering, Vellore Institute of Technology, Vellore, Tamil Nadu, India

Muralidhar Kurni
Department of Computer Science, School of Science, GITAM (Deemed to be Univerity), Hyderabad, Telangana, India

Purva Pravin Likhar
Mahatma Gandhi Institute of Technology, Hyderabad, Telangana, India

Soumyadev Maity
Department of Information Technology, Indian Institute of Information Technology
Allahabad, Prayagraj, Uttar Pradesh, India

Srijanee Mookherji
Indian Institute of Information Technology, Sri City, Andhra Pradesh, India

Ritam Mukherjee
Department of Computer Science and Engineering, School of Engineering and
Technology, Adamas University, Kolkata, West Bengal, India

Debarka Mukhopadhyay
Department of Computer Science and Engineering, School of Engineering and
Technology, Christ Deemed to be University, Bangalore, Karnataka, India

D. Nagadevi
Department of ECE, CBIT, Hyderabad, Telangana, India

Saloni Negi
School of Computer Science and Engineering, Vellore Institute of Technology, Vellore,
Tamil Nadu, India

Muskan Pandey
School of Biotechnology, Gautam Buddha University, Greater Noida, Uttar Pradesh,
India

T. Poongodi
School of Computing Science and Engineering, Galgotias University, Greater Noida,
Delhi-NCR, India

Sanjeev Kumar Prasad
School of Computing Science and Engineering, Galgotias University, Greater Noida,
Delhi-NCR, India

Rajendra Prasath
Indian Institute of Information Technology, Sri City, Andhra Pradesh, India

Partha Pratim Ray
Department of Computer Science and Engineering, National Institute of Technology
Patna, Patna, Bihar, India

Ramani S
School of Computer Science and Engineering, Vellore Institute of Technology, Vellore,
Tamil Nadu, India

Anirban Saha
Department of Computer Science and Engineering, School of Engineering and
Technology, Adamas University, Kolkata, West Bengal, India

K. Saritha
Sri Venkateswara Degree & PG College, Anantapur, Andhra Pradesh, India; Independent Researcher, Ananthapuram, Andhra Pradesh, India

Tanmay Shetty
School of Computer Science and Engineering, Vellore Institute of Technology, Vellore, Tamil Nadu, India

Barkha Singhal
School of Biotechnology, Gautam Buddha University, Greater Noida, Uttar Pradesh, India

K. Somasena Reddy
Department of CSE, JNTUACEA, Anantapur, Andhra Pradesh, India

Odelu Vanga
Indian Institute of Information Technology, Sri City, Andhra Pradesh, India

T. Venkat Narayana Rao
Department of Computer Science and Engineering, Sreenidhi Institute of Science and Technology, Hyderabad, Telangana, India

Sri Vishva E
School of Computer Science and Engineering, Vellore Institute of Technology, Vellore, Tamil Nadu, India

Preface

Blockchain technology has been the most promising alternative in recent years as far as distributed processing and storage of data are concerned. This volume presents the most recent theories and applications on the adjustment and execution of blockchain technology, progressively issue-based logical examination applications. The editors offer the fast headways in architecture, brilliant urban communities, digital physical frameworks, and web of things field. Blockchain-based information fortune in distributed computing and smart transportation frameworks are the main parts of this book. A few use cases with interruption identification frameworks, unmanned aeronautical vehicles, and online computer games are likewise fused. As blockchain for electronically casting a ballot framework and computerized right administration are moderate innovations and are utilized in numerous segments for dependable, savvy, and quick business exchanges, this book is an invited expansion on existing information. This book will address the engineering, plan objectives, difficulties, constraints, and potential answers for the blockchain-based notoriety frameworks. This book additionally joins in the examination of sanitation. It also focuses on the blockchain-based design perspectives of these intelligent architectures for evaluating and interpreting real-world trends. The chapters expand on different models that have shown considerable success in dealing with an extensive range of applications, despite their ability to extract complex hidden features and learn efficient representation in unsupervised environments for blockchain security pattern analysis.

The volume comprises 11 well-versed contributory chapters in different areas of blockchain technology.

Chapter 1 introduces the underlying technology, known as blockchain, of famous cryptocurrencies like Bitcoin. It starts by introducing the term blockchain, its analogies and characteristics. It then contains topics like history of blockchain and benefits of blockchain over traditional technologies. It emphasizes architecture of blockchain and various consensus mechanisms. The latter part of this chapter explores types of blockchain and the blockchain technology stack. It then lists various top blockchains used in contemporary days. It also explains various challenges of using blockchain such as energy consumption, scalability, public perception, etc. This chapter also explores the different types of attacks on blockchain.

The early days of cyberspace expansion saw many people become hesitant to use the internet facility due to two dominant reasons: obscurity and skepticism. The internet soon became a one-stop solution to a diverse range of sectors; a need to resolve issues such as data confidentiality and integrity gained prime importance. In 2008, an online currency called Bitcoin was launched by an anonymous developer or developer community called Satoshi Nakamoto, which was deemed to be a viable alternative to fiat or government-issued currency. What made Bitcoin famous and easily adaptable was the ease of accessibility in the form of a device application or simply "wallet" that included the nodes or "blocks" on which transaction data would be stored and processed instantaneously, and the intention behind it was to create a trustworthy cash system that would give individuals complete ownership of their transactions, not at risk of security breaches. With the advent and success of Bitcoin, new doors opened for other cryptocurrencies and digital assets like Ethereum and Litecoin, and it was observed that unlike fiduciary money, the sustainability of a thorough and transparent record must be maintained in connection with the exchange of digitalized money between any two parties whose anonymity would be preserved. Eventually, this became a turning point and marked the beginning of blockchain technology, which functioned as a distributed ledger system, ensuring secure transactions given its strong and complex cryptographic background strengthened with the help of hashing techniques and timestamps. Chapter 2 delves into this facet of blockchain technology in regard to cyber security.

A cyber-physical system (CPS) is a computer system that integrates real-world objects with embedded technologies to control and monitor physical processes. On the other hand, blockchain technology is a distributed, decentralized framework, which is the core concept behind Bitcoin. Blockchain technology can improve the reliability, security, and robustness of CPS-enabled critical infrastructure systems. Chapter 3 begins with a detailed overview of CPS and blockchain technology followed by a discussion on the various existing use cases of CPS applications.

Chapter 4 relates a new centralized ledger technology with a centralized validation process. It offers a single platform for all categories of real-time transactions and validations, unlike existing conventional blockchain technology. It offers three levels of hashing placed at the generator, server, and validator end for data security from data tampering and two levels of encryption for communication lines between generator-server and server-validator for packet security. This system ensures trustworthiness, authenticity, and CIA (confidentiality, integrity, and availability) to its end users while being real time in execution. The proposed system does not follow a chain-based file architecture. Due to this, no concept of chain break arises, and the problems that arise as a result of chain break in the blockchain are avoided.

Blockchain is a decentralized core architecture, which uses cryptographic validation, also known as hashing function, to link blocks with one another, and this linking plays a major role in ensuring the security, completeness, reliability, and accuracy of the data being stored and transparency in processing. Blockchain also provides a cryptographically safe and secure technique to obtain verified and immutable records in a chain that is chronologically ordered by discrete time stamps. These days, with almost everything becoming digital, the increasing rates of cyber threats, incidents, and policy violations have become a huge concern for organizations. It is only reasonable to use the vast variety of features that are offered by blockchain to assist intrusion detection systems (IDSs). IDSs are mainly used to monitor networks for malicious activities and report such activities. In Chapter 5, the authors discuss the different IDSs, the current situation of IDSs, and how to enhance the IDSs using blockchain.

The internet of things (IoT) has expanded the reachability of pervasive applications in different domains. Smart healthcare is one such area where IoT-based approaches have been successfully demonstrated in the recent past. However, issues related to the scaling of large ad-hoc elements is still a major challenge. Medical delivery drones have come up as a new variant of unmanned aerial vehicle (UAV) to pave holistic orientation into the smart health service paradigm. Lack of augmentation aware notions has resisted the realization of an actual intervention of IoT-based medical delivery via UAVs. Proper architectural frameworks and models are needed to efficiently integrate IoT with the medical delivery drones. However, major security drawbacks should be investigated a priori for health delivery services in coming days. One can use the blockchain-centric approaches to fill this gap in the IoT-based medical delivery drone ecosystem. In Chapter 6, the authors firstly present the details about the drone suppliers and perform a comparative analysis of such drones for medical delivery. Secondly, a state of the art on blockchain-assisted IoT-based drone-centric medical delivery is also presented. Finally, some of the key challenges associated with existing drone delivery mechanisms are highlighted.

A huge majority of digital media in today's age is consumed over the internet. Any digital content uploaded online is extremely vulnerable to leakage through piracy, illegal spread, and sharing of digital copies of files to users who have not paid for the content's consumption. Many times, authentication of content to trace back its source of spread fails due to the anonymity of the said source. The current system of centralized content distribution networks working in conjunction with digital rights management systems to provide and authenticate users consuming digital content is faulty and can be replaced with a far more robust peer-to-peer (P2P) system that operates on blockchain technology. Such a system is illustrated in Chapter 7, which would benefit consumers since content will no longer be held by a centralized server but rather be decentralized geographically, ensuring availability through physical hindrances such as natural disasters or digital blockages such as distributed denial of service attacks, etc. The system will also help digital content creators of various fields such as photography, music, etc., by providing the ability to detect exact points of content breaches as well as maintaining a chain of transactions in case needed in a future investigation.

The past decade has envisaged a paradigmatic shift in the digitalization of executing and recording financial transactions by developing intelligent algorithms secured through cryptography. The architecture of blockchain technology holds tremendous potential for metamorphosing various industrial sectors like healthcare, life sciences, and clinical and medical data management. In recent years, there has been a continuous surge for adoption in the biomanufacturing sector by enhancing supply chain management and customer relationship through blockchain technology. It confers substantial impact on bioprocess design, operational efficiency, reduced maintenance downtime, management of spare part inventory, and continuous online monitoring that has paved the way for inevitable transformation in the biomanufacturing sector. In Chapter 8, the authors highlight the role of blockchain technology in the biomanufacturing sector by highlighting its implementation on various unit operations of the biomanufacturing sector. The technology is still in its nascent stage, but it can be wooed at a global scale for wider applicability to make the biomanufacturing sector more sustainable.

The concept of voting has been in use for many purposes in the past decades. The conventional ballot-based voting (paper and ballot box) approach has many inherent use cases that could lead to severe malpractices and manipulations during and after the voting process. In addition, it would also lead to many debatable situations where the physical voting-related practices could be questionable. To overcome the issues raised in the conventional voting system, an electronic voting (e-voting) system came into being. Although the e-voting approaches are efficient and address the drawbacks of conventional e-voting systems, they raise new challenges to researchers, such as voter identity verification, voter privacy protection, vote verifiability and integrity, and so on. Since blockchain guarantees data security, it can protect the system from coercion attacks so can provide better solutions for transparent and trusted e-voting systems. In Chapter 9, the authors explore various e-voting protocols and present a comparative study of performance, security features, and limitations. Further, they focus on the blockchain-based e-voting protocols to discuss the major achievements and challenges in the blockchain-based e-voting systems.

Blockchain technology is a decentralized distributed ledger that maintains a list of transactions in a P2P network in which the security is provided using cryptographic techniques. The history is recorded in every block, and these are cryptographically connected and secured over time. Moreover, this technology has been used for maintaining cryptocurrencies, digital contracts, land ownership, public records, etc., so far. Future applications are likely to include education, intellectual property, supply chain management, medicine, and science. Also, capital expenditures in blockchain technology are expected to hit USD 13.96 billion by 2022. A blockchain-based approach is presented in Chapter 10 to serve as a perfect solution in which the data security and privacy protection are the major concerns in developing a secure drug supply chain. The performance measures such as central dependency, security, smart contract management, encryption, error rate, user privacy, and traceability are considered for the comparison of the proposed technique with the existing approaches.

Artificial intelligence (AI) and blockchain, these two technologies have recently been the trendiest and most revolutionary progressive technologies. Blockchain technology can automate payments in cryptocurrency and provide admittance in a decentralized, safe, and trustworthy way to shared records, transactions, and log ledgers. Also, with smart contracts, blockchain can handle interactions between participants without an interceder. Furthermore, AI provides intelligence and smart decision-making for human-like machines. Chapter 11 presents a thorough analysis of AI and blockchain integration ability, possibilities, and applications. The incorporation of AI was evaluated, and blockchain will influence industry 4.0. We also recognize and address the open issues of AI and blockchain fusion.

This volume will attract researchers, practitioners, academics, and industry professionals related to design, impact, challenges, solutions, and emerging applications of the blockchain in various domains, thereby serving as an excellent resource for the following areas: smart cities, CPSs, cloud computing, intelligent transportation systems, network security, video gaming, IoT, supply chain, reputation, and financial technology.

September 2021

SK Hafizul Islam
Kalyani, India

Arup Kumar Pal
Dhanbad, India

Debabrata Samanta
Bangalore, India

Siddhartha Bhattacharyya
Birbhum, India

CHAPTER 1

Blockchain architecture, taxonomy, challenges, and applications

Nisanth Reddy Kasi[1], Ramani S[1] and Marimuthu Karuppiah[2]
[1]School of Computer Science and Engineering, Vellore Institute of Technology, Vellore, Tamil Nadu, India; [2]Department of Computer Science and Engineering, SRM Institute of Science and Technology, Delhi-NCR Campus, Ghaziabad, Uttar Pradesh, India

1. Introduction to blockchain

Blockchain is a digitized, distributed ledger for records. It is simply a distributed database recording transactions in chronological order. To tamper with a blockchain is almost impossible. As the name blockchain indicates, a blockchain is nothing but a chain of blocks that stores data. A blockchain stores information in a different way than a typical database. Whenever data should be added, a block is newly created; new data is stored in the block, and then the newly created block will be chained to the previous block. The block creation is done chronologically and in a linear fashion.

There is no particular type of information that should be stored in a blockchain, but the most common application so far for blockchain has been as a record for transactions. The working steps of a blockchain are shown in Fig. 1.1. In blockchain, there is not a central server or third party that has complete control over the network. Blockchain uses a peer-to-peer network to group its computers. This means all the information that is stored in a blockchain is accessible to all the computers present in the network. So, if one person tries to tamper with the data in the blockchain, all others present in the blockchain can cross-reference one other, and that one copy of the blockchain will stand out as the culprit (Wüst and Gervais, 2018).

It is not necessarily impossible to change data in a blockchain. If the majority (i.e., 51%) of the network claims the change of data, then the data can be modified. As the network grows, it is practically impossible to tamper with the data. Even if someone wants to venture on this near impossible mission, the cost of resources required to tamper with data in a

Blockchain Technology for Emerging Applications
ISBN 978-0-323-90193-2
https://doi.org/10.1016/B978-0-323-90193-2.00001-6

1

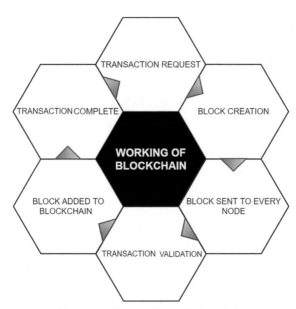

Figure 1.1 The working of blockchain.

blockchain is much more than the outcome. This property where the control is with no one member of the network is called decentralization. It is also possible to create a blockchain that has a centralized architecture.

Blockchain has several applications other than storing transaction data like in cryptocurrencies. Wherever there is a requirement for security, decentralization, or privacy, we can incorporate blockchain technology into that application. Some blockchain applications are in supply chain management, the energy sector, and the business sector. And in the government sector, voting and identity management are two of the applications. In Section 7 a detailed explanation of various blockchain applications are given.

1.1 Motivation

We live in a world where the technology advances every day. Every once in a while, there emerges a technology that completely changes the way that we perceive the world. Generally, a technology is born if there is a need to solve a problem that is not being solved using existing technologies. One such technology that is very much popular today is blockchain. Blockchain is simply a database in which the information is stored as blocks of data. Trust is the basis of any financial transaction. Now, to do any type of financial transaction, we rely on intermediaries such as banks. The trust gap is achieved with the help of intermediaries, and the intermediary demands a fee for their services. But by using blockchain for financial transactions, one can achieve a far greater level of trust and achieve this trust with a fraction of what one pay for intermediaries.

1.2 Blockchain analogy

Let us visualize a huge treasury in a bank. The treasury vault is filled with rows of deposit boxes. Each deposit box is made of glass, allowing everyone to visualize the contents of the deposit boxes, but people only have access to their own box. When a person opens a new deposit box, he or she receives a key that is unique to that box. This is the fundamental concept of cryptocurrencies based on blockchain. Anyone can see the contents of all other addresses.

1.3 Characteristics of blockchain

Each block is built on top of the previous block and uses the block's hash to form a chain. Validating and confirming blocks over the chain is handled by miners. Blocks created are cryptographically sealed over the blockchain, which means that it is nearly impossible to delete and modify data over the blockchain (Xu et al., 2019). Consensus algorithms make sure that all transactions are validated and only added once over the blockchain. The miner receives a reward for running the consensus algorithms; the current reward is 12.5 BTC in the Bitcoin blockchain and 2 ETH in the Ethereum blockchain. All the blocks added are in chronological order and time stamped.

1.4 Summarizing blockchain

A blockchain is a digitized, distributed, consensus-based secure storage of information protected from revision and tampering over the peer-to-peer network. Blockchain is a digitized store for information in the form of transactions. It is distributed. Thus, nobody controls it. Consensus algorithms ensure security and immutability. When new data arrive, they are stored in a block and chained to the blockchain after validation using a consensus mechanism. Data gets recorded in chronological order. Everyone presents over the network can view the transactions. The main elements of blockchain are privacy, security, and efficiency (Fig. 1.2).

1.5 Bitcoin and blockchain

A blockchain is a distributed database of records. Every smart contract or transaction in the public blockchain is confirmed by any one of the

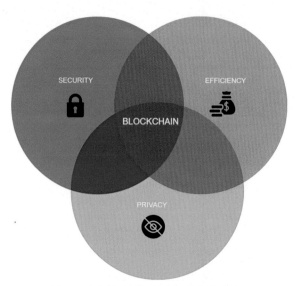

Figure 1.2 Key elements of blockchain.

consensus mechanisms. Transactions are encrypted and cannot be replicated or altered. Currently, the most famous blockchain application is Bitcoin. Blockchain is able to transfer anything from stocks to property rights and cryptocurrency with ease and without the need to go through a third party.

Bitcoin is a digital cryptocurrency, created and withheld digitally on your computer or in a wallet that is virtual. It is distributed, i.e., not centralized, so there are no single entities like persons, organizations, or banks that control the currency. It was started in 2009 to get rid of third-party payment processing intermediaries. The blockchain is the supporting technology that upholds the Bitcoin transaction ledger.

1.6 Wallets, digital signatures, and protocols

A blockchain wallet is similar to a digital wallet in that it allows participants to manage their cryptocurrency. A wallet lets users generate a private key and public address. The private key is used to send the transaction, and a public address is used to receive the transaction. No observable archives of identity about who did what deal or contract with whom are present; only the address of a wallet is visible in the transactions. Different types of blockchain wallets include paper wallets, web wallets, mobile wallets, desktop wallets, etc. Digital signatures are similar to real-world paper signatures as a means to verify a person's identity. Digital signatures use cryptography, which is more secure than handwritten signatures (Xu et al., 2017).

A private key is used to sign messages digitally. The recipient can verify it with the sender's public key. Every transaction that is executed on the blockchain is digitally signed by the sender using their private key. SSL is an example of a digital signature.

1.7 Main contributions of this chapter

The main contributions of this chapter are the following:

(1) The real-life applications of blockchain technology are explained in detail in the latter part of the chapter. Ten applications are listed.

(2) This chapter explains the challenges of blockchain technology like industry challenges and types of blockchain attacks.

1.8 Organization of the chapter

The first section of this chapter gave a basic understanding of blockchain. Section 2 contains the brief history of blockchain. Section 3 describes the advantages of using blockchain over traditional technologies. This section also explores the key benefits of using blockchain such as decentralized control and confidentiality. Section 4 explores the architecture underlying blockchain and various consensus mechanisms like proof of work. This section also discusses the types of blockchain and blockchain ecosystem. Later in this section, various popular blockchains are listed. Section 5 gives the overview of blockchain evolution in fields other than cryptocurrencies like Bitcoin. Section 6 explains the various challenges of blockchain technology, mainly industrial challenges, and attacks against blockchain. Section 7 explores the applications of blockchain in detail. In this section, 10 real-world applications of blockchain are discussed in detail. Section 8 concludes with an assessment of future work.

2. History of blockchain

In early 1990s, the blockchain technology was described with the intent to avoid tampering and time stamp digital data. Almost 20 years later, this technology was adapted by Satoshi Nakamoto for the creation of a cryptocurrency known as Bitcoin. The first practical use case of blockchain technology was Bitcoin.

2.1 Use of blockchain in Bitcoin

Satoshi Nakamoto published a research paper in 2008 entitled "Bitcoin: A peer to peer electronic cash system" that stated that the transactions of this cryptocurrency Bitcoin could take place without the involvement of a third party. With the arrival of Bitcoin in 2008 the blockchain technology came to light even though it had been discovered in the early 1990s. A new protocol was released after a few months that began the concept of a genesis block with 50 coins. This new protocol was an open-source program that gradually became a part of Bitcoin network.

2.2 Ethereum and smart contracts

In 2013, Canadian-Russian programmer Vitalik Buterin, who initially contributed a significant amount of code to Bitcoin codebases, went on to build the cryptocurrency popularly known as Ethereum. He saw many limitations in Bitcoin technology, so he built another cryptocurrency. Unlike Bitcoin, which just records transactions of Bitcoin cryptocurrency, Ethereum helps its users to record digital data of their cars, properties, yachts, contracts, etc.

The launch of Ethereum took place in 2015, and it has the functionality of smart contracts. Based on a set of criteria established in the blockchain, with the use of smart contracts, we can perform logical operations automatically (Syed et al., 2019). For example, a smart contract can be formed to place a bet between two parties. Then, both parties would send cryptocurrency, which is their part of the bet, and upload the contract to the Ethereum blockchain. Each of their cryptocurrencies is held by the software underlying Ethereum blockchain, and after the bet ends, the smart contract would check who is the winner using logical operations and then post the earnings to the winner.

3. Benefits over traditional technologies

Blockchain technology was discovered due to the roadblocks of existing technologies. With the use of blockchain, there exists a decentralized control, in contrast to that of traditional technologies, which support centralized control. The usage of blockchain technology ensures transparency and integrity of its users. The advantages and disadvantages (Fig. 1.3) are discussed later in the chapter in detail. There are a few benefits of blockchain over traditional technology: enhanced security to the user, confidentiality, faster processing, etc.

3.1 Decentralized control

Blockchain technology supports multiple parties that have no trust in each other to share data without the need of a centralized control. It removes the

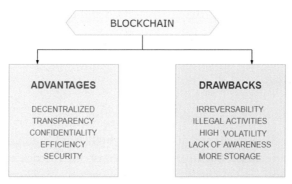

Figure 1.3 Advantages and drawbacks of blockchain.

dangers that are caused by centralized control. With a centralized control over information, anyone with adequate access to the organization can tamper with or corrupt the data within. Cost savings are also provided; usually billions of dollars are spent on safeguarding central repositories from hackers. Blockchain provides a similar public shared system of record concurrently for everybody who is connected to the network. The trust is established by the cryptographic protocols running behind the blockchain technology. All the parties must agree to make a change in blockchain, which is nearly impossible.

3.2 Integrity and transparency

Blockchain technology replaces traditional data storage technology as it is publicly verifiable, aided by transparency and integrity. A user present in a blockchain network can trust that the information they are accessing through a blockchain is tamper-proof and uncorrupted from the instant it was logged and recorded. Every user can authenticate the information added over the blockchain. Blockchain does not leave behind past records, and as the data is added to the blockchain, it appends and grows while also providing current information (Zheng et al., 2018). Merkle trees ensure the integrity of the data by hashing the transactions to a single root.

3.3 Confidentiality

The blockchain is an openly distributed ledger. Yet a private system can be established to maintain confidentiality. Data confidentiality in blockchain guarantee that single entities like persons or organizations that are prohibited from getting information are not approved obtain it. Permissioned blockchains have arisen as a substitute to public blockchain to meet the needs of the industry for having recognized and distinguishable members. Solutions like Hyperledger Fabric blockchain and Block Stream offer rich sets of permissions to maintain confidentiality in the system.

3.4 Faster processing

The traditional banking process takes days to settle, but the blockchain has reduced that time to nearly 2 min or even seconds. Everybody has the access to the same data, and it is easy to build trust among one another without the necessity for any third parties or intermediaries. Moreover, tracking of products could also be made efficient by uploading the data into a blockchain. Digital assets and the trustless system make sure that the data is protected and transacted efficiently.

3.5 Enhanced security

The transactions are encrypted and linked to the previous transactions. Information is stored across a network of computers instead of a single server. Blockchain prevents fraud and unauthorized activity. Cryptography protocols make sure that the data is thoroughly secure. Safeguards are in place from denial of service (DoS) attacks as the data are present on all the nodes connected to the network. The cryptographic fingerprint (hash of the block) is unique for each block.

4. Blockchain architecture

A blockchain holds a chain of blocks in which any type of information can be stored, like in a database. The information that is stored in the blocks and chained together is secure because this information is available to any computer that is present in that network. The computers in this network are grouped together in a peer-to-peer (P2P) architecture, as shown in Fig. 1.4. In simple words, blockchain is a group of computers linked together with no central server. Blockchain is decentralized because the network of computers present in a blockchain has no central server.

4.1 Understanding architecture

Every block in a blockchain has a block header. The block header is useful to differentiate each block in a blockchain network. It contains the time-stamp, version, and Merkle root of the block. One of the common algorithms that checks the legitimacy of a block is proof of work (PoW). To make the PoW operate requires two entities or fields: the difficulty target

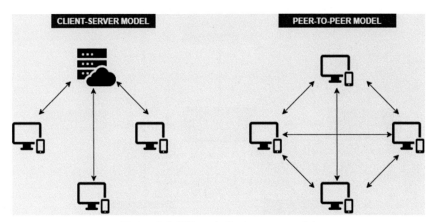

Figure 1.4 P2P and client-server model.

and the nonce. So, the block header should have the PoW fields of difficulty target and nonce. The last field that the block header should include is the previous hash. The blockchain's main property is its immutable nature. This immutable property is made possible by including the previous block hash in the calculation of the present block hash.

By doing so, if anyone wants to change a block in the blockchain, they are forced to change all the other blocks present in the blockchain. Even after replacing all the blocks, one cannot achieve the results that are expected to follow. This feat would be successful if the replacing of blocks took place for at least 51% of nodes present in the network. It is impossible in the case of blockchain as its network is vast, so to change the data in at least 51% of nodes is insurmountable.

4.2 Consensus mechanisms

Blockchain are decentralized systems that contain diverse members who act on condition of inducements they obtain and the data that is accessible to them. When a fresh transaction gets introduced on the network, computers connected to the network have the choice to either take in that transaction to their replica of ledger or to overlook and ignore it. When the 51% or more of the computers that comprise the network decide on a solitary state, the consensus is attained.

Blockchain is not controlled by a central authority, so it has decentralized ledgers. Due to the digital information kept and maintained in these ledgers, bad actors have significant monetary inducements to attempt to cause problems (Lin and Liao, 2017). PoW is a solution that involves

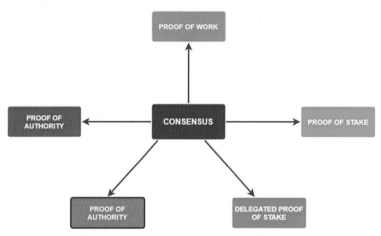

Figure 1.5 Types of consensus mechanisms.

probability, known as the Byzantine Generals problem (Lamport et al., 1982). It follows the longest chain rule where miners shift to the chain that is being more worked upon. When a miner cracks the puzzle and authorizes the block, all the computers present in the network will confirm if the block is binding or valid and append it to their replica of the blockchain. The computers in advance have a necessity to attain a consensus on the validity; only then will the blockchain network synchronize, and the state of the chain of blockchain will update. Various types of consensus mechanisms are shown in Fig. 1.5.

4.3 Various consensus mechanisms

4.3.1 Proof of work

PoW is a type of consensus algorithm where the miners contend to resolve a tough mathematical problem built on a cryptographic algorithm involving hash. This proof shows that a miner spends a lot of resources and time to resolve the difficult mathematical problem. When a block is resolved, the transaction data contained are thereby considered valid and stored in the blockchain.

By mathematical problem, we mean a function involving a hash. In the hash function the miners solve a puzzle to discover the input for which the output is already known. For example, consider integer factorization, which involves in what way to write a number as the product of two numbers, and the guided tour puzzle protocol, which involves the requirement of the calculation of functions that involve hash, if the server is suspected of a DoS attack for some computers in a predefined order (Halaburda, 2018). Miners collect a payment once they crack the difficult mathematical problem, which involves hash functions. For example, in Bitcoin, miners receive 12.5 Bitcoin for solving the puzzle. Miners can also receive transaction fees in addition to rewards.

4.3.2 Proof of stake

Proof of stake (PoS) is an alternative algorithm to authenticate transactions and attain the consensus of a distributed ledger. PoW algorithm pays miners who crack difficult mathematical problems with the final goal of confirming transactions and generating fresh blocks. On the other hand, in the PoS algorithm, the maker of a fresh block is selected in a deterministic way, which depends on their affluence and position in the blockchain (Tapscott and Tapscott, 2017). At the start of the chain, all the digital currencies are created. Their number never changes. Here, in PoS, the miners only take the payment of transaction fees. So, the miners present in the PoS system miners are called forgers.

4.3.3 Delegated proof of stake

People in a specific blockchain network vote for spectators to safeguard their computer network. Let us imagine a reward system where only the top 50 spectators are rewarded for their service, and only the top 10 make a consistent salary. As it creates healthy competition, many want to become a spectator, thus providing hundreds of backup spectators. The strength of the vote of a person is resolved by number of tokens they hold. People who have more tokens will impact the blockchain network more than those who have fewer tokens. If a spectator starts acting like a schmuck or halts undertaking work in safeguarding the blockchain network, persons in the blockchain network can confiscate their votes, which basically means the lousy actor is thrown out of the blockchain community.

Voting is continuously taking place in a delegated PoS consensus mechanism. Delegates are elected as spectators. A delegate becomes a cosigner on an individual account that has access to propose certain changes that are required for the parameters of the network. The genesis account is the name of this account. These network restrictions comprise the whole lot from block sizes to transaction fees, spectator pay, and lump intervals.

4.3.4 Proof of authority

The proof of authority (PoA) consensus mechanism is fundamentally an improved PoS consensus that controls identity as the system of stake rather than token staking. The group of validators is typically supposed to stay relatively small to ensure manageable security and efficiency of the network. Individuals under PoA earn the right to become a validator, which is why there is no incentive to retain the position they hold (Tasatanattakool and Techapanupreeda, 2018), Validators are required to formally verify identity either on the chain or some public domain. The eligibility to become a validator is difficult to obtain, where the individuals need to go through many steps to become a validator.

4.3.5 Proof of weight

Proof of weight (PoW) is a broad consensus mechanism based on the Algorand algorithm, which in turn specifies a new protocol known as Byzantine agreement (BA). BA protocol is highly scalable and secure. The PoW consensus model runs a committee where participants keep on changing, and the committee achieves the consensus for the network. Every user over the network has a weight attached to them, which is determined by the amount of money they hold in their account.

4.4 Types of blockchain

4.4.1 Public blockchain

A public blockchain, as its name indicates, is the blockchain that is available to everyone; in other words, it is a form of blockchain which is for the people, by the people, and of the people. There is no one in charge of the network, and anyone can contribute to reading, writing, and auditing the blockchain. More complex rules are present for safeguarding it from malicious actors. This is the most used blockchain, as shown at the top in Fig. 1.6. All decisions are made using a complex consensus algorithm. Computationally, these blockchain are expensive to mine and commit a block over the network. Examples are Bitcoin and Ethereum (Mettler, 2016).

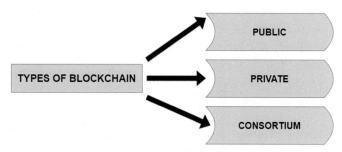

Figure 1.6 Types of blockchain.

4.4.2 Private blockchain

An individual or an organization privately operates a private blockchain, as its name suggests. Unlike public blockchain, there is an administrator or anchor that looks after essential things such as permissions and identities in a private blockchain. The consensus is attained on the notion of the dominant party who can provide mining rights to everyone or just keep those to themselves. Compared to a public blockchain, it is cheaper and faster since a person does not have to employ a huge amount of energy, money, and time to attain a consensus. It is less secure compared with the public blockchain.

4.4.3 Consortium blockchain

A consortium blockchain removes individual independence, which gets conferred in just one unit by means of a private blockchain. Here, in place of a single entity in charge, we have more than one entity in charge. A collection of organizations or representatives can make choices for the profit of the whole consortium blockchain network, as a way of attaining things more quickly and to have more than a single point of checks, which defends the whole blockchain ecosystem. In simple words, it is the best of both private and public blockchains. This blockchain type gives choices for access management and rights while controlling the same blockchain technology and earning its paybacks (Al-Jaroodi and Mohamed, 2019).

4.5 Blockchain technology stack

The stack is the base of all blockchain-based applications. It is a network of nodes spread across the world that runs algorithms to verify and commit transaction over the blockchain. This is a decentralized network and mostly based on open-source cryptography algorithms. This can be created as public, private, or consortium, and it can include certificate authorities and membership services for governments and enterprises.

4.5.1 Overlay networks

This is a network that achieves additional functionality without bootstrapping the original protocols. They benefit from the network effects and build on top of that. Some of the additional functionalities you achieve are smart contracts that involves in crypto agreements between two parties, storage for renting network and side chains which help to transfer tokens from one blockchain to a different blockchain.

4.5.2 User interface

Finally, a user interface is required for your users to connect to a blockchain (Scott et al., 2020). A user interface can be built with existing front-end mechanisms and can easily employ the power of blockchain by using APIs. Some platforms like Hyperledger also provide generators to produce a box user interface for the applications built upon them. Most blockchain platforms also provide connecting services to link applications to blockchain.

4.5.3 Decentralized protocols

This is the essential part of the blockchain technology stack as it makes sure the blockchain layer and overlay networks do not depend on a single entity for validation and transactions. It helps to create decentralized P2P datasets. Decentralized protocols can be based on asset mapping, social identities, verification algorithms, or communication channels.

4.5.4 Support system

For building blockchain applications, APIs are required to interact with the underlying technology (Subramanian, 2017). One can directly build a solution using the existing APIs, without depending and working on a ledger. Most APIs respond to JSON format, so can be easily integrated with existing front-end technologies. You can use open-source APIs like Bitcoin and Ethereum, or you can choose from commercial APIs such as Block.io or BlockCypher for more boxed-up functionalities.

4.6 Blockchain ecosystem

The blockchain ecosystem is currently running some major projects, and more are in the pipeline (Saberi et al., 2019). Some of the major projects on blockchain are Bitcoin (which introduced blockchain to the world), Ethereum (which came with the concept of smart contracts where two parties adhere to certain rules and create a trust, opening the world for more decentralized applications), NEO (which positioned itself as the "Chinese Ethereum," and it bought Python as the main language for the creation of applications), and Stellar (which is trying to make cross-border transactions simpler). Stellar comes with extensive APIs that help developers build applications fast, thus reducing the time to market for applications.

4.6.1 Blockchain miners

To make a blockchain functional and maintain its integrity, a large network of independent nodes around the world is needed to be continuously maintained. In private blockchain, a central organization has the authority over every node on the network. In the case of public blockchain, on the other hand, anyone can set up their computer to act as a node. The owners of these computers are called miners (Guo and Liang, 2016). Since the integrity of the blockchain is directly related to the number of independent nodes on the network, there also needs to be some incentive to mining. Different blockchains utilize different mining systems, but most of them contain some form of an incentive system or a consensus algorithm.

4.6.2 Blockchain developers

Blockchain technology is built through the potential of developers working behind it. A strong team of developers can lead to a successful blockchain project. Currently, there are two types of developers in the blockchain ecosystem: blockchain developers and dApp developers. Blockchain developers build new blockchains with different levels of functionalities and consensus algorithms. dApp developers work with decentralized applications that can run on blockchain, thus providing a similar functionality like Google Play Store over the blockchain technology. The development of smart contracts over the blockchain has opened the possibility for developers to create extensive applications and use cases for industries.

4.6.3 Blockchain users

Blockchain users are average people, like you and me, who make use of the blockchain or cryptocurrency to achieve some results (Niranjanamurthy et al., 2019). They can also be investors who buy cryptocurrencies to sell later. For creating a blockchain user base the technology or cryptocurrency should have some utility related to the problem being tackled. For example, Bitcoin serves as a major utility for payment of goods and services. Currently, there are over 50,000 merchants registered with Bitcoin, including Microsoft, PayPal, and Subway. Bitcoin was the first mover in blockchain, and its high utility as a payment system ensures that a large part of its ecosystem is based upon users.

4.6.4 Blockchain exchanges

Every blockchain project has a robust ecosystem working under it, and it always includes a decentralized exchange. These are developed by the blockchain team or a community of developers. A typical exchange is designed to find the cheapest rates of exchange between any two cryptocurrencies, making it more affordable to trade tokens and cryptocurrencies. Exchanges used for trading also might integrate with hardware wallets, or users can create their own wallet on the exchange website.

4.7 Various top blockchains in the contemporary world

4.7.1 Bitcoin

Bitcoin is a digital payment system and one of the very popular crypto-currencies around the globe. It was founded in early 2010 and released as open-source software. Bitcoin is not operated by a single person or an organization; instead, it is operated by everyone in the network of the Bitcoin blockchain, which is typically a P2P network. Bitcoin gave us the first glimpse of the blockchain, and it is the first decentralized digital currency whose ledger is maintained by blockchain.

Bitcoin transactions take place directly between users, which does not include an intermediate or third party. In this P2P network, nodes verify the transactions that are done by users, and these transactions are recorded in a distributed ledger, which is available to all the nodes in the Bitcoin network. Bitcoin stands out from fiat modes of payment. Some of the features that make the Bitcoin different from fiat currencies are its simple setup process, transparency, anonymity, faster transaction speed, decentralized mechanism, and lower transaction fee (Zhou et al., 2020). The main problem with banks is that they make you go through a complex process to just create an account with them. But in the case of Bitcoin the configuration process is very straightforward, and moreover, it is free of cost. With banks, there is the process called "know your customer" in which you have to show your personal identification to create an account with that bank. But a Bitcoin user does not need to link any personal identification information to their Bitcoin address. In fact, the user can have as many Bitcoin addresses as they wish.

Every Bitcoin transaction is recorded in a linear, public, distributed ledger, in simple terms, a blockchain. Due to this immutable way of storing the transaction information, the Bitcoin once transferred to a Bitcoin address cannot be refunded. As there is no third party or any sort of intermediatory involved in a transaction of Bitcoin, the payment process is much faster than any traditional banking system.

However, Bitcoin charges a small fee for international transfers because of the validity mechanism involved in the transaction processes (Cocco et al., 2017). A large chunk of this fee is claimed by the Bitcoin miners who validate the transaction and store the transaction in a block, which then is chained to the Bitcoin blockchain. The Bitcoin cannot be controlled by a single person or an organization because it is not centralized. The Bitcoin transactions are processed within the network with the help of a group of nodes that work together to mine the Bitcoin cryptocurrency, which does not require any form of a central authority.

4.7.2 Ethereum

Ethereum, which is based on blockchain technology, is an open-source software platform. Ethereum enables developers to build and deploy decentralized applications like smart contracts. It offers a decentralized virtual machine—Ethereum Virtual Machine—that can execute scripts using a globally distributed network of public nodes. It was launched by Vitalik Buterin in late 2013. The development for Ethereum was funded by an online public crowd sale by buying the Ethereum tokens (Ether) between July and August 2014.

The first public beta prerelease was the Olympic network, which provided users with a bounty of 25,000 Ethers for stress testing the limits of the Ethereum blockchain. Ethereum's live blockchain named Frontier was launched on July 30, 2015. The current release is named Homestead and is considered stable. It has led to various improvements such as transaction processing, gas pricing, and security. There are at least two other protocol upgrades planned, i.e., Metropolis and Serenity (PoS).

4.7.3 Hyperledger

Hyperledger is an open-source project created to advance cross-industry blockchain technologies. It is a global collaboration, hosted by The Linux Foundation, including leaders in finance, banking, internet of things (IoT), supply chains, manufacturing, and technology. Hyperledger acts as an operating system for marketplaces, data sharing networks, microcurrencies, and decentralized digital communities. It has the potential to vastly lessen the expense and complications in getting things done in the real world.

4.7.4 Multichain

Multichain was created by Gideon to make available a blockchain solution for organizations to build and develop quickly. Multichain is built upon Bitcoin blockchain but offers the functionality of permissions, streams, and assets, as well as other tools like explorers to interact with the underlying blockchain seamlessly. BankChain is using Multichain as its base.

4.7.5 EOS

EOS is an operating system for marketplaces, data sharing networks, microcurrencies, and decentralized digital communities. It has the potential to vastly lessen the expense and complications in getting things done in the real world (Kalodner et al., 2020). EOS blockchain aims to become a decentralized operating system that can support industrial-scale decentralized applications. EOS is planning to delete transaction fees, and it claims to have the ability to conduct millions of transactions per second. EOS runs on DPOS consensus algorithm.

4.7.6 Corda

Corda is an open-source blockchain aiming to meet requirements for use of blockchain in businesses. Corda offers a solution where a shared ledger can be initiated between parties under a contract. Corda's communications are point-to-point, meaning only participants of a transaction can see it. With Corda's point-to-point architecture, participants only have copies of the transactions where they are observers or participants. A unique ledger is present in every node of Corda's network, which is called a multilateral ledger.

4.7.7 NEO

NEO is a smart economy for the distributed network (Yeoh, 2017). NEO was chosen as the name because neo in Greek means, newness, novelty, and youth. NEO was initially called AntShares (ANS), which was launched in 2014, founded by Da Hongfei and Erik Zhang. AntShares announced on June 22, 2017, that it planned to rebrand itself as NEO. The first initial coin offering (ICO) on the NEO blockchain, Red Pulse Token (RPX), was announced soon after the rebranding finished. Apart from the NEO cryptocurrency itself, the NEO platform has another crypto token, GAS, which was formerly called ANC-Ant coin.

4.7.8 Quorum

Quorum is the brainchild of J.P. Morgan, bringing in an enterprise-focused version of Ethereum. Quorum blockchain delivers private, smart contract implementation and industry-grade output. Quorum uses zk-Snarks cryptography, which allows verification of the computation correctness without even learning what was executed. Quorum uses a hybrid privacy design.

5. Evolution of blockchain in fields other than cryptocurrency

Since the introduction of blockchain technology, there has not been much progress of blockchain technology other than cryptocurrencies. But this technology can be used in various other fields such as politics, music, IoT, supply chain, etc., as shown in Fig. 1.7. Voting is the most important part of

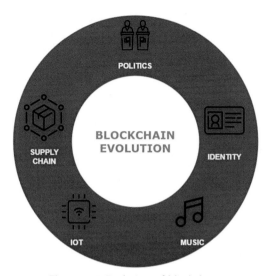

Figure 1.7 Evolution of blockchain.

a democracy. Voter fraud is a critical issue today, which can be easily resolved by using a blockchain. For an instance, a blockchain can be created for voting where each person or node is then added to the blockchain, followed by issuing a single nontransferable token to each node, so each person has a single chance to vote. The tampering of elections in the case of blockchain is impossible because of the large computation power required to change the information at all nodes since one should have complete command over 51% of the network.

In the entertainment industry the movie Braid was the first movie to be produced by doing an ICO (Nguyen and Kim, 2018). In property rental, Rentberry aims to address the common pitfalls and headaches of the traditional rental model. Regarding blockchain in politics, Sierra Leone carried out their elections on blockchain. In education, the Socrates Coin is making big moves to change the traditional approach to a 3D internet. In digital advertising the Basic Attention Token is taking a crack at solving advertisement problems. In the IoT sector, Walton chain is an award-winning Chinese project that seeks to integrate IoT and blockchain technology on an unprecedented scale.

6. Challenges of blockchain

As in every other technology out there, blockchain also has its share of challenges. One of the biggest roadblocks for this emerging technology is illegal activity. Confidentiality is a key factor of blockchain as it protects the users of the network from hacks and also preserves their privacy, but unfortunately, it can also be used for illegal activity. Some other challenges that blockchain faces are high cost, inefficacy of speed, and that it cannot be maintained if the network grows too large.

6.1 Industry challenges with blockchain

6.1.1 Energy consumption

Some major public blockchains use PoW algorithms, which involve the use of the computational power of a machine to solve a complex mathematical puzzle to verify a transaction and add it to a block. Current Bitcoin energy consumption is almost equal that of Ireland. By 2020, it is estimated that Bitcoin will utilize more energy than the entire world currently uses (Kshetri and Voas, 2018). A probable solution for this has emerged in the form of consensus mechanisms like PoW and PoS.

6.1.2 Scalability

Scalability has appeared as a significant issue for blockchain networks like Bitcoin and Ethereum. Blockchains are having issues with efficiently holding a large number of nodes on the network. Moreover, the size of public blockchains keeps on increasing. Currently, Bitcoin ledger size is greater than 100 GB. One possible solution that has emerged is storing a hash of data over the network.

6.1.3 Public perception

Presently, blockchain technology is almost synonymous with Bitcoin. A majority of the public is still unaware of the presence and potential practices of blockchain technology (Chauhan et al., 2018). Since Bitcoin is anonymous, it is used for mysterious transactions of black-market trade, money laundering, and other illegitimate events, giving it a bad reputation. Mainstream adoption is needed to remove the sometimes negative undertones of Bitcoin when misused.

6.1.4 Blockchain standards and regulations

Blockchains are continuously evolving, but countries are still skeptic about them because there is no proper definition for standards and regulations. Enterprises and governments require regulations to protect their customers. To tackle this problem, certain countries are trying to launch their won regulations for the technology. Mass adoption might also standardize the blockchain.

6.2 Attacks against blockchain

6.2.1 Sybil attack

In a Sybil attack, the assailant tries to plug the network with the client's nodes that they control. If this happens, then you would be most likely to join with attacker nodes. Bitcoin never keeps a count of nodes for anything, so if the attacker completely isolates a node from the authentic network, then it can help the attacker in the implementation of other attacks. The potential damage could be that the attacker refuses to relay blocks or possibly the attacker only relays blocks that he creates.

6.2.2 Eclipse attack

This attack is based on distributed application architecture that partitions errands or assignments among users without the necessity for a central server that is coordinating or steady hosts. Crippling a node in such a way means it cannot talk to other nodes in the network. This attack is possible due to design strategy flaws in the blockchain peer's identity and peer selection strategy. Currently, Bitcoin has eight outgoing connections, and Ethereum has 13, which imply one node in Bitcoin only has a view for eight nodes connected to it. So, one node in Bitcoin has to depend on the other eight for the complete view of the network, which can be taken advantage of by a hacker (Sankar et al., 2017).

The potential damage could be double spending, attacks against second layer protocols, or an assailant acquiring services or products without paying by deceiving his victims into thinking that the channel of payment is still open while the other part of the network sees that channel of payment is closed. Smart contracts also may be compromised if peers of the blockchain network see unreliable records over the blockchain.

6.2.3 Time-jacking attack

Time–jacking attack is an extended version of the Sybil attack. In this attack, each computer involved keeps a time counter for the network. The network time counter works on the median time of a node's peers, which is sent in the version message when peers are connected. The network time counter reverts to the system time if the median time varies by more than 70 min from the time of the system (Li et al., 2020).

The potential damage could be that an assailant could possibly speed up or slow down a computer's network time counter by linking multiple nodes and broadcasting imprecise timestamps. Since the time value can be distorted by at most 70 min, the time alteration between the peers would be 140 min.

6.2.4 Fifty-one percent attack

Basically, a 51% attack takes place when a group of miners get control of more than 50% of the mining hash rate of the network, or a group of miners with substantially more computational power can get full control of the network. It is a speculative attack described over Bitcoin blockchain. Bitcoin Gold, when it was among the top cryptocurrencies, suffered a 51% attack and lost (Khan and Salah, 2018).

The assailants would be able to stop fresh transactions in advance, gaining authorizations and making them stop payments among users. Attackers would also be able to redo the transactions that were established while they were in control of the blockchain network, meaning they could double their coins. The mining pool ghash.io was momentarily surpassing 50% of the Bitcoin network computation power in July 2014, leading the pool to obligate to dropping its share of the voluntarily reduced its share of the network.

7. Applications of blockchain

The blockchain technology has several applications, as shown in Fig. 1.8, other than storing transaction data. This technology has already been incorporated by several big companies like Walmart, Pfizer, AIG, and IBM. For instance, IBM has used blockchain in the Food Trust blockchain, which helps trace food products and their location. The reason behind doing this is to check if food is suspected to be poisoned or contaminated. If they went with a traditional database to manage and store the information of the supply chain of food products, it would take forever to trace back where the contamination occurred.

But by storing this data using blockchain, then every part of the journey is recorded and stored in a block that is time stamped, and it is very easy to trace the food product route. This helps to save innumerable lives if the food contamination is massive. Besides the food industry, blockchain can potentially be used in any field. Some of the fields that are using blockchain are banking and finance, currency, healthcare, property records, and state identification (Zhang et al., 2019).

7.1 Mortgages and loans using blockchain

The problem with the current day-to-day loan and mortgage system is that it has a lot of mediators and third parties are involved, typically banks. The process of getting a loan from a bank is very time consuming and

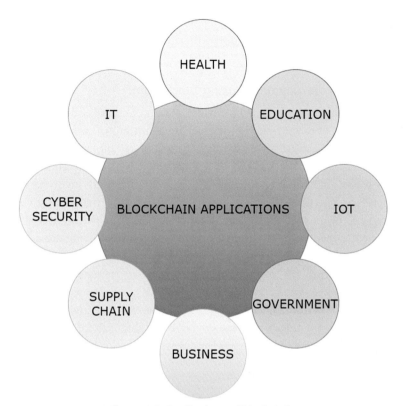

Figure 1.8 Applications of blockchain.

complex and also involves a ton of paperwork. A blockchain-based platform with a network of mortgage and loan lenders seems to be the best course of action for the problem that we are facing with the mortgage and loan system.

This process of using a blockchain requires the lenders and borrowers in the blockchain network to form smart contracts, which then issue tokens for each mortgage or loan issuance. As soon there is a deadline the blockchain automatically implements the details present in the smart contract uploaded by the borrower and lender. The main benefit from using this type of mechanism for mortgage and loan issuance is that it is very cost affective and saves a ton of money and time dealing an intermediatory. The use of a blockchain in this scenario increases the transaction performance, and the speed of each transaction can be increased (Park and Park, 2017). Usually in the case of loans, there are many cases going on in the civil courts, but with the use of a blockchain, the transparency for borrowers and lenders is increased. This proposed method of using a blockchain to process loans and mortgages is much more efficient and straightforward, reducing the processing time.

7.2 Cross-border payments using blockchain

Generally, the problem with the current system of cross-border payments is they cost a lot of money and consume a great amount of time. This process is opaque and the time for each transaction is pretty high. The solution to this problem would be the use of a blockchain with smart contracts and digital assets. The smart contracts take care of the users involved in the financial agreements. The digital assets help to reduce the cost by cutting the capital compliance and operational cost, which helps the user to save money compared to the traditional way of payments involving cross-border payments.

Different types of currencies can be used for transactions for cross-border payments, which typically involve banks. The benefits of using this system are by using a blockchain the transaction becomes faster than a typical transaction. Because of the use of blockchain, there is no involvement of a third party, which helps the user to save a lot of money and also reduces the risk of tampering with the transactions. More security and transparency can be achieved by shifting to blockchain technology. Another alternative to this cross-border payment is the use of digital cryptocurrencies as they solve the liquidity issues of cross-border payments (Karame and Capkun, 2018).

7.3 Stock trading using blockchain

The problem with stock trading using existing technology is that the functioning of stock exchanges includes dealings that consume a lot of time and are very complex. Stock trading is susceptible to risks and is cost inefficient. By using a private blockchain, one can build a trading platform that allows the companies to register and sell their shares digitally over a public blockchain. The investor can get complete transactions benefits and records securely and with ease.

With the use of smart contracts, the stock's movement is recorded, and after one agree to the terms of logical transaction, the money will be deducted from one's account, and the blockchain validates the profit or loss using smart contracts. After validating, the amount would be debited or credited to their account. The security properties settlements can be given by issuing digital tokens. The elimination of intermediaries or any third parties is the main benefit of this methodology of using a private blockchain. There are a couple of benefits of using a private blockchain for stock trading; one of them is that the stock can be traced back to the buyer, and another is that settlements can be done much faster using this technology.

7.4 Online identity management using blockchain

The problem with the existing technologies of online identity management is that it is a time-consuming and costly process. A permission-based blockchain to store digital identities would be the solution to tackle this real-world problem of managing online identities. Based on the immutable nature of a blockchain the user identities cannot be tampered with. The users in this permission-based blockchain have the liberty to choose how one can see them in the blockchain and with whom the personal information can be shared.

This blockchain can use the digital identity in various ways, for example, to apply for loans or mortgages. This helps to maintain a single and ultimate source of identity (Halpin and Piekarska, 2017). The benefits of using this permission-based blockchain are that any intermediatory can be avoided and every user can be provided with same level of security. Information can be accessed anywhere and anytime, as it is a single source of identity. Unlike the traditional way of authenticating identity, there would be no reason for authenticating multiple times, as this is an immutable, legitimate manner of verification.

7.5 Public health security using blockchain

Health is the foremost issue that should be taken into consideration by governments. But the technology that we use to store and maintain public health records is primitive and has many loopholes that can be exploited. The main problems are with authenticating and maintaining public health records. With the use of a public blockchain in which the users are patients, hospitals, and healthcare providers, this problem of storing, maintaining, and authenticating health records can be resolved.

The health records of all patients should be stored and maintained using a public ledger distributed system, a blockchain. After creating a patient record, a key should be set up by the user so one has access to the user's personal health information. The initialization of smart contracts between the hospital and the user is a very good use case application. An IoT device can be used to transfer the data of the patient directly over to the block-chain, so at a later date, the concerned healthcare provider has access to all the patient's health information (Halpin and Piekarska, 2017).

The main benefit of using this blockchain to store and maintain public health records is to have complete data security for the users of this blockchain network. With only the proper permissions can one access or give access of their personal health information to whomever they require, typically healthcare providers and pharmacies. The use of a public block-chain also reduces the complexity of the data sharing agreements compared with traditional public health security.

7.6 Tracing of medicine using blockchain

The problem with traceability of medicine is that there are a lot of counterfeit drugs present on the market that cause a potential danger to people; some of them can even be fatal. With the use of a blockchain for the medicine supply the problem of traceability of medicine could be resolved. A unique identification should be issued to each medicine to help trace every step of the supply chain. For suppliers that have approval of the government a different ledger can be formed, and the documents related to the reliability of the medicine should be stored and maintained in the blockchain for verification and authentication.

In this scenario the use of smart contracts would be appropriate between the distributers and suppliers. The benefits of using a blockchain would when medicine is counterfeit or not based on the data available on the blockchain. Cost can be reduced once counterfeits go out of business. Having fewer counterfeits helps to protect people using medicines as well as helping to preserve the reputations of pharmaceutical companies.

7.7 Rental property using blockchain

The problem with the rental properties is that multiple listing services provide lists that are incorrect and incomplete. Also, the ownership and documents of the rental properties are not well defined. Using a public blockchain for storing and maintaining rental property would be a very good solution, and by using the blockchain the payments of rents and related services would become much easier for all concerned parties.

The use of a public blockchain for storing and maintaining rental re-cords enables records to be stored in one place, and all the transactions and listings could be authenticated independently, and they could be auto-matically submitted by the use of smart contracts. The rental process would be executed with the support of self-implementing smart contracts over the blockchain. Since the transactions between the tenant and landlord can be automatically done by using smart contracts, there is no need for third-party real estate agents or any other sort of intermediatory.

The use of blockchain greatly reduces the risk of alteration of rental records. All this information is stored in every computer present in this network, so in case of any attempt at tampering or altering of data, the data can be retrieved from the blockchain network. The usage of this proposed system reduces trust issues and other miscommunication involved with rental records, saving time and money for both the landlord and tenant.

7.8 Property records using blockchain

The problem with property records is that they are stored and maintained at the local government level. If there is tampering of property records on the government side due to corruption or some natural disaster, there is chance that we can lose our properties. Having centralized control over property records is a sensitive trust issue. Using a multiledger distribution blockchain, where each sector of government stores and maintains the land records per their authority (Dasgupta et al., 2019), allows for a secure environment. These records are accessible to every person whose property records are present in this multiledger blockchain, if they provide correct identification, and there will be no loss of information or corruption of property records since they are stored in a blockchain. The usage of tokens can be encouraged to perform transactions between two parties, like the transfer of ownership of the property records.

Smart contracts can also be used to upload the contract statement, and the blockchain withholds the cryptocurrency or property records and transfers them to the concerned party after validating the contracts of both parties. A benefit of using a multiledger distributed blockchain in the case of property records is that it reduces the trust issues between a government and its people. The use of a multiledger blockchain drastically reduces the risk of tampering with property records. This type of system increases the chances of a middle-class person to invest in small properties. As this is a blockchain, all this information is stored in every computer present in this network, so in case of scandal or natural disaster the data is not lost and can be retrieved from other nodes present in the blockchain network (Karuppiah and Saravanan, 2014, 2015; Karuppiah et al., 2016, 2017, 2019; Kumari et al., 2016; Naeem et al., 2020; Maria et al., 2021; Pradhan et al., 2018; Li et al., 2017).

7.9 Real estate regulations using blockchain

The problems with regulations regarding real estate is that they are not transparent and not being used effectively. The main purpose should be transparency, and there should be universal accessibility to users involved in a real estate contract. But that is not the case in current times. This problem can be resolved by the use of a public blockchain in which the real estate regulations are listed, so they cannot be tampered with, making them accessible to users involved in a contract.

If real estate regulations are listed using a public blockchain, they would be transparent to every party in the value chain. The regulations can be arranged on a public, distributed ledger as a transaction and posted on the public blockchain. Transactions can be done with ease as there is transparency in associated timelines and costs. Using a public blockchain is superior to traditional processes, where even the government profits from the ease and transparency.

7.10 Liquidating real estate assets using blockchain

The problem with liquidation of real estate is that it takes many days to complete a transaction using existing technology. In the current environment, liquidating real estate assets is a hectic process. This problem of taking so much time for a single transaction can be tackled by creating a public or private blockchain that increases the speed of each transaction, as well as being transparent and efficient (Dasgupta et al., 2019).

To sell or buy property over the blockchain, one can be issued tokens to perform transactions. Since these transactions take place using a blockchain, there is less chance for disputes over the ownership of a property. All the transactions that take place in a real estate blockchain can be accessed by anyone in the network and ultimately are transparent. Even financiers and money lenders can get a maximum reach through this blockchain and a new approach to the liquidation of real estate assets. There are also benefits over the traditional process in that there is no third party involved in the transactions, so the transfer of ownership is done within minutes, which saves a lot of time and money.

8. Conclusion and future scope

Blockchain technology is not limited to cryptocurrencies like Bitcoin. It has a vast array of applications in sectors such as government, medicine, energy, etc. Blockchain technology provides decentralization, efficiency, security, and privacy for its applications. In the future, we can see the usage of blockchain technology in almost every sector, which can transform the world to a much safer place. Blockchain removes the trust gap that we have seen for generations. Before, we used intermediaries like banks to do financial transactions, which are not very safe for a variety of reasons such as centralization, lack of transparency, etc. But with the use of crypto-currencies, there is no need to trust an intermediatory, and we can overcome almost all the drawbacks caused by intermediaries.

Blockchain is a rising innovation. Consequently few designers are worried about the standards of computer programming applied to blockchain-based frameworks. By the by, the number and assortment of blockchain executions keeps on expanding. Also, the absence of rules and guidelines on the most proficient method to plan programming structures that incorporate keen agreements as a feature of the framework calls for additional attention. Therefore, adopters should zero in on choosing the arrangement that best meets their requirements and the necessities of their decentralized applications as opposed to growing one more blockchain without any preparation. Using this blockchain technology, there is a less chance to falsify property information, due to the transparency of blockchain, so real estate investment trusts can also be operated by the usage of issuing tokens for properties.

References

Al-Jaroodi, J., Mohamed, N., 2019. Blockchain in industries: a survey. IEEE Access 7, 36500–36515.

Chauhan, A., Malviya, O.P., Verma, M., Mor, T.S., July 2018. Blockchain and scalability. In: 2018 IEEE International Conference on Software Quality, Reliability and Security Companion (QRS-C). IEEE, pp. 122–128.

Cocco, L., Pinna, A., Marchesi, M., 2017. Banking on blockchain: costs savings thanks to the blockchain technology. Future Internet 9 (3), 25.

Dasgupta, D., Shrein, J.M., Gupta, K.D., 2019. A survey of blockchain from security perspective. J. Bank. Financial Technol. 3 (1), 1–17.

Guo, Y., Liang, C., 2016. Blockchain application and outlook in the banking industry. Financial Innov. 2 (1), 1–12.

Halaburda, H., 2018. Blockchain revolution without the blockchain? Commun. ACM 61 (7), 27–29.

Halpin, H., Piekarska, M., April 2017. Introduction to security and privacy on the blockchain. In: 2017 IEEE European Symposium on Security and Privacy Workshops (EuroS&PW). IEEE, pp. 1–3.

Kalodner, H., Möser, M., Lee, K., Goldfeder, S., Plattner, M., Chator, A., Narayanan, A., 2020. BlockSci: design and applications of a blockchain analysis platform. In: 29th Security Symposium ({USENIX} Security 20), pp. 2721–2738.

Karame, G., Capkun, S., 2018. Blockchain security and privacy. IEEE Secur. Priv. 16 (04), 11–12.

Karuppiah, M., Saravanan, R., 2014. A secure remote user mutual authentication scheme using smart cards. J. Inf. Secur. Appl. 19 (4–5), 282–294.

Karuppiah, M., Saravanan, R., 2015. A secure authentication scheme with user anonymity for roaming service in global mobility networks. Wireless Pers. Commun. 84 (3), 2055–2078.

Karuppiah, M., Kumari, S., Das, A.K., Li, X., Wu, F., Basu, S., 2016. A secure lightweight authentication scheme with user anonymity for roaming service in ubiquitous networks. Secur. Commun. Network. 9 (17), 4192–4209.

Karuppiah, M., Kumari, S., Li, X., Wu, F., Das, A.K., Khan, M.K., Basu, S., 2017. A dynamic id-based generic framework for anonymous authentication scheme for roaming service in global mobility networks. Wireless Pers. Commun. 93 (2), 383–407.

Karuppiah, M., Das, A.K., Li, X., Kumari, S., Wu, F., Chaudhry, S.A., Niranchana, R., 2019. Secure remote user mutual authentication scheme with key agreement for cloud environment. Mobile Network. Appl. 24 (3), 1046–1062.

Khan, M.A., Salah, K., 2018. IoT security: review, blockchain solutions, and open challenges. Future Generat. Comput. Syst. 82, 395–411.

Kshetri, N., Voas, J., 2018. Blockchain-enabled e-voting. IEEE Softw. 35 (4), 95–99.

Kumari, S., Karuppiah, M., Li, X., Wu, F., Das, A.K., Odelu, V., 2016. An enhanced and secure trust-extended authentication mechanism for vehicular ad-hoc networks. Secur. Commun. Network. 9 (17), 4255–4271.

Li, X., Niu, J., Bhuiyan, M.Z.A., Wu, F., Karuppiah, M., Kumari, S., 2017. A robust ECC-based provable secure authentication protocol with privacy preserving for industrial internet of things. IEEE Trans. Ind. Inform. 14 (8), 3599–3609.

Lamport, L., Shostak, R., Pease, M., 1982. The Byzantine generals problem. ACM Trans. Program. Languages Syst. (TOPLAS) 4 (3), 382–401.

Li, X., Jiang, P., Chen, T., Luo, X., Wen, Q., 2020. A survey on the security of blockchain systems. Future Generat. Comput. Syst. 107, 841–853.

Lin, I.C., Liao, T.C., 2017. A survey of blockchain security issues and challenges. Int. J. Netw. Secur. 19 (5), 653–659.

Maria, A., Pandi, V., Lazarus, J.D., Karuppiah, M., Christo, M.S., 2021. BBAAS: Blockchain-Based Anonymous Authentication Scheme for Providing Secure Communication in VANETs. Security and Communication Networks.

Mettler, M., September 2016. Blockchain technology in healthcare: the revolution starts here. In: 2016 IEEE 18th International Conference on E-Health Networking, Applications and Services (Healthcom). IEEE, pp. 1–3.

Naeem, M., Chaudhry, S.A., Mahmood, K., Karuppiah, M., Kumari, S., 2020. A scalable and secure RFID mutual authentication protocol using ECC for Internet of Things. Int. J. Commun. Syst. 33 (13), e3906.

Nguyen, G.T., Kim, K., 2018. A survey about consensus algorithms used in blockchain. J.Inf. Process. Syst. 14 (1), 101–128.

Niranjanamurthy, M., Nithya, B.N., Jagannatha, S., 2019. Analysis of blockchain technology: pros, cons and SWOT. Cluster Comput. 22 (6), 14743–14757.

Park, J.H., Park, J.H., 2017. Blockchain security in cloud computing: use cases, challenges, and solutions. Symmetry 9 (8), 164.

Pradhan, A., Karuppiah, M., Niranchana, R., Jerlin, M.A., Rajkumar, S., 2018. Design and analysis of smart card-based authentication scheme for secure transactions. Int. J. Internet Technol. Secur. Trans. 8 (4), 494–515.

Saberi, S., Kouhizadeh, M., Sarkis, J., Shen, L., 2019. Blockchain technology and its relationships to sustainable supply chain management. Int. J. Prod. Res. 57 (7), 2117–2135.

Sankar, L.S., Sindhu, M., Sethumadhavan, M., January 2017. Survey of consensus protocols on blockchain applications. In: 2017 4th International Conference on Advanced Computing and Communication Systems (ICACCS). IEEE, pp. 1—5.

Scott, R., Kaiser, B., Yerukhimovich, A., Clark, J., Cunningham, R., 2020. Blockchain technology and its potential use cases. Commun. ACM 63 (1), 46—53.

Subramanian, H., 2017. Decentralized blockchain-based electronic marketplaces. Commun. ACM 61 (1), 78—84.

Syed, T.A., Alzahrani, A., Jan, S., Siddiqui, M.S., Nadeem, A., Alghamdi, T., 2019. A comparative analysis of blockchain architecture and its applications: problems and recommendations. IEEE Access 7, 176838—176869.

Tapscott, A., Tapscott, D., 2017. How blockchain is changing finance. Harv. Bus. Rev. 1 (9), 2—5.

Tasatanattakool, P., Techapanupreeda, C., 2018. Blockchain: challenges and applications. In: 2018 International Conference on Information Networking (ICOIN). IEEE, pp. 473—475.

Wüst, K., Gervais, A., 2018. Do You Need a Blockchain? 2018 Crypto Valley Conference on Blockchain Technology (CVCBT), Zug, Switzerland, pp. 45—54.

Xu, X., Weber, I., Staples, M., Zhu, L., Bosch, J., Bass, L., Rimba, P., 2017. A taxonomy of blockchain-based systems for architecture design. In: 2017 IEEEinternational Conference on Software Architecture (ICSA). IEEE, pp. 243—252.

Xu, X., Weber, I., Staples, M., 2019. Architecture for Blockchain Applications. Springer, pp. 1—307.

Yeoh, P., 2017. Regulatory issues in blockchain technology. J. Financ. Regul. Compl. 25 (2), 196—208.

Zhang, R., Xue, R., Liu, L., 2019. Security and privacy on blockchain. ACM Comput. Surv. 52 (3), 1—34.

Zheng, Z., Xie, S., Dai, H.N., Chen, X., Wang, H., 2018. Blockchain challenges and opportunities: a survey. Int. J. Web Grid Serv. 14 (4), 352—375.

Zhou, Q., Huang, H., Zheng, Z., Bian, J., 2020. Solutions to scalability of blockchain: a survey. IEEE Access 8, 16440—16455.

CHAPTER 2

Blockchain: a new perspective in cyber technology

T. Venkat Narayana Rao[1], Purva Pravin Likhar[2], Muralidhar Kurni[3] and K. Saritha[4]

[1]Department of Computer Science and Engineering, Sreenidhi Institute of Science and Technology, Hyderabad, Telangana, India; [2]Mahatma Gandhi Institute of Technology, Hyderabad, Telangana, India; [3]Department of Computer Science, School of Science, GITAM (Deemed to be Univerity), Hyderabad, Telangana, India; [4]Independent Researcher, Ananthapuram, Andhra Pradesh, India

1. Introduction

Development is an inevitable condition of humankind. With each day passing, millions of people find themselves in the continuous process of searching for solutions to billions of problems that require global attention. The exchange of cash has been a long-standing issue. The rise of banks and other intermediary people like brokers has contributed to cash exchange, making it a more complex problem to ensure legitimate transactions between any two parties.

It was 2008 when a solution finally surfaced to put the problem at hand to rest, as shown in Fig. 2.1. *Bitcoin* soon enjoyed huge success and became the most famous cryptocurrency, with its market reaching billions of dollars in less than a decade after its invention (Damak, 2018). To facilitate the transactions involving Bitcoin, a special data storage structure called *blockchain* was designed, and soon enough, this technology was used in other spheres (Frizzo-Barker et al., 2020).

1.1 Blockchain technology and its history

As the saying "Rome was not built in a day" goes, blockchains were not invented and developed in the 21st century. This technology dates to 1982 when Cryptographer David Chaum proposed a protocol similar to blockchain (Zhang et al., 2019). A few years later, Stuart Harbor and Scott Stornetta described a "cryptographically secure" chain of blocks in 1991, and their work concentrated on timestamping documents. They aimed to design a system that would maintain the integrity of these documents. In 1992, *Merkle trees* were incorporated into the design, which facilitated collecting several documents into a single *block*, improving the system's

Blockchain Technology for Emerging Applications
ISBN 978-0-323-90193-2
https://doi.org/10.1016/B978-0-323-90193-2.00004-1

33

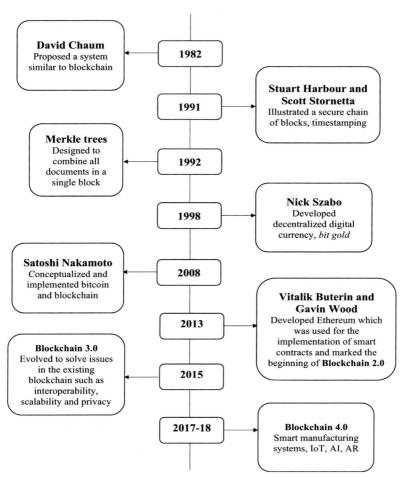

Figure 2.1 Blockchain technology evolution.

efficiency (Yangui et al., 2019). Digital currencies came into the picture in 1998 when a renowned computer scientist, Nick Szabo, started working on and designing something called *bit gold*, decentralized entities (Nian and Chuen, 2015). Finally, in 2008, the theory of blockchains and bitcoins was conceptualized and deployed under the name Satoshi Nakamoto, an anonymous developer or community of developers (Caradonna, 2020). Nakamoto authored the Bitcoin white paper and designed a system that used hashing techniques to timestamp blocks without a third party's involvement. It is speculated by many that Nick Szabo is, in fact, Satoshi Nakamoto since bit gold is said to be a direct precursor to Bitcoin architecture.

While it was not the first time an online currency was proposed, Bitcoin solved problems beyond imagination. It could be used as a form of virtual cash that could be sent peer to peer without a bank or other authorities and assisted the ledger's maintenance by an unbiased party. The engine that runs this ledger is known as "blockchain," and the first block of Bitcoin ever mined , the *genesis block*, was created by Nakamoto in 2009, and this block is known to be the foundation for all other blocks in the Bitcoin blockchain (Forsstr, 2015). As years passed, blockchain came into use for applications beyond currency and has been classified into four progressive eras. While Blockchain 1.0 was primarily focused on cryptocurrencies, Blockchain 2.0 included smart contracts, smart property, security trading, banking, and other finance areas. Blockchain 3.0 marked the technology usage in healthcare and biomedicine, arts, culture, science, and technology. The era of Blockchain 4.0 allowed decentralizing of IT systems and expanding these on cross-business processes like supply chain management, asset and resource management, and financial management (Xu et al., 2019).

2. Blockchain architecture

Blockchain refers to a sequence of blocks that contains a list of all immutable transactions occurring in a distributed network of nodes avoiding a single point of failure and denies the empowerment of a central authority to control its working. It is also referred to as a public distributed ledger system. This means that each node on the network possesses a copy of the shared data, so if any one of the nodes attempts to alter the data, it will not go unnoticed.

Fig. 2.2 represents a simple blockchain with a sequence of three blocks (Ismail and Materwala, 2019). As can be seen, each block contains a parent block hash. This hash value contains the identity of its previous block. If any blocks are removed, replaced, or misplaced with other blocks in the chain, they can be easily identified by verifying with this value. It is to be noted that the genesis block does not have a parent block, so the parent block hash value equals 0.

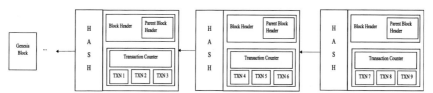

Figure 2.2 Simple blockchain.

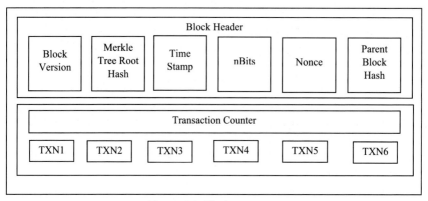

Figure 2.3 Block structure.

Fig. 2.3 represents the structure of a typical block. Each block consists of two main parts: *block header* and *block body*.

2.1 Block header

The block header contains the following fields:

a. Block version: This indicates which set of block validation rules or protocols are to be followed.

b. Merkle tree root hash: It is the hash values of all transactions present in the block body.

c. Timestamp: It provides the current time in seconds since January 1, 1970.

d. nBits: This is the target threshold of a valid block hash.

e. Nonce: It is a 4-byte field that starts with 0 and increases with each hash calculation made.

f. Parent block hash: As discussed earlier, it is a 256-bit hash value that points to the previous block.

2.2 Block body

A block body comprises two fields: the transaction counter and the transactions *TXN*. Depending on the size of each transaction's block and size, the maximum number of transactions may vary (Fig. 2.4).

To validate the transactions, blockchain makes use of asymmetric cryptography or public-key cryptosystems. These mechanisms make use of a digital signature to verify the authenticity of transactions. The typical digital signature algorithm used in the blockchain is the elliptic curve digital signature algorithm. For example, when a user A wants to send a message to another user B, the following process occurs (Fig. 2.5).

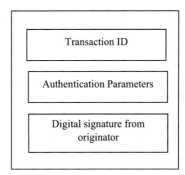

Figure 2.4 Transaction.

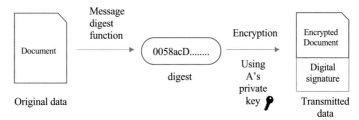

Figure 2.5 Signing.

On the original document, a message digest function is applied that creates a digest value, after which using the sender A's private key, the document is encrypted and a digital signature is attached.

After the receiver B receives the document, the same message digest function is applied that was applied on the originator end to obtain a digest value. Using B's public key, the transmitted document is decrypted and another digest value is obtained. If these values are the same, the signature is verified and added to the transactions block, as shown in Fig. 2.6.

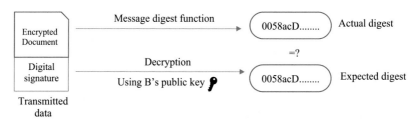

Figure 2.6 Verifying.

It is important to note that an additional database is also maintained by all the nodes known as the *Unspent Transaction Outputs* cache (UTXO) aside from the blockchain. It is a ledger with the records of funds available for every address and acts as a cache for the blockchain. As new transactions occur, UTXO gets updated: funds from sending addresses are subtracted and added to the receiving addresses. The Bitcoin Node software uses a key-value store, LevelDB, to hold a copy of the UTXO.

3. Blockchain concepts

Blockchain is a technology based on two essential concepts: *hashing* and *timestamping* (Sabry et al., 2019).

3.1 Hash functions

A hash function uses an algorithm that transforms an input of arbitrary length into a fixed-length hash value. Hash values generated are the same for the same input value. Hash functions map input to output, so small differences in input produce large differences in the result and are often used in computing since they locate data quickly using hash tables. Bitcoins use cryptographic hash functions, also known as secure hash functions, to perform consensus operations. These functions possess additional features over and above usual hash properties, such as the following:

- One-way function or resistance: If a hash value is given, finding the input data must be infeasible.
- Poor resistance to collisions: Given an input, finding another input with the same hash value must be computationally too tedious.
- Good resistance to collisions: It is computationally infeasible that they point to the same hash given two data points.

Bitcoin uses *SHA-256²* as its proof-of-work function (which will be discussed later in the chapter). SHA-256² refers to the application of the hashing algorithm SHA-256 twice. As evident as it is, SHA-256 produces an output that is 256 bits long and meets the preimage resistance requirement (Fig. 2.7).

In the Merkle-Damgård construction, cryptographic hashing functions are built using a compression function as a building block to accept arbitrary length input, where the compression function refers to the scrambling of the input by a variety of shifting and mixing operations. Merkle-Damgård has shown that if the compression is collision-resistant, then the whole

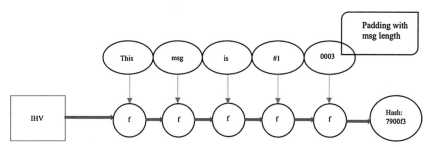

Figure 2.7 Merkle-Damgard construction.

construction is also. Referring to Fig. 2.7, and with the compression function labeled f, it is to be noted that f operates on 256 bits in the case of SHA-256. The compression function takes two inputs: a block of input data or a message and an intermediate hash value. To compute the hash value using SHA-256, input data is broken into blocks of length 256 bits with the end of the message padded with zeroes. The intermediate hash value is given to IHV (initial hash value), and the compression value is applied to each block by applying the hash value from the previous step to the next step. Finally, the last value yields the whole input's SHA-256 hash.

The Merkle-Damgard structure is prone to *length extension attacks*. Ferguson et al. suggested that one way of fighting the length extension problem would be to hash the message twice, and it is believed that Nakamoto chose SHA-256² instead of SHA-256 for the same reason.

3.2 Timestamp

A digital timestamp is the same as a physical timestamp. It establish that some information, like a digital document, remained at a particular point in time, and it serves useful when two parties agree to a contract or transactions take place over a digital medium. Usually, the information in the timestamp is the hash of the data that is to be secured. This has several advantages:

(i) The timestamp information is kept private and separate from the medium that is used to secure the timestamp.

(ii) It decreases storage costs since a hash is considerably smaller than the information it generates.

(iii) Digital signatures work best on data whose size is already determined.

There are many ways through which a timestamp can be secured. The easiest way would be to send a trusted party a copy of the information, and they would store this data and the time of reception in a safe place. The problem with such a method is that a trusted third party may lose the database or be compromised. Another way would be to rely on a *time-stamping authority* (TSA), a trusted third party, to sign the data and the time when the data was communicated with its private key. This signature would be sent back to the original owner, but the timestamp will lose its integrity if the TSA collaborates with another party.

A third method would involve publishing the hash of the data in a public place, such as the newspaper. If an attacker wishes to alter any of the transactions, it will collide with the hash published in a public newspaper, as shown in Fig. 2.8. A TSA could use this idea too, but it would prove costly to publish a hash for every transaction. Instead, hashes of multiple data can be combined to achieve economies of scale. This can be executed efficiently by using Merkle trees, covered in Section 7.

Another refinement to further secure timestamps could be the usage of lined timestamps, as shown in Fig. 2.9. The main aim behind this is that if the hash to be published is connected to the hash already published, it will help protect the older hash. An attacker with malicious intent would now have to face a double collision if he/she desires to alter data from an older hash, and after another step in the chain, the collision would be triple and so on. Thus, the security of this chain increases exponentially.

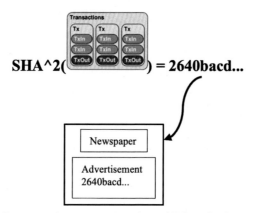

Figure 2.8 Timestamping transactions by publishing hash in newspapers.

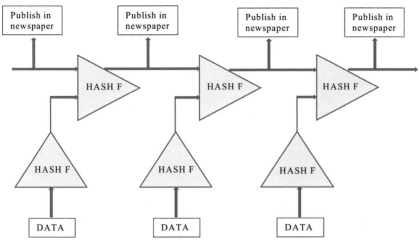

Figure 2.9 Linked timestamps.

Let us review some simple Java code to create a block to the blockchain.

```java
// creating a block in a blockchain

import java.util.Date;

public class Block {
        private String hash;
        private String previoushash;
        private String data;
        private long TimeStamp;
        private int nonce;

        //constructor
        public Block(String data, String previoushash, long TimeStamp) {
                this.data = data;
                this.previoushash = previoushash;
                this.TimeStamp = new Date().getTime();
                this.hash = calcBlockHash();
        }

        //function to calculate hash
        public String calcBlockHash() {

                String calchash = crypt.sha256(previoushash +
                Long.toString(TimeStamp) + data);

                return calchash;
        }
}
```

In this code, four main attributes are seen that are used to create a block:
- *previoushash*: hash of the previous block
- *data*: actual content in the block, which may include numbers, strings, or a combination of both
- *TimeStamp*: the time of the creation of the block
- *hash*: the hash value of the current block
- *nonce*: used for cryptography

The method *calcBlockHash()* uses the user-defined class *crypt* to calculate the hash of the current block by concatenating *previoushash*, *TimeStamp*, and *data* values. This value is stored in a variable, *calchash*, which is then returned (Fig. 2.9).

Generating hash values:

```
// generating hash of the present block

public class crypt {

        public static String sha256(String input) {

                try {
                        MessageDigest md = MessageDigest.getInstance("SHA-
                256");

                        int i = 0;
                        String hex;

                        byte[] hash = md.digest(input.getBytes("UTF-8"));
                        StringBuffer hexhash = new StringBuffer();

                        while ( i < hash.length) {
                                hex = Integer.toHexString(0xff & hash[i]);

                                if (hex.length()==1)
                                        hexhash.append('0');

                                hexhash.append(hex);
                                i++;
                        }

                        return hexhash.toString();
                }

                catch (Exception e) {
                        throw new RuntimeException(e);
                }
        }
}
```

In this snippet, the following points must be noted:

- Using *MessageDigest*, an instance of the hash function SHA-256 is obtained.
- Then, a hash value for our input data, stored in a local variable *input*, is generated in the form of a byte array, *hash*.
- Finally, this byte array is transformed into a hexadecimal hash, *hexhash*, which is then converted into a string.

The principle behind the blockchain technology is mutual trust or consensus, and the algorithms in the next section are the last pieces of the puzzle to achieve it.

4. Consensus algorithms

Before diving into the algorithms, it is important to briefly understand the meaning and importance of consensus in blockchain technology.

4.1 What is the consensus?

The Byzantine Generals (BG) Problem occurred in the 13th century, which involved generals with their armies attempting to capture an encircled city. The attack would prove to be successful if all the armies attacked the city at the same time. Since all the generals belonged to different armies, coordination would be the main problem because their only way of communication would be through messengers. It is also possible that any of the generals may be traitors and may intercept the messages between two parties and attempt to modify them to cause the attack to fail. How to avoid single point failure, make a coordinated attack, and build trust among peers form the basis of today's blockchains.

Consensus refers to mutual trust or understanding between parties to agree on what is true. Consensus mechanisms or algorithms are strategies that a group of computers deploys in blockchains to achieve a common point of agreement or a single state of the network (Wang et al., 2019). There are many techniques to address this issue, which will be discussed further.

4.2 Consensus algorithm: Proof of Work (PoW)

In a decentralized network, a node is selected to record all the transactions within the network. The simplest way to select this node is to make a random selection, but its problem is that it is prone to attacks. Therefore, if a node is interested in publishing a block of transactions, it must do much computational work to prove that it is unlikely to attack the network. This forms the basis of PoW. It is a strategy that deploys the nodes in the network to calculate the block header's hash. As discussed in the blockchain architecture, each block contains a nonce value, and the nodes would make changes to the nonce frequently to get different hash values. The consensus demands that the estimated value must be equal to or less than a specific given value. Once a node reaches this target value, it broadcasts the block to all the other nodes in the network, and all the nodes are supposed to confirm the accuracy of the hash value mutually. If it is validated, this new block is appended by all the nodes to their blockchains, and this process takes place every 10 min. The nodes contributing their computing ability to the partial hash inversion power are termed miners, and this process is called mining. In simple terms, mining is the process of guessing a nonce that generates a hash with the first x number of zeroes.

The following program aims to make the mining concept clear and use a brute force approach to achieve this goal.

```
//mining the block

public String miningblock (int prefix) {
        String prefstr = new String (new char[prefix]).replace('\0',
        '0');

        while (!hash.susbstring(0, prefix).equals(prefstr)) {
                nonce++;
                hash = calcBlockHash();

        }
        return hash;

}
```

In the code, the following process is seen:
- Define the desired prefix.
- Then, check whether the solution has been obtained.
- If the solution has not been found, increment the nonce and calculate the hash using *calcBlockHash()*.
- This process continues until the required result is attained.
  Fig. 2.10 illustrates the PoW working.

The question is *why would anyone want to go through a complex problem and solve it computationally and keep the blockchain growing?* This is because miners

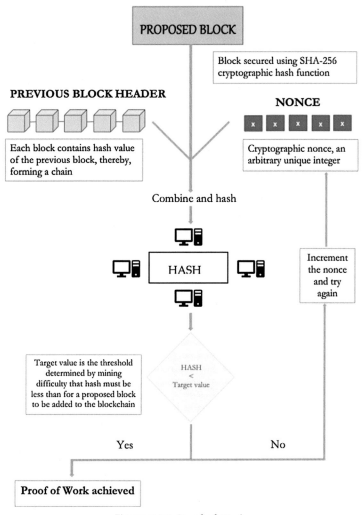

Figure 2.10 Proof of Work.

receive *mining rewards* in the form of coins or any other way that the application may want to reward its participants. The winning miner is given the block reward and the transaction fees every 10 min.

Sometimes, two miners may arrive at the same block by finding the nonce at the same time. This may result in *forking*. This results in network division, and some miners regard one branch as valid, while others follow

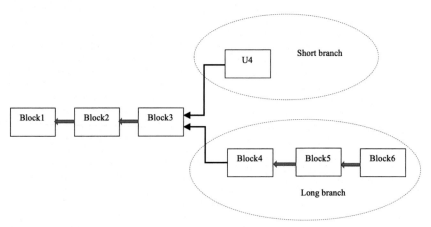

Figure 2.11 Forking.

the different branch of execution. The procedure specifies that the right branch is the longest, as seen in Fig. 2.13. Therefore, the other branch, *U4*, is discarded (known as *orphan blocks*), and miners stop working on it.

The problem with PoW is that computing calculations waste many resources. To mitigate these issues, some PoW protocols have been designed to include a side application.

4.3 Consensus algorithm: proof of stake (PoS)

PoS is an alternative to PoW, which locks crypto assets to protect the network. Miners in PoS are asked to prove their possession of the currency. The basic concept of PoS is focused on a randomly chosen state of validators who "stake" the native network tokens by locking them into the blockchain to generate and accept blocks. Validators are compensated directly proportional to their total stake, incentivizing nodes to validate the network based on a return on investment. Then, based on their stakes, validators are picked to follow their next blocks. While often programmed with random functions to prevent front-running consensus, a greater amount staked by a validator gives them a higher probability of producing the next block. Proposed blocks by validators are then propagated or broadcasted to the rest of the set, verifying and appending the blockchain's accepted block, as shown in Fig. 2.11.

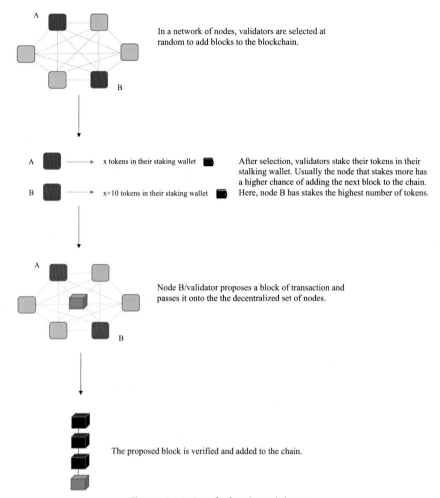

In a network of nodes, validators are selected at random to add blocks to the blockchain.

A → x tokens in their staking wallet

B → x+10 tokens in their staking wallet

After selection, validators stake their tokens in their stalking wallet. Usually the node that stakes more has a higher chance of adding the next block to the chain. Here, node B has stakes the highest number of tokens.

Node B/validator proposes a block of transaction and passes it onto the the decentralized set of nodes.

The proposed block is verified and added to the chain.

Figure 2.12 Proof of stake validators.

It is usually believed that people with greater amounts are less likely to attack the network, but this gives dominance to the richest person. Therefore, many solutions were identified with a combination of the stake size to decide which one will forge the next block, like the lowest hash values, the age of the set of coins, etc. Many blockchains adopt PoW initially and ultimately transform into PoS, like the one Ethereum has been

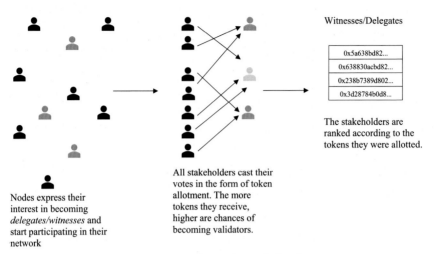

Witnesses/Delegates

0x5a638bd82...
0x638830acbd82...
0x238b7389d802...
0x3d28784b0d8...

The stakeholders are ranked according to the tokens they were allotted.

All stakeholders cast their votes in the form of token allotment. The more tokens they receive, higher are chances of becoming validators.

Nodes express their interest in becoming *delegates/witnesses* and start participating in their network

Figure 2.13 Delegated proof of stake.

developing. This kind of hybrid model is known as *Casper*. Unlike in PoW, miners in PoS are not rewarded with a mining reward. Instead, they charge a transaction fee or a network fee to add blocks to the blockchain.

4.4 Consensus algorithm: delegated proof of stake (DPoS)

The significant difference between DPoS and PoS is that DPoS is representative democratic. In the sense that stakeholders elect their delegates to generate and validate their blocks, they appoint them as validators. Since the nodes are fewer in number, validation takes less time, so transactions are made faster. Additionally, delegates are free to tune block size and block intervals, and users may vote dishonestly to delegate if needed (Figs. 2. 12 and 2.13).

4.5 Consensus algorithm: Practical Byzantine Fault Tolerance (PBFT)

PBFT is a replication algorithm proposed to tolerate *Byzantine faults*, the problems that occurred in the BG problem, and it is known to handle one-third of these faults. The whole process is divided into three parts: *preprepared*, *prepared*, and *committed*. In each round, a *primary* (0) is selected according to some set conditions and is responsible for ordering transactions; a client *C*

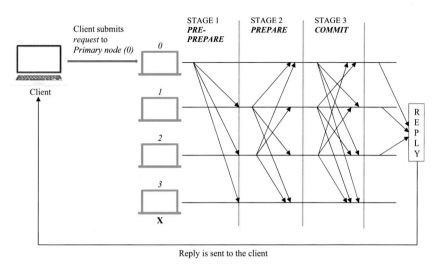

Figure 2.14 Practical Byzantine Fault Tolerance.

submits a request to the primary node. The primary sends messages to everyone (*nodes 1,2,3, wherein the third node may have lost connection and dropped from the network*). Other nodes accept the message as long as it is valid. Increasingly, these messages often contain signatures and sequence numbers to determine message validity (Fig. 2.14). If a node accepts a prepared message, it recognizes it by sending a prepared message to everyone. The receiving nodes accept these prepared messages as long as they are true. A node is then called prepared if it received the original request from the main, preprepared message and saw 2f prepare messages (received from other nodes), making it 2f+1, where f is the Byzantine fault number. After nodes have been prepared, they send a commit message to the rest of the nodes, and if a node receives valid commit messages from f+1, they perform the client's request and send the reply to the client. On the other hand, the client waits for f+1 answers and declares them correct. A node would reach the next step if it obtained two-thirds of all nodes. PBFT demands that the network knows each node and queries other nodes.

Table 2.1 explains the comparison among the algorithms discussed based on the mentioned criteria.

Table 2.1 Consensus algorithms comparison.

Property Algorithm	PoW (proof of work)	PoS (proof of stake)	DPoS (delegated proof of stake)	PBFT (Practical Byzantine Fault Tolerance)
Energy saving	No	Partial	Partial	Yes
Tolerated power of adversary	<25% computing	<51% stake	<51% validators	<33.3% faulty replicas
Application of algorithm	Bitcoin	Peercoin	Bitshares	Hyperledger fabric

5. Blockchain validity

Before diving into how to check if a block on a blockchain is valid, these blocks must be stored to be verified later. In the program below, these blocks are stored in an array list of *blockchain*.

```java
//to store blocks of a blockchain, we make use of ArrayList

import java.util.ArrayList;

public class Storingblocks {

        //creating ArrayList object
        public static ArrayList<Block> blckchain = new ArrayList<Block>();

        public static void main (String[] args) {

                blckchain.add(new Block("1st block", "0"));
                blckchain.add(new Block("2nd block",
        blckchain.get(blckchain.size()-1.hash));
                blckchain.add(new Block("3rd block",
        blckchain.get(blckchain.size()-1.hash));
                blckchain.add(new Block("2nd block",
        blckchain.get(blckchain.size()-1.hash));
                blckchain.add(new Block("2nd block",
        blckchain.get(blckchain.size()-1.hash));

        }
    }
```

```
//validate blocks on blockchain

public static Boolean ChainValidity() {
        Block presentblock;
        Block prevblock;

        for(int i=1; i < blckchain.size(); i++) {

                //storing the current and previous block

                presentblock = blckchain.get(i);
                prevblock = blckchain.get(i-1);

                //checking if present hash equals to calculate hash or not

                if (!presentblock.hash
                        .equals(presentblock.
                                calcBlockHash())) {

                        System.out.println("Hashes are unequal");
                        return false;
                }

                //checking if previous hash equals to calculated previous
                //hash value or not

                if (!prevblock.hash
                        .equals(presentblock.prevhash)) {

                        System.out.println("Previous hash values are
                        unequal");
                        return false;
                }
        }

        //if all hashes are equal to their respective calculated hashes,
        //then it the blockchain is completely verified

        return true;
}
```

6. Blockchain attacks

A double-spend attack happens when two separate transactions try to expend the same funds. Usually, the protocol defends this attack by deciding the valid transaction as the one that makes its way to the blockchain. Thus, this issue is addressed in a decentralized manner without the intervention of a single central authority. A transaction is further made safe when more blocks are stacked on top of the block where it was first included. Therefore, if an attacker wishes to alter a particular block, he will have to mine all the blocks to make way to the desired block (Moubarak et al., 2018). Since adding blocks is a continuous process, the attacker would have to redo all the precedent work and keep pace with the new blocks added to the blockchain. The only way to accomplish such a task is to command a hash rate as high as the other hash rates of the network. The hash rate refers to hash rates for blocks in the blockchain. This attack is known as a 51% attack, and an attacker who controls less than half of the network is still possible. The likelihood of success depends on the hash rate regulation of the attacker and the number of blocks to dig in, and this likelihood decreases exponentially. If the attacker can monitor >50% of the network hash rate, the likelihood of success becomes 100%. A 51% attacker can change transactions he controls and trigger double spending on those assets but cannot change the transaction receiver, as the elliptic curve cryptography (ECC) signature protects it.

A race attack happens by checking some nodes when a vendor accepts payment of an unconfirmed transaction. The attacker may submit a transaction to vendor-near nodes and a different transaction to several other network nodes. Thus, only the nodes closest to the vendor reveal the transaction sending funds to the vendor, while the remaining network contains double spending in their mempool. To defend against this attack, a vendor should wait for the transaction to be at least one block (Moubarak et al., 2018).

Bitcoin developer Hal Finney discovered the Finney attack. Moreover, a miner is required to premine one transaction into a newly created, unreleased block and spend the coins. If the payment is still unconfirmed, the new block will include a double-spending transaction. The solution to solve the Finney attack is to wait for at least six confirmations.

Attackers may also try to perform a DoS (denial of service) attack on the network by generating surplus transactions to fund themselves and stop legitimate transactions. However, this offense is unlikely to happen since the number of free transactions an attacker can send to the network is of a limited number, the fees to complete this payment would have to compete with the fees of a legitimate transaction, and these transactions must be made above a certain threshold.

7. Merkle trees

The data structure proposed by Ralph Merkle in 1982 is one Merkle tree or hash tree. Nakamoto assumed the concept of Merkle trees to timestamp

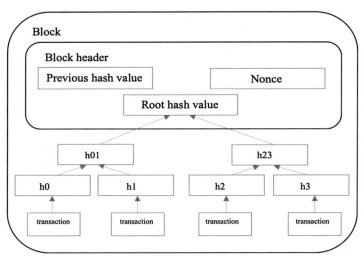

Figure 2.15 Merkle tree of transactions for a block.

a block of transactions. These trees are commonly used in file-sharing applications to keep track of blocks of files (Mercan et al., 2020). Fig. 2.15 shows how Merkle trees compute the hash value of a block. Initially, a binary tree, where each parent node has two children, is formed with hashes of individual transactions as leaves denoted by h0, … h. The hash of the parent node is denoted by the hash of its two children, i.e., h01 = H(h0), where H stands for SHA–256 hash function. Finally, the hash of the root node, Merkle root, is calculated, and now this can be appended to the block header (refer to Fig. 2.15).

Transaction authentication is one of the main drawbacks of the Merkle tree. Assume that a node would like to search whether a t3 is a block transaction. A node can accomplish this task in log(n) time when n is the number of nodes. The node has to measure h3, h23, and the root hash and verify the root hash stored on the block according to Fig. 2.15. This means the node can only search the unique branch of Merkle.

8. How secure is blockchain?

The original version of blockchain uses the SHA–256 algorithm, which was already discussed earlier in the chapter. Despite being secure, SHA–256 faced inefficiency issues due to which specialized hardware, *mining rigs*, were developed to handle the processing of transactions and confirm and rely on valid transactions by solving mathematical problems called *hashes*. Apart from hashes, the cryptographic information on each block of records contains a unique timestamp, making the blockchain more secure (Bashir, 2018).

Imagine a person adding links to the chain of blocks, and someone comes along, chooses a link in the middle of the chain, and starts adding his blocks to the link. This results in forking (refer to Fig. 2.13). Blockchains can be forked for various reasons, like falsely altering a record on the preexisting chain, or someone may wish to take control of the whole system. It is simple enough to compare the hash and timestamp of the block to verify the original, valid record in both cases. This scenario happened in 2013 due to a faulty update, but the swift reaction by blockchain developers and warning miners showed that it is possible to recognize and isolate fraudulent forks quickly. An alert expert on the blockchain can isolate a node that has gone rogue or shows signs of tampering without compromising the rest of the system, which benefits from having a decentralized system.

9. Challenges and recent advances

Given the potential of blockchain, it faces quite a few challenges that hinder its use. Some shortcomings and advances in the areas are as follows (Chen, 2018; Zheng et al., 2017; Pajooh et al., 2021).

9.1 Scalability

Blockchain becomes bulkier as the number of transactions grows daily. Each node must have the details of transactions to validate and verify on the blockchain. Due to the block and time interval's original size to generate a new block, blockchain can process only seven transactions per second. Moreover, because the block's capacity is less, small transactions might get postponed because miners prefer transactions with higher transaction fees. There were two methods designed to fight this problem:

a. storage optimization of blocks by adopting a novel cryptocurrency scheme that ensures removal of old transactions by networks using *Ver-Sum*, which allows lightweight clients to outsource expensive computation over large inputs;

b. redesigning blockchain through *Bitcoin-NG* (next generation), whose main idea is to divide a conventional block into a key block for leader election and microbook to store transactions.

9.2 Selfish mining

In this strategy, selfish miners keep their mined blocks without broadcasting, and this private branch would be revealed only when some conditions are met. The private branch would ultimately grow longer than the current public chain; all the miners in the network would admit it; therefore, the honest miners would be wasting their energy and resources on a useless branch, and selfish miners would be mining on their unpublished private chain without anyone to compete with. Therefore, selfish miners would be earning more. To fix this problem, Heilman proposed a novel approach for honest miners to decide which branch to follow with random beacons and timestamps. Another approach would be to generate and accept each block within a maximum interval of time. This approach, known as *ZeroBlock*, would disable selfish miners from achieving more than expected revenue (Li, 2019).

9.3 Privacy leakage

It is a lesser-known fact that blockchain cannot guarantee transactional privacy because the values of all transactions and balances for each public key are made publicly available. New research has revealed that a user's Bitcoin transactions can be connected to his personal information. A method was proposed to connect user pseudonyms to IP addresses even when users use firewalls to protect their identity. However, the origin of the transaction could still be found. Since then, multiple methods have come into the picture to solve this issue:

a. Mixing: It refers to the strategy that provides anonymity to users by exchanging funds from multiple source addresses to multiple destination addresses, so intermediary nodes can be used to transfer data between two parties. For example, consider A with address a wants to transfer funds to B possessing address b. If it sends money to B directly, their relationship might be revealed. On the other hand, if A sends money to a trusted intermediary C with multiple inputs $c1$, $c2$, $c3$, etc., and multiple outputs $d1$, $d2$, $d3$, b, etc., deliver the money to B, it becomes hard to reveal the relationship between A and B. However, there may come a point where these intermediary nodes like C may behave dishonestly. Mixcoin devises a simple method to avoid such behavior. The intermediate node encrypts user information, including fund amount and transfer date, with its private key, and if the intermediate node fails to send the money, anybody could verify that the intermediary cheated. This method, however, detects theft but fails to prevent it. Coinjoin depends on a central server to shuffle output addresses to prevent theft. An improvisation to this, CoinShuffle uses decryption mix nets for address mixing and shuffling.

b. Anonymous: In Zerocoin, a zero-knowledge proof mechanism is used. The origin of payments is unlinked from their transactions, so graph analyses cannot be made. In Zerocash, zk-SNARKS (zero-knowledge succinct noninteractive arguments of knowledge) is leveraged, so the transaction amount and the coin values that a user possesses are hidden.

10. Emerging applications of blockchain

Blockchain technology has been in use mostly in the financial domain. Specific industries have contributed tools to help financial institutions and governments in monitoring the exchange of cryptocurrency. They detect frauds, money laundering, and compliance violation issues, helping the general public to invest their trust in blockchains. Thanks to the rise in Blockchain 2.0, Blockchain 3.0, and Blockchain 4.0, others have been trying to apply this technology in their field. To enhance their systems and improve their performance, conventional industries can use blockchain for their secure storage facilities. The following areas have benefitted from blockchain extensively (Li, 2019) (Bassi et al., 2020):

10.1 Blockchain and Internet-of-Things (IoT)

The past few years witnessed many evolutions, among which blockchains and the IoT happened to impact the world significantly. IoT has become a sensation worldwide due to its unique network of physically connected devices (which contain components such as chips, sensors, codes, software, and exchange data) via the internet. Since devices are connected via the internet, there lies a possibility that this exchange of information might face security and privacy issues. This is where blockchain technology can come into use. It is essential to ensure that the information flowing between the devices is safe and protected from unwanted parties. Many industries have developed software and hardware that are connected and operated via blockchain. Some benefits in this area include encryption of ledger data, real-time distribution of information between blockchain-connected devices, and monetization of machines based on timestamps. Following are some of the IoT systems that use Blockchain in their day-to-day use:

- Energy CPS: Energy grid systems come under complex cyber-physical systems or CPS, which direct some of the main functions such as energy generation, distribution, and utility in a bidirectional way. The main aim of blockchain technology is to provide a secure environment for interactions in such systems.
- Vehicular CPS: Many smart transportation systems, including unmanned aerial vehicles and autonomous driving cars, have been invented to solve traffic and road safety issues. Security and privacy are main drawbacks, so blockchain technology has been in use to leverage these intelligent systems due to their decentralized and immutable characteristics.
- Smart homes: We see several inventions regarding sensor-based lights, electrical systems such as fans and door locks, and devices that help other home operations. It is necessary to ensure that the right party is in command to dictate these devices' actions. Blockchain technology can be used to provide the right users with control of their devices.
- Internet of battlefield things: IoT has also been used in defense situations under the acronym IoBT. Smart defense vehicles and combat equipment with sensors are used to enable battlefield operations. Blockchain technology can, therefore, help in conducting secure and reliable commands for IoBT.
- Industrial IoT: IioT enables the integration of wireless components connected via the internet with processes that support industrial activities. These industrial operations comprise examination, monitoring, analysis, production, management, and distribution of items manufactured. These processes must be given equal importance to attain efficiency, safety, and quality, which is where blockchains are deployed.

10.2 Smart contracts

Smart contracts contain functions that consist of a set of instructions that are embedded with conditional statements. These instructions are self-executable, which means that the contracts execute the actions specified under the condition if the condition is met. Blockchain-based smart contracts are like agreements between parties who are obliged by the terms specified. The agreement is automatically implemented on the fulfillment of the conditions. When a new block is supposed to be added to the chain, miners do the computation work, and once all the users verify it, it is concatenated to the chain. Thus, smart contracts work only if there is mutual consensus in the group, thereby stressing the network of node decentralization.

10.3 Blockchain in education

Due to its strong cybersecurity capabilities, blockchain technology has made its place extensively in educational industry usage. Although its application in education is still in its early stages, blockchain can be widely used to issue, validate, and share data. Since blockchain comprises a digitalized, decentralized, and secure ledger, one can have their educational records under their authority and share these credentials with interested parties. Documents such as e-transcripts, digital degrees, and e-certificates can be easily exchanged among individuals or groups, like Nespore, who developed a blockchain certificate sharing platform to ease this process. Since blockchain technology keeps a complete record of a student's profile in data blocks in sequential order by timestamps, managing and verifying data becomes comfortable with full transparency and authenticity. Data blocks old and new cannot be deleted or tampered with, so it acts as a foolproof virtual infrastructure for storage of credentials and achievements indefinitely.

Furthermore, the ubiquitous learning or U-learning system was introduced, which equipped students with an engaging and collaborative learning environment with high security with blockchains, which facilitated web-based distance education. This reduces costs, procedures, and unnecessary paperwork in schools, colleges, and universities. Blockchain technology aims to end a high-cost, trustless, inefficient data management paper-based system and provide a secure, authoritative, transparent system, so applications like EduCTX that are blockchain-based higher education credit platforms have grown popular.

Even though blockchain offers many advantages to the academic sector, there are quite a few limitations. Since there are thousands of students whose records need to be maintained, educational organizations need to keep track of all these records. Due to the increased block size, the latency of transactions increases, making the system slow and repetitive, thereby giving rise to scalability problems. In addition to this, deploying blockchain also includes infrastructure costs, computing power costs, and time costs. There is also a possibility of security issues rising due to constant system updating to add newer features. Despite these issues, blockchain technology has been applied in many educational processes such as the following:

- Admissions: Students can easily fill out various applications and other formalities of different institutions across the world.
- University library and related services: With the advent of blockchain, library authorities can easily monitor the movement of books and students who have borrowed books. Obsolete methods of recordkeeping such as register maintenance can now be discarded with systematic ledger technology.
- Alumni contact: All necessary communication with students is stored in the form of blocks, which helps develop a good rapport with the alumni.
- Nonacademic achievement detail maintenance: Apart from education, the details of a student's extracurricular activities can be maintained as a part of his/her records, thereby facilitating a complete record of a student's merits.
- Intellectual property protection: Since many researchers in a university may be working on similar projects, it is possible that two parties may collide over intellectual property rights due to plagiarism. The use of blockchain avoids such a hassle by publishing research content while keeping an eye on citations and reuse.

10.4 Blockchain in healthcare

Although the medical industry is one of the last to put into use the latest technology, it is safe to say that blockchains might offer some advantages to the sector. The utility of blockchains can be expanded to medical fields such as pharmaceuticals, genome medicine, neurosciences, and clinical studies. Managing patient records so they are private and standardizing and looking for patterns among the huge, structured blocks of health data are main reasons for digitizing these details. Sensitive information related to patients and doctors must be transferred safely among parties without middlemen, and the accountability of all parties must be held. Due to blockchain-based smart contracts, the shared data parameters are maintained, and health plans are customized for patients. This would also help improve the security and privacy of these records by handing over their access to patients, making them available and retrievable from any part of the world. The patient could then monitor their health with their complete data record, which can be used for reference elsewhere stored in the InterPlanetary File System (IPFS). Another advantage to the healthcare industry would be managing the whole process of drug manufacture and distribution. Most blockchain projects employed in hospitals are built on IPFS to utilize encryption and minimize data redundancy with the help of off-chain cloud components using crypto algorithms.

Various blockchain-supporting companies have started offering data monetization and tokenization services. For example, Nebula Genomics provides genome sequencing for free to stock a blockchain-based genetic marketplace. On sequencing their genomes, users can charge an amount to any person who wants to access it, and these tokens can be redeemed for future products and services. Another blockchain company named Genomes.io allows users to sequence their genomes and stores them securely, allowing access to only a select group of people. Users can sell their genetic data in parts and, at the same time, prevent their data from falling into the wrong hands. In collaboration with an fast healthcare interoperability resources (FHIR) enabled EHR (electronic health record) aggregator mobile application, Health Wizz allows users to safely aggregate, organize, exchange, and trade their tokenized medical data. This helps patients to exchange their data with organizations related to healthcare safely. Medicalchain, an HER blockchain company, allows doctors and other healthcare workers and healthcare-related institutes like hospitals, dispensaries, and pharmacies to access patient EHRs.

Since blockchains are decentralized, immutable, trustable sources that are robust and secure, several points can benefit a health industry:

- Improved medical record management: Unalterable and source-verifiable patient records are the prime advantages of having blockchains.
- Enhanced insurance claim processes: Eliminating middlemen with transparent blockchain records and detecting fraudulent insurance claims will become easier since records could be verified easily and checked if the claim can be qualified.
- Accelerated clinical and biomedical research: Since the patient data is timestamped and accurate, the right authority can use these records for research purposes.
- Advanced healthcare data ledger: Manufacturer and ownership transferring, drug detection, and prevention systems in pharmaceutical supply chains add more positive points of using a blockchain.

10.5 Blockchain in supply chains, transportation, and logistics

From the advent of blockchain, it has been used in many applications, including supply chain management (SCM). SCM refers to the management of a product from its point of origin to the point of consumption. These affairs must be handled with much care to maximize value and minimize time. Especially since the coronavirus pandemic hit, many things have been made digital. The most common problems that global SCM faces are tracking and tracing, opacity, and ambiguity. It has become essential to allow a solid link between consumers, their products, and values to maximize the profit that traditional systems have failed to offer. With the use of blockchains, it can be easy to identify the source of the final goods. This information can be easily verified since blockchains cannot be tamper with. Since records are timestamped, consumers can know the exact time at which each process in the chain took place, and due to transparency, the relationship between the producer and consumer is highly improved. The main factors that influence the application of blockchains into SCM are the following:

- trust
- efficiency
- cost–effectiveness
- authority and control
- sense of privacy
- scalability

The structural design of blockchains helps provide SCM resilience by identifying risks associated with any supply chain, mitigating the impacts of any disturbances caused in the supply chain, and providing encryption to data, thereby safeguarding it. Since security is a significant concern, blockchains help enhance IoT-based intrusion detection where product bar codes can ease the interaction between various components in the process and seamless communication using RFID (radio frequency identification) protocol. Smart contracts are used to verify and allow actions by the devices, and any action outside the scope of this application is not carried out. Shipping giants like Maersk teamed with IBM and Walmart have infused RFID systems to trace consumer products. Shipping firms like DHL have also found their application in blockchain by using a digital ledger of shipments, the progress of their shipped goods, and maintenance of the integrity of transactions. In areas of product management, blockchains have had a more significant role to play. Every day, tons of goods are produced, and our obsolete systems are incapable of storing such information. Blockchains ensure that the exact pricing from raw materials to the completed goods is made known to the public.

Real-world projects like originChain have started to restructure their traditional databases to blockchains to provide tamper-proof traceability of imported products. While blockchain commercialization looks promising, the supply chain and logistics areas are still far from unlocking the true potential of blockchains in their fields.

10.6 Blockchain in the agri-food sector

The distribution of agricultural products had faced many issues in earlier times. Thanks to blockchain technology, the food being circulated across various levels is provided with security due to its transparency. In addition to this, since blockchains are low-cost, fast, and robust, they can be easily applied to the agricultural supply chain. Since each block is unique, identifiers can be assigned to each product, which would be then added to the block, and this is where the IoT can have a significant role to play. These identifiers could contain information about the type of product, its source, its cost, its expiry date, and the way it was distributed. Due to its immutable nature, food transactions could be scrutinized at each point, thereby promoting easy sharing of food details.

The trade of agricultural items involves many parties, i.e., the producers, processors, packers, traders, wholesalers, retailers, and consumers. It is possible that since information is passed through so many levels, problems related to synchronization among various stakeholders might rise and might lead to differences in content about the same product. Blockchains have paved a way to solve this problem by integrating all the data of different levels into a single block, allowing symmetry of information throughout. Furthermore, the food labels could be easily verified using their identifiers to prevent swindles.

AgriBlockIoT is a blockchain-based system that uses Ethereum and Hyperledger Sawtooth implementations, which allows the traceability of food using IoT devices. As discussed earlier, RFID technology has found its use in agri-food sectors too by tracing the items using simple components like labels and tags that contain related information stored in databases.

10.7 Blockchain in technology and cybersecurity

The integration of cloud platforms with blockchain is an essential step toward solving the technology sector's most significant problems since clouds and IoTs are incredibly prone to threats due to their centralized nature. The entire process can now be automated and therefore avoid single point of failure issues.

Various organizations throughout the world find it challenging to share their threat information since there is a possibility that competitors may use the information to break into their systems. However, information can be shared easily when there is a two-key pair since only the public key is released publicly and the private key is known only to authorized members of the blockchain. With the usage of decentralized credential solutions, cybersecurity risks in IoT devices have seen a drop. Usage of biometric and password-free solutions instead of a password being stored on a centralized system has been trending and has made IoT devices almost virtually unhackable.

10.8 Blockchain in identity management

Blockchain technology has found extensive usage in identity management in the following forms:

- Certificates: Records of important certificates for birth, marriage, or death, etc., and other kinds of registrations such as work permits and pensions must be kept safe and secure. These details must last a long time, so traditional storage structures must be avoided to eliminate the risks of alteration. Such issues can be resolved with the use of public ledging systems such as blockchain. Another adaptation to this can be to encrypt these certificates.
- Academic records and transcripts: Blockchains can store educational records and memorandums of students by keeping them verifiable and immutable.
- Property rights: In the entertainment industry, originalities are the only valuables for artists. The original work of the artists and their rights must be preserved. This may seem like a challenge to create an accurate database to allot rights. Blockchain technology and smart contracts prohibit fraudulent people from claiming someone else's work as theirs, thereby allowing ownership to the right party.
- Citizenship rights: Citizenship identification information such as passports and social security numbers is now digitalized, and the information is stored safely in blockchains. Owners of these can now be verified from anywhere in the world since digitalized passports are now available to government authorities. Blockchains may also benefit the voting system by allowing voters to cast a vote securely from anywhere in the world.

- Personal identity: Blockchains can be used to safeguard users' identity by encrypting their data and securing it from attackers. A person's identity is stored in a digital form that can be accessed from anywhere, replacing traditional physical card identifications.

11. Conclusion and future scope

This chapter discussed the history and events that led to the emergence of Bitcoin and blockchains, the architecture of blocks, different kinds of consensus algorithms, blockchain attacks, Merkle trees, blockchain security, and challenges.

Each algorithm has been known to serve various needs, and a developer has to pick the one that meets his/her needs the best.

- PoW is known for its simplicity and resistance to a wide range of cyberattacks.
- PoS is a more energy-saving alternative to PoW and reduces the complexity of the issues at hand by quite a significant rate.
- Due to the limited number of nodes, the DPoS can manage high volume transactions and has fast confirmation rates.
- PBFT is energy efficient, does not need multiple confirmations, and provides low rewarding variance.

Due to its decentralized design, blockchain is extremely resilient and completely transparent and has found its application in many sectors apart from finance and will continue to be a powerful force, as discussed in this chapter. This technology has made it a point to cross all its limitations and show a potential direction, thereby changing the whole dynamic around artificial intelligence.

The potential areas where blockchain can make unpredictable advancements are big data analytics, decentralization, and blockchain testing.

11.1 Big data analytics

Since blockchain focuses primarily on security and distributed storage, it could be used for data management in the coming years. It could also validate the authenticity of the data. This case would significantly help the health sector where patient data must be kept untampered and protected from theft. In the data analytics domain, transactions on the blockchain can perform operations on big data. Since data is huge and may predict a pattern, analytics could forecast stock prices and trading.

11.2 Decentralization

Blockchain was designed to be a decentralized system. However, miners in the process are centralized. It is estimated that the top five mining pools collectively own more than 51% of the Bitcoin network's total hash. To prevent selfish mining, blockchain may develop methods to solve this problem.

11.3 Blockchain testing

Since blockchain has come into use in different fields, users have begun to include them in their business, so it has become necessary to test which kind of blockchain would suit the users' requirements. This has given rise to blockchain testing mechanisms. A typical blockchain testing mechanism can be divided into two phases: *the standardization* and *testing phases*. During the standardization phase, the blockchain is created and agreed upon by a set of criteria to be fulfilled, and in the testing phase, a different criterion is set on which blockchain testing needs to be performed.

Apart from the consensus algorithms discussed, there are newer algorithms like Proof of Authority (PoA), Proof of Elapsed Time (PoET), Proof of Burn (PoB), and Proof of Capacity (PoC), a few of which are still in the developing stage, and the rest have been just finding their ground so they go beyond the scope of this chapter.

References

Bashir, I., 2018. Mastering Blockchain. Packt Publishing, Birmingham. www.packtpub.com.

Bassi, M.A., Lopez, M.A., Confalone, L., Gaudio, R.M., Lombardo, L., Lauritano, D., 2020. Blockchain: emerging applications and use cases. In: Nature, vol. 388, pp. 539–547.

Caradonna, T., 2020. Blockchain and society. Informatik-Spektrum 43 (1), 40–52. https://doi.org/10.1007/s00287-020-01246-7.

Chen, X., 2018. Blockchain challenges and opportunities: a survey Zibin Zheng and Shaoan Xie Hong-Ning Dai Huaimin Wang. IEEE Int. Symp High Perform. Distrib. Comp. Proc. 14 (4), 352–375.

Damak, M., 2018. The Future of Banking: Cryptocurrencies Will Need Some Rules to Change the Game. S&P Global. https://www.spglobal.com/our-insights/The-Future-of-Banking-Cryptocurrencies-Will-Need-Some-Rules-to-Change-the-Game.html.

Forsstr, S., December, 2015. Blockchain Research Report.

Frizzo-Barker, J., Chow-White, P.A., Adams, P.R., Mentanko, J., Ha, D., Green, S., 2020. Blockchain as a disruptive technology for business: a systematic review. Int. J. Inf. Manag. 51 (November), 0–1. https://doi.org/10.1016/j.ijinfomgt.2019.10.014.

Ismail, L., Materwala, H., 2019. A review of blockchain architecture and consensus protocols: use cases, challenges, and solutions. Symmetry 11 (10). https://doi.org/10.3390/sym11101198.

Li, Y., 2019. Emerging blockchain-based applications and techniques. Serv. Oriented Comput. Appl. 13 (4), 279–285. https://doi.org/10.1007/s11761-019-00281-x.

Mercan, S., Cebe, M., Tekiner, E., Akkaya, K., Chang, M., Uluagac, S., 2020. A cost-efficient IoT forensics framework with blockchain. In: IEEE International Conference on Blockchain and Cryptocurrency, ICBC 2020, April. https://doi.org/10.1109/ICBC48266.2020.9169397.

Moubarak, J., Filiol, E., Chamoun, M., 2018. On blockchain security and relevant attacks. In: 2018 IEEE Middle East and North Africa Communications Conference, MEN-ACOMM 2018, pp. 1–6. https://doi.org/10.1109/MENACOMM.2018.8371010.

Nian, L.P., Chuen, D.L.K., 2015. Introduction to bitcoin. In: Handbook of Digital Currency: Bitcoin, Innovation, Financial Instruments, and Big Data, April, 5–30. https://doi.org/10.1016/B978-0-12-802117-0.00001-1.

Pajooh, H.H., Rashid, M., Alam, F., Demidenko, S., 2021. Hyperledger fabric blockchain for securing the edge Internet-of-Things. Sensors (Switzerland) 21 (2), 1–29. https://doi.org/10.3390/s21020359.

Sabry, S.S., Kaittan, N.M., Ali, I.M., 2019. The road to the blockchain technology: concept and types. Period. Eng. Nat. Sci. 7 (4), 1821–1832. https://doi.org/10.21533/pen.v7i4.935.

Wang, W., Hoang, D.T., Hu, P., Xiong, Z., Niyato, D., Wang, P., Wen, Y., Kim, D.I., January 2019. A survey on consensus mechanisms and mining strategy management in blockchain networks. IEEE Access 7, 22328–22370. https://doi.org/10.1109/ACCESS.2019.2896108.

Xu, M., Chen, X., Kou, G., 2019. A systematic review of blockchain. Financial Innovation 5 (1). https://doi.org/10.1186/s40854-019-0147-z.

Yangui, S., Bouguettaya, A., Xue, X., Faci, N., Gaaloul, W., Yu, Q., Zhou, Z., Hernandez, N., 2019. In: Y. N., E., Steffen, B. (Eds.), Service-Oriented Computing – ICSOC 2019 Workshops. https://doi.org/10.1007/978-3-030-45989-5.

Zhang, R., Xue, R., Liu, L., 2019. Security and Privacy on Blockchain, vol. 1. ArXiv, 1.

Zheng, Z., Xie, S., Dai, H., Chen, X., Wang, H., 2017. An overview of blockchain technology: architecture, consensus, and future trends. In: Proceedings – 2017 IEEE 6th International Congress on Big Data, BigData Congress 2017, pp. 557–564. https://doi.org/10.1109/BigDataCongress.2017.85.

CHAPTER 3

Characteristics, advances, and challenges in blockchain-enabled cyber-physical systems

Manohar Sai Burra and Soumyadev Maity
Department of Information Technology, Indian Institute of Information Technology Allahabad, Prayagraj, Uttar Pradesh, India

1. Introduction

With advancements in science and technology, the world is becoming a global village. At present, there is tremendous growth in the digital transformation of many products and activities. The days have transformed from people connecting through the internet toward any physical object with software embedded connecting to the internet. We now call this paradigm the internet of things (IoT). The integration of physical processes, computation, the internet, and control of these physical objects through actuators is called the cyber-physical system (CPS) (Sztipanovits et al., 2011). CPS is a feedback system where the data from physical objects affect computation, and this results in affecting the control and vice versa (Derler et al., 2013). IoT, CPS, and the industrial internet of things (IIoT) have many overlapping features and characteristics in design, deployment, and management.

CPSs play a crucial role in improving the performance of many products and activities in areas such as next-generation mobile systems, vehicular networks (VANET), smart homes, and industrial automation. With the increased use of CPS technology, it is important to secure communication and control of the system (Cardenas et al., 2009). CPSs are usually deployed with the internet as the backbone network. So the CPS should withstand cyberattacks coming through the internet. The CPS architecture focuses on building resilient systems that recover and provide services at any instance of a cyberattack (Zheng et al., 2017).

CPSs are a complex integration of physical processes, computation, and actuators of resource-constrained devices, which results in newer challenges in designing, deploying, and managing these systems. The prime focus while realizing a CPS should be on measuring the system's resilient capabilities, reviewing the quantitative and qualitative factors for assessing the system, and providing cyber resilience strategies per the assessment (Ding et al., 2015).

Blockchain Technology for Emerging Applications
ISBN 978-0-323-90193-2
https://doi.org/10.1016/B978-0-323-90193-2.00008-9

The CPS involves complex interactions of various processes between the cyber and physical world. CPS involves multiple disciplinary approaches that merge computer science, mechatronics, electronics, cybernetics, mathematics, logic, and more. These interactions bring in newer complexities to the CPS system design and development. To achieve reliability for such systems is a tough task. Blockchain technology has become a boon to establish consensus and achieve reliability among these processes of the CPS (Bach et al., 2018). Most of the blockchain-related consensus algorithms employ proof-of-work (PoW) or proof-of-stake (PoS) or a hybrid of these techniques. PoW requires a prover party to perform a certain moderately hard but feasible task (computation) that must be easy for the verifier to check the proof or vice versa. PoS requires that an individual can validate or mine block transactions based on available assets such as coins in coin mining.

Blockchain has gained popularity as a secure electronic distributed ledger since the introduction of Bitcoin. But it has progressed far beyond digital currency and into other areas of application. Many domain areas requiring the storage and retrieval of transaction data use blockchain technology. One of the important types of blockchain technology is smart contracts, which allows essential automation of workflow in many systems. This smart contract allows two entities to execute an agreement that will be irreversible, transparent, and traceable.

The main contributions of this chapter are the following:

1. We have reviewed and provided a detailed comparison of various existing blockchain-enabled CPS schemes based on different characteristic properties.
2. We have identified various challenges in blockchain-enabled CPSs.
3. We have reviewed and discussed the possible security attacks and the likelihood of blockchain-enabled CPSs.
4. Additionally, we have also provided a brief introduction to blockchain and CPSs.

The rest of the paper is organized as follows: Sections 2 and 3 discuss the background for both CPS and blockchain in detail. Section 4 describes various blockchain-enabled CPS frameworks. Section 5 provides a comparative analysis of various existing blockchain-enabled CPS schemes based on different characteristic properties. Section 6 states the various technical and nontechnical challenges and some specific security attacks. Finally, we conclude the chapter in Section 7.

2. Background of CPS

With the increase in the number of digital devices globally, there is a growing demand for CPS-based applications worldwide. It requires accurate coordination and a combination of both computational and physical resources to deliver performance. It plays a crucial role in transforming critical infrastructure systems such as traffic management, personalized healthcare, autonomous automobiles, smart grids, the industrial internet, the IoT, and many others through innovative, intelligent services. In CPS, there is complex information transfer and exchange among various physical processes. These complex interactions require consensus among the processes for the reliable and efficient performance of critical infrastructure systems. This section discusses various use cases in CPSs integrated into the networks. We discuss the following scenarios: (1) healthcare systems, (2) transportation and vehicular ad-hoc networks, (3) urban infrastructure, and (4) defense systems.

2.1 Healthcare systems

In the healthcare sector, CPS enables the development of newer medical devices that are implantable equipment and wearable sensors that collect health data from humans to form wireless body area networks. An effective health data analysis can provide better timely disease diagnosis and improve the overall quality of life. Further, these personal healthcare devices would assist hospitals in providing economically viable services (Haque et al., 2014; Kurde et al., 2019; Zhang et al., 2015).

Fig. 3.1 shows a CPS-enabled healthcare system where the user wears a sensor device that collects health data and transfers it to the connected mobile device. The mobile device forwards the data securely to a cloud server through the internet. The various other entities such as the doctor can obtain health data to perform diagnoses or the emergency services can be called automatically when continuous data analysis shows signs of an emergency health issue.

2.2 Transportation and vehicular ad-hoc networks

In the automobile industry, there is advancement in the integration of communication and computation technologies into vehicles. Autonomous and smart vehicles can be built that will reduce the load on human driving and bring increased safety and ease of travel. Further, CPS can boost growth in smart highways, vehicular networks, railroad systems, and airspace management in the aviation sector (Abid et al., 2011; Mehmood et al., 2020).

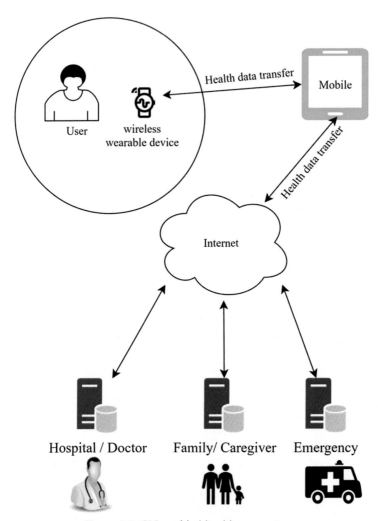

Figure 3.1 CPS-enabled healthcare system.

Fig. 3.2 shows a vehicular ad–hoc network. There are three types of communication: (1) vehicle to vehicle (V2V) communication, (2) vehicle to infrastructure (V2I) communication, (3) infrastructure to infrastructure (I2I) communication. CPS technology provides benefits to improve traffic congestion through embedding sensors onto vehicles that continuously collect data and upload onto the server for traffic analysis, and these servers provide control data for interactive traffic control systems, ultimately preventing accidents and reducing traffic congestion.

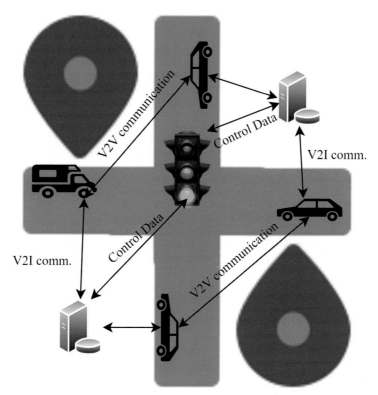

Figure 3.2 CPS-enabled transportation and VANET.

2.3 Urban infrastructure

In civil infrastructure development such as dams, sewage management, wastewater treatment, and many more examples, CPS can provide continuous monitoring, assessment, and control over these systems. Smart grids can be built to treat wastewater and manage water resources efficiently. In a large bridge or dam, CPS can provide early warning signs on the structural damages of infrastructure and thus save lives and prevent property damage (Saetta et al., 2019; Sun et al., 2018).

Fig. 3.3 shows a water treatment and management system where the water from natural water body sources is treated to provide drinking water to users. The computing server and control system will monitor, analyze, and send control data to other entities to improve the performance and efficiency of the water treatment system.

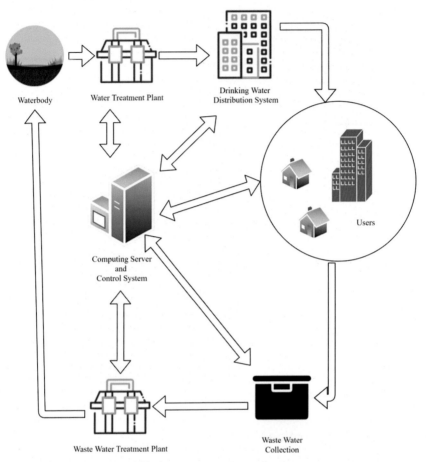

Figure 3.3 CPS-enabled water treatment and management system.

2.4 Defense systems

Warfare can greatly damage both the living and their property. Today nations are striving to create tools and technology to win wars with less damage. CPS can enable in development of smart precision-guided weapons, smart unmanned vehicles, and wireless wearable computing devices. This will reduce the number of soldiers involved in direct combat but increase remote warfare capabilities (Gill, 2008).

Today, individuals and businesses are directly or indirectly utilizing these systems. There is an increasing demand for control and automation in complex processes, specifically where human life is in danger while performing hazardous tasks. We could employ CPSs to eliminate the human need to perform such hazardous tasks as investigating volcanic sites, detecting mining areas, or handling radioactive elements. Further, industries utilizing a CPS could improve their overall efficiency, performance, and economy.

3. Background of blockchain

Blockchain is the underlying concept behind Bitcoin cryptocurrency (Nakamoto and Bitcoin, 2008). Today, there are hundreds of cryptocurrencies that employ blockchain to create, store, and verify transactions (Corbet et al., 2018). Blockchain is a distributed and decentralized database, so it differs from the database of a traditional financial instrument (Sarmah, 2018). In the early stages, the role of blockchain was limited to its application in creating cryptocurrencies. Today, blockchain finds its use in many newer areas, including and not limited to healthcare, smart contracts, the IoT, CPS, and IIoT (Alladi et al., 2019; Dedeoglu et al., 2020; Panarello et al., 2018).

Fig. 3.4 shows the blockchain structure of Bitcoin. Each block is a composition of the previous block hash, timestamp, nonce, and Merkle root of all the transactions in that block. These blocks are interlinked together to form a blockchain. The first block of the blockchain is called the genesis block, and it does not contain any previous hash value. The blockchain is a secure ledger of verifiable records. A new block can only be

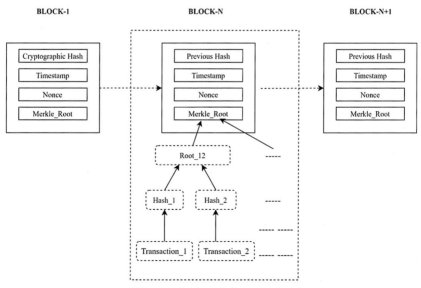

Figure 3.4 Blockchain structure.

added through a PoW mechanism and this requires solving for a pattern in the hash and thus may require high computational power. The PoW itself takes significant time compared to the verification of PoW, which takes very little time. Any malicious entity that wants to replace a block in the chain must solve for subsequent resulting chains in the blockchain, and this could take exponential time so cannot realistically be performed. Therefore the blockchain is a tamperproof ledger of records.

3.1 Types of consensus algorithms

Blockchain technology is one of the important techniques to build consensus algorithms. These algorithms are responsible for achieving reliability even in a complex system with high interactions and faulty processes. Two of the methods to achieve consensus are discussed next (Bach et al., 2018; Mingxiao et al., 2017):

- Proof-of-work: As described earlier, PoW involves entities called miners to solve a puzzle. The solution to the puzzle is called the nonce. Here, the miners can take advantage of distributed parallel computation to achieve the solution faster. Once the solution is available, the miners publish the nonce value to claim the rewards. Generally, in blockchain-based cryptocurrency, the currency is given as the reward.
- Proof-of-stake: The PoS mechanism was created as an alternative mechanism to reduce the computational power required to add a block to the blockchain. The PoS allows miners to mine with respect to the stake they hold. For example, a miner with a 3% stake can only mine 3% of the blocks in the blockchain. This allows miners with good stakes to mine more and those with less to mine fewer. This promotes miners to increase stakes to mine the blocks.

3.2 Essential features of blockchain technology

- Immutability: Many of the blockchain users maintain full nodes. This is quite different from a traditional centralized ledger. Any addition or validation of the block requires consensus from the majority of the users. Moreover, a block in the chain cannot be replaced since it requires changing the other blocks in the chain. This process requires exponential time, so the ledger is immutable.
- Decentralization: The immutability and decentralization go hand in hand. The blockchain ledger is not owned by any central authority. Many users have a copy of all the blocks of the blockchain, and any

entity maintaining a complete ledger is called a full node. As no single entity governs the blockchain, the fear of monopoly is eliminated, creating trust among all the participating entities of the blockchain. Most of the work involved in building a blockchain can be automated, thereby reducing the risk of human error. The blockchain technology employed in cryptocurrency and asset management can provide users with complete control over their coins and assets without the need for any third-party entity involvement. Through decentralization comes transparency, since any transaction in the blockchain can be validated with only public values.

- Improved security: Blockchain technology employs cryptographic techniques to achieve strong security. It employs encryption and signature mechanisms to accurately validate transactions in the blockchain. The core technique used in the blockchain is hashing, where the hash function employed is a secure one-way hash function that transforms original data to a different form to protect the actual data as well as enabling easier verification and processing.
- Privacy: Blockchain technology inherently provides privacy for user information. The ledger, which is available to all the entities, does not contain sensitive information of its users. It usually contains public data, which does not create privacy concerns for the users. Any user can perform a transaction without the need to provide personal, sensitive information.

4. Blockchain-enabled cyber-physical systems

In this section, we will discuss the advancement of blockchain technology in various CPS-enhanced areas.

4.1 Supply chain management

The adoption of blockchain in supply chain management (SCM) is growing rapidly. These SCM systems have a large number of participating entities, which creates complex interactions, so requires better mechanisms to address the various issues involved. The integration of blockchain in the SCM systems provides mechanisms to reduce operational costs, improve quality, and create sustainable and flexible systems. The primary use of blockchain in these SCM systems traces back to accountability and transparency. With CPS enhancing SCM, various components such as sensors, integrated circuits, global positioning tags, barcodes, and radio-frequency identification tags can be used to track the location of the shipments, parcels, and products. This brings out techniques to efficiently track real-time goods from source to destination (Blossey et al., 2019; Saberi et al., 2019).

Queiroz and Fosso Wamba (2019) have shed light on the behavior of various entities involved in SCM across India and the United States on the adoption of blockchain. They have proposed a novel model that established a clear difference of behaviors of adopters in both India and the United States. Montecchi et al. (2019) developed a framework for SCM to address the issues of the provenance of goods through the integration of blockchain. Their framework contained a wheel of four assurances: the first is the origin of goods assurance; the second is custody of assurance, which enables a consumer to track the goods throughout the entire supply chain; the third is integrity assurance; and finally, the fourth is authenticity assurance. In Toyoda et al. (2017) the authors have proposed blockchain-based techniques to fight counterfeiting in post-SCM.

Fig. 3.5 shows the SCM network of apple juice beverage production. Here, blockchain can be employed at each step of the process, where the ledger data from every step can be later verified to identify the location of any entity involved. For example, if a batch of apple juice produced has been tampered with, then we can use the help of the ledger to track back into every step of the production process to identify the possible location of tampering. This will help the SCM industry to trace and audit the systems.

4.2 Healthcare sector

Due to the ever-growing population, there is an ever-growing demand for healthcare services across the world. The healthcare sector requires stringent mechanisms to protect patient data confidentiality. In the world of interconnected smart devices and people, there is a greater need to secure communication and provide privacy of data at every instance of health data management. There are some distinctive requirements for the healthcare sector, and these include but are not limited to secure health data transfer, authentication of patient data, and interoperability. Many healthcare institutions worldwide maintain electronic health records of patients. These records are either at the hospital repository or stored at a third-party server. There exist mechanisms for multiple institutions to access patient data on a shared basis, but there are very few mechanisms to protect privacy. There is a need for patient-centric health data sharing that includes security and privacy (Hathaliya et al., 2019; Kassab et al., 2019; McGhin et al., 2019; Zhang et al., 2017).

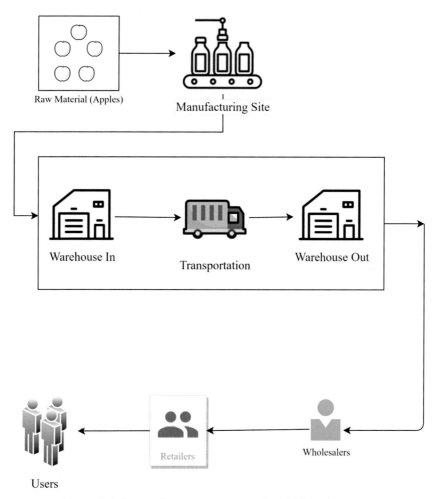

Figure 3.5 Supply chain management of apple juice beverage.

Blockchain can provide decentralized storage of medical records, which enhances the quality of data and enables faster access time and patient-driven interoperability. Li et al. (2018) proposed a medical data preservation system using blockchain technology, where if any record is found to be tampered with, it can be easily verified. They even have employed cryptographic techniques to secure sensitive user information. Yue et al. (2016) proposed a patient-driven health data monitoring and control that protects the privacy of users. The authors have implemented the same through a user interface application. They also provide mechanisms to employ third-party entities for computation purposes without any privacy issues through the use of multiparty computation. Ekblaw et al. (2016) have proposed a prototype for medical health data handling and use. They provided mechanisms to allow hospitals and patients to give metadata from the health records for big data analysis without impacting data privacy. The data analysis can provide insights into the health status of various patients and diseases.

In the insurance industry, blockchain can enable a ledger of immutable records, where the blocks contain data related to a set of health-related events as they took place, and this allows easier verification of events. Further, no entity can change the sequence of events in the blockchain nor change the data in the blockchain, thus giving both the insurance company and the insured better mechanisms of the claim process. Raikwar et al. (2018) have identified various blockchain-enabled use cases for insurance processes. They have utilized smart contract mechanisms to simulate real-world insurance policies across multiple endorsers. Gatteschi et al. (2018) elaborated on the possibilities of blockchain integration in the insurance sector considering various factors that are involved.

4.3 Emerging industrial control systems

Today, we have a new emerging market in an industrial sector called the industrial internet of things where the physical components of the industry are enabled with intelligent software systems that can be controlled through the internet. Moreover, there is a great demand to automate the processes through the use of computing capabilities. Today, the IIoT has grown larger than imagined a decade ago, where every piece of equipment in the industrial sector can be integrated into the IIoT. These can range from machines in manufacturing industries to sensors nodes in wireless networks. The IIoT network architecture is not standardized, distributed, nor open in nature. This heterogeneous architecture creates challenges in designing reliable and efficient communication among the entities in the IIoT system.

Blockchain is one technology that can bring greater automation into IIoT with efficacy. There are numerous works that have employed smart contract techniques to improve operations and productivity in the IIoT sector. These blockchain-based techniques provide consensus among the various entities involved in the IIoT architecture and help in automating many human-monitored activities. The authors in Wang et al. (2020) have proposed a consensus mechanism that is built over the reputation of the nodes as a key attribute to determine the incentives for every valid proof generated. Liu et al. (2019) proposed an efficient lightweight proof mechanism for resource-constrained nodes of IIoT systems. This mechanism reduces the workload on nodes to establish consensus among the low-power computing-enabled physical devices. They have employed a concept named "synergistic multiple proofs" that reduces the unlimited growth of a general blockchain structure to efficiently work for power-constrained networks.

Due to the ever-growing information technology-enabled critical infrastructure networks, there is always increasing concerns on the security, privacy, and reliability of these networks. Wu et al. (2020) have discussed the various important opportunities and challenges that are created due to the integration of blockchain and edge computing into the critical infrastructure of IIoT networks. They have proposed a layer-by-layer architecture for the blockchain- and edge-computing-enabled critical infrastructure networks. Wan et al. (2019) have proposed a blockchain-enabled semi-decentralized smart factory architecture to provide solutions for the privacy and security in these IIoT networks. The authors in Guan et al. (2020) built a decentralized two-tier architecture for IIoT networks for energy trading purposes. Their approach utilizes PoS consensus mechanisms to enable efficient and secure energy trading methods. Kumari et al. (2020) provided a peer-to-peer consensus mechanism through blockchain to improve the reliability, quality of service (QoS), and efficiency of the IIoT environment.

4.4 Smart cities

With the growth in the use of information technology in a multitude of domains, a smart city is no exception. Today, there is a lot of research focused to develop and deploy IT infrastructure into smart city networks. These networks involve communication among a huge number of nodes with varying degrees of characteristics and features. These nodes share various resources and require a high degree of coordination to work efficiently. Smart cities can improve the overall QoSs a user can receive. The definition of smart city networks can differ from different sources, but ultimately this architecture tries to benefit humans to improve their quality of life. Due to the complexity and high degree of nodes in a smart city, the security, reliability, and privacy of these networks remain an open challenge even today though there is significant work done (Liu et al., 2021; Mora et al., 2018).

Blockchain technology has provided opportunities for research to design and develop efficient mechanisms to solve various communication- and security-related problems. Sun et al. (2016) proposed a blockchain-integrated, three-level framework that involves technology, humans, and organization to address the problems of reliable sharing services in the smart city scenarios. The authors in Hakak et al. (2020) have discussed the various characteristic features of blockchain technology and its use in smart city networks. They proposed a novel conceptual framework to provide data security that utilizes blockchain technology in the smart city network. Sharma and Hyuk Park (2018) proposed an innovative multidimensional framework that uses blockchain technology and software-defined networks for the smart city network. They provide the important solutions and methods that can be deployed within a smart city network to address the architectural challenges. Their consensus mechanism employs PoW concepts to establish a distributed and decentralized secure communication in a smart city network.

Data integrity and privacy is a basic requirement of smart city networks. A lot of data in these networks can be sensitive user data that requires various techniques to provide security against malicious entities. The authors in Makhdoom et al. (2020) present a novel privacy-preserving mechanism to protect user data from reaching attackers. They utilize a distributed blockchain network where there are different channels in these networks. Each channel contains specific entities and processes responsible for access control of the users within these networks. Their consensus mechanisms are reward-based, where they have introduced a coin named "PrivyCoin" to provide rewards for users sharing their data to different authorized entities. Liang et al. (2018) in their paper provide important security aspects of a smart city network. They specifically discuss in detail the scenarios of blockchain-enabled smart cities through the various attack surfaces possible. The transportation or vehicular networks are a part of the smart city. There is research work in building blockchain-enabled vehicular ad-hoc networks, to provide efficient privacy-preserving authentication, verification, and decentralization (Lin et al., 2020; Nadeem et al., 2019; Wagner and McMillin, 2020; Yang et al., 2019).

5. Characteristics of blockchain-enabled CPS systems

Table 3.1 summarizes the various characteristic properties of various blockchain-enabled CPS systems. Lyu et al. (2020) proposed a framework

Table 3.1 Characteristics of blockchain-enabled CPS systems.

Authors	Characteristics	Sector
Lyu et al. (2020)	• Decentralization • Access control • Data sharing • Data auditing	Information-centric networking
Gordon and Catalini (2018)	• Data aggregation • Patient identity verification • Digital access • Data immutability • Data liquidity	Healthcare industry
Xia et al. (2017)	• Data sharing • Trust-less environment • Big data • Cloud integration	Healthcare industry
Huh et al. (2017)	• Smart contract • RSA cryptography • Etherum • Tamperroof	Internet of things
Stefan et al. (2018)	• Data integrity • Nonrepudiation • Verifiability • Decentralization	Generic CPS architecture
Xu et al. (2019)	• Authentication • Access control • Smart contract • Micro services • Smart surveillance	IoT-enhanced public safety systems
Sodhro et al. (2020)	• Convergence • Interoperability • Reliability • Decentralization	IIoT
Behzad et al. (2020)	• Sustainability • Smart contract • Energy management • Tokenization	Supply chain management
Oscar Novo (2018)	• Accessibility • Scalability • Transparency • Mobility • Concurrency • Lightweight	IoT

Continued

Table 3.1 Characteristics of blockchain-enabled CPS systems.—cont'd

Authors	Characteristics	Sector
Ibba et al. (2017)	• Data storage and management • Immutability • Availability • Smart contract	Smart cities
Lei et al. (2017)	• Distributed key management • Decentralized • Key exchange • Traffic efficiency	Intelligent transportation systems
Ismail et al. (2019)	• Lightweight • Anti-forking • Scalable • Traceable	Healthcare

for data sharing, data revocation, and audit by a user securely through the use of blockchain technology in information-centric networking. The authors in Gordon and Catalini (2018) have proposed mechanisms to provide patient-driven interoperability in the healthcare industry. Where this scheme can enable patient-centric data sharing without the fear of privacy concerns, it uses blockchain technology to achieve these properties. Xia et al. (2017) proposed a blockchain-driven control, audit, and data provenance of shared healthcare big data among the various cloud service providers. Huh et al. (2017) have employed blockchain-based Ethereum technology to design and develop smart contracts for IoT devices.

Stefan et al. (2018) have proposed a blockchain-enabled information monitoring system where the data source error in the CPS architecture can be easily detected. Xu et al. (2019) designed authentication and access control mechanisms using blockchain technology to provide secure decentralized data sharing micro services in IoT-enhanced public safety systems. The authors in Sodhro et al. (2020) have proposed a pseudo-random-based key management technique with the integration of blockchain technology for IIoT architecture to provide reliable, interoperable, and convergence of services among the various entities. Behzad et al. (2020) addressed the various uses of blockchain technology in SCM to provide sustainable monitoring and reporting of various activities.

Oscar Novo (2018) has proposed a lightweight, decentralized, distributed, blockchain-enabled system for access management in the IoT.

The authors in Ibba et al. (2017) have designed a "Citysense" application that utilizes blockchain technology to manage sensor data efficiently. These sensors collect environment quality indicators that include pollutants and temperature. Lei et al. (2017) have developed distributed key management techniques for intelligent transportation systems using blockchain technology. Ismail et al. (2019) proposed lightweight blockchain architecture for healthcare data management in resource-constrained networks. Their scheme does not have the forking problem as in a traditional blockchain.

6. Challenges in blockchain-enabled CPS systems

There are various challenges concerning blockchain-enabled CPSs. A few of them are listed next.

6.1 The nontechnical challenges

- There is poor knowledge transfer between academia and industry. There is a gap between the current state of theoretical research and practical implementation. There is a need to minimize the gap to get the best out of blockchain for the good of society.
- There is a lack of investment by businesses due to limited standardization of policies and practices. There are restrictions by various government entities on the use of blockchain and cryptocurrency in the public domain.
- Many existing technologies in various industries do not support migration to blockchain-enabled mechanisms. Since blockchain is evolving with time, many old legacy systems do not support newer blockchain-based technologies, making it difficult for certain organizations to adapt to the blockchain.
- The users, particularly in the healthcare sector, need to be educated before adopting blockchain technology since the data involved is sensitive in nature. Some users may agree and some may not. Largely, blockchain technology has been adopted in the public domain, and there should be caution when using blockchain for healthcare applications.
- Blockchain is not a solution to every problem. Though there is a lot of research going on regarding blockchain technology, there are many instances where blockchain is being hard fitted for some processes where it might not actually provide any positive results.

6.2 The technical challenges

- The immutability property may be a disadvantage for systems with unreliable data generation mechanisms. This property will not allow making changes to the records entered into the blockchain.
- The computing resources required for certain consensus algorithms are high. Resource constraint networks may not be able to utilize blockchain technology considering the high computational burden on the participating nodes in the network.
- Most of the research in blockchain-enabled CPS is on paper; only a few applications exist in practice.
- Some domains generate huge amounts of data, and the recording of all the data onto the blockchain can be cumbersome and costly.
- Security and privacy issues arise where blockchain records sensitive, confidential data, and user identities.
- Not every domain can adopt blockchain efficiently. There should be a detailed analysis of blockchain applications before designing systems.
- Integration and coordination of data generated by different entities of a system needs to be recorded into the blockchain in a synchronized manner.
- In some systems, there is high complexity involved while integrating blockchain technology.

6.3 Security attacks and their likelihood on blockchain-enabled CPS systems

We discuss a few security threats and their likelihood on blockchain-enabled CPS systems:

- Sniffing attack (Shi et al., 2019): The attackers in a network try the passive analysis of transaction data in blockchain to guess the identities of the user. The attack is likely to happen in a public blockchain.
- The 51% attack (Yoon, 2019): Any entity that controls 51% of computational resources or participating entities in the blockchain will control the blockchain. The attack is possible for small networks and is most unlikely for large, decentralized networks.
- The distributed denial of service (Saad et al., 2018): Attackers flood fake data to record into the blockchain network, which will exhaust resources of the network. If the block contains a hash value, then it may not impact the availability of resources to entities, but if the block contains other extra information, then each malicious entity can flood the network with fake data, likely creating an unnecessary burden on the network.

- Sybil attack (Zhang and Lee, 2019): The malicious entities create multiple identities in a network. This does not have any significant impact on the blockchain structure.
- Public ID spoofing (Hong, 2020): An attacker tries to replace the public key of other entities of a blockchain network. This attack is most unlikely to happen.
- Security vulnerabilities (de Leon et al., 2017): A poorly implemented blockchain network application is likely to suffer from various types of cyberattacks including and not limited to trojans, malware, and viruses.
- Eclipse attack (Wust and Gervais, 2016): In this attack, the attacker nodes compromise the blockchain ledger at an honest node. This is achieved when the honest node interacts with only the malicious nodes to update the blockchain in a peer-to-peer network.

7. Conclusion and future scope

In this book chapter, we first provided the preliminary background of blockchain and CPSs. Then we explained various works in blockchain-enabled CPSs in the areas of SCM, the healthcare sector, emerging industrial control systems, and smart cities. Then we stated important characteristics of blockchain-enabled CPSs considering different approaches by various authors in different areas of CPS. We discussed, in brief, the various technical and nontechnical challenges in blockchain-enabled CPSs. We have detailed some security attacks and their likelihood in the blockchain-enabled CPSs.

Blockchain is a great technology that has various important features, though the current state of practical implementation in various areas of CPS is in its infancy. There is strong scope for blockchain to evolve and be adopted at various levels in the near future. The theoretical research on blockchain uses in different areas is at its full pace.

References

Abid, H., Thi Thu Phuong, L., Wang, J., Lee, S., Qaisar, S., 2011. V-Cloud: vehicular cyber-physical systems and cloud computing. In: Proceedings of the 4th International Symposium on Applied Sciences in Biomedical and Communication Technologies, pp. 1—5.
Alladi, T., Chamola, V., Parizi, R.M., Raymond Choo, K.-K., 2019. Blockchain applications for industry 4.0 and industrial IoT: a review. IEEE Access 7, 176935—176951.

Bach, L.M., Mihaljevic, B., Zagar, M., 2018. Comparative analysis of blockchain consensus algorithms. In: 2018 41st International Convention on Information and Communication Technology, Electronics and Microelectronics (MIPRO). IEEE, pp. 1545–1550.

Blossey, G., Eisenhardt, J., Hahn, G., 2019. Blockchain technology in supply chain management: an application perspective. In: Proceedings of the 52nd Hawaii International Conference on System Sciences.

Cardenas, A., Amin, S., Bruno, S., Giani, A., Adrian, P., Sastry, S., 2009. Challenges for securing cyber physical systems. In: Workshop on Future Directions in Cyber-Physical Systems Security, vol. 5, p. 1.

Corbet, S., Meegan, A., Larkin, C., Lucey, B., Yarovaya, L., 2018. Exploring the dynamic relationships between cryptocurrencies and other financial assets. Econ. Lett. 165, 28–34.

de Leon, D.C., Stalick, A.Q., Jillepalli, A.A., Haney, M.A., Sheldon, F.T., 2017. Blockchain: properties and misconceptions. Asian Pacific J. Innov. Entrep. 11 (3), 286–300.

Dedeoglu, V., Ali, D., Raja, J., Michelin, R.A., Lunardi, R.C., Kanhere, S.S., Zorzo, A.F., 2020. A journey in applying blockchain for cyberphysical systems. In: 2020 International Conference on COMmunication Systems & NETworkS (COMSNETS). IEEE, pp. 383–390.

Derler, P., Lee, E.A., Tripakis, S., Martin, T., 2013. Cyber-physical system design contracts. In: Proceedings of the ACM/IEEE 4th International Conference on Cyber-Physical Systems, pp. 109–118.

Ding, J., Lindstrom, B., Mathiason, G., Andler, S.F., 2015. Towards threat modeling for CPS-based critical infrastructure protection. In: Proceedings of the 22nd International Emergency Management Society (TIEMS) Annual Conference, Rome, Italy, vol. 22.

Ekblaw, A., Azaria, A., Halamka, J.D., Lippman, A., 2016. A case study for blockchain in healthcare: "MedRec" prototype for electronic health records and medical research data. In: Proceedings of IEEE Open & Big Data Conference, vol. 13, p. 13.

Esmaeilian, B., Sarkis, J., Lewis, K., Behdad, S., 2020. Blockchain for the future of sustainable supply chain management in industry 4.0. Resour. Conserv. Recycl. 163, 105064.

Gatteschi, V., Lamberti, F., Demartini, C., Pranteda, C., Santamaría, V., 2018. Blockchain and smart contracts for insurance: is the technology mature enough? Future Internet 10 (2), 20.

Gill, H., 2008. From vision to reality: cyber-physical systems. In: HCSS National Workshop on New Research Directions for High Confidence Transportation CPS: Automotive, Aviation, and Rail, pp. 18–20. USA: Austin.

Gordon, W.J., Catalini, C., 2018. Blockchain technology for healthcare: facilitating the transition to patient-driven interoperability. Comput. Struct. Biotechnol. J. 16, 224–230.

Gries, S., Meyer, O., Wessling, F., Hesenius, M., Gruhn, V., 2018. Using blockchain technology to ensure trustful information flow monitoring in cps. In: 2018 IEEE International Conference on Software Architecture Companion (ICSA-C). IEEE, pp. 35–38.

Guan, Z., Lu, X., Wang, N., Wu, J., Du, X., Guizani, M., 2020. Towards secure and efficient energy trading in IIoT-enabled energy internet: a blockchain approach. Future Gener. Comput. Syst. 110, 686–695.

Hakak, S., Zada Khan, W., Amin Gilkar, G., ran, M.I., Guizani, N., 2020. Securing smart cities through blockchain technology: architecture, requirements, and challenges. IEEE Network 34 (1), 8–14.

Haque, S.A., Aziz, S.M., Rahman, M., 2014. Review of cyber-physical system in healthcare. Int. J. Distrib. Sens. Netw. 10 (4), 217415.

Hathaliya, J., Sharma, P., Tanwar, S., Gupta, R., 2019. Blockchain-based remote patient monitoring in healthcare 4.0. In: 2019 IEEE 9th International Conference on Advanced Computing (IACC). IEEE, pp. 87–91.

Hong, S., 2020. P2P networking based internet of things (IoT) sensor node authentication by Blockchain. Peer Peer Netw. Appl. 13 (2), 579–589.

Huh, S., Cho, S., Kim, S., 2017. Managing IoT devices using blockchain platform. In: 2017 19th International Conference on Advanced Communication Technology (ICACT). IEEE, pp. 464–467.

Ibba, S., Pinna, A., Seu, M., Eros Pani, F., 2017. City Sense: blockchain-oriented smart cities. In: Proceedings of the XP2017 Scientific Workshops, pp. 1–5.

Ismail, L., Materwala, H., Zeadally, S., 2019. Lightweight blockchain for healthcare. IEEE Access 7, 149935–149951.

Kassab, M.H., DeFranco, J., Malas, T., Laplante, P., Vicente Graciano Neto, V., 2019. Exploring research in blockchain for healthcare and a roadmap for the future. IEEE Trans. Emerg. Topics Comput.

Kumari, A., Tanwar, S., Tyagi, S., Kumar, N., 2020. Blockchain-Based Massive Data Dissemination Handling in IIoT Environment. IEEE Network.

Kurde, S., Shimpi, J., Pawar, R., Tingare, B., 2019. Cyber physical systems (CPS) and design automation for healthcare system: a new Era of cyber computation for healthcare system. Structure 6 (12).

Lei, A., Cruickshank, H., Cao, Y., Asuquo, P., Chibueze, P., Ogah, A., Sun, Z., 2017. Blockchain-based dynamic key management for heterogeneous intelligent transportation systems. IEEE Internet Things J. 4 (6), 1832–1843.

Li, H., Zhu, L., Shen, M., Gao, F., Tao, X., Liu, S., 2018. Blockchain-based data preservation system for medical data. J. Med. Syst. 42 (8), 1–13.

Liang, X., Shetty, S., Tosh, D., 2018. Exploring the attack surfaces in blockchain enabled smart cities. In: 2018 IEEE International Smart Cities Conference (ISC2). IEEE, pp. 1–8.

Lin, C., He, D., Huang, X., Kumar, N., Raymond Choo, K.-K., 2020. BCPPA: a blockchain-based conditional privacy-preserving authentication protocol for vehicular ad hoc networks. In: IEEE Transactions on Intelligent Transportation Systems.

Liu, Y., Wang, K., Lin, Y., Xu, W., 2019. LightChain: a lightweight blockchain system for industrial internet of things. IEEE Trans. Industr. Inform. 15 (6), 3571–3581.

Liu, Z., Chi, Z., Mohamed, O., Peter, D., 2021. Blockchain and building information management (BIM) for sustainable building development within the context of smart cities. Sustainability 13 (4), 2090.

Lyu, Q., Qi, Y., Zhang, X., Liu, H., Wang, Q., Zheng, N., 2020. SBAC: a secure blockchain-based access control framework for information-centric networking. J. Netw. Comput. Appl. 149, 102444.

Makhdoom, I., Zhou, I., Abolhasan, M., Lipman, J., Ni, W., 2020. PrivySharing: a blockchain-based framework for privacy-preserving and secure data sharing in smart cities. Comput. Secur. 88, 101653.

McGhin, T., Raymond Choo, K.-K., Liu, C.Z., He, D., 2019. Blockchain in healthcare applications: research challenges and opportunities. J. Netw. Comput. Appl. 135, 62–75.

Mehmood, A., Ahmed, S.H., Sarkar, M., 2020. Cyber-physical systems in vehicular communications. In: Cyber Warfare and Terrorism: Concepts, Methodologies, Tools, and Applications. IGI Global, pp. 411–431.

Mingxiao, D., Ma, X., Zhang, Z., Wang, X., Chen, Q., 2017. A review on consensus algorithm of blockchain. In: 2017 IEEE International Conference on Systems, Man, and Cybernetics (SMC). IEEE, pp. 2567–2572.

Montecchi, M., Kirk, P., Etter, M., 2019. It's real, trust me! establishing supply chain provenance using blockchain. Bus. Horiz. 62 (3), 283—293.

Mora, O.B., Rivera, R., Larios, V.M., Raul Beltran-Ram´irez, J., Maciel, R., Ochoa, A., 2018. A use case in cybersecurity based in blockchain to deal with the security and privacy of citizens and smart cities cyberinfrastructures. In: 2018 IEEE International Smart Cities Conference (ISC2). IEEE, pp. 1—4.

Nadeem, S., Rizwan, M., Ahmad, F., Manzoor, J., 2019. Securing cognitive radio vehicular ad hoc network with fog node based distributed blockchain cloud architecture. Int. J. Adv. Comput. Sci. Appl. 10 (1), 288—295.

Nakamoto, S., Bitcoin, A., 2008. A Peer-To-Peer Electronic Cash System. Bitcoin. https://bitcoin.org/bitcoin.pdf4.

Novo, O., 2018. Blockchain meets IoT: an architecture for scalable access management in IoT. IEEE Internet Things J. 5 (2), 1184—1195.

Panarello, A., Tapas, N., Merlino, G., Longo, F., Puliafito, A., 2018. Blockchain and IoT integration: a systematic survey. Sensors 18 (8), 2575.

Queiroz, M.M., Fosso Wamba, S., 2019. Blockchain adoption challenges in supply chain: an empirical investigation of the main drivers in India and the USA. Int. J. Inf. Manag. 46, 70—82.

Raikwar, M., Mazumdar, S., Ruj, S., Gupta, S.S., Chattopadhyay, A., Lam, K.-Y., 2018. A blockchain framework for insurance processes. In: 2018 9th IFIP International Conference on New Technologies, Mobility and Security (NTMS). IEEE, pp. 1—4.

Saad, M., Thai, M.T., Mohaisen, A., 2018. POSTER: deterring DDoS attacks on blockchain-based cryptocurrencies through mempool optimization. In: Proceedings of the 2018 on Asia Conference on Computer and Communications Security, pp. 809—811.

Saberi, S., Kouhizadeh, M., Sarkis, J., Shen, L., 2019. Blockchain technology and its relationships to sustainable supply chain management. Int. J. Prod. Res. 57 (7), 2117—2135.

Saetta, D., Padda, A., Li, X., Leyva, C., Pitu, B., Mirchan, D., Dragan, B., Boyer, T.H., 2019. Water and wastewater building CPS: creation of cyber-physical wastewater collection system centered on urine diversion. IEEE Access 7, 182477—182488.

Sarmah, S.S., 2018. Understanding blockchain technology. Comput. Sci. Eng. 8 (2), 23—29.

Sharma, P.K., Hyuk Park, J., 2018. Blockchain based hybrid network architecture for the smart city. Future Generat. Comput. Syst. 86, 650—655.

Shi, L., Yang, L., Liu, T., Jia, L., Shan, B., Chen, H., 2019. Dynamic distributed honeypot based on blockchain. IEEE Access 7, 72234—72246.

Sodhro, A.H., Pirbhulal, S., Muzammal, M., Luo, Z., 2020. Towards blockchain-enabled security technique for industrial internet of things based decentralized applications. J. Grid Comput. 1—14.

Sun, J., Yan, J., Zhang, K.Z.K., 2016. "Blockchain-based sharing services: what blockchain technology can contribute to smart cities. Financial Innov. 2 (1), 1—9.

Sun, C., Cembrano, G., Puig, V., Meseguer, J., 2018. Cyber-physical systems for real-time management in the urban water cycle. In: 2018 International Workshop on Cyber-Physical Systems for Smart Water Networks (CySWater). IEEE, pp. 5—8.

Sztipanovits, J., Koutsoukos, X., Karsai, G., Kotten stette, N., Antsaklis, P., Gupta, V., Goodwine, B., Baras, J., Wang, S., 2011. Toward a science of cyber-physical system integration. Proc. IEEE 100 (1), 29—44.

Toyoda, K., Mathiopoulos, P.T., Sasase, I., Ohtsuki, T., 2017. A novel blockchain-based product ownership management system (POMS) for anti-counterfeits in the post supply chain. IEEE Access 5, 17465—17477.

Wagner, M., McMillin, B., 2020. An efficient blockchain authentication scheme for vehicular ad-hoc networks. In: International Conference on Critical Infrastructure Protection. Springer, Cham, pp. 87–109.

Wan, J., Li, J., Imran, M., Li, D., 2019. A blockchain-based solution for enhancing security and privacy in smart factory. IEEE Trans. Industr. Inform. 15 (6), 3652–3660.

Wang, E.K., Liang, Z., Chen, C.-M., Kumari, S., Khurram Khan, M., 2020. PoRX: a reputation incentive scheme for blockchain consensus of IIoT. Future Generat. Comput. Syst. 102, 140–151.

Wu, Y., Dai, H.-N., Wang, H., 2020. Convergence of blockchain and edge computing for secure and scalable IIoT critical infrastructures in Industry 4.0. IEEE Internet Things J.

Wust, K., Gervais, A., 2016. Ethereum Eclipse Attacks. ETH Zurich.

Xia, Q.I., Boateng Sifah, E., Omono Asamoah, K., Gao, J., Du, X., Guizani, M., 2017. MeDShare: trust-less medical data sharing among cloud service providers via blockchain. IEEE Access 5, 14757–14767.

Xu, R., Yahya Nikouei, S., Chen, Y., Blasch, E., Alexander, A., 2019. Blendmas: a blockchain-enabled decentralized microservices architecture for smart public safety. In: 2019 IEEE International Conference on Blockchain (Blockchain). IEEE, pp. 564–571.

Yang, Y., He, D., Wang, H., Zhou, L., 2019. An Efficient Blockchain-Based Batch Verification Scheme for Vehicular Ad Hoc Networks. Transactions on Emerging Telecommunications Technologies.

Yoon, H.-J., 2019. Blockchain technology and healthcare. Healthc. Inform. Res. 25 (2), 59–60.

Yue, X., Wang, H., Jin, D., Li, M., Jiang, W., 2016. Health care data gateways: found healthcare intelligence on blockchain with novel privacy risk control. J. Med. Syst. 40 (10), 1–8.

Zhang, S., Lee, J.-H., 2019. Double-spending with a sybil attack in the bitcoin decentralized network. IEEE Trans. Industr. Inform. 15 (10), 5715–5722.

Zhang, Y., Qiu, M., Tsai, C.-W., Hassan, M.M., Alamri, A., 2015. Health-CPS: healthcare cyber-physical system assisted by cloud and big data. IEEE Syst. J. 11 (1), 88–95.

Zhang, P., Walker, M.A., White, J., Schmidt, D.C., Gunther, L., 2017. Metrics for assessing blockchain-based healthcare decentralized apps. In: 2017 IEEE 19th International Conference on E-Health Networking, Applications and Services (Healthcom). IEEE, pp. 1–4.

Zheng, Z., Xie, S., Dai, H., Chen, X., Wang, H., 2017. An overview of blockchain technology: architecture, consensus, and future trends. In: 2017 IEEE International Congress on Big Data (BigData Congress). IEEE, pp. 557–564.

CHAPTER 4

A novel secured ledger platform for real-time transactions

Debarka Mukhopadhyay[1], Tanmay Chakraborty[2], Anirban Saha[3] and Ritam Mukherjee[3]

[1]Department of Computer Science and Engineering, School of Engineering and Technology, Christ Deemed to be University, Bangalore, Karnataka, India; [2]Department of Electronics and Communication Engineering, School of Engineering and Technology, Adamas University, Kolkata, West Bengal, India; [3]Department of Computer Science and Engineering, School of Engineering and Technology, Adamas University, Kolkata, West Bengal, India

1. Introduction

The invention of blockchain first served as public transaction ledger of the cryptocurrency Bitcoin (Haber and Stornetta, 1991). It came into force through the inventor Satoshi Nakamoto in the year 1991 (Peters et al., 2015). The design of Bitcoin inspired researchers to solve the double-spending problem without the need of a trusted authority or central server. It is a growing list of records that are connected via secured link. Each record, broadly called a block, consists of a hash of the previous block, a time stamp, and transaction data. It is a distributed, decentralized, and public digital ledger useful to keep track of transactions and allows participants to verify and audit transactions independently and inexpensively. A peer-to-peer network and timestamp server manage blockchain database, which is authenticated by mass collaboration powered by collective self-interest. Blockchain finds its application in multiple domains like health-care (Tripathi et al., 2020), data sharing (Shen et al., 2019), supply chain, internet of things (IoT), finance, mobility sharing, etc. (Al-Jaroodi and Mohamed, 2019). Blockchain technology may also be integrated into multiple areas as a distributed ledger for cryptocurrencies, smart contracts, financial services, supply chain, and much more. In Holotescu (2018), the author suggested its usefulness over educational actors and policy makers wanting to explore and to integrate blockchain in institutional projects and curricula.

In Huh et al. (2017), the authors expressed their observations in situations where more than thousands or tens of thousands of IoT devices are connected that the existing model of server-client may have some

Blockchain Technology for Emerging Applications
ISBN 978-0-323-90193-2
https://doi.org/10.1016/B978-0-323-90193-2.00011-9

limitations and issues in synchronization. They proposed a method using blockchain to build the IoT system. Here blockchain can control and configure IoT devices. In Watanabe et al. (2015) a proposal was made to use blockchain technology for recording contracts. A new protocol using the technology was described that makes it possible to confirm that contractor consent had been obtained and to archive the contractual document in the blockchain. In another work (Azaria et al., 2016), a modular design integrated with providers' existing, local data storage solutions, facilitating interoperability and making their system convenient and adaptable. They incentivized medical stakeholders (researchers, public health authorities, etc.) to participate in the network as blockchain miners. This provided them with access to aggregate anonymized data with mining rewards in return for sustaining and securing the network via proof of work. MedRec thus enables the emergence of data economics, supplying big data to empower researchers while engaging patients and providers in the choice to release metadata. One article (Turk and Klinc, 2017) incorporates a survey on blockchain technology. It expressed that a construction site blockchain could improve the reliability and trustworthiness of construction logbooks, works performed, and material quantities recorded. In the facility maintenance phase, blockchain's main potential is the secure storage of sensor data, which are sensitive to privacy.

A lightweight blockchain architecture has been proposed (Ismail et al., 2019) for healthcare applications. Other similar work (Hathaliya et al., 2019; Dwivedi et al., 2019) describes a remote patient monitoring application with blockchain and wearable sensors. Other works (Onik et al., 2019; Chen et al., 2019; Su et al., 2020) suggested the use of blockchain in sharing and storing electronic medical records, clinical trial data, and insurance information in the healthcare industry. They proposed a patient-centric data sharing model where the patient is the owner of their own data and chooses to share it with the shareholders as necessary (Al Omar et al., 2019; Leeming et al., 2019). In Abdellatif et al. (2020), edge computing and blockchain were merged together for applications in epidemic discovering, remote monitoring of patients, and fast emergency response. Tele-medical application of blockchain was introduced in Celesti et al. (2020). The authors proposed a tele-medical laboratory service where IoT-based medical devices would be utilized by technicians to perform clinical tests on patients, and the data would be shared over a blockchain and cloud system with the doctors and other hospitals and stakeholders (Ray et al., 2021). Application of blockchain in the healthcare management system has been proposed in other works (Fusco et al., 2020; Jennath et al., 2020). A scalable blockchain architecture with smart contracts was proposed to make IoT networks more secure and better preserve privacy (Satamraju et al., 2020; Abdullah and Jones, 2019; Rathee et al., 2019). As a use case, device authentication, authorization, access-control, and data management for medical purposes were taken. A cross-platform blockchain application having a low energy footprint with multiple stakeholders like patients, hospitals, and pharmaceutical and insurance companies was proposed in Munoz et al. (2019). Their solution followed the EU data regulations for data and privacy protection. A blockchain based tele-surgery framework was proposed in Gupta et al. (2019). They exploited smart contracts to establish trust between all the parties involved.

Combating counterfeit goods is a global problem (Korotkov, 2019). With the onset of blockchain, an effective solution to this problem came to light (Leng et al., 2020). A blockchain framework has been proposed for detecting counterfeit medicine (Saxena et al., 2020; Kumar et al., 2019). Blockchain applications in mobility are gaining momentum in smart cities (Katkova et al., 2020). In Bagloee et al. (2019), a tradable mobility permit based on Bitcoin and Etherium was introduced using tickets for public transportation. Mobility as a service takes into consideration a network of all public transportation systems where only a single permit can be utilized for riding (Nguyen et al., 2019; Vega Medel, 2020). It is possible to achieve a system like this with the help of blockchain (Bothos et al., 2019). A blockchain scheme for group mobility management was proposed (Lai and Ding, 2019). Pollution tracking, car monitoring, and emission control are some important factors involved in car maintenance and registration purposes (Distefano et al.). A blockchain-based architecture to emission monitoring has been proposed in Eckert et al. (2020). Ensuring fuel efficiency of commercial vehicles has been a problem for a long time, and a work (Anwar et al., 2019) tries to tackle it by using blockchain. Smart metering systems in e-mobility is another domain that has been explored with blockchain (Olivares-Rojas et al., 2020).

There have been tremendous advancements in the financial industry involving blockchain (Ali et al., 2020; Baker and Werbach, 2019). It has transcended beyond cryptocurrencies to distributed banking, asset management, and portfolio maintenance (Polyviou et al., 2019; Wang et al., 2017). This change has impacted a lot of business models of different companies as well (Morkunas et al., 2019). Blockchain in agritech is another common area of application (Kamilaris et al., 2019, 2021). Often the consumer is keen to know from where their food comes from, what fertilizers have been utilized to grow it, what is the shelf life of that food, as well as nutrient content, etc. A blockchain-based system is able to give answers to those questions directly (Demestichas et al., 2020). The blockchain-based traceability is able to track food items from inception to consumption (Kamble et al., 2020) (Singh et al., 2020a). In Hang et al. (2020), a fish farm platform was proposed utilizing the concept of blockchain to collect data and maintain data integrity. Blockchain has also found a sweet spot in applications related to law, policy, forensics, and contracts (Temte, 2019; Wanhua, 2020; Dasaklis et al., 2020). In an attempt to involve consumers who produce electricity in the electricity market, a blockchain network was proposed in Diestelmeier (2019). Smart contracts are also being employed in real estate dealings (Seigneur et al., 2020). Blockchain, artificial intelligence, and IoT are transforming smart cities rapidly (Singh et al., 2020b; Gill et al., 2019). In Makhdoom et al. (2020), a privacy-preserving data sharing model was proposed for smart cities. It leverages blockchain to secure public data sharing and enable privacy. Data verification from CCTV cameras of a smart city using IoT and blockchain to prevent crime has been proposed (Khan et al., 2020). A dynamic pricing strategy for energy pricing in a smart city using blockchain helps make smart city energy governance a lot easier (Khattak et al., 2020).

Even though it is so well known, there are some principle drawbacks in the core of blockchain technology, which will be discussed in the further sections. The existing public blockchain technology exhibits a single layer of hashing and incorporates no encryption algorithms for their transactions. Hence, it ascertains partially secured transactions based on one level of hashing to ensure openness to all parties. The property of openness exposes privacy of the users, so we employed a double-layer encryption procedure. The first layer encompasses AES encryption methodology with a randomly generated key at the user end, and the second layer of encryption process is performed at the server end. Data security is ensured through three layers of hashing unlike conventional blockchain networks. The first layer of hashing is initiated at the user end to ensure tamper-proof transmission. The second and third layers are performed at the server side before initiating the validation process to ensure the highest level of data security. Unlike the existing blockchain technology, our proposal ensures real-time transaction and validation even when scaled up. Again unlike conventional blockchain technology, this invention allows multiple applications to perform under single platform. Other than the distinguishing features as mentioned, this invention carries the rest of the features of a blockchain technology. The rest of this paper is organized as follows: Section 2 discusses the brief detailing of the proposed work, followed by Section 3 that analyzes the performance of the system and compares it with some state-of-the-art models. Beside this, Section 4 describes certain use cases of the proposed technology, and the chapter is concluded in Section 5.

2. Proposed work

The work presented in this chapter unveils a novel technology that can be utilized in place of conventional blockchain. In addition to services provided by a normal blockchain technology, it provides the highest security through two layers of encryption, higher authenticity through three layers of hashing utilized for validation, and also gives a platform to trace the complete activity performed by a trusted module over a particular project for future reference. The proposed system does not follow a chain-based file architecture. Due to this, no concept of chain break arises, and the problems that arise as a result of chain break in blockchain are avoided. This system ensures trustworthiness, authenticity, and CIA (confidentiality, integrity, and availability) to its end users while being real time in execution.

The proposed system overview is captured in Fig. 4.1. In the total working environment, there exists a distributed cloud server, a generator, and several validators called trusted modules. These trusted modules continuously communicate with one another while abiding to some

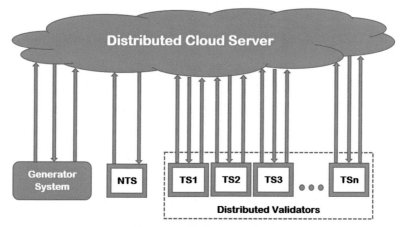

Figure 4.1 System overview.

security rules. If any nontrusted module appears to start communication, the server as a responsible entity shall deny the service requested by the nontrusted module without exposing its data files.

2.1 Communication between generator and server

Fig. 4.2 illustrates the communication between the generator and the server for a single transaction. While generating a combination of data and hash value, namely a node, the generator first sends a request to the server for a random key. After successful authentication, the server generates a random key and sends it to the generator. An encryption process with the data will be carried out at the generator end before it is to be transmitted over the network to the server requesting for further processing.

2.2 Communication between validator and server

Fig. 4.3 depicts communication between the server and validators. A validator, when ready to validate data, modifies its status flag. The server,

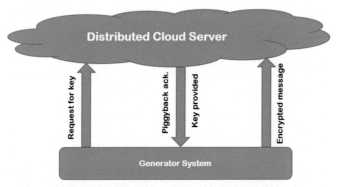

Figure 4.2 Generator-server communication.

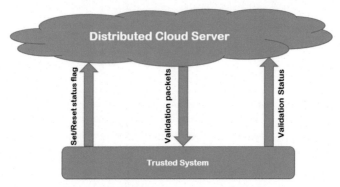

Figure 4.3 Validator-server communication.

when it finds any validator ready, starts sending unvalidated packets toward the validators. The validators on completion of the process of validation send validation status of each packet to the server. While going for a break, validators modify the flag to zero and communicate directly with the server.

2.3 Communication with nontrusted module

Fig. 4.4 depicts a communication attempt by any nontrusted system for gathering protected information from the server. The server plays the role of a moderator and declines any request made by the unauthenticated or nontrusted system. This increases the overall security of the proposed system and prevents unwanted data leakages.

2.4 Functional units of generator module

Fig. 4.5 shows internal data flow of a generator. When a transaction as an event is initiated at the Plain Text Generator, two different operations shall

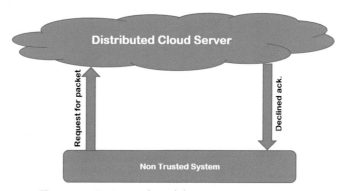

Figure 4.4 Nontrusted module-server communication.

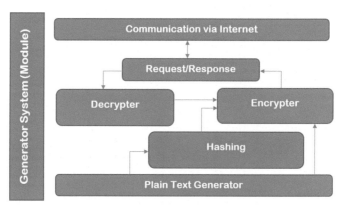

Figure 4.5 Data flow graph for generator.

follow. First and foremost a hash value is generated on data and is forwarded to the Encrypter, which requests a random key from the server. The generated random key is received in encrypted form, which is forwarded to the Decrypter that decrypts the key and communicates the key with the Encrypter. On receiving the key, the encrypter encrypts the combination of plain text and hash value. The Encrypter now communicates the encrypted data to the server.

2.5 Functional units of validator module

Fig. 4.6 illustrates internal data flow for the Validator module. Upon receiving an unvalidated data from the server, it gets stored in the local storage and the validation process gets started. The validation process is completely automated and undergoes four main operations, which are decryption, splitting, hash value computing, and checking for level-wise validation status. These four operations are iterated twice in the same sequence utilizing the local storage during the process. Then the last level of validation is initiated where the data fetched from the local storage is decrypted and split for checking the validation status. This final validation status is communicated to the server. If the validation fails at any stage, the further process is terminated and a negative status is sent to the server.

2.6 Functional units of server module

The internal data flow within the cloud server is demonstrated by Fig. 4.7. At first, the server provides access to the Registration/Login Module to the system accessing the service. Any system that is registered for the service needs to login, and others needs to register per their required service. This

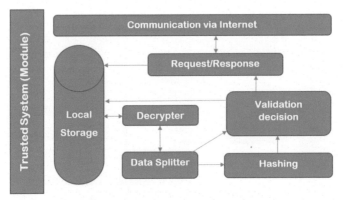

Figure 4.6 Data flow graph for validator.

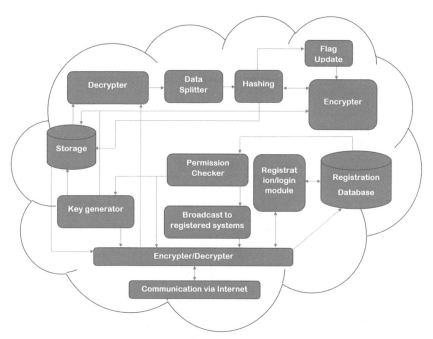

Figure 4.7 Data flow graph for cloud server.

module directly communicates to the Registration Database, which provides the permission details to the Permission Checker, which is further utilized in a later stage. Apart from this service, the server provides the intermediate services to support the proposed platform. This starts when a generator requests a key to initiate a transaction. Upon receiving this request, the server checks the permission from the Permission Checker and ignites the Key Generator module upon successful permission checking. This generated key is transmitted to the generator through a network-level encryption. The cipher text generated by the generator is received by the server and gets forwarded to the local storage. Even a duplicate copy of the cipher text is transmitted to the Decrypter module, which is followed by the Data Splitting module that separates the transaction details from the hash. Now the data is hashed and the hash value is compared with the previous one. If both hash values match, then a status flag is set to 1; otherwise, it is set to 0. This is further followed by the Encrypter module along with hashing modules two times with intermediate interaction with the storage and key generator modules. Then the ultimate details get stored in the Storage module with unvalidated status. This complete process enables the security concept of two-layer encryption and three-layer hashing. Meanwhile, a number of validators are active with validation permission. Now, the unvalidated data are broadcasted to the validators online by the Broadcast to Registered System module upon proper interaction with the Permission Checking module. Once the validators provide feedback, it gets stored. Depending upon the amount of positive and negative feedback from the validators, the ultimate validation status gets updated in the storage module, which basically determines the transaction status.

3. Result and discussion

The proposed system is implemented as an embedded system, and the results show that the system is lightweight and agile. The generator, cloud server, and validators are developed separately and made to communicate with each other over the internet. The system was found to be real time with a time lag of less than 1 s (from generation to validation) including network delay. With a faster network, the delay would become less, which will reduce the overall system delay.

Table 4.1 shows a detailed analysis of the proposed technology when compared with other state-of-the-art ledger-based platforms. With the implementation of dual layers of encryption, the data transmissions are secured to the highest extent. And three layers of hashing ensures data privacy. The proposed methodology does not restrict the number of transactions per second, as it maintains a log book instead of chain structure. Due to adaptation of the log book concept in a ledger platform, several concerns, arising as a result of chain or graph structure, can be avoided. Examples of such concerns include chain break and isolated graph generation due to data hampering.

4. Use cases

1. Healthcare monitoring ecosystem application: We have a patient-centric ecosystem where all medical shops, hospitals, diagnostic centers, patient families, doctors, insurance companies, etc., become parties of the system after they are registered with the application. The application layer should allow different parties to register according to their organizations for proper system maintenance. When a patient registers himself with the application, a permanent patient ID is generated with the help

Table 4.1 Comparison chart.

Methodology	Blockchain (El Ioini and Pahl, 2018)	Sidechain (El Ioini and Pahl, 2018)	Tangle (El Ioini and Pahl, 2018)	Hashgraph (El Ioini and Pahl, 2018)	Proposed
Data structure	Array	List of linked lists	DAG	DAG	Log file
Consensus	PoW: SHA256 hash	PoW: Ethash	PoW: Hashcash	Virtual voting	3 layers of hash
Transactions	Grouped into blocks	Two chains of blocks	Single transaction	Gossip events	Contiguous data
Transactions per second	4 to 7	Limited	500 to 800	>200,000	Unbounded
Validation time	Order of minutes	Order of minutes	Order of seconds	Order of seconds	Order of milliseconds
Privacy	Low	High	Low	Low	Highest
Security	High	High	High	High	Highest

of the disclosed technology. Now, when the treatment starts, the doctor (as a generator) accesses the application layer and communicates with the proposed server through local cloud server and uploads the required documents that need to be sent to the patient (prescription). This ignites the disclosed technology to start its processing, which validates (finds out) any tampering with the document and provides the feedback to the local cloud server. These documents are stored in the patient's application wallet, and selected data from the wallet can be shared with relevant parties according to patient's desire of what data to share, providing application-layer security. Sharing may take place by account number or generator number to indicate which organization should receive the data from the patient via the proposed server. The local server can pull data through API end points of the proposed database (database has transaction instances with generator ID). The moment anything needs to be updated, it takes place in the proposed server upon successful validation. This process continues for subsequent updating, i.e., updates from the doctor, insurance company, medical facility, etc. All communications provided by the proposed server are real-time, secured, and scalable per need.

2. Mobility as a service: We have a traveler-centric ecosystem where all mobility-providing companies become parties of the system after they are registered with the application. The application layer should allow different parties to register according to their organizations for proper system maintenance. When a customer registers with the application, a permanent customer ID is generated with the help of the proposed technology. Now, when the customer initiates a ticket booking with a certain amount of credits, tokens, or stable coins, an initial checking to see if they have the required amount of coins needs to be made. Upon successful checking a transaction needs to be initiated with the proposed technology, and upon receiving successful feedback, a barcode or QR code needs to be generated that would have a certain amount of credits. The payment system of tokens needs to be maintained in the local database where the local database would act as the ledger for the ecosystem. Once the booking process is complete the customer can travel with the barcode or QR code, and each party in the ecosystem will be able to deduct their amount from the credit available in the code. Transferring of credits needs to be again initiated in the application once the QR is scanned by a valid and authentic generator. Credits from the QR code's account will be transferred to the scanning party's

account via the disclosed ledger technology. Upon trip completion the QR will be discarded and relevant data can be stored in the local cloud server for future processing. All communications provided by the proposed server are real-time, secured, and scalable per need.

5. Conclusion

The work revealed here indicates its superiority over existing blockchain technology. It is a platform where multiple transactions of various categories can be performed under one hood. It is a provider of highly secured transaction where three layers of hashing and two layers encryption are incorporated. Three layers of hashing are initiated to prevent tampering of data while communicating between server and generator, within server, and between server and validator. The two layers of encryption manages a man in the middle attack or packet sniffing attack between generator and server and server and validator. The platform provides real-time validation results unlike other existing systems. It also ensures CIA (confidentiality, integrity, and availability) to its end users besides having all other the features except chaining of a blockchain technology.

References

Abdellatif, A.A., Al-Marridi, A.Z., Mohamed, A., Erbad, A., Chiasserini, C.F., Refaey, A., 2020. ssHealth: toward secure, blockchain-enabled healthcare systems. IEEE Netw. 34 (4), 312−319. https://doi.org/10.1109/MNET.011.1900553.

Abdullah, T., Jones, A., 2019. eHealth: challenges far integrating blockchain within healthcare. In: IEEE 12th International Conference on Global Security, Safety and Sustainability (ICGS3). IEEE, pp. 1−9.

Al Omar, A., Bhuiyan, M.Z.A., Basu, A., Kiyomoto, S., Rahman, M.S., 2019. Privacy-friendly platform for healthcare data in cloud based on blockchain environment. Future Gener. Comput. Syst. 95, 511−521.

Ali, O., Ally, M., Dwivedi, Y., et al., 2020. The state of play of blockchain technology in the financial services sector: a systematic literature review. Int. J. Inf. Manag. 54, 102199.

Al-Jaroodi, J., Mohamed, N., 2019. Industrial applications of blockchain. In: IEEE 9th Annual Computing and Communication Workshop and Conference (CCWC). IEEE, pp. 0550−0555.

Anwar, H., Arasu, M., Ahmed, Q., 2019. Ensuring fuel economy performance of commercial vehicle fleets using blockchain technology. SAE Int. J. Adv. Curr. Pract. Mobil. 1, 1510−1516.

Azaria, A., Ekblaw, A., Vieira, T., Lippman, A., 2016. Medrec: using blockchain for medical data access and permission management. In: 2nd International Conference on Open and Big Data (OBD), pp. 25−30. https://doi.org/10.1109/OBD.2016.11.

Bagloee, S.A., Tavana, M., Withers, G., Patriksson, M., Asadi, M., 2019. Tradable mobility permit with Bitcoin and Eethereum—A Blockchain application in transportation. Internet Things 8, 100103.

Baker, C., Werbach, K., 2019. Blockchain in financial services. In: FINTECH. Edward Elgar Publishing.

Bothos, E., Magoutas, B., Arnaoutaki, K., Mentzas, G., 2019. Leveraging blockchain for open mobility-as-a-service ecosystems. In: IEEE/WIC/ACM International Conference on Web Intelligence-Companion Volume, pp. 292—296.

Celesti, A., Ruggeri, A., Fazio, M., Galletta, A., Villari, M., Romano, A., 2020. Blockchain-based healthcare work ow for tele-medical laboratory in federated hospital IoT clouds. Sensors 20 (9), 2590.

Chen, H.S., Jarrell, J.T., Carpenter, K.A., Cohen, D.S., Huang, X., 2019. Blockchain in healthcare: a patient-centered model. Biomed. J. Sci. Tech. Res. 20 (3), 15017.

Dasaklis, T.K., Casino, F., Patsakis, C., 2020. SoK: blockchain solutions for forensics arXiv preprint arXiv:2005.12640.

Demestichas, K., Peppes, N., Alexakis, T., Adamopoulou, E., 2020. Blockchain in agriculture traceability systems: a review. Appl. Sci. 10 (12), 4113.

Diestelmeier, L., 2019. Changing power: shifting the role of electricity consumers with blockchain technology—policy implications for eu electricity law. Energy Pol. 128, 189—196.

Distefano, S., Di Giacomo, A., Mazzara, M. Trustworthiness for Transportation Ecosystems: The Blockchain Vehicle Information System.

Dwivedi, A.D., Srivastava, G., Dhar, S., Singh, R., 2019. A decentralized privacy-preserving healthcare blockchain for IoT. Sensors 19 (2), 326.

Eckert, J., Lopez, D., Azevedo, C.L., Farooq, B., 2020. A blockchain-based user-centric emission monitor-ing and trading system for multi-modal mobility. In: Forum on Integrated and Sustainable Transportation Systems (FISTS). IEEE, pp. 328—334.

El Ioini, N., Pahl, C., 2018. A review of distributed ledger technologies. In: OTM Confederated International Conferences on the Move to Meaningful Internet Systems. Springer, pp. 277—288.

Fusco, A., Dicuonzo, G., DellAtti, V., Tatullo, M., 2020. Blockchain in healthcare: insights on covid-19. Int. J. Environ. Res. Publ. Health 17 (19), 7167.

Gill, S.S., Tuli, S., Xu, M., Singh, I., Singh, K.V., Lindsay, D., Tuli, S., Smirnova, D., Singh, M., Jain, U., et al., 2019. Transformative e ects of iot, blockchain and artificial intelligence on cloud computing: evolution, vision, trends and open challenges. Internet Things 8, 100118.

Gupta, R., Tanwar, S., Tyagi, S., Kumar, N., Obaidat, M.S., Sadoun, B., 2019. Habits: blockchain-based telesurgery framework for healthcare 4.0. In: International Conference on Computer, Information and Telecommunication Systems (CITS), pp. 1—5. https://doi.org/10.1109/CITS.2019.8862127.

Haber, S., Stornetta, W.S., 1991. How to time-stamp a digital document. J. Cryptol. 3 (2), 99—111. https://doi.org/10.1007/BF00196791.

Hang, L., Ullah, I., Kim, D.-H., 2020. A secure sh farm platform based on blockchain for agriculture data integrity. Comput. Electron. Agric. 170, 105251.

Hathaliya, J., Sharma, P., Tanwar, S., Gupta, R., 2019. Blockchain-based remote patient monitoring in healthcare 4.0. In: IEEE 9th International Conference on Advanced Computing (IACC), pp. 87—91. https://doi.org/10.1109/IACC48062.2019.8971593.

Holotescu, C., 2018. Understanding Blockchain Technology and How to Get Involved.

Huh, S., Cho, S., Kim, S., 2017. Managing IoT devices using blockchain platform. In: 19th International Conference on Advanced Communication Technology (ICACT), pp. 464—467. https://doi.org/10.23919/ICACT.2017.7890132.

Ismail, L., Materwala, H., Zeadally, S., 2019. Lightweight blockchain for healthcare. IEEE Access 7, 149935−149951. https://doi.org/10.1109/ACCESS.2019.2947613.

Jennath, H., Anoop, V., Asharaf, S., 2020. Blockchain for healthcare: securing patient data and enabling trusted artificial intelligence. Int. J. Interact. Multimed. Artif. Intell. 6, 15−23.

Kamble, S.S., Gunasekaran, A., Sharma, R., 2020. Modeling the blockchain enabled traceability in agriculture supply chain. Int. J. Inf. Manag. 52, 101967.

Kamilaris, A., Fonts, A., Prenafeta-Bold, F.X., 2019. The rise of blockchain technology in agriculture and food supply chains. Trends Food Sci. Technol. 91, 640−652.

Kamilaris, A., Cole, I.R., Prenafeta-Boldu, F.X., 2021. Blockchain in agriculture. In: Food Technology Disruptions. Elsevier, pp. 247−284.

Katkova, M., Tregubov, V., Kapustina, N., Yussuf, A., Pilipchuk, N., 2020. Application of blockchain-based technology for smart transport system. In: Russian Conference on Digital Economy and Knowledge Management (RuDEcK 2020). Atlantis Press, pp. 261−267.

Khan, P.W., Byun, Y.-C., Park, N., 2020. A data verification system for CCTV surveillance cameras using blockchain technology in smart cities. Electronics 9 (3), 484.

Khattak, H.A., Tehreem, K., Almogren, A., Ameer, Z., Din, I.U., Adnan, M., 2020. Dynamic pricing in industrial internet of things: blockchain application for energy management in smart cities. J. Inf. Secur. Appl. 55, 102615.

Korotkov, M., 2019. The Problem of Counterfeiting and Fashion Piracy.

Kumar, A., Choudhary, D., Raju, M.S., Chaudhary, D.K., Sagar, R.K., 2019. Combating counterfeit drugs: a quantitative analysis on cracking down the fake drug industry by using blockchain technology. In: 9th International Conference on Cloud Computing, Data Science & Engineering (Confluence). IEEE, pp. 174−178.

Lai, C., Ding, Y., 2019. A secure blockchain-based group mobility management scheme in VANETs. In: IEEE/CIC International Conference on Communications in China (ICCC). IEEE, pp. 340−345.

Leeming, G., Cunningham, J., Ainsworth, J., 2019. A ledger of me: personalizing healthcare using blockchain technology. Front. Med. 6, 171.

Leng, J., Ruan, G., Jiang, P., Xu, K., Liu, Q., Zhou, X., Liu, C., 2020. Blockchain-empowered sustainable manufacturing and product lifecycle management in industry 4.0: a survey. Renew. Sustain. Energy Rev. 132, 110112.

Makhdoom, I., Zhou, I., Abolhasan, M., Lipman, J., Ni, W., 2020. PrivySharing: a blockchain-based frame-work for privacy-preserving and secure data sharing in smart cities. Comput. Secur. 88, 101653.

Morkunas, V.J., Paschen, J., Boon, E., 2019. How blockchain technologies impact your business model. Bus. Horiz. 62 (3), 295−306.

Munoz, D.-J., Constantinescu, D.-A., Asenjo, R., Fuentes, L., 2019. Clinicappchain: a low-cost blockchain hyperledger solution for healthcare. In: International Congress on Blockchain and Applications. Springer, pp. 36−44.

Nguyen, T.H., Partala, J., Pirttikangas, S., 2019. Blockchain-based mobility-as-a-service. In: 28th International Conference on Computer Communication and Networks (ICCCN). IEEE, pp. 1−6.

Olivares-Rojas, J.C., Reyes-Archundia, E., Gutierrez-Gnecchi, J.A., Molina-Moreno, I., 2020. A Survey on Smart Metering Systems Using Blockchain for E-Mobility, arXiv preprint arXiv:2009.09075.

Onik, M.M.H., Aich, S., Yang, J., Kim, C.-S., Kim, H.-C., 2019. Blockchain in healthcare: challenges and solutions. In: Big Data Analytics for Intelligent Healthcare Management. Elsevier, pp. 197−226.

Peters, G.W., Panayi, E., Chapelle, A., 2015. Trends in crypto-currencies and blockchain technologies: a monetary theory and regulation perspective. J. Cryptol. 3 (2), 99–111. https://doi.org/10.2139/ssrn.2646618.

Polyviou, A., Velanas, P., Soldatos, J., 2019. Blockchain technology: financial sector applications beyond cryptocurrencies. In: Multidisciplinary Digital, vol. 28. Publishing Institute Proceedings, p. 7.

Rathee, G., Sharma, A., Saini, H., Kumar, R., Iqbal, R., 2019. A Hybrid Framework for Multimedia Data Processing in Iot-Healthcare Using Blockchain Technology. Multimedia Tools and Applications, pp. 1–23.

Ray, P.P., Dash, D., Salah, K., Kumar, N., 2021. Blockchain for IoT-based healthcare: background, consensus, platforms, and use cases. IEEE Syst. J. 15 (1), 85–94.

Satamraju, K.P., et al., 2020. Proof of concept of scalable integration of internet of things and blockchain in healthcare. Sensors 20 (5), 1389.

Saxena, N., Thomas, I., Gope, P., Burnap, P., Kumar, N., 2020. PharmaCrypt: blockchain for critical pharmaceutical industry to counterfeit drugs. Computer 53 (7), 29–44.

Seigneur, J.-M., Pusterla, S., Socquet-Clerc, X., 2020. Blockchain real estate relational value survey. In: Proceedings of the 35th Annual ACM Symposium on Applied Computing, pp. 279–285.

Shen, B., Guo, J., Yang, Y., 2019. MedChain: Efficient healthcare data sharing via blockchain. Appl. Sci. 9 (6), 1207.

Singh, S.K., Rathore, S., Park, J.H., 2020a. Blockiotintelligence: a blockchain-enabled intelligent IoT architecture with artificial intelligence. Future Generat. Comput. Syst. 110, 721–743.

Singh, S., Sharma, P.K., Yoon, B., Shojafar, M., Cho, G.H., Ra, I.-H., 2020b. Convergence of blockchain and artificial intelligence in IoT network for the sustainable smart city. Sustaina. Cities Soc. 63, 102364.

Su, Q., Zhang, R., Xue, R., Li, P., 2020. Revocable attribute-based signature for blockchain-based healthcare system. IEEE Access 8, 127884–127896.

Temte, M.N., 2019. Blockchain challenges traditional contract law: just how smart are smart contracts. Wyo. L. Rev. 19, 87.

Tripathi, G., Ahad, M.A., Paiva, S., 2020. S2HS-a blockchain based approach for smart healthcare system. In: Healthcare, vol. 8. Elsevier, p. 100391.

Turk, Z., Klinc, R., 2017. In: Procedia Engineering, vol. 196, pp. 638–645.

Vega Medel, G., 2020. A blockchain-based mobility as a service concept design with the adoption of autonomous vehicles: an exploratory study of the most elemental systems, requirements and possible configurations.

Wang, Y., Kim, D.-K., Jeong, D., 2017. A survey of the application of blockchain in multiple fields of financial services. J. Inf. Process. Syst. 16 (4).

Wanhua, L., 2020. Research and application of blockchain technology in transportation administrative law enforcement. In: IEEE 5th Information Technology and Mechatronics Engineering Conference (ITOEC). IEEE, pp. 766–770.

Watanabe, H., Fujimura, S., Nakadaira, A., Miyazaki, Y., Akutsu, A., Kishigami, J.J., 2015. Blockchain contract: a complete consensus using blockchain. In: 2015 IEEE 4th Global Conference on Consumer Electronics (GCCE), pp. 577–578. https://doi.org/10.1109/GCCE.2015.7398721.

CHAPTER 5

Blockchain for intrusion detection systems

Tanmay Shetty[1], Saloni Negi[1], Anushka Kulshrestha[1], Shaifali Choudhary[1], Ramani S[1] and Marimuthu Karuppiah[2]
[1]School of Computer Science and Engineering, Vellore Institute of Technology, Vellore, Tamil Nadu, India; [2]Department of Computer Science and Engineering, SRM Institute of Science and Technology, Delhi-NCR Campus, Ghaziabad, Uttar Pradesh, India

1. Introduction

Nowadays, much work is done online, giving rise to cyber-attack. These attacks have become advanced and very complicated. To overcome these problems and detect suspicious or malicious activities in a short time, intrusion detection systems (IDSs) are being used and implemented in different fields (such as health, banking, and education). If such an activity occurs, it is collected by security information and event management systems. In some cases, these IDS are capable of responding to such activity. So, to understand the importance of blockchain in an IDS, we first need to understand what intrusion detection actually is and why we need it. An important step is to select a suitable IDS technology, which is basically of two types: network intrusion detection (NIDS) or host-based intrusion detection (HIDS). The IDS analyzes networks for any malicious activity. It is positioned on network telecommunications like Ethernet and monitors the contents of packets passively. It looks for volume, source, and destination of the traffic, and it verifies the packets that should be present in the network and the ones that should not be present and then alerts the user upon suspicious activity (Kumar and Singh, 2020). It monitors important operating system files. It looks for resources each program accesses, authentication tables, changes that are made in memory at particular locations, RAM storage state information, and log-related files. It also monitors dynamic behavior and state of the system and compares that with what it actually should be.

Detection approaches are divided into two parts: signature-based IDS and anomaly-based IDS.

Blockchain Technology for Emerging Applications
ISBN 978-0-323-90193-2
https://doi.org/10.1016/B978-0-323-90193-2.00003-X

1.1 Signature-based IDS

This is used to detect threats known to us. It relies on a preprogrammed list of known threats. This technique looks at specific patterns like malicious byte sequences. It can detect known attacks, but it is not efficient when it comes to detect new or unknown threats like novel viruses.

1.2 Anomaly-based IDS

This is used to detect changes in behavior. The system is trained with a normalized baseline, which is basically a normal behavior. The activity is then compared against this baseline. If any event occurs that does not belong to this baseline, an alarm is triggered. This technique is efficient to detect unknown attacks.

These IDSs have proven that they are capable of preventing and protecting network segments. They are hence deployed on the networks in different machines and devices for protection against cyber threats. However, since nowadays much has become digital and network based, the rate of intrusions and their complexity has also increased. In such cases a single IDS proves to be very ineffective in protecting the whole network from attacks. A single IDS can easily let a sequence of attacks pass through (Wu et al., 2003). If we are not able to find the attack or virus at the proper time, it could cost major damage to the system and network. To overcome such issues, we should use collaborative intrusion detection systems/networks (CIDSs/CIDNs). Here, we see where we can use blockchain. The properties that blockchain exhibits are useful in the context of a CIDS. Specifically, the critical component of blockchain technology for CIDS applications is its mechanism of validating and storing data with no need for a central, trusted authority. As it possesses the unique feature of keeping data and information in different blocks and different systems using algorithms, it becomes difficult for an attacker to gain access to information because data is stored in different locations.

1.3 Organization of the paper

The remainder of this chapter is structured as follows. Section 2 of this chapter explains IDSs and their functionalities. Along with this, it explains different forms of IDSs. In Section 3, the blockchain is explained in detail. Also it discusses the reasons why blockchain is secure and reliable; this is due to the different consensus mechanisms that it uses to verify each transaction. Section 4 focus on HIDS and its working. In Section 5, blockchain-based intrusion detection is explained as well as challenges related to the intrusion detection system and how blockchain helps IDS and is a solution to the challenges faced in IDS. Section 6 focuses on a collaborative IDS and how blockchain can be a solution to problems like sharing of data and trust management in CIDS. Section 7 discusses the applications of IDS, mainly Snort, and the designing of Snort-based CIDS with blockchain. Section 8 deals with the limitations of both IDS and blockchain. Section 9 illustrates how IDSs and firewalls, both being related to the security of the network, are different from each other. In Section 10 is discussed the capabilities of blockchain and how much help it will be in the near future.

2. Intrusion detection system

The main objective of intrusion detection (ID) is to recognize any kind of virus or malicious activity that can be found in the host or in a network. There are various processes to approach the IDS, but Fig. 5.1 shows the general process of an IDS. The figure shows the different parts of the process in how the system is capable of detecting an anomaly in the host or network (Scarfone and Mell, 2007).

ID gives details about the information gathered by monitoring the network and all kinds of system events with any incidents. Basically, an IDS can provide following functions.

2.1 Information gathering

As IDS monitors the system and network. It can collect all kinds of local information for the target. This information gathered can be processed and stored, which can further be used in managing the system (Kanth, 2019).

2.2 Generating the alert

The major role of an IDS is that it gives an alert to the information security administrator if any kind of attack or incident happens. It is necessary to keep a record at the time when it is attacked so it is effective (Kanth, 2019).

As we have seen, an IDS can be classified into NIDS or HIDS, so a network can be deployed on location like a wireless-based IDS that can

Figure 5.1 General process of an IDS.

monitor suspicious activity by monitoring wireless network packets through different kinds of protocols. Nowadays, IDS products use these two types of detection, providing more security and protection. The setup of such a network is shown in Fig. 5.2. There are five different forms of IDSs.

2.3 Network intrusion detection system

NIDSs are set up at specific points inside the network to analyze the traffic of data from all devices connected in the network. They carry the task of observing traffic on the subnet of the organization and matching the traffic data that is moved inside the network with a set of known cyber-attacks. Once an attack is recognized, an alert message can be sent to the security administrator. For example, NIDSs can be deployed on the firewall so we can notice if someone attacks it and be notified (Hu, 2010).

Once they are installed in the network, they start gathering information from a host console and check with the network for identification of permitted host computers, applications, and operating systems that are commonly used throughout the network. They also maintain a log on characteristics of normal traffic present in the network to identify any malicious activity or any changes in the network. They can also prevent different attacks like denial-of-service (DoS) attacks in a variety of ways, for example, by sending a TCP packet connection to prevent an attack, limiting bandwidth range and usage, or even by rejecting malicious activity or files present in the network. The setup of an NIDS is shown in Fig. 5.3 (Hu, 2010).

This gives various information of network traffic packets and different types of network protocols. The packets that are captured are analyzed by knowledge-based or behavioral-based approaches. In a knowledge-based approach, if packets match with a past record of attack, then it is an attack (Hu, 2010).

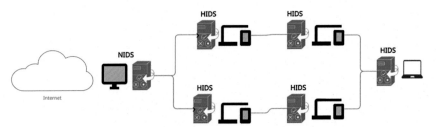

Figure 5.2 Network environment of HIDS and NIDS.

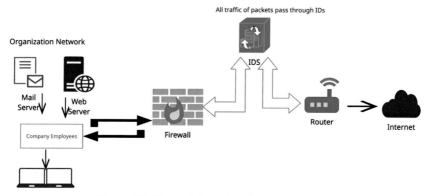

Figure 5.3 Network intrusion detection system.

2.4 Host intrusion detection system

An HIDS runs on each host or device inside the network. An HIDS keeps a record of all the incoming as well as outgoing packets from every device and notifies the security administrator in case there is any unwanted activity such as a malicious file or code being detected. A record of snapshots is maintained that consists of existing system snapshots and present system snapshots, so when any unwanted activity happens, it can compare these snapshots. If anyone tries to edit or delete the analytical system files, it will send an alert to the security administrator, so an investigation can be performed. For example, a laptop provided by a company to its employee for work may not have changes to any existing files or layout. The setup of an HIDS can be done as shown in Fig. 5.4 (Hu, 2010).

Regarding misuse, an HIDS can detect any kind of attack by the patterns of previous computer activities compared to current computer activities like CPU usage, memory used, and which files are access against the rules of host-based intrusions (Hu, 2010).

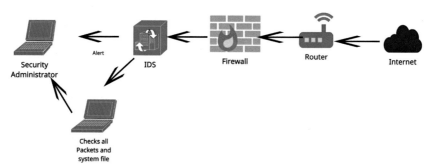

Figure 5.4 Host-based intrusion detection system.

2.5 Protocol-based intrusion detection system

PIDS is a device or sensor that detects the presence of an attacker trying to breach the physical parameter. It consists of a system that would consistently stay at the front end of a server; it is controlled and interprets protocols between a user device and the server, which can be a database. It mainly focuses on trying to secure the web server by keeping a record of monitoring the HTTPS protocol.

2.6 Application protocol-based intrusion detection system

It monitors and analyzes the important or specific applications present in a computer or device itself. Generally, this system is present within a group of servers. It monitors and interprets the application-specific protocols, thus identifying the intervention. For example, as it communicates with a database on the web server, this will track SQL protocol specifically displayed in middleware.

2.7 Hybrid intrusion detection system

As the name suggests, a hybrid intrusion detection system is made of two or more IDS techniques, e.g., Network intrusion detection system (NIDS) and HIDS. This is done to increase efficiency, as it allows detecting both known and unknown attacks. In this, a complete view of the network is created by combining host agent or system data with network information. This system is more effective in comparison to other IDSs.

3. About blockchain

Think of blockchain as a database with exception of its way of storing information and data. It is also referred to as distributed ledger technology (DLT) and follows peer-to-peer (p2p) topology. A DLT is a technology or system that stores digital data and records the transaction and its details in multiple places (servers) at the same time. So unlike traditional database systems, there is no central place where data is stored. Blockchain technology makes a transaction transparent by using decentralization, cryptography, and consensus mechanisms. Here, the digital assets are not copied or transferred. Instead, they are distributed over the network, and assets are decentralized, which means they can be accessed in real time.

The most common analogy to understand blockchain would be Google Docs. When we grant access to other people, the document is not copied; instead, it is distributed. If anyone makes changes to the document, it is affected in real time. Other people do not have to wait while someone else is reading or writing. The same is the case with blockchain, but at a larger scale and more complex than this. In a world with blockchain technologies being followed, we can imagine that every transaction will be in digital code and will be stored in a shared database, decentralizing the network and making it accessible in real time, yet protecting it from alterations by hackers, deletion, or revisions. This is a world where bankers will no longer be required to identify, validate, store, and share payment information as it could all be done digitally using blockchain. The security aspects are discussed later in this chapter.

There are different types of blockchains based on your requirement. For example, if Bitcoin is considered, we need a blockchain that can be accessible by the public, so they can become one node and verify others and trade. But in the case of banks, the transactions need to be secured and only authorized members should have the right to access this confidential information. So in this scenario a blockchain that has limited authorization will be used. Different types of blockchain are detailed next.

3.1 Public blockchain

The public blockchain, also called a permissionless distributed ledger system, is a nonrestrictive blockchain system. Public blockchain systems are safe as long as participants follow security rules. A person can become an authorized participant by signing in on a blockchain platform. A participant or node can then access present as well as past records, verify a transaction by consensus mechanism, and do mining. These three are the most important tasks in blockchain, with mining and exchanging cryptocurrencies being the most basic use of a public blockchain. Examples include Bitcoin and Ethereum.

3.2 Private blockchain

A private blockchain, also called a permissioned blockchain, operates in a closed network. This type of blockchain is used in organizations where only a few people are allowed to be authorized to participate. This type of blockchain is the same as public but with more restriction and fewer users participating.

3.3 Consortium blockchain

This is a type of semi-decentralized blockchain that is managed by more than one blockchain network. It is like a permissioned blockchain. In this type of blockchain, more than one organization can act as a node and exchange information or do mining. This type is mostly used in banks and government organizations.

3.4 Hybrid blockchain

This is a combination of public and private blockchains. This allows the user to control who can have permission to access data stored in the blockchain. Here a transaction in private mode can be verified in public.

Blockchain is not limited to cryptocurrency. It can be used to run websites using decentralized domains living on blockchain. Fig. 5.5 shows the blockchain of permissionless and permissioned, where an example is censoring the internet. A lot of countries hide information from their citizens about the outside world. VPN seems to be a solution, but governments often have the power to shut down VPNs. So a better solution is decentralized domains using blockchain, where websites are not hosted from only one location, so they are difficult to take down. This helps in fighting censorship.

3.5 Blockchain in security

Blockchain is a DLT, in which data are structured in the form of blocks and each block is chained together (Fig. 5.6). Blockchain is based on principles of cryptography, decentralization, and consensus, which ensures trust in transactions, a major limitation of IDSs.

Each block is connected to all the blocks before it in a cryptographic chain, as shown in Fig. 5.7. All the transactions within blocks are validated and agreed upon by consensus mechanism to ensure that each transaction is true

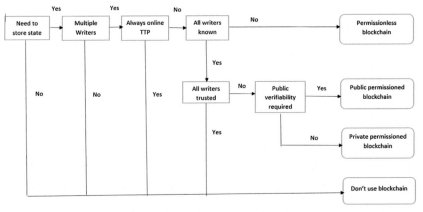

Figure 5.5 Permissionless and permissioned blockchain.

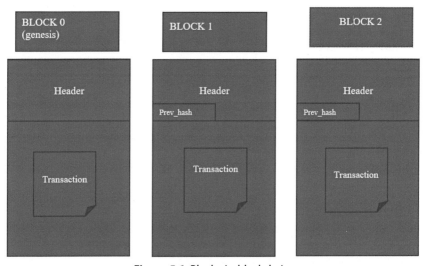

Figure 5.6 Blocks in blockchain.

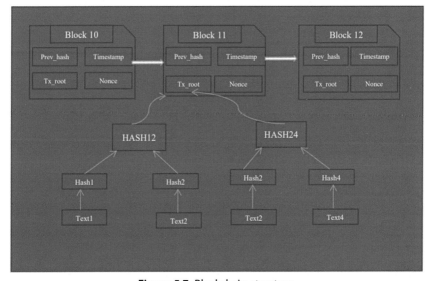

Figure 5.7 Blockchain structure.

and correct. Blockchain enables decentralization, which means members participate in a distributed network. This implies that a single user cannot change the record of a transaction, thus also providing security. The reason for this will be discussed subsequently. To understand the security concepts in blockchain, we need to understand its major components, presented next.

3.5.1 Block

Blockchain is composed of different blocks chained together. Each block has some basic elements:

I. Data with nonce. Unless the data is mined, it is signed to a nonce and a hash. Nonce is a 32-bit random number, which is created when a block is generated. This nonce creates the block header hash.

II. Hash is 256-bit number starting with many zeroes.

On creating the first block, the nonce creates a cryptographic hash.

3.5.2 Miners

Miners create new blocks on the chain through a process called mining. Each block consists of a nonce and hash, which is always unique, and it also references the previous block by hash. Basically, if you want to mine a new block, you have to change all the blocks, so mining is difficult. This provides safety to transactions. This is sometimes referred to as "safety in math." To carry out mining, miners use special software.

3.5.3 Nodes

Decentralization is one of the most important concepts of blockchain. As we know, blockchain is a DLT, in which no one computer can own the chain. Instead the chain is connected by different nodes, where each node has its own copy of the blockchain. Nodes can be devices that keep copies of the blockchain and keep the network working.

Blockchains are transparent, so each transaction can be viewed and checked. Each participant has a unique identification number that shows its transaction. The network must check and approve newly mined blocks for the chain based on different algorithms. Blockchain provides integrity of transactions. This is achieved by cryptographic validation called hashing function, which links all blocks to one another in the chain. When any modification is done to the transaction in a block, it will cause the hash function in the next block to be invalidated, as each block has a hash function of the previous block. If a hacker wants to modify a transaction, he will have to mine the block and re-mine all other blocks that come after it, which is a tedious task and requires huge amounts of time and computing power. Integrity is one of the greatest merits of blockchain.

Blockchain provides reliability through verification of each transaction by consensus mechanism. Blockchain is considered secure and verified. This is possible because of consensus protocol, an important part of blockchain. A consensus algorithm is a procedure that all peers and nodes in the network follow to reach common agreement about the state of the distributed ledger. Consensus protocol looks for every new block added to the blockchain by making sure that it is one along with the version that is agreed by all the nodes in the blockchain, thus, providing reliability and trust in the network. The consensus protocol has different objectives like coming to the same agreement, collaboration, cooperation, and providing equal rights to every node.

3.6 Consensus algorithms

3.6.1 Proof of work (PoW)

Bitcoin and Ethereum use this algorithm. The main use of this algorithm is to solve mathematical puzzles that are complex in nature. It is used to generate blocks by selecting the miner. This mathematical puzzle requires high computation power and enormous time. According to this algorithm the node that solves the puzzle first will mine the block.

3.6.2 Proof of stake (PoS)

This is a different approach to PoW. In PoW, to carry out verification, miners have to solve the mathematical puzzle. The first node to decrypt the puzzle gets the coin or to generate the next block. This requires high power. It has been approximated that one Bitcoin transaction will use enough energy to fuel 1.57 American households. Thus, to solve this issue, PoS attributed mining power (i.e., the ability of a miner or node to solve the mathematical puzzle) to a proportion of coins held by the miner. A block is validated in this way by putting a wager on whether or not it will be attached to the chain. Validators are awarded in proportion to their stakes based on actual blocks added, and their stakes are increased accordingly. Finally, a validator is selected based on its economic condition to add a new block to the network's chain. To reach an agreement in the case of PoS, an incentive scheme is used.

3.6.3 Practical Byzantine Fault Tolerance (PBFT)

This consensus algorithm focuses on providing a safeguard against system failures by collecting responses from correct as well as faulty nodes. This protocol is designed for asynchronous systems, to lower the overhead time. Its aim is to solve problems in a distributed network to reach a consensus even when nodes does not respond or respond incorrectly.

3.6.4 Proof of burn (PoB)

This algorithm is like setting priorities. Validators are required to sacrifice their long-term goals to achieve a short-term goal of mining the next block.

Here, validators "burn" their coins, which basically means that they have to send their coins to an IP address from where the coins cannot come back. The more they sacrifice (burn their coins), the more chance they have to be selected to mine the next block. This is a different approach from PoW.

3.6.5 Proof of capacity (PoC)

Rather than investing in costly hardware or burning, validators are expected to invest their hard drive space in this protocol. The more space they have, the more likely they are to be chosen to mine the next block.

3.6.6 Proof of elapsed time (PoET)

PoET is the most equitable algorithm since each validator has the opportunity to build their own block. Any node must wait for an unknown period of time before adding their proof of waiting time to the block, which is then connected to the network. The validator with the shortest waiting period is chosen, and his or her block is added to the blockchain.

3.7 Blockchain in IDS

In the last few years, many industries have been focusing on deploying blockchain-based applications. Most of these are used for some specific cases that have certain unique and particularly detailed blockchain requirements along with some uniquely detailed and customized characteristics.

For instance, there have been a lot of cases that were built on the basis of improving security and privacy among different divisions in a particular system. So, the major focus of such cases is to store the data completely privately (Zyskind et al., 2015). Similarly, most implementations use proprietary schemes with the cryptography application. This method ensures full privacy security and anonymity between different transactions (Li et al., 2013).

Technologies centered on blockchain are mostly used to store data in a decentralized way that can ensure security of the data. It is therefore of great importance to find out how blockchain systems can be deployed in IDSs.

Blockchain-based CIDN frameworks are designed for certain methods. In some the set of alarms that are not legitimate, also called false alarms, that are obtained from IDSs are considered blockchain transactions. In some cases, for safety against intrusions in blockchain, a unique communication protocol is used. This provides a stable transaction connection for the alarms being generated in a specific block (Alexopoulos et al., 2017). CIoTA framework was also developed by some researchers to utilize the methodologies of blockchain for collaborative anomaly detection (Golomb et al., 2018). Blockchain applications can also be protected with the help of IDS agents such as decision agent, monitor agent, manager agent, and action agent. These agents can be added to the security node for monitoring and analyzing purposes.

4. Host-based intrusion detection system

An HIDS helps us in detection of unauthorized use of the network and abnormal and malicious activities on the host. As we know, an IDS helps us in maintaining the security of a system by capturing and analyzing network traffic to detect suspicious activities (Axelsson, 2000; Debar et al., 1999; Holtz et al., 2011). An IDS works mainly on two approaches: anomaly detection and misuse/signature detection. We have different kinds of IDSs, as seen previously in the chapter. Based on the requirements of the organization, the kind of IDS that is to be used is selected. Sometimes, types of IDSs that work for different approaches are combined to get overall protection.

4.1 Working of an IDS in an HIDS

In organizations or anywhere where there is a large network, multiple NIDS are positioned and installed across the network. These systems share among themselves the log and alert information that they collect overtime. This type of arrangement and positioning is generally known as a distributed intrusion detection system (DIDS). The type of information or data and the amount of information to be shared among the systems is configured beforehand by the network administrator and should be modified and updated frequently according to the patterns of attacks being detected. These systems help the administrator get an overall view of network attacks (Ghribi et al., 2018). These IDSs help the administrators to analyze the threats and alerts of the whole network and then to recognize the complicated patterns of attack. Based on these attack patterns, certain signatures and sets of rules are created. They are then given to the IDS to secure the network segment from such attacks in the future (Titorenko and Frolov, 2018; Anwer et al., 2018; Kato and Klyuev, 2017).

These days the attack patterns have become more complex, and with the increasing variation in the size of networks, the number of attacks is also growing. To identify and prevent intruders and malicious activities, the administrator should know how the attack began, where it generated, what the attacker did, and what the level of attack was. Because the whole framework is dependent on DIDS, it should be flexible and strong enough to detect the attacks quickly.

5. Blockchain-based intrusion detection

Attackers these days apply more complex, complicated, and advanced techniques to attack systems and to avoid getting detected. Misconfigured network segments can also compromise security given by the multiple IDSs that are connected to the centralized server and may result in giving un-authentic logs or alerts (Alexopoulos et al., 2017). So, to make the whole system trustworthy and robust, a reliable solution according to many researchers and industrialists is blockchain.

The following are some of the challenges that a DIDS faces, and we will see how blockchain can be used to solve them (Yang et al., 2018; Shvachko et al., 2010; Lee and Lee, 2012).

5.1 Challenges in distributed intrusion detection systems
5.1.1 Integrity
The first challenge is the integrity or the authenticity of the alert that is being generated by an IDS. For the smooth working of IDSs and proper protection of the network, it is of utmost importance that the logs and the alerts generated by the system are unmodifiable and inaccessible by any attacker.

5.1.2 Consensus
All the IDSs that are in the network should have a common set of rules about the type of alert and quality of the alert that is to be generated.

5.1.3 Scalability
For centralized servers, their computational demands should be altered according to the size of the network.

5.1.4 Privacy
Only the participating IDS should have control over the accessibility of data regarding which alert is generated. For the proper functioning of the whole system, it is also important for the central server to remain secure and reliable; it should not be affected by any intruders. The central server has the most important task of collecting all the logs and alerts from the IDS for easy analysis of data and decision-making. Hence, it is the most important challenge that should be satisfied (Meng et al., 2018; Kim et al., 2018).

5.2 Blockchain-based solution

The way blockchain could be implemented is by having a distributed ledger that is secured and protected for the purpose of sharing of logs and alerts that are generated by individual IDSs. The alerts that are generated by the IDS will then be stored in the blockchain and are called transactions. The IDSs that are in connection with the centralized server then run a protocol that validates all the transactions that occurred. Only after validation is the transaction added to the blockchain, as shown Fig. 5.8. This kind of arrangement acts as a guarantee that only the alerts that are authenticated and validated will be updated in the server. These alerts cannot be modified and are visible to all the IDSs present in the network (Foroushani and Yue, 2018; Titorenko and Frolov, 2018).

The diagram shows the transfer of alerts to the cloud-based centralized server, using the alert exchange layer. The alerts are then validated by the blockchain consensus layer, and if their authenticity is proved the transaction is updated in the blockchain of all the IDSs. In Fig. 5.8, all the IDSs are connected to a DIDS that acts as a regulator between all the IDSs present in the network. Whenever any modification takes place in any of the IDSs in the network, an alert is generated, which goes to the distributed IDSs. This checks the authenticity of the generated alert and makes sure that the alert generated is genuine and is not the result of any malicious

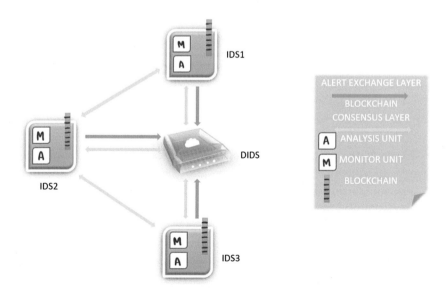

Figure 5.8 DIDS architecture using blockchain and cloud.

activity. Only after the authentication and validation of the generated alert will the DIDS allow the changes to be saved and updated in the blockchain. The figure thus shows how the DIDS regulates the activities that occur in any of the IDSs in the network and makes sure that all the IDSs in the network have up-to-date data in the respective blockchain.

5.3 Why a cloud-based centralized server?

Different scenarios may require different sized networks. It is important to maintain the performance and scalability of a DIDS even if the network is really large. In large networks, the load on the centralized sever will increase as all the IDSs dump their logs to it, and it becomes big data. To solve the challenge of analyzing such large data in real time, we need a cloud-based centralized server that is cost-effective and scalable.

6. Collaborative intrusion detection system

The discovery of collaborative intrusion detection involving CIDNs and CIDSs was carried out practically. Performance improvement was the main objective that could be surpassed easily by complex attacks like DoS attacks. The main reason is that IDSs usually do not have information about their protected area. The framework of a CIDS allows the various areas of the IDS to understand the context by data exchanging with one another. Collaborative programs can be classified into these types:

(a) hierarchic systems such as DIDS (Snapp et al., 1991) and EMERALD (Porras and Neumann, 1997)

(b) subscribe systems such as Distributed Overlay for Monitoring InterNet Outbreaks (DOMINO) (Barford et al., 2004) and COSSACK (Papadopoulos et al., 2003)

(c) P2P querying-based systems like Netbait (Chun et al., 2003) and PIER (Huebsch et al., 2005)

Event Monitoring Enabling Responses to Problems with Anomalous Live Disturbances (EMERALD) (Porras and Neumann, 1997) is detection of malicious incidents in a layer of layers that are not visible on a large network. Similarly, DIDS was developed (Snapp et al., 1991). It pointed out disadvantages by combining centralized data analysis, data reduction, and distributed monitoring. Papadopoulos et al. founded COSSACK (Papadopoulos et al., 2003), which focused on zero human intervention to intelligently reduce distributed denial-of-service (DDoS) attacks. Yegneswaran et al. founded DOMINO (Barford et al., 2004), which can increase the effectiveness of detection by directing interactions between illegal sites or heterogeneous nodes. PIER (Huebsch et al., 2005) is an internet-scale query engine that can support the most widely distributed and ongoing queries and can be used as a platform to build a set of information centric applications.

In Fig. 5.9 the architecture of a CIDN is shown. In this, a node, such as node A, can exchange data needed for one another node (such as nodes B, C, D). A node is often made up of many parts or components: a collaboration component, P2P communication, and an IDS module component. Especially, functions of intrusion detection can be performed by the IDS module, including functions such as recording events and network traffic monitoring. The component of collaboration is responsible for helping the node in exchanging required data with other nodes and performing specific tasks such as trust computation. The objective of the P2P communication component is to help in establishing a physical communication with another IDS node.

6.1 Working model of CIDS

The elementary detectors (EDs), the message queue (MQ), the connection tracker, the manager, and the response engine are the components of the CIDS operating model. The EDs are specialized intrusion detectors dispersed throughout the system. To communicate with one another, all of the system's components use MQ, which employs TCP as the data

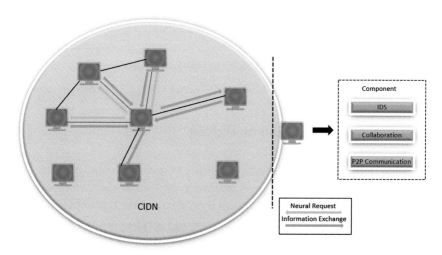

Figure 5.9 CIDN architecture.

transport. The connection tracker is a kernel-level entity that keeps track of the mapping of a port number to the process ID of the process that is currently connected to that port. The manager is the workhorse, and it is in charge of combining data from several detectors and making a system-wide decision in the presence of an intrusion.

6.2 Collaborative intrusion detection challenges

Studies on ID have been done for approximately 40 years, and the conclusions show that sharing of data and the computation of trust in collaborative environments remain two major challenges.

6.2.1 Sharing of data

Sharing of data is one of the major problems of the collaborative process because it is not a small or easy task to allow all participants to trust one another. For instance, some amount of trust can be built by the help of Public Key Infrastructure (PKI) technology, but it does not work every time in terms of detecting intrusion. In addition, due to some concerns of privacy, some participants are reluctant to pass or share information. Without sufficient data, they cannot perform algorithms of detection and create a model for the detection of suspicious or malicious events.

6.2.2 Management of trust

It is evident that CIDNs/CIDSs are at risk of internal attacks, where intruders authorize access to the network. Typically, computer dependencies are usually used to measure levels of trust between other nodes. In doing so, a server (central) is set up to collect traffic data and node behavior and calculate the value of trust for each and every node. Management of trust will be a problem when an organization is large because it is very difficult to find a third party that is reliable; that is, the server (central) can be compromised.

6.3 Solution for CIDs using blockchain

6.3.1 Sharing of data

The problem of sharing of data is mainly due to two things: trust and confidentiality of data. The term mutual trust means that when data or information is shared, working groups should have trust that others will not disclose any information. For example, two IT organizations would make an agreement that they will not share or disclose any data with other parties. Privacy of data indicates that the shared data may contain specific information related to a real company, i.e., traffic shared including packet payloads and IP addresses that could be used to transfer organizational privacy.

Blockchain can be used as a solution to this problem. Especially, sharing of data can be taken as a series of transactions. First, the groups must form an agreement for sharing of data, and each group should digitally sign it. After that, a blockchain box agreement can be kept that is consistent and public. In this case, other groups can also access the box of blockchain, read the agreement, and verify the data identity. The constant appearance of the agreement ensures that one group cannot reject it by disagreement. It is similar to using blockchain in the healthcare sector (Sotos and Houlding, 2017). An open accounting system is able to provide trust between the many working groups.

6.3.2 Trust computation

Generally, centralized, hierarchic, and distributed are the types of collaborative network architecture. In the literature, structures that are distributed have been widely discussed, whereas the two others are believed to have a problem of failure and a problem of one point of failure. In CIDN, warning exchanges are very important between the different IDS nodes, which can determine if anything is wrong.

The technology of blockchain can help to reduce this problem. For example, a blockchain-based CIDS that was introduced by Alexopoulos et al. (2017) uses blockchain so trust can be increased between IDS nodes. They view the alerts (raw alerts) generated by each IDS dot as a transaction of blockchain, which can be repeated between CIDN affiliate sites. After that, all collaborative nodes accept a sequence of rules to verify the authenticity of the functions before placing them on board. This function can ensure that warnings stored in the blockchain are disputed.

7. Applications of IDS: Snort

Snort is an open-source software. It is used for IDS or Intrusion Prevention Systems (IPS). It can perform real-time traffic analysis on IP. It has other features like protocol analysis, searching the content and matching it over the network-based system. The Snort program has the ability to detect a variety of attacks, such as OS fingerprinting, semantic URL attacks, buffer overflows, server message block probes, and stealth port scans, among others.

We can configure Snort into three different modes:

7.1 Sniffer mode

In sniffer mode, it will run a program that will scan the packets present in the network that will be shown on the console.

7.2 Packet logger mode

In this mode, it will run the program to log packets present in the network to a storage device like disk, hard drive, or pen drive.

7.3 NIDS mode

In this mode, the running software has the ability to track packets in network traffic and analyze them using a set of rules specified by the user. The running software will then take a specific action in response to what has been found.

7.4 Designing a Snort-based CID with blockchain

This section highlights the deployment and extensive use of software-defined networking (SDN). The model has a blockchain-based CID-based network topology. Snort IDS is used as an HIDS and a Ryu versatile network-based NIDS. The main goal is to defend against attacks that are performed internally and to improve the detection of attacks and their accuracy with the help of blockchain through a Snort node between the control plane of the application and the entire node's signature database. As a unique hash function, they compiled and connected the entire job's ID. This hash number is used by each Snort node, and the new ID is used for delivery. Similarly, for the next Snort position in the current blockchain, the hash value of a block and transaction ID of the last used block will then be used as the hash value for new blocks (Karuppiah and Saravanan, 2014).

Fig. 5.10 depicts information of the blockchain network between CIDN nodes. Here Snort1 to Snort2 and Snort2 to Snort3 nodes can interact with each other with the help of a hash table that has the public and private keys. In this network topology, Snort1 node is connected to Snort2 by hash value, and Snort2 is connected with Snort3 in the same manner. In this way, Snort nodes can communicate with each other by assigned transaction (Karuppiah and Saravanan, 2014).

This system can detect various kinds of DDoS attacks, which are the following: DDoS floods, SSH attacks (this represents SSH exploits), FTP attacks such as brute force type, HTTP attacks (which perform HTTP floods on the attacker's system), ICMP attacks such as Smurf, ARP attacks (which perform

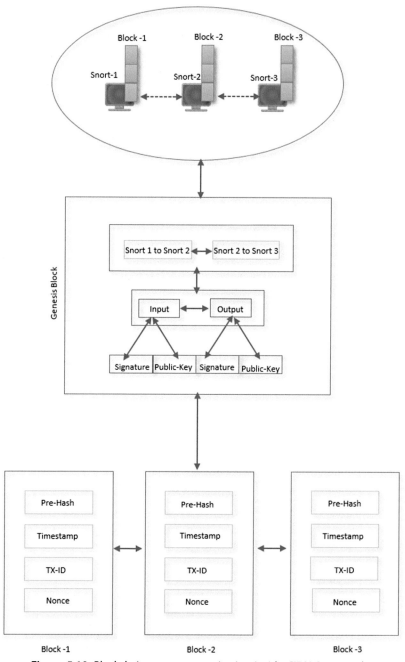

Figure 5.10 Blockchain trust communication inside CIDN Snort nodes.

ARP spoofing), and scan attacks that scan all ports. Their design consists of three different components: Ryu controller, IDS nodes, and blockchain certificates trust, as shown in Fig. 5.11. It has the flexibility of three VM's, like VM–1 that contains the integration of SDN Ryu and Snort and VM–2 that depicts the network domain, in which network emulation is used to simulate a virtual CIDN. There are three Snort IDS locations on the CIDN. Direct attacks on CIDN–1 and CIDN–2 nodes are launched using VM–3. Only a capture adapter is used for this virtual machine (Ujjan et al., 2019).

7.5 Evaluation of this design

The proposed system's performance in an SDN–based environment uses the CIDN to measure the collective-based Snort CDN performance of the

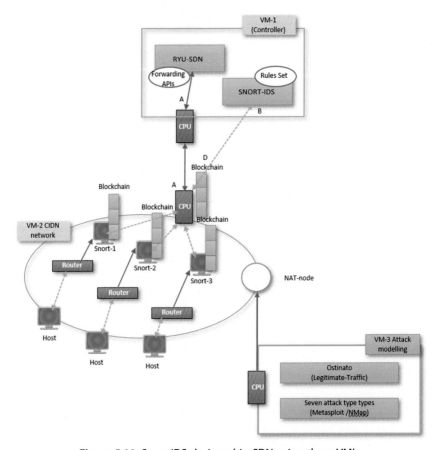

Figure 5.11 Snort IDS designed in SDN using three VM's.

network with implementation of blockchain. It makes use of blockchain in Snort nodes, which track, detect, and share the rule set with all neighboring nodes that are present in the Snort signature (Ujjan et al., 2019).

7.5.1 Attack modeling

HTTP, FTP, and SSH resources were used on VM-3 as a server for attack modeling. Seven different types of malicious traffic were created by using Metasploit and Kali Linux. The intention was to generate malicious traffic. CIDN IDS positions were inserted into all major attacks and the official route. All blockchain-based IDSs began testing dangerous and permitted traffic and issued warnings when input traffic matched a rule set by blockchain for Snort IDS, causing network traffic to be disrupted (Ujjan et al., 2019).

7.5.2 Evaluation with poisonous and permitted traffic in a CIDN

The output of a Snort IDS that has been collaborated with a blockchain-based CIDN has been investigated. The CIDN was used to look at the output of malicious and permitted traffic. There were three Snort IDS nodes with blockchain collaboration. Each node was also connected to an SDN-based switch. In the CIDN, there were seven different types of malicious attacks, with each node employing the Snort signature rule set. To test the CIDN detection accuracy, we only used three nodes in the network. Metrics for IDS results are given (Ujjan et al., 2019).

1. true positive (TP)
2. true negative (TN)
3. false positive (FP)
4. false negative (FN)

Snort IDS nodes that collaborated in CIDN had a default set of rules. They used seven different attack combinations with permitted traffic. Using a trusted blockchain, they allowed a collaborated IDS to get the set of rules from the Ryu controller in the period's second run. The proposed developed model's overall detection efficiency was assessed using a blockchain-based backend framework that allowed each IDS node to incorporate new signatures from Ryu, allowing for more accurate and efficient detection (Ujjan et al., 2019).

7.5.3 Analysis of a CIDN with permitted traffic

The setup used a CIDN that comprised three Snort IDS used for designing a Snort CID. In this, Snort nodes used blockchain in collaboration with the nodes. To see how the proposed idea of design worked, they watched when all Snort IDS were put together and analyzed their performance with the help of permitted traffic, which they created. The utilization of the CPU in the CIDN with blockchain when all Snort IDS were together was analyzed and contained three Snort IDSs nodes, Snortnode1, Snortnode2, Snortnode3, each of which used a shared processor unit rather than the entire CPU. Furthermore, since Snort is a signature-based IDS, it has limited processing power when it used as a standalone IDS during periods of high network traffic. As a result, the CIDN network was able to correctly detect intrusions with a low number of false triggers. A Snort IDS can also accept new indications from the Ryu controller due to the blockchain-based approach. Overall, we can observe that when they integrated all Snort nodes, the proposed design of the system's processing of packets is feasibly enhanced, allowing it to capture different forms of attacks quickly (Ujjan et al., 2019).

8. Limitations

8.1 IDS limitations

Studies on ID have been for a very long time, but still there are various unresolved problems in applications of real time that could significantly reduce detection function (Wang and Liu, 2015).

8.1.1 Traffic overhead with handling capability limited

Overload packets will dramatically reduce the detection system's efficiency in high-traffic networks. A significant number of network packets should be discarded if traffic exceeds the IDS processing power. For example, the computational burden is proportional to the size of the packet payload.

8.1.2 Signature coverage in limited range

The capability of detection when signature-based relies largely on signatures that are accessible. In another way it can be said that the number and quality of signatures sent determine detection results. Signatures, on the other hand, are usually restricted and cannot cover all reported attacks and abuses.

8.1.3 Incorrect profile establishment

With detection that is anomaly-based, it is very difficult to create a standard correct profile as it has strong traffic. Specifically, IDSs that are anomaly-based many times use ML methods for creating a profile. Data training, specifically that with data attacks that are severely limited within performance, leads to incorrect classification of ML.

8.1.4 Major false warnings

It is important for the IDS to give timely alerts to security managers when there is a problem with the network. False alarms, on the other hand, are a significant problem during detection due to immature signatures and incorrect profiles, which can significantly reduce detection efficiency and add to security analyst workload. For example, a big organization may produce over 10,000 fake warnings in a day.

8.2 Blockchain limitations

As summarized in Fig. 5.12, blockchain technology is a modern approach that still faces some problems and limitations.

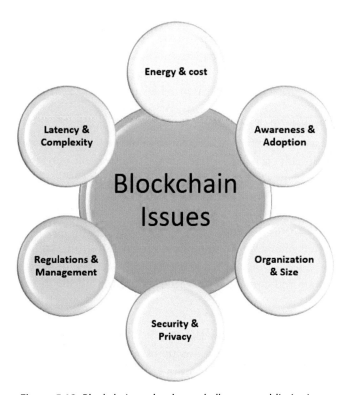

Figure 5.12 Blockchain technology: challenges and limitations.

8.2.1 Cost and energy

The power of computation is concerning with the usage of blockchain (Yli-Huumo et al., 2016). Take Bitcoin mines as an example: they require a high level of power to validate and calculate transactions. Liu and Wang (Wang and Liu, 2015) found that power of computation was added to the individual miner initially, but it could increase significantly as the network changed.

8.2.2 Security and privacy

Applications related to blockchain to be linked to known brands require smart transactions and contacts, which raises privacy concerns about data stored in a ledger that is shared. In addition, the technology of blockchain itself can be an attraction for cyber criminals, so it can suffer from many attacks such as DDoS (Karuppiah and Saravanan, 2014, 2015; Karuppiah et al., 2016, 2017, 2019; Kumari et al., 2016; Naeem et al., 2020; Maria et al., 2021; Pradhan et al., 2018; Li et al., 2017).

8.2.3 Complexity and latency

As we know, with the distributed nature of blockchain transactions, they will take several hours to complete before all parties have reviewed the corresponding ledgers. This delay could trigger a great deal of confusion among business partners, as well as provide an incentive for cyber criminals.

8.2.4 Awareness and adoption

The lack of understanding and acceptance of blockchain technology is one of the most important challenges. For example, many people need to know how it is useful and secure. The blockchain's potential growth is dependent on how many teams implement the technology, but this is still an open question.

8.2.5 Size and organization

Many different organizations use their own standards to create blockchains. The increased size of distributed ledgers could lead to significant reduction of performance and compared to current frameworks make blockchain less efficient.

8.2.6 Management and regulations

In advanced technology, regulations are usually far behind. For completing transactions on blockchain, due to the lack of standards and for better efficiency, Bitcoin blockchain has exceeded existing regulations. Applications of blockchain are expected to work within the rules.

8.3 General IDS limitations

- The effectiveness of IDSs can be severely affected by noise. The bad packets that are generated from software bugs, corrupted DNS data, and the local packets that somehow escaped create a very high rate of false alarms, thereby reducing the effectiveness of the system.
- In most cases the number of real attacks is lower, especially when compared to the number of times the alarm goes off. Hence, most alarms are false alarms, and a lot of energy and time can be spent in categorizing the attack as real or false, leading to a real attack being missed or ignored.
- The library of signatures and the set of rules should be changed and updated as regularly as possible to mitigate and reduce the threats. Many times, the library might get outdated with only certain types of attack patterns stored in it or they might be only for a specific version of software. These outdated databases can make the system more vulnerable to attacks that use newer methodologies and techniques
- In the case of signature-based IDSs, there often is a lag between discovering a new threat and then applying the signatures generated to the IDS, so during this time the IDS may become vulnerable to similar attacks.
- IDS is completely dependent on the signatures and the set of rules that are provided to it, so if any attacker gets into the network even after the IDS is configured properly, the IDS can do nothing to prevent the malpractice. Therefore, IDS cannot compensate for a poor set of network protocols or weak authentication methodologies used.
- An encrypted packet that is not discovered until more significant network intrusions are detected can intrude the network and will not be identified by the IDS.
- Using IDS in networks will only be beneficial if the IP address of the packet being analyzed and monitored is correct, as the IDS works only on the basis of the network address that is being provided to it by the packets. If the IP address of the packets is spoofed or is falsified, the IDS will not be able to protect the network from the intruder.
- As NIDS are needed to analyses the packets as soon as they are captured, they can be susceptible to the same attacks to which the network host is vulnerable. The NIDS may also crash due to attacks by invalid data and TCP/IP.

9. Comparison with firewalls

Though IDSs and firewalls are both related to security of the network, IDS is different from a firewall in terms of a traditional network firewall; that is, different from a next-generation network, to allow or deny any network communication it uses the same rules. It completely blocks entry by assuming the correct rules are set. In fact, to prevent intrusion and not signaling of attacks from within the network, the firewall tries to restrict access between networks. Once intrusion has occurred, the IDS describes the suspected intrusion and signs the alarm. Attacks from within the system are also monitored by the IDS. They are detected by examining communications of networks and identifying patterns (which are also known as signatures) of common attacks on computers, as well as taking steps to notify operators. An IPS is the system that terminates the connection and performs access control like a firewall of an application layer.

10. Conclusion and future scope

With such capabilities, it is expected that blockchain will definitely emerge across different industries and domains like IOT, machine learning etc. With more use of proof-of-concept, the technology will validate itself. When combined with ID the technology will make huge impacts in possibly every digital transaction in the world and impact trade-offs and costs. A major application would be sharing of data, which is a huge problem for large, distributed organizations as performance, trust, and data privacy need to be improved. There are not a lot of real-time exchange applications available, so data sharing and alert exchange need to be improved. Blockchain is an emerging technology in field of data management. It is unlike any traditional data management system, where real-time information exchange, decentralization, and distributed ledgers are not available. Blockchain for ID is one of the trending areas of research and has a huge potential to affect the world. Our chapter focused on understanding the concepts of blockchain regarding ways in which it helps in security and IDSs.

References

Alexopoulos, N., Vasilomanolakis, E., Réka Ivánkó, N., Mühlhäuser, M., 2017. Towards blockchain-based collaborative intrusion detection systems. In: International Conference on Critical Information Infrastructures Security. Springer, Cham, pp. 107–118.
Anwer, H.M., Farouk, M., Abdel-Hamid, A., 2018. A framework for efficient network anomaly intrusion detection with features selection. In: 2018 9th International Conference on Information and Communication Systems (ICICS). IEEE, pp. 157–162.

Axelsson, S., 2000. Intrusion Detection Systems: A Survey and Taxonomy, vol. 99. Technical report.

Barford, V.Y.P., Jha, S., Li, Z., Chen, Y., Beach, A., 2004. Global intrusion detection in the domino overlay system. In: Proceeding of NDSS, vol. 4.

Chun, B.N., Lee, J., Weatherspoon, H., Chun, B.N., 2003. Netbait: A Distributed Worm Detection service. Intel Research Berkeley Technical Report IRB-TR-03 33.

Debar, H., Dacier, M., Wespi, A., 1999. Towards a taxonomy of intrusion-detection systems. Comput. Network. 31 (8), 805–822.

Foroushani, Z.A., Yue, L., 2018. Intrusion detection system by using hybrid algorithm of data mining technique. In: Proceedings of the 2018 7th International Conference on Software and Computer Applications, pp. 119–123.

Ghribi, S., Meddeb Makhlouf, A., Zarai, F., 2018. C-DIDS: a cooperative and distributed intrusion detection system in cloud environment. In: 2018 14th International Wireless Communications & Mobile Computing Conference (IWCMC). IEEE, pp. 267–272.

Golomb, T., Mirsky, Y., Elovici, Y., 2018. CIoTA: Collaborative IoT Anomaly Detection via Blockchain arXiv preprint arXiv:1803.03807.

Holtz, M.D., David, B., Timóteo de Sousa Júnior, R., 2011. Building scalable distributed intrusion detection systems based on the mapreduce framework. Telecomunicacoes (Santa Rita do Sapucai) 13 (2), 22–31.

Hu, J., 2010. Host-based anomaly intrusion detection. In: Handbook of Information and Communication Security. Springer, Berlin, Heidelberg, pp. 235–255.

Huebsch, R., Chun, B., Hellerstein, J.M., Thau Loo, B., Maniatis, P., Roscoe, T., Scott, S., Stoica, I., Yumerefendi, A.R., 2005. The Architecture of Pier: An Internet-Scale Query Processor.

Kanth, V.K., 2019. Blockchain for Use in Collaborative Intrusion Detection Systems. PhD Diss. Naval Postgraduate School.

Karuppiah, M., Saravanan, R., 2014. A secure remote user mutual authentication scheme using smart cards. J. Inf. Secur. Appl. 19 (4–5), 282–294.

Karuppiah, M., Saravanan, R., 2015. A secure authentication scheme with user anonymity for roaming service in global mobility networks. Wireless Pers. Commun. 84 (3), 2055–2078.

Karuppiah, M., Kumari, S., Das, A.K., Li, X., Wu, F., Basu, S., 2016. A secure lightweight authentication scheme with user anonymity for roaming service in ubiquitous networks. Secur. Commun. Network. 9 (17), 4192–4209.

Karuppiah, M., Kumari, S., Li, X., Wu, F., Das, A.K., Khan, M.K., Basu, S., 2017. A dynamic id-based generic framework for anonymous authentication scheme for roaming service in global mobility networks. Wireless Pers. Commun. 93 (2), 383–407.

Karuppiah, M., Das, A.K., Li, X., Kumari, S., Wu, F., Chaudhry, S.A., Niranchana, R., 2019. Secure remote user mutual authentication scheme with key agreement for cloud environment. Mobile Network. Appl. 24 (3), 1046–1062.

Kato, K., Klyuev, V., 2017. Development of a network intrusion detection system using Apache Hadoop and Spark. In: 2017 IEEE Conference on Dependable and Secure Computing. IEEE, pp. 416–423.

Kim, S., Kim, B., Kim, H.J., 2018. Intrusion detection and mitigation system using blockchain analysis for bitcoin exchange. In: Proceedings of the 2018 International Conference on Cloud Computing and Internet of Things, pp. 40–44.

Kumar, M., Singh, A.K., 2020. Distributed intrusion detection system using blockchain and cloud computing infrastructure. In: 2020 4th International Conference on Trends in Electronics and Informatics (ICOEI)(48184). IEEE, pp. 248–252.

Kumari, S., Karuppiah, M., Li, X., Wu, F., Das, A.K., Odelu, V., 2016. An enhanced and secure trust-extended authentication mechanism for vehicular ad-hoc networks. Secur. Commun. Network. 9 (17), 4255–4271.

Lee, Y., Lee, Y., 2012. Toward scalable internet traffic measurement and analysis with hadoop. Comput. Commun. Rev. 43 (1), 5–13.

Li, W., Meng, Y., Kwok, L.-F., 2013. Enhancing trust evaluation using intrusion sensitivity in collaborative intrusion detection networks: feasibility and challenges. In: 2013 Ninth International Conference on Computational Intelligence and Security. IEEE, pp. 518—522.

Li, X., Niu, J., Bhuiyan, M.Z.A., Wu, F., Karuppiah, M., Kumari, S., 2017. A robust ECC-based provable secure authentication protocol with privacy preserving for industrial internet of things. IEEE Trans. Ind. Inf. 14 (8), 3599—3609.

Maria, A., Pandi, V., Lazarus, J.D., Karuppiah, M., Christo, M.S., 2021. BBAAS: Blockchain-Based Anonymous Authentication Scheme for Providing Secure Communication in VANETs. Security and Communication Networks.

Meng, W., Wolfgang Tischhauser, E., Wang, Q., Wang, Y., Han, J., 2018. When intrusion detection meets blockchain technology: a review. Ieee Access 6, 10179—10188.

Naeem, M., Chaudhry, S.A., Mahmood, K., Karuppiah, M., Kumari, S., 2020. A scalable and secure RFID mutual authentication protocol using ECC for Internet of Things. Int. J. Commun. Syst. 33 (13), e3906.

Papadopoulos, C., Lindell, R., Mehringer, J., Hussain, A., Govindan, R., 2003. Cossack: coordinated suppression of simultaneous attacks. In: Proceedings DARPA Information Survivability Conference and Exposition, vol. 1. IEEE, pp. 2—13.

Porras, P.A., Neumann, P.G., 1997. EMERALD: event monitoring enabling response to anomalous live disturbances. In: Proceedings of the 20th National Information Systems Security Conference, vol. 3, pp. 353—365.

Pradhan, A., Karuppiah, M., Niranchana, R., Jerlin, M.A., Rajkumar, S., 2018. Design and analysis of smart card-based authentication scheme for secure transactions. Int. J. Internet Technol. Secur. Trans. 8 (4), 494—515.

Scarfone, K., Mell, P., 2007. Guide to Intrusion Detection and Prevention Systems (IDPS), vol. 800. NIST Special Publication, p. 94.

Shvachko, K., Kuang, H., Radia, S., Chansler, R., 2010. The hadoop distributed file system. In: 2010 IEEE 26th Symposium on Mass Storage Systems and Technologies (MSST). IEEE, pp. 1—10.

Snapp, S.R., James, B., Dias, G., Terrance, L., Goan, L., Todd, H., Ho, C.-L., Levitt, K.N., 1991. DIDS (Distributed Intrusion Detection System)-Motivation, Architecture, and an Early Prototype.

Sotos, J., Houlding, D., 2017. Blockchains for data sharing in clinical research: trust in a trustless world. Intel, Santa Clara, CA, USA, Blockchain Appl. Note 1.

Titorenko, A.A., Frolov, A.A., 2018. Analysis of modern intrusion detection system. In: 2018 IEEE Conference of Russian Young Researchers in Electrical and Electronic Engineering (EIConRus). IEEE, pp. 142—143.

Ujjan, R.M.A., Zeeshan, P., Dahal, K., 2019. Snort based collaborative intrusion detection system using blockchain in SDN. In: 2019 13th International Conference on Software, Knowledge, Information Management and Applications (SKIMA). IEEE, pp. 1—8.

Wang, L., Liu, Y., 2015. Exploring miner evolution in bitcoin network. In: International Conference on Passive and Active Network Measurement. Springer, Cham, pp. 290—302.

Wu, Y.-S., Foo, B., Mei, Y., Bagchi, S., 2003. Collaborative intrusion detection system (CIDS): a framework for accurate and efficient IDS. In: 19th Annual Computer Security Applications Conference, 2003. Proceedings. IEEE, pp. 234—244.

Yang, J., Shen, C., Chi, Y., Xu, P., Sun, W., 2018. An extensible Hadoop framework for monitoring performance metrics and events of OpenStack cloud. In: 2018 IEEE 3rd International Conference on Big Data Analysis (ICBDA). IEEE, pp. 222—226.

Yli-Huumo, J., Ko, D., Choi, S., Park, S., Smolander, K., 2016. Where is current research on blockchain technology?—a systematic review. PLoS One 11, e0163477—10.

Zyskind, G., Nathan, O., Pentland, A., 2015. Enigma: Decentralized Computation Platform with Guaranteed Privacy arXiv preprint arXiv:1506.03471.

CHAPTER 6

Blockchain for IoT-based medical delivery drones: state of the art, issues, and future prospects

Partha Pratim Ray and Dinesh Dash
Department of Computer Science and Engineering, National Institute of Technology Patna, Patna, Bihar, India

Nomenclature

AIRA	Autonomous intelligent robot agent
ATC	Air traffic control
BCoT	Blockchain of things
BVLOS	Beyond visual line of sight
CC	Command and control
eVTOL	Electric vertical takeoff and landing
HIRO	Healthcare integrated rescue operations
IDS	Intrusion detection system
IoDT	Internet of drone things
IPFS	Interplanetary file system
KPI	Key performance indicator
LoS	Line of sight
MAS	Multiagent systems
SDU	University of Southern Denmark
SOP	Standard operating procedure
UAS	Unmanned aerial system
UHF	Ultra high frequency
UPDWG	UAV for payload delivery working group
VHF	Very high frequency
VTOL	Vertical takeoff and landing

1. Introduction

The internet of things (IoT) refers to the ecosystem that allows billions of distributed things to exchange information by using sensors, actuators, microcontrollers, and network backhaul (Pawar et al., 2021; Hemalatha, 2021; Frikha et al., 2021; Sadeeq and Zeebaree, 2021). Since its inception, IoT

Blockchain Technology for Emerging Applications
ISBN 978-0-323-90193-2
https://doi.org/10.1016/B978-0-323-90193-2.00002-8

137

has been successfully deployed in a wide range of smart applications, e.g., healthcare, agriculture, transportation, military, and industry (Ratta et al., 2021; Gul et al., 2021; Liang and Ji, 2021). It has evolved due to convergence of a multitude of heterogeneous technologies comprising pervasive computing, ubiquitous computing, embedded systems, and wireless sensor networks (Chinaei et al., 2021; Alzubi, 2021; Mourya et al., 2021; Guo et al., 2021). The main aim of IoT is to automate things with an aware workflow. For example, a pulse sensor can measure the pulse rate of a person and send the information to a remote cloud for further processing. Robotic elements are integrated with the IoT-based infrastructure to deploy in the industry 4.0 use cases (Gimenez et al., 2021; Lv and Singh, 2021; Philip et al., 2021). Recently, drones have been getting significant attention from many organizations and startups to use them as a key component in some prospective business models (Saranya, 2021; Maitra et al., 2021; Abbas et al., 2021; Majeed et al., 2021; Bhuvaneshwait et al., 2021), especially for the delivery of medical items to remote outdoor locations. A drone is designed to serve remote locations without a human pilot. Drones are equipped with communication technologies to establish connections with the ground command and control (CC stations) (Kumar et al., 2021; Kumar and Tripathi, 2021; Shukla et al., 2021; Chen et al., 2021; Jeong et al., 2021; Velmurugadass et al., 2021; Chittoor et al., 2021). Ordinarily a drone is an autonomous thing that was earlier used for military applications. Nowadays, drones are easily available in various forms, factors, and cost. Drones can be found in following types: multirotor, fixed wing, single rotor, and hybrid vertical takeoff and landing (VTOL) (Nehme et al., 2021; Miglani and Kumar, 2021; Singh et al., 2021; Shynu et al., 2021; Evita et al., 2021). Drones can be accommodated with high resolution cameras and sensory elements to capture images, collect information, monitor target zones, and provide control signals. Drones can fly at different heights above sea level (600, 1500, 3000, and 5000 m) based on design and regulatory constraints (Jamil et al., 2021; Kiran et al., 2021; Saxena et al., 2021; Aruna, 2021; Svedin et al., 2021). Propulsion can be controlled by internal combustion engines, rotary engines, and lithium-polymer battery assembly (Ribeiro et al., 2021). They can be designed as real-time things that are accompanied with smart, embedded microcontroller boards, e.g., Raspberry Pi and Beagle boards (Rominger et al., 2021; Homier et al., 2021).

Smart medical item delivery is an important use case of the smart healthcare domain that can be upgraded with the inherent capability of autonomy and real timeliness (Liu and Szirányi, 2021). Drones are being considered the key player of this application to deliver medical objects to remote locations (Martins et al., 2021). Drones can be accommodated with blood, pathology samples, vaccines, smart IoT–based health sensors, and related medical items to support patients located distant from a standard medical facility such as a hospital (Da Xu et al., 2021; Yaqoob et al., 2021; Comtet and Johannessen, 2021). Such an approach can benefit the health condition of citizens all over the world, especially in low-income or developing countries (Tarr et al., 2021). However, there exists some key research issues that can hinder the process of adoption of drones for the purpose of medical delivery (Saraf et al., 2021). For example, existing medical delivery faces the following challenges: user data privacy, data security, tampering of sensitive medical records, delay in package delivery, and lack of transparency.

Blockchain technology can be used to minimize such issues along with IoT and drones for medical delivery (Shuaib et al., 2021). A blockchain is a growing list of digital records, i.e., blocks. Each block of a blockchain contains a timestamp, transaction history, nonce, and hash values to point to the previous block (Iqbal et al., 2021). Thus, a change in a random block would change the hash associated with it, leading to mismatch with other blocks of the chain (Chelladurai and Pandian, 2021). Blockchain uses peer-to-peer network architecture to share data in distributed ledgers. A node that is acting as a ledger needs to adhere to the protocols to validate the blocks before using it (Gul et al., 2021). The blockchain allows the decentralization, transparency, and consensus algorithm mechanisms to cater tamper-proof, immutable data storage and access (Fatokun et al., 2021). Blockchain technology is used in many applications such as financial services, cryptocurrencies, supply chain management, anticounterfeiting, video games, energy trading, and healthcare (Pavithran et al., 2021; Ali et al., 2021; Santos et al., 2021; Farahani et al., 2021; Awan et al., 2021). Blockchains are normally classified into three types: public, private, and hybrid. Public blockchain has fewer restrictions over accessing the blocks of the chain by any user. Private blockchains are permissioned and require an entity to authenticate before accessing the blocks (Attraian and Hashemi, 2021; Yang et al., 2021; Khubrani, 2021). Distributed ledger technology refers to the use of private blockchains. Hybrid blockchains have a combination of centralized and decentralized attributes. There exists another special type of blockchain, called sidechain, that can run in parallel to the primary blockchain. Blockchains should ensure the use of consensus algorithms that enable distributed coordination between decentralized entities (Serrano, 2021; Soni and Singh, 2021; Alqaralleh et al., 2021;

Pathak et al., 2021; Panda et al., 2021; Meier et al., 2021). Sometimes, voting is done among the participating entities to reach agreement. Fig. 6.1 presents drone-based medical delivery using IoT and blockchain.

The major research questions of this study are as follows:

- RQ1: Can drones serve the medical industry?
- RQ2: Are drones compatible with health services?
- RQ3: What type of drones are available for medical aid?
- RQ4: What is the comparative structure of such drones?
- RQ5: What are important use cases for medical drone delivery?
- RQ6: What are the key challenges of medical delivery drones?
- RQ7: Can we provide future direction in this context?

Drones can be enabled with blockchains and IoT to enrich the prospects of medical delivery opportunities to remote places. In this paper, we discuss the prospects of using drones as a key component in the purpose of medical item delivery. First, we discuss the existing drone suppliers for medical delivery and compare such drones based on model name, method of flight, propulsion, power source, payload capacity, payload volume, maximum flight time with full payload, radio links, delivery method, and role. Second, we present the status of drone-based medical delivery services based on an in-depth review of available literature. Third, we depict major challenges associated with the present scenario and leverage future directions.

The key contributions of the chapter are as follows:

- to evaluate available drones for medical delivery
- to assess the state of the art on drone-based blockchain-IoT enabled medical delivery
- to present key research challenges and provide future prospects

The rest of the chapter is organized as follows. Section 2 presents related works on the given topic of discussion. Section 3 evaluates drones under deployments for medical delivery. Section 4 provides an in-depth review on classifications of medical delivery approaches based on blockchain and IoT. Section 5 discusses research challenges and delivers future directions. Section 6 concludes the chapter.

2. Related works

Blockchain can be used with 5G technology for demonstration of various applications. Nguyen (Nguyen et al., 2020) described that cloud and edge computing are integrated with network function virtualization for enabling 5G-aware service provisioning. Device-to-device communication is used to

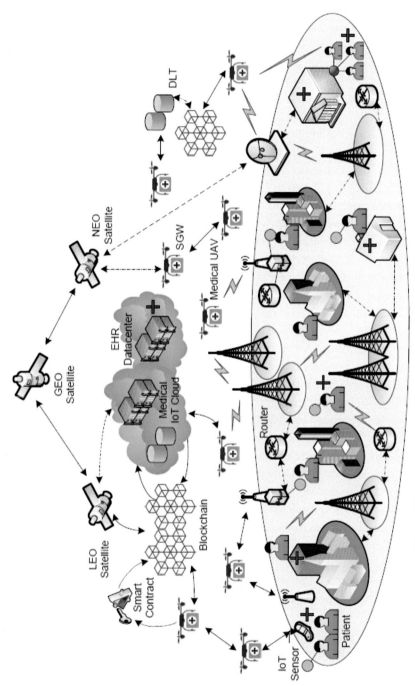

Figure 6.1 Drone-based medical delivery architecture using IoT and blockchain.

showcase the network slicing scheme for efficient management of numerous use cases using 5G-based blockchain. This study discusses vital notions of 5G-assisted blockchain deployment scenarios that includes resource management, federated learning approach, privacy concerns, data sharing, spectrum management, and network virtualization. This work presents the way the UAVs should be aligned with the 5G-blockchain ecosystem. We find that this article is silent about the medical delivery-specific domain of application.

Beyond 5G (B5G) technology can be integrated with a blockchain and drones for alleviating the green internet of things (Alsamhi et al., 2021a,b). The Alsamhi study shows that drones can fly near IoT-based devices. Thus, the drones can be useful to minimize the overall power consumption by the IoT devices. This study showcases various approaches where IoT, blockchain, and drones can fit together for supporting a wide range of applications, such as, monitoring, surveillance, transportation, public safety, healthcare, and environmental prevention. However, this work does not deal with the medical delivery aspect, where drones can be highly involved.

We find that IoT can improve industrial applications, especially industry 4.0, by using smart sensors, actuators, microcontrollers, and decision-making algorithms. An in-depth survey on IoT and its implications on blockchain is presented in a work by Dai et al. (2019). This work synthesizes IoT as a blockchain of things (BCoT) to amalgamate with futuristic use cases. We notice this study did not specify drone-based medical delivery approaches. A related tertiary study on blockchain-IoT was discussed in Xu (Xu et al., 2020). However, no mention of drone-based medical delivery was found in that study either.

We observe that McGovern (2020) discussed several factors and types of data needed by the blockchain-UAV ecosystem. It presented how drones, operators, and hospitals together can support healthcare applications. This study proposed a case study where organ supplying was envisaged with help of blockchain-assisted drones. In this case study, hospitals first write organ-supplying information in the blockchain, which is then read by the air traffic control (ATC) to allow drone operators to start the organ delivery. A drone then ships the organ to the destination hospital where authorized staff receive the organ after validating the transaction process over the blockchain.

In Ferrag and Maglaras (2019), the DeliveryCoin, a cryptocurrency, was proposed to allow blockchain-based drone-assisted delivery of goods. DeliveryCoin uses a strong Diffie-Hellman algorithm to achieve a secure consensus algorithm among various drones. An intrusion detection system (IDS) was integrated with the proposed blockchain ecosystem to allow 5G technology for establishing communication between drones and control centers. A machine learning—based IDS was proposed by Khan et al. (2021) where predictive analytics was incorporated to detect IDS in a decentralized fashion.

Deep learning (DL) technique is a popular way to make complex decisions based on given input. In Gumaei et al. (2021), such an architecture was proposed that can deal with DL-enabled decision-making capability in drones. This study presents that 5G can be considered an important communication technology to perform delay-aware drone identification and flight mode detection on the go. We could not find the medical delivery aspect in that study. In another work (Fraga-Lamas et al., 2019), a review on IoT-based DL techniques was conducted to make the UAVs self-aware of obstacles and avoid collisions on the fly. This work presented an architecture that considered DL-based unmanned aerial system (UAS) for futuristic application deployments.

Trust management was included in a novel drone-based blockchain system for measurement and protection of critical infrastructure (Barka et al., 2019). Besides performing a survey, the major contribution of this work was to propose a blockchain-based framework to confirm the trust and security of IoT-integrated UAVs.

A feasibility analysis of financial risk was performed (Hiebert et al., 2020) while considering drones as key enablers of smart healthcare applications. However, there was no mention about the possibility of medical delivery by drones under a blockchain-IoT environment.

Privacy preservation was mandated by Wu et al. (2021), where a blockchain-based 5G-enabled infrastructure was proposed. The study was designed around the pandemic situation where collection and dissemination of large data can be seamlessly done by drones. This study presented an approach to secure the information and make the drone communication aware of privacy.

We observe that Islam et al. (2021) presented a blockchain-aware system that can supervise some decision-making tasks with help of artificial intelligence technique. This study was conducted while considering a pandemic situation like COVID-19. This study discussed the internet of drone things (IoDT) to revolutionize a smart healthcare application during times of epidemic. It employed a lightweight blockchain platform on the drones to collect IoT-based data from remote locations and monitoring of

COVID-19 standard operating procedure (SOP) with poor network connectivity. A two-phase security algorithm was deployed to adopt the consensus algorithms under a resource-constrained scenario.

In another study (Fernández-Caramés et al., 2019), we find an approach to deal with big data–driven supply chain management by using UAVs and blockchain. The main aim of the study was to design an industry 4.0 warehouse that can be monitored for current status about the inventory. Further, the component on traceability was implied to make the whole supply chain feasible, cost effective, and reliable.

A discussion on UAV and blockchain was made by Kosuda et al. (2020). The study presented the utilization of commercial UAS operators under the aegis of a blockchain-based ecosystem. It was envisaged that the UAS can be aligned with unmanned traffic management for incorporation of IoT, 5G, and artificial intelligence toward smart, UAV-assisted operation management. A similar discussion was found in Han et al. (2021) where emergence of drone-aware trends was investigated. More emphasis was given to the utilization of mobile edge computing on top of drones on the fly so blockchain technology can be used to bring a novel application paradigm.

In Ray and Nguyen (2020), an in-depth review was conducted to investigate the status of blockchain-assisted medical drone delivery under the 5G-IoT ecosystem. This study presented a multimodal approach where medical drone delivery could be possible by using 5G and IoT. A satellite-based 5G-IoT drone architecture was proposed that was supported by the blockchain to maintain the logs of medical delivery.

2.1 Research gap

We found several research gaps after extensive surveys of related works. First, we find that the majority of the literature is silent about the drone suppliers for medical delivery operations. Second, existing literature does not conform to the use of blockchain for medical delivery via drones. Third, tere are minimal investigations on IoT-edge-centric ecosystem design for medical drone delivery. Finally, there is a lacuna in prospective use cases in this context.

2.2 Lessons learned

We learned that related works covered blockchain, 5G, IoT, and drone-aware studies. It was noticed that most of the works except Ray and Nguyen (2020) did no investigation of drone-based medical delivery.

The novelty of this paper can be expressed as follows: explicit investigation of drone suppliers for medical delivery, review of present status on drone-based medical delivery, implications of blockchain and IoT on the present situation of drone-aware medical delivery, and assessment of existing challenges.

3. Drone suppliers for medical delivery

Several drone suppliers are actively working toward delivery of medical items and services to different parts of the globe. Such drone suppliers have come up with a new consortium called the UAV for Payload Delivery Working Group (UPDWG). The UPDWG includes multiple stakeholders belonging to academic institutions, nonprofit organizations, lenders, private companies, and UAV suppliers. UPDWG allows four-phase inclusion of drones consisting of technology demonstration, safety and feasibility testing, effectiveness measurement, and impact expansion. Most of the medical delivery services are confined within a few countries such as Ghana, Madagascar, Malawi, Rwanda, Vanuatu, and Democratic Republic of the Congo. However, some drone suppliers are in the initial phases of UPDWG and are testing their prototypes in following countries: South Africa, Sweden, Italy, United Kingdom, Mozambique, Canada, Nepal, Botswana, France, Kazakhstan, Germany, Netherlands, Senegal, Tanzania, and United States of America (UPDWG, 2021). Such drones can carry different types of payloads that include saline bags, blood, medications, vaccines, first aid kits, diagnostic samples, tuberculosis sputum samples, syringes, defibrillators, oxytocin, and essential portable medical products. We present a list of the drone suppliers that have completed all four phases of testing and are now included in the official technology database of the UPDWG (MD3, 2021).

- Matternet

    Matternet is a Berlin-based drone supplier that deploys beyond visual line of sight (BVLOS). It provides an end-to-end (E2E) Matternet M2 drone for facilitation of medical item delivery between health stations. It uses Matternet station and Matternet cloud platform to perform tasks such as, monitoring, CC, customer response, and on-demand routing (Matternet, 2021).

- Vertical Technologies

    Vertical Technologies uses VTOL drones, which are available in various models to perform mapping, viewing, inspection, and cargo operations. It depends on the DeltaQuad VTOL drones that can fly up to 150 km by using an auxiliary battery with 1.2-kg payload. Delta-Quad drones can fly both in snowy and rainy conditions and have less than 1-min field assembly duration (Vertical, 2021).

- DJI

  DJI uses DJL Air 2S aircraft with 595-g payload weight. It has a maximum ascent speed of 6 m/s both in S and N modes. It can fly above 5000 m sea level with hovering time of 30 min. In a no wind condition, the drone can travel 18.5 km. The drone has a high accuracy hovering range with foldable aircraft arms. It uses one CMOS camera sensor with 20 megapixels and 100−3200 ISO automatic video range. It provides smartphone apps for CC of the drone with advanced safety and obstacle sensing (DJI, 2021).

- Cloudline

  Cloudline drone suppliers can serve with 10-kg medical payload and around 50-km flying range. Such drones can attain 9 knots during head-winds and 40 km/h during cruise speed. It uses a Cloudship I drone with an electric rotor with a built-in ultra high frequency (UHF) radio communication module. It uses landing-based medical package delivery (Cloudline, 2021).

- Germandrones

  Germandrones uses a reliable flight management system having auto-pilot, ground station, and data interconnection systems. It provides live video cameras including Nextvision Colibri II, Merio Temis XL, and photo cameras (Sony Alpha series, MicaSense Altum, PhaseOne iXM-100). Several fixed wing drones are used to enable long flight time and distances (Germandrones, 2021). It uses 4G data transmission technologies for high-quality video data propagation. It deploys a Song-bird drone that can provide VTOL for medical delivery.

- Phoenix-Wings

  Phoenix-Wings supplies the PWOne, which is the smallest VTOL drone that can carry 500 g of payload for 40 km. Manta Ray is another drone belonging to the Phoenix-Wings that is used for long-range (55−95 km) heavy-duty (10-kg) package delivery (Phoenix, 2021).

- UAV Factory

  UAV Factory deploys the Penguin B, a fixed wing drone with an internal combustion engine. It has satellite communication modules for establishing data transmission with the drone stations. It uses para-chutes to deliver medical items to the destination. Penguin C is a type of long-endurance (16−20 h) drone that can fly with a line-of-sight (LoS) range of 100 km. It is capable of carrying 2 kg of payload with a maximum cruise speed of 19−22 m/s at 5000 m above sea level (UAV, 2021).

- Vayu

  Vayu provides the VTOL-based drones for moderate payload delivery. There exist two models (X5 and G1) that can work on battery or petrol power sources (Vayu, 2021). X5 uses UHF radio and G1 uses satellite communication, 3G, and 4G LTE. Average endurance of travel is 480 h with a full payload having 2−5 kg.

- NextWing

  NextWing supplies two types of drones (NXT 1 and NXT 11) for delivery, survey, and security applications. They contain insulated cargo that can hold medical shipments and safeguard it from external environmental impacts (Nextwing, 2021). They comprise high–resolution cameras (e.g., 42 megapixel, SLR sensors) to capture images and sense obstacles. NXT 1 can carry 1 kg of payload, whereas NXT 11 can deliver 11 kg of payload to the destination. The speed is around 90−95 km/h with a long range (70−190 km).

- Swoop Aero

  Swoop Aero supplies scalable drones to serve medical delivery anywhere on the planet. Swoop Aero supports the delivery of pathologies, pharmaceuticals, vaccines, and urgent blood to locations where they are needed (Swoop, 2021). It depends on the digital twin of the deployed drone. The underlying system helps to communicate the physical hardware to the digital twin.

- Wingcopter

  Wingcopter provides a multitude of applications based on the two drones (W198 and W178). It can support mapping, inspection, intersite logistics, and medical item delivery. W178 and W198 have a wingspan of 178 and 198 cm, respectively. W178 can hover 100 km with 2 kg of payload and 120 km without any payload (Wingcopter, 2021). W198 can fly 110 km without payload and 75 km with a 5-kg payload. Both W178 and W198 can fly 5000 m above sea level. Their average fixed wing speed is 148 km/h. Both support cellular and satellite telemetry for ground station connectivity.

- Zipline

  Zipline is one of the most popular medical delivery drone suppliers in the world. It has different generations of drones (first, second, and third) that are based on fixed wing design and electric motors (Zipline, 2021). It uses parachutes to deliver medical items to the destination. Zipline is used in both deliveries and integrated on-demand delivery services. It has served many flights in Ghana in the past. Zipline is well known for its high resilience, scale, speed, and range.

- University of Southern Denmark

    University of Southern Denmark (SDU) has designed both fixed and multirotor health drones for medical delivery. Recently, it originated the GENIUS project to deploy 5G-based drone communication networking by following the BVLOS mechanism. Currently, the SDU drones can carry lightweight payload (100–300 g) with battery-supported endurance (SDU, 2021). It can fly 20–45 km with payload to deliver the package to the destination. It is supported with an electric motor and can communicate via UHF radio.

- Aurora Aerial

    Aurora Aerial deploys different versions of drones (AAC-1000, AAT-1000, AAT-1200, AAF-1000) for medical delivery. The drones can carry 5–36 kg of payload with endurance of 40–130 km (Aurora, 2021). The majority of their drones follow the multirotor design, whereas AAF-1000 uses helicopter design. Both AAC and AAT models fly on the basis of electric motors, whereas AAF can fly on internal combustion engines. All the drones use landing facilities for medical delivery.

- Healthcare Integrated Rescue Operations (HIRO)

    HIRO is a telemedicine supplier that depends on its drone the HIRO for medical delivery. The HIRO drones are internally guided and use the BLOV mechanism. Such drones are useful for medical search and rescue operations. It uses a multirotor design for a more than 40-mile flight distance (HIRO, 2021).

- AerialMetric

    Aerial Metric deploys the Savior 330 drone, which is an electric VTOL (eVTOL) fixed wing UAV that runs on an electric motor. It can carry 10 kg of payload with 130 km of flight distance. It also uses parachutes to deliver the medical items to the destination. The drone can fly at 5000 m above sea level and the speed is 150 km/h (Aerialmetric, 2021). When the payload weight is minimized, it can fly for 300 km with 3-h battery backup. Besides, it is equipped with UHF radio, 4G LTE, and satellite communication modules.

- Quantum Systems

  Quantum systems uses three major designs of drones (Trinity F90+ UAS, Vector UAS, and Scorpion UAS). All the drones are equipped with eVTOL techniques and electric motors (Quantum, 2021). Trinity F90+ comprises RGB and NDVI payload sensors for mapping of areas. It follows 2.4 GH telemetry and has a 7-km CC range. The Vector can fly for 120 min covering a 15-km range. The Scorpion is built on top of a tricopter UAV design and has 0−15 m/s cruise speed and 45 min of flight.

- Windracers

  Windracers deploys a fixed wing UAV called ULTRA (Windracers, 2021). ULTRA flies based on the internal combustion engine fueled by petrol. It can carry 100 kg of payload for a 240-km range. It comprises UHF radio, very high frequency (VHF) radio, satellite communications, and 4G LTE for establishing connectivity with base stations. It delivers medical packages by using both parachute and landing approaches. It can capture multispectral imagery besides collecting samples from the patients.

- RigiTech

  RigiTech drones (RiGiOne) are controlled by the Rigi cloud management system. Such drones are equipped with VTOL specification and can fly 75 km (Rigitech, 2021). The payload volume is 15 L, which is fueled by a battery. It can carry 2 kg of solid payload to a landing facility. It can perform both delivery and collection of samples.

- Avy

  Avy uses their flagship drone, Aera, that is a VTOL fixed wing system. It is fueled by a battery to run an electric motor. Maximum payload is 1.5 kg for 55-km range (Avy, 2021). It depends on a landing feature to deliver the shipments. Figs. 6.2 and 6.3 present various drones. Table 6.1 compares medical delivery drones.

4. Blockchain-IoT aware drone-based medical delivery

In this section, we list the most important notions of blockchain-assisted medical delivery with the help of IoT and drones. We present key classifications of drone-aware medical delivery such as last mile delivery, collaborative and multiagent delivery, epidemic support delivery, forensic delivery,

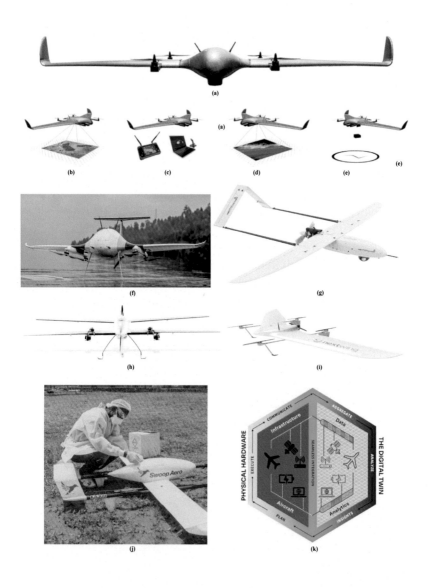

Figure 6.2 (A) DeltaQuad VTOL applications; (B) mapping; (C) viewing; (D) inspection; (E) cargo delivery; (F) Manta Ray; (G) Penguin C; (H) Vayu X5; (I) NextWing NXT 1; (J) Swoop Aero drone is fitted with medical shipment; (K) Swoop Aero digital twin management architecture. *(Courtesy of (A) Vertucal, 2021. https://www.deltaquad.com/. (Accessed 26 June 2021), (H) Vayu, 2021. https://vaayudrones.com/. (Accessed 26 June 2021), (I) Nextwing, 2021. https://flynextwing.com/. (Accessed 26 June 2021), and (K) Swoop, 2021. https://swoop.aero/. (Accessed 26 June 2021)).*

Figure 6.3 (A) Wingcopter; (B) Zipline; (C) SDU drone; (D) Aurora Aerial AAC-1000 drone; (E) Trinity F90+; (F) Vector; (G) Scorpion; (H) Windracer's ULTRA; (I) Aera drone. *(Courtesy of (A) Wingcopter, 2021. https://wingcopter.com/. (Accessed 26 June 2021), (B) Zipline, 2021. https://flyzipline.com/. (Accessed 26 June 2021), (C) SDU, 2021. https:// www.sdu.dk/en/forskning/sduuascenter. (Accessed 26 June 2021), (D) Aurora, 2021. https://www.auroraaerial.aero/. (Accessed 26 June 2021), (E–G) Quantum, 2021. https:// www.quantum-systems.com/. (Accessed 26 June 2021), (H) Wingcopter, 2021. https:// wingcopter.com/. (Accessed 26 June 2021), and (I) Swoop, 2021. https://swoop.aero/. (Accessed 26 June 2021)).*

Table 6.1 Comparison of drones for medical delivery.

Drone supplier	Model name	Method of flight	Propulsion	Power source	Payload capacity (g)	Payload volume (cm)	Maximum flight time with full payload (min)	Radio links	Delivery method	Role
Matternet	M2	Multirotor	Electric motor	Battery	3	22 × 14 × 14	10	Autonomous	Landing	Delivery only
Vertical Technologies	Delta Quad	VTOL fixed wing	Electric motor	Battery	1	16 × 12 × 7	10	LTE (3G/4G)	Landing	Delivery only
DJI	M600 plus	Multirotor	Electric motor	Battery	3	22 × 14 × 14	12	LTE (3G/4G)	Landing	Delivery and collection
DJI	M600	Multirotor	Electric motor	Battery	6	22 × 14 × 16	29	Autonomous	Landing	Delivery, collection, video, still and multispectral imagery
Cloudline	Cloudship I	Other	Electric motor	Battery	4.5	470 × 180 × 180	208	UHF radio	Landing	Delivery and collection
Germandrones	Songbird	VTOL fixed wing	Electric motor	Battery	4.5	15 × 12 × 20	60	UHF radio	Landing	Delivery, collection, video, and multispectral imagery
Phoenix-Wings	Manta Ray SR	VTOL fixed wing	Electric motor	Battery	10	39.5 × 36.5 × 21	45	UHF radio	Landing	Delivery and collection
UAV Factory	Penguin B	Fixed wing	Internal combustion engine	Petrol	2	18 × 13 × 8	120	Satcom	Parachute	Delivery only
Vayu	X5	VTOL fixed wing	Electric motor	Battery	2	55 × 15 × 14		UHF radio	Landing	Delivery and collection

Company	Model	Type	Propulsion	Power	Payload	Dimensions	Range	Communication	Landing	Service
Vayu	G1	VTOL fixed wing	Hybrid	Battery and petrol	5	22.6 × 22.2 × 14	480	Satcom, LTE (3G/4G)	Landing	Delivery and collection
NextWing	VTL3D	VTOL fixed wing	Electric motor	Battery	1	10 × 10 × 12			Landing	Delivery and collection
Swoop Aero	Kookaburra	VTOL fixed wing	Electric motor	Battery	3	19 × 12 × 9	60	Satcom, LTE (3G/4G)	Landing	Delivery and collection
Wingcopter	178 Heavy Lift	VTOL fixed wing	Electric motor	Battery	6	178 × 132 × 52	22.5	LTE (3G/4G)	Winch	Delivery only
Wingcopter	178 Heavy Lift Skyports	VTOL fixed wing	Electric motor	Battery	6	81 × 37 × 20	25	LTE (3G/4G), UHF radio	Landing	Delivery and collection
Zipline	Zip UAV 1st Generation, Zip UAV 2nd Generation, Zip UAV 3rd Generation	Fixed wing	Electric motor	Battery	1.75	25 × 25 × 15	180	LTE (3G/4G), UHF radio, VHF radio, and Satcom	Parachute	Delivery only
University of Southern Denmark	HealthDrone Fixed Wing	Fixed wing	Electric motor	Battery	0.1	12 × 12 × 3	45	LTE (3G/4G)	Landing	Delivery only
University of Southern Denmark	HealthDrone Multirotor	Multirotor	Electric motor	Battery	0.3	10 × 10 × 5	20	UHF radio	Landing	Delivery and collection
Aurora aerial	AAT-1200 Thunderbolt	Multirotor	Electric motor	Battery	9.1	40 × 40 × 40	20	UHF radio	Landing	Delivery only
Aurora aerial	AAC-1000 Thunderbolt	Multirotor	Electric motor	Battery	5	45 × 40 × 40	40	LTE (3G/4G)	Landing	Delivery and collection
								LTE (3G/4G)		

Continued

Table 6.1 Comparison of drones for medical delivery.—cont'd

Drone supplier	Model name	Method of flight	Propulsion	Power source	Payload capacity (g)	Payload volume (cm)	Maximum flight time with full payload (min)	Radio links	Delivery method	Role
Aurora aerial	AAF-1000 Mfit	Helicopter	Internal combustion engine	Diesel	36	N/A	120	Autonomous	Landing	Delivery, collection, video, still and multispectral imagery
AerialMetric	Savior 330	VTOL fixed wing	Electric motor	Battery	10	41 × 41 × 8.5	130	LTE (3G/4G), UHF radio, Satcom	Parachute	Delivery and video
Quantum systems	Trinity F90+	VTOL fixed wing	Electric motor	Battery	0.5	12.5 × 8.2 × 10.8	90	UHF radio	Landing	Delivery only
Quantum systems	Tron	VTOL fixed wing	Electric motor	Battery	2	24.9 × 8.7 × 9.7	60	UHF radio	Landing	Delivery only
Windracers	ULTRA	Fixed wing	Internal combustion engine	Petrol	100	N/A	240	LTE (3G/4G), UHF radio, VHF radio, Satcom, autonomous	Parachute and landing	Delivery, collection, video, still and multispectral imagery
RigiTech	RigiOne	VTOL fixed wing	Electric motor	Battery	2	45 × 21 × 16	30	LTE (3G/4G), UHF radio	Landing	Delivery and collection
Avy	Aera	VTOL fixed wing	Electric motor	Battery	1.5	15.5 × 23 × 65	55	LTE andand Satcom	Landing	Delivery and collection, video, still and multispectral imagery, other

smart city delivery, and 5G-AI-assisted delivery. We provide detailed explanations on each of the major types of drone-based delivery that can benefit the current smart healthcare domain with a futuristic orientation.

4.1 Last mile delivery

Last mile delivery is a prominent application of medical drone delivery where drones are expected to deliver medical items to remote locations. A number of key performance indicators (KPIs) can be listed to evaluate the significance of the last mile medical delivery by a drone. For example, such KPIs can be classified into three major types: time of delivery, cost of delivery, and efficiency of the drone. Important KPIs can be considered as follows: number of stops on the fly, on-time delivery, cost per delivery, miles per watt of power, predicted versus actual distance traveled by drones, shipment accuracy, drone in motion on air, and drone in static condition on air. Route planning is an important component for KPIs of last mile delivery.

Last mile delivery use cases must be formulated against the order fulfillment versus delivery approach notions. Thus, IoT can play a vital role to support the monitoring of drones, controlling, optimization, automation, and learning of the context. Blockchain technology herein can improve the data transparency, minimal risk of fraud, immutable transactions, and secure data storage (Marco, 2018).

A three-phase decentralized drone management architecture was proposed by Ahmad et al. (2021). The architecture uses phase-1 for gathering medical data from IoT-based sensors. The data is then forwarded to other drone or blockchain platforms via drones for further processing. Drones must return to the origin when the delivery is complete. Smart contracts are used to manage the whole scenario in a seamless manner. Fig. 6.4 presents the three-phase drone delivery architecture with detailed interactions.

4.2 Collaborative and multiagent delivery

Multiagent systems (MAS) comprise autonomous agents, i.e., drones to exchange data within the group. In a study (Kapitonov et al., 2017), an MAS-based drone delivery system was proposed: autonomous intelligent robot agent (AIRA). This model helps to assist UAVs in a multitude of IoT-based applications. The AIRA system uses a docker cluster to serve cognitive services with the help of a package advisor, market analytics, and adapter analysis. The Ethereum and interplanetary file system (IPFS) are

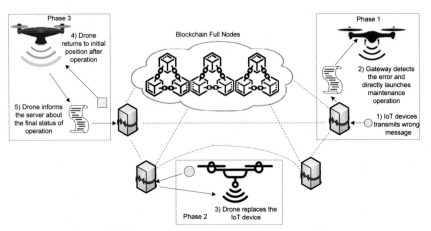

Figure 6.4 Three-phase medical drone delivery architecture.

combined to alleviate the AIRA kernels to provide seamless drone management for medical delivery purposes. AIRA uses MAS for leveraging communication with the blockchain platform via a peer-to-peer network. The system empowers the drones with efficient owner's rule and localized identity management.

Multidrone collaboration framework has become a popular approach encountered in medical delivery applications. We can use the end-to-end delivery scheme where blockchain platforms can act as the core of decentralized data storage. The system works on request and response workflow where location, trajectory, timing, and other necessary information is stored in the blockchain network. Drones can alleviate the utility of blockchains for performing various types of medical delivery scenarios. Drones that follow multirobot design need to follow the localized intelligent edge computing that allows them to decide instantly based on the gathered information about a context.

RobotChain (Alsamhi et al., 2021a,b) is such a multiagent drone architecture that uses private, public, and consortium blockchains for medical delivery. Fig. 6.5 presents the RobotChain architecture for medical drone delivery.

4.3 Epidemic support delivery

The world has witnessed the wrath of COVID-19 as a devastating epidemic. Blockchain, IoT, and drones are being used to counter COVID-19 in different parts of the world. For example, contactless delivery of medicines to COVID-19-affected patients can be done by drones. We also

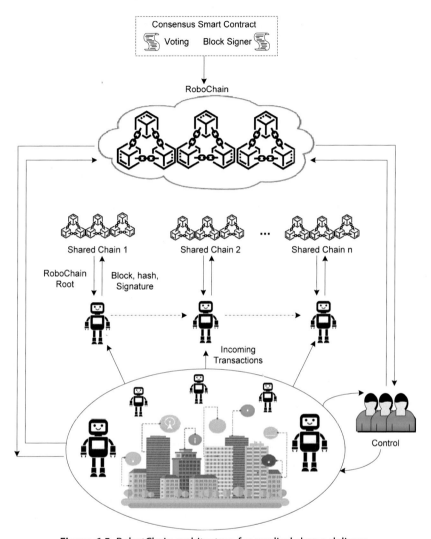

Figure 6.5 RobotChain architecture for medical drone delivery.

find that drones have been used in other applications such as food distribution during COVID-19 lockdown, delivery of vaccines by using supply chain management, COVID-19 patient information sharing, and awareness campaigning for COVID-19 (Kalla et al., 2020). Various types of consensus algorithms are used in such aspects. For instance, proof of work and proof of stake are used in contact tracing, patient information sharing, food distribution, and automated contactless surveillance. We notice that Ethereum and Hyperledger Fabric are the most used blockchain platforms in such scenarios. In Gupta et al. (2021), a UAV-based drone-centric medical delivery architecture was proposed to combat COVID-19. This architecture uses a four-layered approach considering COVID-19, virtualization, network control, and application layers. Drones collect and monitor the COVID-19 situation and forward the information to the virtual infrastructure manager. A virtual drone swarm network is envisaged herein to manage the delivery of the drones. The network control plane performs network monitoring, access control, dynamic routing, and switching between various software-defined network controllers. Smart contracts are deployed in each of the four layers, which are connected with the Ethereum blockchain. Fig. 6.6 presents software-enabled multi-swarming UAV architecture for medical delivery. In Kumar et al. (2021), a drone-based control, monitoring, and analysis architecture was proposed. The architecture uses a COVID-19-centric CC room for management of the overall drone delivery process. Drones are equipped with IoT-based data collection sensors. Drone signaling systems communicate with the centralized control room for necessary command procurement. Drones send the information to the edge, fog, or cloud platforms per their vicinity and availability of services. Thermal imagery sensors can sense whether a patient is wearing a mask and whether the patient's body temperature is within the normal range. In Firouzi et al. (2021), a number of issues are discussed in the

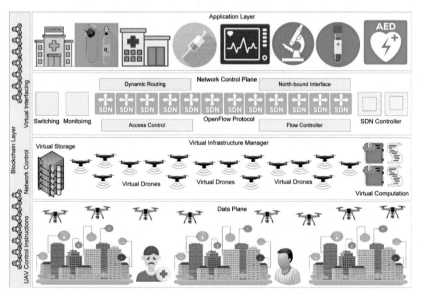

Figure 6.6 Software-enabled multi-swarming UAV medical delivery architecture.

drone-assisted COVID-19 combat scenario. Also, a pandemic-tracking smartphone app is used to update COVID-19 safety status about a patient and check the mask inventory.

4.4 Forensic delivery

Drones can be useful for both forensic and paramedical delivery operations. In Yu et al. (2019), a self-adaptive architecture called LiveBox was proposed to deal with forensic aware drone operations. In this software design, drones are equipped with a LiveBox that can be controlled from a central station. The LiveBox ground station is responsible for detecting the drones and updating the logs based on the collection information. Third-party stakeholders can access the LiveBox cloud services to check the status of the drones and perform queries. It can verify the consensus algorithm using hashing keys and make context-aware decisions. A smart contract performs recovery of flight data based on tamper-proof evidence. The LiveBox uses four-stage feedback that includes monitoring, analysis, planning, and execution. The proposed software can address two key research issues: stringent forensic application deployment ability of the drones and live forensic analysis while following regulatory corridors (no-fly zone, restricted zone, private zone, etc.). It uses a self-adaptive reporting algorithm to measure the accurate geolocations when it falls under the drone fly zone. Fig. 6.7 presents the LiveBox architecture.

4.5 Smart city delivery

Smart city, aware, drone-based medical delivery is a promising application where various types of healthcare services can be provided. For example, blockchain can be used to create a health bank that can be accessed with the help of DApps. We can also share medical data by using a medical record keeping blockchain. Blockchain can be used for the medical data storage,

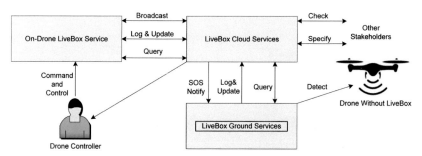

Figure 6.7 LiveBox forensic medical drone delivery architecture.

which can be useful for medical delivery use cases. Drones can be linked with the cloud-based blockchain platforms to provide such medical services in a smart city framework (Aggarwal et al., 2019). Medical professionals can access the blockchain storage with consent from the patient. Drones can be aligned with the IoT-based smart health sensors that can be used for gathering and monitoring of real-time health status.

A typical example of a smart city drone delivery use case can be described as follows. IoT-based smart sensors collect health data from the patients, which is then transmitted to the authorized drones for further forwarding to the mobile edge computing (MEC) platforms. All of the information is processed at the MECs and stored in the blockchain infrastructure. In Islam et al. (2019), a smart city, aware, blockchain architecture is proposed: BHMUS. BHMUS uses MEC to process citizen-centric health data by using drones. The drones gather data from citizens that is processed at the MEC-enabled base stations. Existing cellular networks are used to convey such data transmission between distributed MEC-enabled base stations. Each of the base stations is equipped with a blockchain that takes control of localized data storage. The whole architecture is served by standard enterprise cloud platforms. Fig. 6.8 presents a smart city—enabled drone delivery architecture.

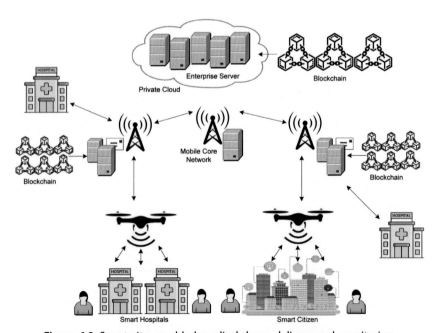

Figure 6.8 Smart city—enabled medical drone delivery and monitoring.

Smart city aware drone delivery must be safeguarded from possible threats and attacks that include cryptographic vulnerability, propagation delay, distributed denial of service attacks, infrastructure security, data integrity, data privacy, and smartphone-aware attacks (Singh et al., 2020). Smart city–based intelligent infrastructure needs to be revised in terms of the following key aspects, transmit management of drones, patient information, crash prevention, arterial management, commercial drone operation, freight management, and incident management.

4.6 5G- and AI-assisted delivery

Blockchain can be integrated with 5G and artificial intelligence (AI) to empower drone-based medical delivery. A study by Gupta et al. (2020) proposed a three-layer architecture to allow various delivery applications by using drones. A UAV layer is used to support the delivery-aware applications, e.g., healthcare, smart grid, smart city, and military surveillance. It is supported by an edge-AI layer that integrates the UAV layer to the blockchain layer. The edge-AI layer performs the decision-making based on the received information from the drones. The communication technology that is used in this architecture relies on the 5G infrastructure to minimize the latency of data transmission. Further, cloud platforms are used to analyze the filtered information that is not served by the edge-AI systems. The blockchain layer provides the security of the information collected and processed by the drones and the edge-AI layers. Blockchain allows the utilization of a UAV smart contract to communicate with the Ethereum blockchain platform. Fig. 6.9 presents the three-layer blockchain-assisted medical drone delivery architecture.

A study by Bera et al. (2020) proposed the BSD2C-IoD architecture to enable delivery operations by using drones. In this architecture, the control room sends a registration request to the registration authority (RA) and receives the acknowledgment from the RA. The prospective drone is registered with the service, which then starts delivery operations with constant communication with the ground stations. Ground stations send the block creation information to the peer-to-peer ground station network for efficient management of blocks in the remote blockchain center. This architecture uses an internet of drone (IoD) scheme for secure data delivery to remote locations.

We find key benefits of using 5G and AI in the blockchain-drone delivery ecosystem as follows: decentralized automation, scalability, identity management, autonomy, security, reliability, and secure code deployment (Mistry et al., 2020). Use of 5G and AI can improve medical delivery

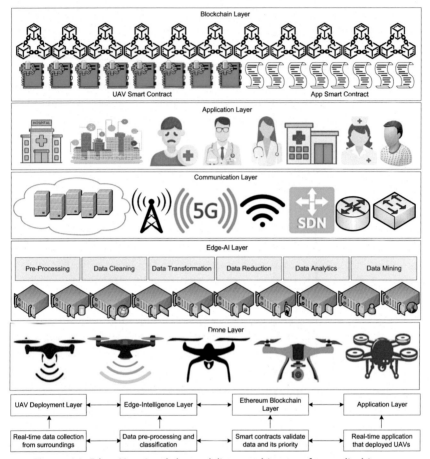

Figure 6.9 Edge-AI-assisted drone delivery architecture for medical items.

applications with the following features: dynamic deployment ability, drone swarm network, and design of aerial base stations. However, optimization of drone weight, battery capacity, and computing ability remain key issues (Han et al., 2021) (Table 6.2).

5. Key issues and future direction

5.1 Health record storage cost

Medical drone delivery can face huge costs for medical data due to storage in the blockchain platforms. At the present, very few blockchains exist that provide minimal cost per transactions (Rabah, 2018). In such a context, expenditure due to health data transactions can impact new startups and

Table 6.2 Different types of medical delivery of drones.

Application	Medical use	Medicinal items	Drone site	Advantages	Limitations
Palliative care	Delivery of controlled drugs and medicines	Injectable medicines	Remote site, outdoor	Control	Security, safety
Diagnosis	Specialized diagnostic test kits delivery	Blood, tissue, pathology samples	Indoor, clinical use	Centralized supply	Range, safety
Diagnostic	Nuclear imaging	Short half-life radionuclide	Indoor, clinical use	Rapid transfer from remote location	Safety, security
Emergency care	Overdose of medicine	Prothrombin	Outdoor, remote site	Rapid transfer to remote site	Delivery speed, cruise speed
Emergency care	Cardiac arrest	Adrenaline, lidocaine, atropine	Outdoor, remote site	Rapid transfer to remote site	Delivery speed, cruise speed
Emergency care	Asthma attack	Salbutamol, nebulizer	Outdoor, remote site	Rapid transfer to remote site	Delivery speed, cruise speed
Emergency care	Snake bite	Antivenom, antidotes	Outdoor, remote site	Rapid transfer to remote site	Delivery speed, cruise speed, range, stability
Emergency care	Burn	Live maggots	Outdoor, remote site	Centralized supply to remote site	Range
Emergency care	Clotting agent	Live leeches	Outdoor, remote site	Centralized supply to remote site	Range

Continued

Table 6.2 Different types of medical delivery of drones.—cont'd

Application	Medical use	Medicinal items	Drone site	Advantages	Limitations
Emergency care	Allergic reaction	Epi pen	Outdoor, remote site	Rapid transfer to remote site	Range, medicine stability
Emergency care	Suspected sepsis	IV antidote	Outdoor, remote site	Rapid transfer to remote site	Range, medicine stability
Emergency care	Chemotherapy	Short half-life radionuclide	Indoor, clinical use	Rapid transfer from remote site	Security, safety
Emergency care	Disease outbreak	Vaccine	Outdoor, remote location	Remote delivery	Range, stability, medicine stability
Emergency care	Organ delivery	Heart, kidney, eye, liver	Outdoor, remote location, hospitals	Rapid transfer to remote site	Range, organ stability, speed of delivery, guarantee of delivery
Emergency care	Blood delivery	Blood packets	Outdoor, remote location, hospitals	Rapid transfer to remote site	Range, blood stability, speed of delivery, guarantee of delivery
Regular use	Patient guidance	Medical support with voice	Outdoor, hospital out area	Centralized control	Stability

technology deployments. Novel techniques should be sought to use public blockchains, but proper security and privacy issues need to be addressed beforehand.

5.2 Energy management

Energy consumption by the drones during flight and charging could be a major problem in the coming days. Normally, drones get charged by standard alternating current—centric electrical modules. This can indirectly increase fossil fuel consumption. New methods must be developed that can use renewable energy sources to charge the UAVs. However, cost and circuit complexity should be optimized simultaneously.

5.3 Ecologic condition

Use of drones for medical delivery can populate open air space that can hinder the normal working of natural ecology. Thus, ecologic conditions must be balanced before deployment of drones for medical delivery. We should focus on the dismantling of drones when they expire. Proper renewal strategy should be provided before using drones for healthcare applications.

5.4 Legal disputes

Drones may enter such locations or geographic zones that are either restricted or avoided, e.g., military bases or industrial buildings. In that case, the drone operators may face legal issues (Jain et al., 2019). Drone suppliers and operators must follow strict geographic fencing algorithms to safeguard the drones from possible legal disputes. Further, drones should be programmed to handle medicinal products and deliver the shipments to appropriate destinations. Notwithstanding these points, drone suppliers may face legal disputes.

5.5 Latency and throughput

Drone-based medical delivery needs to have latency-aware systems. For example, emergency organ delivery applications should avoid any type of latency (network or speed) to avoid health hazards to the patient. Throughput of drone-based delivery depends on the amount of delivery successfully completed against a given time window. Thus, drone operators should follow a priority basis medical delivery scheme to minimize the issues related to latency.

5.6 Resource utilization

IoT works on a resource-constrained framework. Thus, IoT- enabled drone networks must be aware of resource-constrained design. We should find solutions that can mitigate and optimize the existing resource utilization for medical delivery. Drones should not over depend on IoT-based resources to make them compulsorily work in an overclocked manner. Further solutions should be sought to look into the underutilization of the available resources.

5.7 Vulnerability

Drones are expected to fly in the open air and remote fields. In such a context, drones can face vulnerable conditions by manual attack or military fire. Drones may also be considered in the scenario where climatic conditions are against the proper workflow of their in-built mandates. Thus, vulnerable prediction analytics and recovery of drones need to be incorporated into the network design (Alladi et al., 2020). Blockchains can help to account for tamper-proof data storage to eradicate the vulnerable behavior of humans or nature to safeguard private health information.

5.8 Standard architecture

There is no standard architecture that exists to date that can guide the proper deployment of drones under the aegis of blockchain and IoT. In such a context, initiatives should be taken by international organizations to come up with a standard architecture following a rigid protocol-aware formulation.

5.9 Incentive for participation

Ordinarily, blockchains provide incentives to miners in terms of crypto-currency, i.e., economic benefit. Drone-aware medical delivery should be empowered with incentivization schemes for all stakeholders (Al-Marridi et al., 2021; Xu et al., 2021; Manu et al., 2021; Johari et al., 2021). It would boost their involvement to contribute for safety, privacy, and vulnerability-free passage through the open air. For example, a miner who gives prior information about a possible obstacle or vulnerable attack can be given a token of cryptocurrency. Thus, a holistic ecosystem can be devised where stakeholders from all categories can join the blockchain and improve the delivery service.

5.10 Regulatory constraints

To date, there are no fixed regulations that are applicable in all the countries of the world. This hinders the process of deployment and utilization of various bands of frequency spectrum in different locations (Sujihelen, 2021; Reinert and Corser, 2021; Sharma et al., 2021; Chouhan et al., 2021). Further, there is no fixed rule for hovering drones in the open air. Some countries allow drones to fly at 5000 m above sea level. But sometimes, it may not be possible due to some technical or administrative reasons. Further, consideration should be paved to include insurance companies to compensate for accidents or destruction of drones while on duty for delivery. We expect that soon policy makers from all countries will design regulations that can be modified based on a consensus algorithm mechanism.

5.11 Technology adoption

Adoption of technology for medical use cases is not an easy task. It is often observed that people from different educational backgrounds and economic stature take such matters in a completely unexpected manner. Utilization of drones for medical delivery can face social inertia that can hinder the acceptance of such technology (Ch et al., 2020). We expect that proper campaigning and awareness about public safety can ensure the minimization of resistance to technology adoption in society.

5.12 Future direction

Vulnerability prevention should be the first step toward futuristic drone-centric medical delivery applications. We should focus on various levels of vulnerabilities, e.g., communication channel level, transceiver level, and control center level. Use of fuzzy logic and advanced DL can benefit vulnerability prediction, detection, and recovery simultaneously (Eichleay et al., 2019). We need to further think of using layered blockchain architecture where the workflow should start from the data layer, i.e., gathering data from IoT-based devices. The information should then be traversed to the next layers, such as the network layer. It can work as the key to all communication activities and cover all types of heterogeneity protocols to allow IoT devices to cooperate. Higher layers of such blockchain architecture may consist of consensus algorithm layer, incentive layer, smart contract layer, and application layer. Various consensus algorithms must be incorporated into the consensus algorithm layer to provide a flexible approach to serve a multitude of medical delivery applications (Thiels et al., 2015; Razdan and Sharma, 2021; Barnawi et al., 2021). An insurance mechanism and allocation of cryptocurrency token can be accommodated in the incentive layer. Smart contracts can be deployed in the contract layer, which can finally reach to the application layer, where the actual medical delivery use case would take place. Emphasis should be given to the following aspects to improve the existing drone delivery ecosystems: creation of new business models, collision-free UAV movement guarantee, uniform load (medical data) sharing (Ling and Draghic, 2019), data entity authentication, and lightweight consensus algorithm design (Rahman et al., 2021; Irshad et al., 2021). Upcoming drone delivery startups may need to fulfill cooperation and faster synchronization schemes between drones and remote CC centers. Decentralized decision-making would be another important avenue that can enhance the acceptance and availability of drone-based health services. Utilization of multidrone (swarms) techniques can alleviate the channel utilization with enriched security and transparency (Du et al., 2021; Saxena et al., 2021; Guggenberger et al., 2021). UAV-based cloud or fog platforms can be considered as another future direction to make medical delivery accessible to every citizen. Internet agnostic network design techniques could expand the reachability of the drones for efficient deployment at the extreme last mile scenario. Dew computing paradigm could be considered the perfect match for devising the dew-IoT drone cluster implementation that merely depends on the internet backhaul for exchange of data (Ray, 2017). Virtual circuit-based risk assessment models may be investigated for eradication of unprecedented failure of drones due to technical issues.

6. Conclusion

In this article, we present an in-depth review of drones for possible deployment in the medical delivery use cases. We envisage that drones would be accepted to encounter the gradually increasing requirement of medical delivery at lower cost and higher security than what exists today. We expect that proper incorporation of lightweight blockchain-based frameworks may harness transparency as well as privacy, alleviating medical delivery applications. Existing drone suppliers are doing fantastic jobs to lift up drone-assisted medical care, though because of lack of latency-mitigating technologies and proper planning, they seem to be resisted by general social inertia. It is however understood that upon certain changes in the socio-technologic paradigm, drones are certainly going to revolutionize the delivery domain to make healthcare smarter.

References

Abbas, A., Alroobaea, R., Krichen, M., Rubaiee, S., Vimal, S., Almansour, F.M., 2021. Blockchain-assisted secured data management framework for health information analysis based on Internet of Medical Things. Personal Ubiquitous Comput. 1—14.

Aerialmetric, 2021. https://aerialmetric.com/. Accessed on June 26, 2021.

Aggarwal, S., Chaudhary, R., Aujla, G.S., Kumar, N., Choo, K.K.R., Zomaya, A.Y., 2019. Blockchain for smart communities: applications, challenges and opportunities. J. Netw. Comput. Appl. 144, 13—48.

Ahmad, R.W., Hasan, H., Yaqoob, I., Salah, K., Jayaraman, R., Omar, M., 2021. Blockchain for aerospace and defense: opportunities and open research challenges. Comput. Ind. Eng. 151, 106982.

Al-Marridi, A.Z., Mohamed, A., Erbad, A., 2021. Reinforcement Learning Approaches for Efficient and Secure Blockchain-Powered Smart Health Systems. Computer Networks, p. 108279.

Ali, M., Karimipour, H., Tariq, M., 2021. Integration of Blockchain and Federated Learning for Internet of Things: Recent Advances and Future Challenges. Computers & Security, p. 102355.

Alladi, T., Chamola, V., Sahu, N., Guizani, M., 2020. Applications of blockchain in unmanned aerial vehicles: a review. Veh. Commun. 23, 100249.

Alqaralleh, B.A., Vaiyapuri, T., Parvathy, V.S., Gupta, D., Khanna, A., Shankar, K., 2021. Blockchain-assisted secure image transmission and diagnosis model on Internet of Medical Things Environment. Personal Ubiquitous Comput. 1—11.

Alsamhi, S.H., Afghah, F., Sahal, R., Hawbani, A., Al-qaness, A.A., Lee, B., Guizani, M., 2021a. Green Internet of Things Using UAVs in B5G Networks: A Review of Applications and Strategies. Ad Hoc Networks, p. 102505.

Alsamhi, S.H., Lee, B., Guizani, M., Kumar, N., Qiao, Y., Liu, X., 2021b. Blockchain for Decentralized Multi-drone to Combat COVID-19 and Future Pandemics: Framework and Proposed Solutions. Transactions on Emerging Telecommunications Technologies, p. e4255.

Alzubi, J.A., 2021. Blockchain-based lamport merkle digital signature: authentication tool in IoT healthcare. Comput. Commun. 170, 200—208.

Aruna, E., 2021. Survey on use of blockchain technology in cloud storage for the security of healthcare systems. Turkish J. Comp. Math. Educ. (TURCOMAT) 12 (13), 3326—3332.

Attarian, R., Hashemi, S., 2021. An anonymity communication protocol for security and privacy of clients in IoT-based mobile health transactions. Comput. Network. 190, 107976.

Aurora, 2021. https://www.auroraaerial.aero/. Accessed on June 26, 2021.

Avy, 2021. https://avy.eu/. Accessed on June 26, 2021.

Awan, S., Ahmed, S., Ullah, F., Nawaz, A., Khan, A., Uddin, M.I., et al., 2021. IoT with BlockChain: a futuristic approach in agriculture and food supply chain. Wireless Commun. Mobile Comput. 2021, 14. https://doi.org/10.1155/2021/5580179, 5580179.

Barka, E., Kerrache, C.A., Benkraouda, H., Shuaib, K., Ahmad, F., Kurugollu, F., 2019. Towards a Trusted Unmanned Aerial System Using Blockchain for the Protection of Critical Infrastructure. Transactions on Emerging Telecommunications Technologies, p. e3706.

Barnawi, A., Chhikara, P., Tekchandani, R., Kumar, N., Alzahrani, B., 2021. Artificial intelligence-enabled Internet of Things-based system for COVID-19 screening using aerial thermal imaging. Future Generat. Comput. Syst. 124, 119−132. https://doi.org/10.1016/j.future.2021.05.019. Epub 2021 May 26. PMCID: 34075265; PMCID: PMC8152244.

Bera, B., Saha, S., Das, A.K., Kumar, N., Lorenz, P., Alazab, M., 2020. Blockchain-envisioned secure data delivery and collection scheme for 5G-based IoT-enabled Internet of drones environment. IEEE Trans. Veh. Technol. 69 (8), 9097−9111.

Bhuvaneshwari, C., Saranyadevi, G., Vani, R., Manjunathan, A., February 2021. Development of high yield farming using IoT based UAV. In: IOP Conference Series: Materials Science and Engineering, vol. 1055. IOP Publishing, p. 012007. No. 1.

Ch, R., Srivastava, G., Gadekallu, T.R., Maddikunta, P.K.R., Bhattacharya, S., 2020. Security and privacy of UAV data using blockchain technology. J. Inf. Secur. Appl. 55, 102670.

Chelladurai, U., Pandian, S., 2021. A novel blockchain based electronic health record automation system for healthcare. J. Ambient Intell. Humaniz. Comput. 1−11.

Chen, C.M., Deng, X., Gan, W., Chen, J., Islam, S.H., 2021. A secure blockchain-based group key agreement protocol for IoT. J. Supercomput. 1−23.

Chinaei, M.H., Gharakheili, H.H., Sivaraman, V., 2021. Optimal witnessing of healthcare IoT data using blockchain logging contract. IEEE Internet Things J. 8 (12), 10117−10130. https://doi.org/10.1109/JIOT.2021.3051433.

Chittoor, P.K., Chokkalingam, B., Mihet-Popa, L., 2021. A review on UAV wireless charging: fundamentals, applications, charging techniques and standards. IEEE Access 9, 69235−69266.

Chouhan, A.S., Qaseem, M.S., Basheer, Q.M.A., Mehdia, M.A., 2021. Blockchain based EHR system architecture and the need of blockchain in healthcare. Mater. Today Proc. https://doi.org/10.1016/j.matpr.2021.06.114. ISSN 2214-7853.

Cloudline, 2021. https://flycloudline.com/. Accessed on June 26, 2021.

Comtet, H.E., Johannessen, K.A., 2021. The moderating role of pro-innovative leadership and gender as an enabler for future drone transports in healthcare systems. Int. J. Environ. Res. Publ. Health 18 (5), 2637.

Da Xu, L., Lu, Y., Li, L., 2021. Embedding blockchain technology into IoT for security: a survey. IEEE Internet Things J. 8 (13), 10452−10473.

Dai, H.N., Zheng, Z., Zhang, Y., 2019. Blockchain for internet of things: a survey. IEEE Internet Things J. 6 (5), 8076−8094.

DJI, 2021. https://www.dji.com/. Accessed on June 26, 2021.

Du, Y., Wang, Z., Leung, V., 2021. Blockchain-enabled edge intelligence for IoT: background, emerging trends and open issues. Future Internet 13 (2), 48.

Eichleay, M., Evens, E., Stankevitz, K., Parker, C., 2019. Using the unmanned aerial vehicle delivery decision tool to consider transporting medical supplies via Drone. Glob. Health: Sci. Practice 7 (4), 500−506.

Evita, M., Zakiyyaduddin, A., Srigutomo, W., Aminah, N.S., Meilano, I., Djamal, M., February 2021. Photogrammetry using intelligent-battery UAV in different weather for volcano early warning system Application. In: Journal of Physics: Conference Series, vol. 1772. IOP Publishing, p. 012017, 1.

Farahani, B., Firouzi, F., Luecking, M., 2021. The convergence of IoT and distributed ledger technologies (DLT): opportunities, challenges, and solutions. J. Netw. Comput. Appl. 177, 102936.

Fatokun, T., Nag, A., Sharma, S., 2021. Towards a blockchain assisted patient owned system for electronic health records. Electronics 10 (5), 580.

Fernández-Caramés, T.M., Blanco-Novoa, O., Froiz-Míguez, I., Fraga-Lamas, P., 2019. Towards an autonomous industry 4.0 warehouse: a UAV and blockchain-based system for inventory and traceability applications in big data-driven supply chain management. Sensors 19 (10), 2394.

Ferrag, M.A., Maglaras, L., 2019. DeliveryCoin: an IDS and blockchain-based delivery framework for drone-delivered services. Computers 8 (3), 58.

Firouzi, F., Farahani, B., Daneshmand, M., Grise, K., Song, J.S., Saracco, R., et al., 2021. Harnessing the power of smart and connected health to tackle COVID-19: IoT, AI, robotics, and blockchain for a better world. IEEE Internet Things J. 8 (16), 12826−12846. https://doi.org/10.1109/jiot.2021.3073904.

Fraga-Lamas, P., Ramos, L., Mondéjar-Guerra, V., Fernández-Caramés, T.M., 2019. A review on IoT deep learning UAV systems for autonomous obstacle detection and collision avoidance. Rem. Sens. 11 (18), 2144.

Frikha, T., Chaari, A., Chaabane, F., Cheikhrouhou, O., Zaguia, A., 2021. Healthcare and fitness data management using the IoT-based blockchain platform. J. Healthc. Eng. 2021, 12. https://doi.org/10.1155/2021/9978863, 9978863.

Germandrones, 2021. https://www.germandrones.com/. Accessed on June 26, 2021.

Gimenez-Aguilar, M., de Fuentes, J.M., Gonzalez-Manzano, L., Arroyo, D., 2021. Achieving cybersecurity in blockchain-based systems: a survey. Future Generat. Comput. Syst. 124, 91−118.

Guggenberger, T., Lockl, J., Röglinger, M., Schlatt, V., Sedlmeir, J., Stoetzer, J.C., Völter, F., 2021. Emerging digital technologies to combat future crises: learnings from COVID-19 to be prepared for the future. Int. J. Innovat. Technol. Manag. 2140002.

Gul, M.J., Subramanian, B., Paul, A., Kim, J., 2021. Blockchain for public health care in smart society. Microprocess. Microsyst. 80, 103524.

Gumaei, A., Al-Rakhami, M., Hassan, M.M., Pace, P., Alai, G., Lin, K., Fortino, G., 2021. Deep learning and blockchain with edge computing for 5G-enabled drone identification and flight mode detection. IEEE Netw. 35 (1), 94−100.

Guo, Y., Zhao, Z., He, K., Lai, S., Xia, J., Fan, L., 2021. Efficient and flexible management for industrial Internet of Things: a federated learning approach. Comput. Network. 192, 108122.

Gupta, R., Kumari, A., Tanwar, S., 2020. Fusion of Blockchain and Artificial Intelligence for Secure Drone Networking Underlying 5G Communications. Transactions on Emerging Telecommunications Technologies, p. e4176.

Gupta, R., Kumari, A., Tanwar, S., Kumar, N., 2021. Blockchain-Envisioned Softwarized Multi-Swarming UAVs to Tackle COVID-I9 Situations. IEEE Network, pp. 160−167.

Han, J., Ribeiro, I.D.L., Magaia, N., Preto, J., Segundo, A.H.F.N., de Macêdo, A.R.L., de Albuquerque, V.H.C., 2021. Emerging drone trends for blockchain-based 5G networks: open issues and future perspectives. IEEE Netw. 35 (1), 38−43.

Hemalatha, P., 2021. Monitoring and securing the healthcare data harnessing IOT and blockchain technology. Turkish J. Comput. Math. Educ. (TURCOMAT) 12 (2), 2554−2561.

Hiebert, B., Nouvet, E., Jeyabalan, V., Donelle, L., 2020. The application of drones in healthcare and health-related services in North America: a scoping review. Drones 4 (3), 30.

HIRO, 2021. https://unmanned-aerial.com/hiro-telemedical-drone-continues-advancing-inches-closer-production/. Accessed on June 26, 2021.

Homier, V., Brouard, D., Nolan, M., Roy, M.A., Pelletier, P., McDonald, M., et al., 2021. Drone versus ground delivery of simulated blood products to an urban trauma center: the Montreal Medi-Drone pilot study. J. Trauma Acute Care Surg. 90 (3), 515.

Iqbal, N., Jamil, F., Ahmad, S., Kim, D., 2021. A novel blockchain-based integrity and reliable veterinary clinic information management system using predictive analytics for provisioning of quality health services. IEEE Access 9, 8069–8098.

Irshad, A., Chaudhry, S.A., Ghani, A., Bilal, M., 2021. A Secure Blockchain-Oriented Data Delivery and Collection Scheme for 5G-Enabled IoD Environment. Computer Networks, p. 108219.

Islam, A., Shin, S.Y., 2019. BHMUS: blockchain based secure outdoor health monitoring scheme using UAV in smart city. In: 2019 7th International Conference on Information and Communication Technology (ICoICT). IEEE, pp. 1–6. https://doi.org/10.1109/icoict.2019.8835373.

Islam, A., Rahim, T., Masuduzzaman, M.D., Shin, S.Y., 2021. A blockchain-based artificial intelligence-empowered contagious pandemic situation supervision scheme using internet of drone things. IEEE Wirel. Commun.

Jain, K., Khoshelham, K., Zhu, X., Tiwari, A., 2019. Proceedings of UASG. https://doi.org/10.1007/978-3-030-37393-1.

Jamil, F., Kahng, H.K., Kim, S., Kim, D.H., 2021. Towards secure fitness framework based on IoT-enabled blockchain network integrated with machine learning algorithms. Sensors 21 (5), 1640.

Jeong, S., Shen, J.H., Ahn, B., 2021. A study on smart healthcare monitoring using IoT based on blockchain. Wireless Commun. Mobile Comput. 2021, 9. https://doi.org/10.1155/2021/9932091, 9932091.

Johari, R., Kumar, V., Gupta, K., Vidyarthi, D.P., 2021. BLOSOM: BLOckchain Technology for Security of Medical Records. ICT Express.

Kalla, A., Hewa, T., Mishra, R.A., Ylianttila, M., Liyanage, M., 2020. The role of blockchain to fight against COVID-19. IEEE Eng. Manag. Rev. 48 (3), 85–96.

Kapitonov, A., Lonshakov, S., Krupenkin, A., Berman, I., 2017. Blockchain-based Protocol of Autonomous Business Activity for Multi-Agent Systems Consisting of UAVs. 2017 Workshop on Research, Education and Development of Unmanned Aerial Systems (RED-UAS), Linköping, Sweden. October 3–5, 2017.

Khan, A.A., Khan, M.M., Khan, K.M., Arshad, J., Ahmad, F., 2021. A Blockchain-Based Decentralized Machine Learning Framework for Collaborative Intrusion Detection within UAVs. Computer Networks, p. 108217.

Khubrani, M.M., 2021. A framework for blockchain-based smart health system. Turkish J. Comput. Math. Educ. (TURCOMAT) 12 (9), 2609–2614.

Kiran Dash, K., Nayak, B., Kumar Mohanta, B., 2021. An approach to securely store electronic health record (EHR) using blockchain with proxy re-encryption and behavioral analysis. In: Machine Learning and Information Processing: Proceedings of ICMLIP 2020. Springer Singapore, pp. 415–423.

Kosuda, M., Lipovsky, P., Yang, W., Bai, M., Novotnak, J., Szöke, Z., 2020, September. Discussion on blockchain applications in unmanned aerial systems domain. In: 2020 New Trends in Aviation Development (NTAD). IEEE, pp. 142–145.

Kumar, R., Tripathi, R., 2021. Towards design and implementation of security and privacy framework for internet of medical things (IOMT) by leveraging blockchain and IPFS technology. J. Supercomput. 77 (3), 1–40. https://doi.org/10.1007/s11227-020-03570-x.

Kumar, A., Sharma, K., Singh, H., Naugriya, S.G., Gill, S.S., Buyya, R., 2021. A drone-based networked system and methods for combating coronavirus disease (COVID-19) pandemic. Future Generat. Comput. Syst. 115, 1–19.

Liang, W., Ji, N., 2021. Privacy challenges of IoT-based blockchain: a systematic review. Cluster Comput. 1–19.

Ling, G., Draghic, N., 2019. Aerial drones for blood delivery. Transfusion 59 (S2), 1608–1611.

Liu, C., Szirányi, T., 2021. Real-time human detection and gesture recognition for on-board UAV rescue. Sensors 21 (6), 2180.

Lv, Z., Singh, A.K., 2021. Big data analysis of Internet of Things system. ACM Trans. Internet Technol. 21 (2), 1–15.

Maitra, S., Yanambaka, V.P., Puthal, D., Abdelgawad, A., Yelamarthi, K., 2021. Integration of Internet of Things and blockchain toward portability and low-energy consumption. Trans. Emerg. Telecommun. Technol. 32 (6), e4103.

Majeed, U., Khan, L.U., Yaqoob, I., Kazmi, S.A., Salah, K., Hong, C.S., 2021. Blockchain for IoT-based smart cities: recent advances, requirements, and future challenges. J. Netw. Comput. Appl. 103007.

Manu, M.R., Musthafa, N., Menon, D., Sindhu, S., Varma, S., 2021. Blockchain-based health care applications. In: Convergence of Blockchain Technology and E-Business. CRC Press, pp. 141–154.

Marco, A.D., 2018. Case Study: Assessment of the Possibility of Adoption and Impact of Blockchain, IoT and Drones Technology in the Different Types of Last-Mile Delivery. Online. https://webthesis.biblio.polito.it/7276/1/tesi.pdf. Accessed on June 28, 2021.

Martins, R., Duarte, J., Branco, J.C., Teixeira, T., Vasconcelos, S., Fernandes, M., et al., 2021. Book of Abstracts of the 4th Symposium on Occupational Safety and Health. Matternet, 2021. https://mttr.net/. Accessed on June 26, 2021.

McGovern, S., 2020. Blockchain for Unmanned Aircraft Systems (No. DOT-VNTSC-20-04). John A. Volpe National Transportation Systems Center (US).

MD3, 2021. Medical Drone Delivery Database. https://www.updwg.org/wp-content/uploads/2021/06/UPDWG-Medical-Drone-Delivery-Database-June-2021.xlsx. Accessed on June 26, 2021.

Meier, P., Beinke, J.H., Fitte, C., Teuteberg, F., 2021. Generating design knowledge for blockchain-based access control to personal health records. Inf. Syst. E Bus. Manag. 19 (1), 13–41.

Miglani, A., Kumar, N., 2021. Blockchain management and machine learning adaptation for IoT environment in 5G and beyond networks: a systematic review. Comput. Commun. https://doi.org/10.1016/j.comcom.2021.07.009.

Mistry, I., Tanwar, S., Tyagi, S., Kumar, N., 2020. Blockchain for 5G-enabled IoT for industrial automation: a systematic review, solutions, and challenges. Mech. Syst. Signal Process. 135, 106382.

Mourya, A.K., Alankar, B., Kaur, H., 2021. Blockchain technology and its implementation challenges with IoT for healthcare industries. In: Advances in Intelligent Computing and Communication. Springer, Singapore, pp. 221–229.

Nehme, E., El Sibai, R., Abdo, J.B., Taylor, A.R., Demerjian, J., 2021. Converged AI, IoT, and blockchain technologies: a conceptual ethics framework. AI and Ethics 1–15.

Nextwing, 2021. https://flynextwing.com/. Accessed on June 26, 2021.

Nguyen, D.C., Pathirana, P.N., Ding, M., Seneviratne, A., 2020. Blockchain for 5G and beyond networks: a state of the art survey. J. Netw. Comput. Appl. 102693.

Panda, S.S., Jena, D., Mohanta, B.K., Ramasubbareddy, S., Daneshmand, M., Gandomi, A.H., 2021. Authentication and key management in distributed IoT using blockchain technology. IEEE Internet Things J. https://doi.org/10.1109/JIOT.2020.3008906.

Pathak, N., Mukherjee, A., Misra, S., 2021. AerialBlocks: blockchain-enabled UAV virtualization for industrial IoT. IEEE Internet Things Mag. 4 (1), 72–77.

Pavithran, D., Al-Karaki, J.N., Shaalan, K., 2021. Edge-based blockchain architecture for event-driven IoT using hierarchical identity based encryption. Inf. Process. Manag. 58 (3), 102528.

Pawar, P., Parolia, N., Shinde, S., Edoh, T.O., Singh, M., 2021. eHealthChain—a blockchain-based personal health information management system. Ann. Telecommun. 1—13.

Philip, N.Y., Rodrigues, J.J., Wang, H., Fong, S.J., Chen, J., 2021. Internet of Things for in-home health monitoring systems: current advances, challenges and future directions. IEEE J. Sel. Area. Commun. 39 (2), 300—310.

Phoenix, 2021. https://www.phoenixairunmanned.com/. Accessed on June 26, 2021.

Quantum, 2021. https://www.quantum-systems.com/. Accessed on June 26, 2021.

Rabah, K., 2018. Convergence of AI, IoT, big data and blockchain: a review. Lake Inst. J. 1 (1), 1—18.

Rahman, M.A., Hossain, M.S., Showail, A.J., Alrajeh, N.A., Alhamid, M.F., 2021. A secure, private, and explainable IoHT framework to support sustainable health monitoring in a smart city. Sustain. Cities Soc. 103083.

Ratta, P., Kaur, A., Sharma, S., Shabaz, M., Dhiman, G., 2021. Application of blockchain and internet of things in healthcare and medical sector: applications, challenges, and future perspectives. J. Food Qual. 2021, 20. https://doi.org/10.1155/2021/7608296, 7608296.

Ray, P.P., 2017. An introduction to dew computing: definition, concept and implications. IEEE Access 6, 723—737.

Ray, P.P., Nguyen, K., August 2020. A review on blockchain for medical delivery drones in 5G-IoT era: progress and challenges. In: 2020 IEEE/CIC International Conference on Communications in China (ICCC Workshops). IEEE, pp. 29—34.

Razdan, S., Sharma, S., 2021. Internet of Medical Things (IoMT): Overview, Emerging Technologies, and Case Studies. IETE Technical Review, pp. 1—14.

Reinert, J., Corser, G., March 2021. Classification of blockchain implementation in mobile electronic health records and internet of medical things devices research. In: SoutheastCon 2021. IEEE, pp. 01—05.

Ribeiro, R., Ramos, J., Safadinho, D., Reis, A., Rabadão, C., Barroso, J., Pereira, A., 2021. Web AR solution for UAV pilot training and usability testing. Sensors 21 (4), 1456.

Rigitech, 2021. UAV for Payload Delivery Working Group. https://www.updwg.org/md3/. Accessed on June 26, 2021.

Rominger, K.R., DeNittis, A., Meyer, S.E., 2021. Using drone imagery analysis in rare plant demographic studies. J. Nat. Conserv. 126020.

Sadeeq, M.A., Zeebaree, S., 2021. Energy management for internet of things via distributed systems. J. Appl. Sci. Technol. Trends 2 (02), 59—71.

Santos, J.A., Inácio, P.R., Silva, B.M., 2021. Towards the use of blockchain in mobile health services and applications. J. Med. Syst. 45 (2), 1—10.

Saraf, V., Senapati, L., Swarnkar, T., 2021. Application and progress of drone technology in the COVID-19 pandemic: a comprehensive review. Comput. Model. Data Anal. COVID-19 Res. 47—66.

Saranya, S., 2021. Go-win: COVID-19 vaccine supply chain smart management system using BlockChain, IoT and cloud technologies. Turkish J. Comput. Math. Educ. (TURCOMAT) 12 (12), 1460—1464.

Saxena, S., Bhushan, B., Ahad, M.A., 2021. Blockchain based solutions to secure IoT: background, integration trends and a way forward. J. Netw. Comput. Appl. 103050.

SDU, 2021. https://www.sdu.dk/en/forskning/sduuascenter. Accessed on June 26, 2021.

Serrano, W., 2021. The blockchain random neural network for cybersecure IoT and 5G infrastructure in smart cities. J. Netw. Comput. Appl. 175, 102909.

Sharma, P., Jindal, R., Borah, M.D., 2021. Healthify: a blockchain-based distributed application for health care. In: Applications of Blockchain in Healthcare. Springer, Singapore, pp. 171—198.

Shuaib, M., Alam, S., Alam, M.S., Nasir, M.S., 2021. Compliance with HIPAA and GDPR in blockchain-based electronic health record. Mater. Today Proc. https://doi.org/10.1016/j.matpr.2021.03.059.

Shukla, S., Thakur, S., Hussain, S., Breslin, J.G., Jameel, S.M., 2021. Identification and Authentication in Healthcare Internet-Of-Things Using Integrated Fog Computing Based Blockchain Model. Internet of Things, p. 100422.

Shynu, P.G., Menon, V.G., Kumar, R.L., Kadry, S., Nam, Y., 2021. Blockchain-based secure healthcare application for diabetic-cardio disease prediction in fog computing. IEEE Access 9, 45706−45720.

Singh, S., Sharma, P.K., Yoon, B., Shojafar, M., Cho, G.H., Ra, I.H., 2020. Convergence of blockchain and artificial intelligence in IoT network for the sustainable smart city. Sustain. Cities Soc. 63, 102364.

Singh, P., Masud, M., Hossain, M.S., Kaur, A., 2021. Cross-domain secure data sharing using blockchain for industrial IoT. J. Parallel Distr. Comput. 156, 176−184. https://doi.org/10.1016/j.jpdc.2021.05.007.

Soni, M., Singh, D.K., 2021. Blockchain-based security & privacy for biomedical and healthcare information exchange systems. Mater. Today: Proc. https://doi.org/10.1016/j.matpr.2021.04.105X.

Sujihelen, L., June 2021. A study on blockchain and the healthcare system. In: 2021 5th International Conference on Trends in Electronics and Informatics (ICOEI). IEEE, pp. 518−521.

Svedin, J., Bernland, A., Gustafsson, A., Claar, E., Luong, J., 2021. Small UAV-based SAR system using low-cost radar, position, and attitude sensors with onboard imaging capability. Int. J. Microw. Wirel. Technol. 1−12.

Swoop, 2021. https://swoop.aero/. Accessed on June 26, 2021.

Thiels, C.A., Aho, J.M., Zietlow, S.P., Jenkins, D.H., 2015. Use of unmanned aerial vehicles for medical product transport. Air Med. J. 34 (2), 104−108.

Tarr, A.A., Perera, A.G., Chahl, J., Chell, C., Ogunwa, T., Paynter, K., 2021. Drones—healthcare, humanitarian efforts and recreational use. In: Drone Law and Policy. Routledge, pp. 35−54.

UAV, 2021. https://uavfactory.com/. Accessed on June 26, 2021.

UPDWG, 2021. UAV for Payload Delivery Working Group. https://www.updwg.org/md3/. Accessed on June 26, 2021.

Vayu, 2021. https://vaayudrones.com/. Accessed on June 26, 2021.

Velmurugadass, P., Dhanasekaran, S., Anand, S.S., Vasudevan, V., 2021. Enhancing Blockchain security in cloud computing with IoT environment using ECIES and cryptography hash algorithm. Mater. Today: Proc. 37, 2653−2659.

Vertical, 2021. https://www.deltaquad.com/. Accessed on June 26, 2021.

Wingcopter, 2021. https://wingcopter.com/. Accessed on June 26, 2021.

Wu, Y., Dai, H.N., Wang, H., Choo, K.K.R., 2021. Blockchain-based privacy preservation for 5g-enabled drone communications. IEEE Netw. 35 (1), 50−56.

Xu, Q., Chen, X., Li, S., Zhang, H., Babar, M.A., Tran, N.K., December 2020. Blockchain-based solutions for IoT: a tertiary study. In: 2020 IEEE 20th International Conference on Software Quality, Reliability and Security Companion (QRS-C). IEEE, pp. 124−131.

Xu, B., Xu, L.D., Wang, Y., Cai, H., 2021. A distributed dynamic authorisation method for Internet+ medical & healthcare data access based on consortium blockchain. Enterprise Inf. Syst. 1−19.

Yang, X., Yang, X., Yi, X., Khalil, I., Zhou, X., He, D., et al., 2021. Blockchain-based secure and lightweight authentication for internet of things. IEEE Internet Things J. https://doi.org/10.1109/JIOT.2021.3098007.

Yaqoob, I., Salah, K., Jayaraman, R., Al-Hammadi, Y., 2021. Blockchain for healthcare data management: opportunities, challenges, and future recommendations. Neural Comput. Appl. 1–16.

Yu, Y., Barthaud, D., Price, B.A., Bandara, A.K., Zisman, A., Nuseibeh, B., 2019. LiveBox: a self-adaptive forensic-ready service for drones. IEEE Access 7, 148401–148412.

Zipline, 2021. https://flyzipline.com/. Accessed on June 26, 2021.

CHAPTER 7

Blockchain for digital rights management

Ramani S[1], Sri Vishva E[1], Lakshit Dua[1], Arya Abrol[1] and Marimuthu Karuppiah[2]

[1]School of Computer Science and Engineering, Vellore Institute of Technology, Vellore, Tamil Nadu, India; [2]Department of Computer Science and Engineering, SRM Institute of Science and Technology, Delhi-NCR Campus, Ghaziabad, Uttar Pradesh, India

1. Introduction

The emergence of the internet has brought in a huge number of resources in the form of information and sources of entertainment. Apart from being a hub for social media and communication gateway, it also acts as a source of virtual technology, giving a better experience to the users all around. Even though it acts as a revolution in its own way, it possesses certain disadvantages. The availability of millions of resources on the internet gives users a way to copy and share content as well as falsely providing ownership for the same. This increases the chances of piracy and a waste of talent and recognition to the real owners. Apart from massive availability of resources, it is equally important to add a layer of protection over the content available, so the internet becomes a safe place to share authentic content and provide desirable recognition.

One of the most important ways to curb the issue of piracy on the internet is digital rights management (DRM). DRM is a process of combining different secure technologies to provide protection to the owners and secure their ownership rights. It provides certain rules and guidelines across all forms of digitized content, mainly regarding the process of distribution and sharing. The data are converted into different formats and are flagged in such a way that they are available only to trustworthy devices and users. This prevents unauthorized users from being able to access content and illegally share precious digital content. These guidelines can also restrict useful processes such as backup maintenance, accessing the content of different devices by the same owner, and so on.

Blockchain Technology for Emerging Applications
ISBN 978-0-323-90193-2
https://doi.org/10.1016/B978-0-323-90193-2.00010-7
177

DRM is the technology that inhibits piracy and unauthorized use of right-protected material. DRM is applied on all levels of software and hardware from company logos to artistic works, digital sound, images, etc. (Ma et al., 2018a,b).

In recent times, digital rights management systems (DRMS) have become more useful and proven themself time and again effective in various fields of digital technology production, development, and distribution. When the first DRM was discussed in the early 21st century, there was not clear guidance on what is defined as digital content and the law related with it, but as we now use more and more proprietary technology, the laws have become stringent, leading to a clear set of standard guiding procedures.

At first DRMSs were being applied only to research papers, blueprints, and information systems, but now, DRMSs are being employed beyond these industries.

Nowadays, DRMSs could be applied to most of the hardware components as the designs are made using digital technology. In the case of agricultural technology, John Deere used the Digital Millennium Copyright Act (Congress, 1998) to prevent local mechanics from recreating their fairly simple machinery parts. The world of DRM goes hand in hand with the intellectual property rights and finance sector. DRM management, often not discussed elaborately, is really important in the case of research and development, especially in the fields of science, engineering, technology, and medicine.

DRMS is one of the fastest growing technologies employed. The recent development of peer-to-peer (P2P) file sharing systems based on IPFS and blockchain technology (Vimal and Srivatsa, 2019), such as Torrents sites piracy, has become a huge aggravation for digital content creators. The digital content creation industry is expected to have market cap of USD 397,390 million by 2026 (Swatman et al., 2006). This figure does not include the mainstream digital content industries such as entertainment, e-books, patents, etc., but by including, the monetary value involved would reach a huge figure, proving that there should a much more secure way of handling DRM.

In the COVID-19 scenario, as more and more businesses are being carried out over the internet, there is more possibility of internet theft. This is where we should hugely rely on the technology of blockchain.

Having discussed the intricacies of DRM systems from the origin of such systems to current applications, we can clearly make out that as technology of both content creation and digital piracy moves forward, we need a more trusted model of rights verification that is able to build up flexible storage to meet enormous demand for content around the world, and obviously has a robust DRM protection scheme for fast identity verification and a conditional useful feature for tracing violations back to the original source of the content leak. Apart from these very apparent benefits of said P2P DRM system, another benefit will come to the customer's side. They will have an indefinite access to content that they purchase even after the content serving organization has been shut down.

2. Illustrations

To make DRM safe and efficient, it is very important to integrate the same with blockchain technology. This new process of using DRM with blockchain is also being introduced by many companies to protect copyrighted content. As bad as videos of unlawful distribution of rights in the blockchain and the loss of record-keeping rights have gotten, some new concepts have been introduced using the DRM blockchain.

A visual distribution system is introduced such as a blockchain and a functional version. A distributed blockchain-based license was also implemented and designed, but there was a flaw that the platform should have high performance to manage the top acquisition keys simultaneously.

The blockchain-based DRMS was proposed, but the design was not holonomic because only transaction details were recorded in the blockchain. After DRM analysis and DRM requirements came the DRM blockchain-based system, which supports ownership and privacy protection and conditional management compliance. The state-of-the-art machine is used to build a naming and storage system and to install crowds based on blocks where it helps to build a blockchain-based DRM platform.

2.1 Cryptocurrencies

Blockchain science can go hand in hand with the introduction of digital currency, which can add the economic layer to the blockchain. This 'scientific science" can be used to make micropayments to publishers who do not feed their content. It can also bring rewards for scientific work, such as peer review, statistical support, laboratory exchanges, the release of specific research, or hosting of data. Finally, initial coin donations, a form of refund using cryptocurrencies, can be used to fund all research projects. In this way, the crypto economy can be transformed into a science that shows value suitability for multiple jobs.

2.2 Content distribution and DRM

The role of the blockchain has been largely researched (i.e., nonacademic), where online migration has led to a change in the distribution of revenue from content creators and publishers to hosting companies, communications giants, and advertising consultants. To some extent, this change is due to the natural feature of the World Wide Web, namely the use of hyperlinks.

Hyperlinks are one-way content links: they do not point back to users who click them. Therefore, there is no way to allow small automatic payments (micropayments) to be used. Given this, the only options for publishers are to either open content and support business modelling in advertising or to place unpaid payments on expensive credit card bills. Micropayments can also create another way for business models prominent in educational publishing (subscriptions and open access), each coming with its own challenges.

2.3 Storing research data

The low-blockchain environment paves the way for the creation of a database for research activities from all research environments that can be shared collaboratively. Although creating this database is technically possible with current database technology, there is a requirement from the central gatekeeper as well. The owner of such a data store makes its fulfilment less likely. This low-level data store will show that whenever a researcher, for example, uploads data, performs statistical analysis, writes and presents an article, or reviews a manuscript, this will be automatically tracked and recorded, researched, and very productive. The risk of fraud will also be reduced. In addition, it will be repeated. It is much easier to gather reliable and complete data on the performance of research, so researchers, as well as universities, can allow for the construction of higher and more reliable metrics more. In addition, it will allow metrics to be based on tasks that are not yet fully developed (e.g., peer review).

3. DRM requirement

Over the ages the evolution in techniques of producing content and distribution of the same in general has gradually become simpler for both consumer and producer. Earlier, to listen to music, one had to visit a music store nearby and purchase a cassette loaded with the songs or their choice and had to purchase a cassette player to play the song. Today it takes a matter of seconds to download and listen to songs through a mobile phone and the wonderful possibilities of an internet connection. In the traditional case of DRM, it mainly focuses on preventing illegal usage of digital content without paying any monetary benefit to the concerned content creator.

There was a physical aspect that the content and rights of the content once sold did not provide the creator a lasting benefit but rather only a one-time payment, the rest going to the middlemen that distributed the content. Once the content gets encrypted, there is no possibility for auditing the content in it. In recent times, as distribution of content has crossed physical barriers, the need for verification of content and the credibility of the creator has tremendously increased. For example, to prevent underage kids from watching movies with violence, illegal, or sexual content in them, thereby enforcing proper certification of movies, verification of authenticity of online distribution sources is needed since the internet in all of its glory is a free space to trade and distribute such content and much more (Karuppiah and Saravanan, 2014, 2015; Karuppiah et al., 2016, 2017, 2019; Kumari et al., 2016; Naeem et al., 2020; Maria et al., 2021; Pradhan et al., 2018; Li et al., 2017). Many such scenarios give rise to a new set of security and requirements in DRM as follows:

- content verifiability along with tamper proofness
- privacy of identity for digital content provider
- protecting the access of content
- usage control of content
- trademarking and licensing
- detection of violation

3.1 Content verifiability along with tamper proofness

Content made available for public purchase has to go through some legal procedures and audit before being hosted on a public platform. It has to follow rules such as the platform specifying that the content be verifiable as well as auditable. It should also be made clear to the platform's owners and distributors what clear track was taken to acquire the content, as a sequence of how it exchanged hands or the chain of custody of the content being uploaded.

Once it has been verified that the content has been acquired from a legal source, it is then checked thoroughly for vulgarity in accordance to content distribution acts. If the content is being reported as abuse or vulgar the hosting platform must be in position to hold the creator accountable for this, to prove that tamper-proof evidence is required. This eliminates any future need to detect and seal leaks of content as the content acquired is ultimately leak-proof since no party can exchange ownership by simply downloading and tampering with creator metadata.

3.2 Privacy of identity for digital content provider

The rights management system must be in a position to prevent an adversary from exploiting the privacy and access of the user. It must also be in position to hold a user accountable for his action like spreading abuses, rumors, violence, hate speech, etc. In general, there should not be any bias toward anyone in the system.

3.3 Protecting the access of content

Before the content is uploaded to hosting platforms, it must have some protection to prevent piracy and to prevent someone else claiming the credit for another's work. Usually, cryptographic encryption or watermarking is done to ensure this.

3.4 Usage control of content

As the access to content is prevented, it should include sophisticated management mechanisms for further usage of content and also to track its usage.

3.5 Trademarking and licensing

When a user uses the content available in the hosting platform, he/she agrees to the terms and conditions of the license under which the content is published. The license specifies the terms such as usage times, period, domain, rental, translation, or watermark that defines the ownership of the content.

3.6 Detection of violation

During the usage of the content, the user should always be bound by the terms and conditions specified by the license. The DRMS should be in a position to monitor and track when violation happens.

4. Parts of a traditional DRM

A traditional DRM system has multiple components that have immense functionalities that need to be properly understood. The main components of a traditional DRM system are as follows (Fig. 7.1).

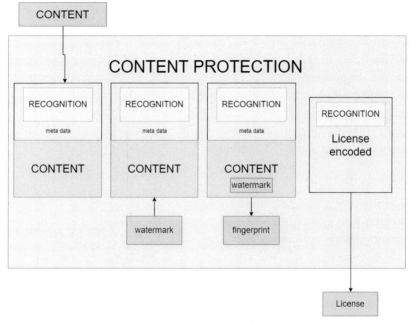

Figure 7.1 Components of a DRM.

4.1 Content recognizer

The main property of a content recognizer is to remain consistent. It is often said, even if the rights of the content change, the content recognizer should always remain consistent. To maintain consistency and generate persistent systems, the content recognizer uses standard identification schemes for numbering and copyrighting such as International Standard Book Number (ISBN), International Standard Serial Number, and Digital Object Identifier System, etc.

4.2 Meta data

The meta data include different schemes that are used also with the content recognizer to provide more insight about the content and how to access the information.

4.3 Watermark

A watermark is another important technology to prevent the unauthorized access and copying of data and for identifying and tracking data. Most watermarks use a traditional approach to use lower amplitude signals that are inserted into the content directly. The watermark can be easily identified using different methods that can be correlated by authorized hardware and software stores.

This technology helps to easily detect copies of data being sold illegally that are not properly protected from such kinds of attacks. However, it is very important to ensure that the watermarks injected into the content do not hamper the content and are not easily identifiable by hackers and attackers. It is also important to detect and remove fake and falsely added watermarks from authentic content.

4.4 Fingerprints

Fingerprints are generally used to address data based on its content by matching it to components of data stores or databases. It is very different from watermarks in many ways:

- Watermarks get injected into the system, whereas fingerprints do not get injected, so they do not change any content.
- Watermarks require the availability of content to get injected; fingerprints do not need the content to be available.
- If any kind of changes in the content take place the watermarks need to be properly processed again over the data as well as all copies that are distributed across the internet, which is not at all required in fingerprints.
- Fingerprints need to be stored for any kind of new content that is to be added in the database, which is not required in watermarks.

4.5 Containers

Containers provide security for the content. They use different algorithms like hashing algorithms to secure the content. The digital certificates coupled along with these encryption algorithms also help in providing confidentiality for the data.

4.6 Security licenses

These are used by users specially to mention their authoritative laws and rights that guarantee integrity of the content. The security license is only available to a particular device and is not easily transferred to any other device.

4.7 EUP

End user player (EUP) is another component of the DRM. It acts as a way to make the rights of the user to the content digitally available across the network. It is used to restrict any kind of actions to the content by the ones accessing the content. These components act as the backbone of the DRM technology and also help in providing security, integrity, confidentiality, and secure availability of the content across the internet. Even after so many layers of protection, DRM technology still has loopholes that make it desirable to use blockchain along with it to increase security of content.

5. Compatibility of blockchain for DRM

5.1 Immutability

Immutability is one of the most important properties of blockchain. It states that the blockchain technology is permanent and write-only. Every node maintains a copy of the ledger, so if some new content is being added or updated, every node has to check the validity of it and add it to the ledger. This makes sure that DRM is transparent and free of corruption. A public blockchain can be used in case of public DRM, whereas enterprises can use private or consortium blockchain for ensuring privacy from outsiders and maintaining its inner transparency.

5.2 Decentralized

A decentralized network means that it does not have any governing authority or single person on top; rather a group of nodes maintains the blockchain, making it decentralized. We can store content, as we have direct access over it with our private key. The decentralized network ensures that everyone has equal rights and power regarding their assets. This ensures that our chain experiences less failure, good user control, is less prone to break down, has no third-party, zero scams, and has a high level of transparency and authentic nature. This is key for a nonbiased DRM.

5.3 Enhanced security

As we have gotten rid of central authority, it just does not mean that anyone can modify the characteristics of DRM. Usage of cryptographic hash functions adds a layer of security. We know that hashing is irreversible, so if an adversary wants to destroy the DRM chain, he/she would have to modify all data stored on every block of every node in the network. There could be billions of people, where every individual has the same copy of the ledger. Updating the hash in millions of computers is next to impossible and costly.

5.4 Distributed ledger

Usually a distributed ledger will provide all the information about a transaction and its user, thereby ensuring fairness in the system. Because of this distributed power of computing across the computers a better outcome is ensured. This helps the DRM to achieve no malicious changes, managership, and quick response.

5.5 Consensus

Every DRM blockchain is powered because of the consensus algorithms. The architecture is essentially designed, and consensus algorithms are the core for this architecture. Consensus in blockchain makes it essential for the decision-making process. This takes care of choosing the next node and repairing its earlier mistakes. This consensus algorithm is responsible for maintaining the trustworthiness of the DRM chain.

5.6 Faster responses

Traditional hosting platforms are quite slow. Sometimes it can take days to process an upload and get benefits from it. It also can easily be corrupted. Blockchain provides a faster approach compared to traditional DRM systems. This way a user performs uploading relatively faster, which saves a lot of time in the long run.

With all the aforementioned advantages, blockchain is a perfect companion to DRMS. Generally the effect of blockchain impacts the way in which the digital world works to another level (Singh and Kumar Tripathi, 2019) (Fig. 7.2).

6. Various cryptographic hash functions in blockchain

6.1 MD5 algorithm

The MD5 algorithmic function, also called the MD5 message digest algorithm, was invented in the late 1990s by mathematician Ronal Rivest. It is the successor to the MD4 algorithm and proves to be much more effective as well as efficient. At first, it was only employed to be used as a crypto hash, but it was found to suffer from vulnerabilities so extensive that a relatively weak machine was able to crack it and produce collisions in polynomial time. However, now widely used as a checksum algorithm to prevent an advisory changing the content of the blockchain, it still is suitable for other noncryptographic applications and for operations with regard to partitioned databases.

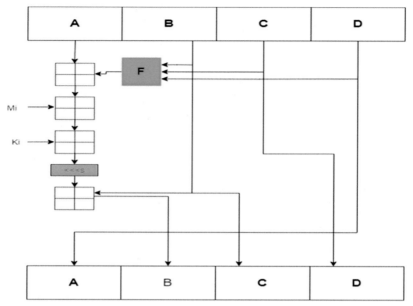

Figure 7.2 MD5 algorithm working.

Talking about suffering from vulnerabilities, what are these and how does MD5 perform in relation to them? Hash functions employed in cryptography are considered powerful based on many features, one of them being their property to not feasibly produce multiple messages with similar hash values.

A collision attack can usually find the solution in seconds of the MD5 hash. With advancement of the off-the-shelf GPU and TPU the complexity to find the collision is tremendously reduced. It took 218 operations to find the collision. It is still widely used for simple use cases even after the warnings by cybersecurity experts and is mostly depreciated.

6.2 SHA-0 algorithm

The SHA-0 hashing function produces a 160-bit hash value. The hash values are then given to a digital signature algorithm (DSA), which then authenticates or generates the signature for the hash values that are fed into it. It was first published as a message digest algorithm and was much more effective than its predecessor MD series.

A collision usually can be found in 261 operations; later improvised attacks found collisions in 236 operations. The US National Institute of

Standards and Technology stopped recommending SHA-0 from the year 1996. Although the use of SHA-0 is highly discouraged, researchers are still working on SHA-0 as it is predecessor of SHA-1.

6.3 SHA-1 algorithm

The SHA-1 hashing algorithm function generates a 160-bit hash value. It proved to be better than its predecessor SHA-0. It was designed by a US federal agency and then made open. Google published that it has made successful collision attacks on SHA-1. At last, it took 263 operations to find the collision. It took equivalent to the computing power of 6500 years on a CPU and 110 years on a single GPU computation. Theoretically speaking, SHAttered attack is 100,000 times faster than the brute force attack used to perform a collision attack on the SHA-1 algorithm. The NSIT and other cybersecurity experts have depreciated its use on any collision avoidance requirements.

6.4 SHA-2 algorithm

The SHA-2 has similar hash functions with varied block sizes, such as SHA-256 with 32-byte words and SHA-512 with 64-byte words. It consists of SHA-244, SHA-256, SHA-384, SHA-512, SHA-512/224, and SHA-512/256. SHA-2 hash function is widely used in security applications and protocols including TLS, SSL, PGP, and IPsec. It uses from 64 to 80 rounds of cryptography operations, and it is commonly used to validate and sign digital security certificates and documents.

6.5 SHA-256 algorithm

This algorithm is used to get a constant 256 bit every time. It is the algorithm that is used in blockchain technology. The complexity of this algorithm is 2211.5. This hash function's collision resistance complexity is highly important for the security of this DRMS using blockchain (Fig 7.3).

7. Methodologies and technology in use

Some of the blockchain technologies for DRM are as follows.

The blockchain system is being used to manage and protect rights of videos and graphics, as stated by Kishigami in their paper (Watanabe et al., 2016). This helps users to manage copyrights and maintain permissions to use graphics and other content. To view the content, the client should not be offline and should also have a transaction ID to decrypt the content.

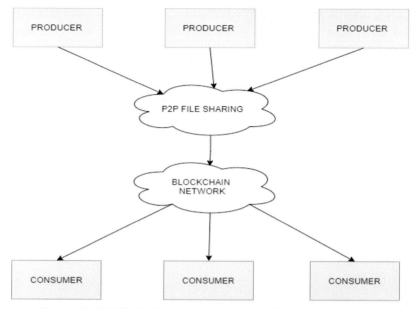

Figure 7.3 P2P file sharing architecture using blockchain technology.

Blockchain technology is also used to validate the license of software applications. There are mainly two methods of blockchain for validation processes. First is the master model of Bitcoin, helping the user to store more information like time limit of expiry, etc. The other model, called the Bespoke model, is used for one user having one license. This technology will be further used for holders having multiple licenses available.

The ownership of image records is also performed using blockchain technology. The records are stored in the form of timestamps and other services, which helps in storing the information of the image owner. A machine learning algorithm is used to find out images being used in different websites without the permission of the owner.

The Ethereum blockchain technology is used in copyrighting music content. Copyrighting involves protecting payments, music compositions, owner rights, distribution rights, and most importantly production costs. Peer music is another technology being used for music copyrighting for the peer tracks. The muse blockchain being used here provides cryptocurrency to different users on the basis of consumption by different content creators and music artists.

DECENT is a customized blockchain technology that uses delegative proof of stake for distributing content. It helps to create a system where content is rated and cannot be changed or modified. It builds custom tokens allowing the artists to create further methods for earning cryptocurrency.

8. Effects and applications of using blockchain in DRM

8.1 Effects

8.1.1 Discoverability of copyrights

Users can query for different copyrights and their history in blockchain. This can be done with the help of unique identifiers that will be used for identification. Collection of the copyright history will help to deduce a route of ownership rights.

8.1.2 Privacy

The specifics of production copyrights are only present securely with the owner. Cryptography technology states that the content present in them cannot be retrieved using a hash digest in a copyright record. Hence, the detailed content present in the design can be protected.

8.1.3 Efficient method

The authorization of the copyrights using the blockchain consensus algorithms is very efficient. In the Bitcoin network, where the processing speed is considered relatively low, it takes about a week to complete all the copyright registrations for the whole year. This is relatively lower in comparison to the present methods of copyright management.

8.1.4 Maintenance of security and fairness of copyright trading

If anyone tries to provide false information while registering for a copyright, fraudulent evidence left will definitely get caught by the blockchain technology. In this case, the buyer will get punished by authorities for the fraud records and information provided by them using their digital signatures. Fraudulent copyright records are not protected. The use of blockchain will hence guarantee the fairness and security in copyright management. It will also help in maintaining authenticity of copyrights to a certain extent.

8.1.5 Protection from repetitive registrations

If a user registers the same work multiple times, it will generate multiple IDs for the same work. Even though he will have multiple copies of his work, the person will not be able to sell the work again and again, thus stealing the work recognition that has been sold once. The repeated trading of the same work, on the contrary, will leave digital evidence of piracy in the blockchain technology.

8.1.6 Default in reception

Copyrighted data can be obtained by the buyer only when he sends the private key and then receives its delivery and decrypts it. If the buyer has not requested the decryption and delivery, the actual information will never be retrieved through any other method. Therefore, the security of the information can be provided. A buyer sets a contract to set a deadline to sign for delivery and decrypt it. If the deadline is not met, the default process will get started.

8.2 Applications

8.2.1 Educational learning passports

Today, with the development and increase in the number of sources available to learn, it is difficult to maintain records of all the lifelong learnings and achievements. Blockchain technology with DRM integration can be used to permanently store achievements, certifications, and records digitally in the form of educational passports, which will act as a proof of educational experience for individuals. The advent of educational passports with unique identification factors will help increase the value of certifications and additional educational skills that can be acquired by an individual (Guo et al., 2019).

8.2.2 Multimedia community of educational resources

Blockchain technology can also be used as a measure to maintain rights and security of educational resources, thus creating a secure community of educational resources by authorized and experienced people in the industry. Learners will also be able to securely share their learning resources through the multimedia community as educational creators, which will further help to increase availability of educational resources (Van Rossum, 2018).

8.2.3 Copyrighting multimedia works

The application of blockchain technology can also be extended to apply to protection and digital rights maintenance of multimedia works, which will help in developing a web of diverse multimedia resources and their digital rights maintenance. Law and technology have a tedious relationship. In recent times, with the boom of development in technology, development in legal fields is being accelerated, while the technology is also being shaped because of law. The development of law for copyrights proves these efforts as its enforcement and development are usually closely inspired by the technologic state of the art. With the emergence and ease of use of blockchain technology and blockchain-based contracts, some people perceive a recent wave of technical transmutation that could have a long-standing impact on copyright law. Indeed, it is recommended that these technologies help us to provide new technologic mechanisms for the sole purpose of managing the intellectual property rights that can now be implemented in current scenarios with a wave of development in over-the-top media services (Cho and Jeong, 2019).

8.2.4 DRM in the music industry

Blockchain technology can offer solutions to problems inside the music industry that are often reported by artists, composers, and producers. The technology may not be able to help solve all the problems, but it may show a way out of the current problem between artists and middlemen by getting rid of the outdated and old procedure. This will help an artist to show their original content without any hesitation, enabling a more secure way of licensing their work and having their copyrights properly secured.

Blockchain may help in transforming the music industry, such as challenging the economic models and bringing about a more equal place for all artists, not just record labels and production houses.

8.2.5 Blockchain and copyright law

At its core, blockchain is in fact a shared and in sync database that is supported by an algorithm, and there are multiple nodes involved in this ecosystem, where each node contains an exact copy of the complete database. The blockchain achieves a high level of resilience since every node has a copy of the blockchain, whereby even if one node gets corrupted, we can be sure that the chain remains intact. In such cases the possibility of a single point of failure is avoided. The technology derives its name from the fact that it is ordered as a chain of individual blocks. Every block comprises the transactions that happen during the digital media being procured, maintained, and delivered. Every transaction is transformed into a block as it reaches a certain size; this gets appended to the existing ledger by a process of hashing. Not just any node can append their block; as mentioned earlier, a node proposes a block, which is displayed to every other block in the ecosystem. Then a node assumes a role of miner, which plays a key role in hash generation (Savelyev, 2018).

The blocks contain different important components in them including a timestamp, a hash of the previous block (which creates a chain of sequential blocks of transaction in chronological order), and the hash of all transactions contained in the block (its "fingerprint"). Since only data can be added to the blockchain, we can safely say that it is only an appending data structure.

There are actually quite a few different flavors of blockchain based on their technicality and governing constraints: "private and permission" and "public and nonpermission." In a public chain, any individual can download the ledger and start using it. The transaction is open to the public. This provides more transparency but also comes with a disadvantage of less privacy. In the case of private chains, it is the opposite: there is an authentication process before anyone can use the chain, which provides more privacy. The private chain is sometimes called an enterprise chain. In the case of using blockchain in DRM, a combination of both would be fruitful (O'Dwyer, 2020).

Simply, a narrative smart contract is a set of self-executing programs that process input as it gets triggered. It is a small set of computer scripts that are deployed in blockchain. As smart contracts are currently being discussed alongside blockchain, similar techniques have been used by DRM for a long time. As we mentioned earlier, DRM implants copyright law into the digital content by suppressing the user's ability to copy, view, print, play, or other works. For example, audio files embedded with DRM technology are not subjected to the double spending attack because they consist of a basic smart contract, which references a centralized web network (for example, Spotify's server programmed to enforce the terms and conditions of the application).

The blockchain technology in copyright law mainly works around the following basic logic: 1. There is the ability to identify digital content and monitor it, thereby protecting the fluidity of the document. 2. The idea is to promote transparency and disintermediate the occurrence of transactions. 3. There is the ability of blockchain to be adapted as a DRMS.

The early origins of blockchain and DRM are quite distinct. The first was developed as a P2P network for the Bitcoin community. Nevertheless, as tension arose between DRM and copyright law, a similar case is likely bound to happen between blockchain and blockchain contracts. This is an important point that we have to remember. Distributed ledger technology (DLT) is still immature and can be easily molded. The further development also lies in configuration of DLT chosen for implementation. There is also a minor danger that we might lose the public policy aspect of blockchain, like DRM, which must be taken into mind during development (Finck and Moscon, 2019).

9. Methodologies for coupling DRM with blockchain

9.1 Blockchain implementation in the design industry (Lu et al., 2019)

Design works of the digital age need to be protected by digital technology, but this proposition fails ahead of advanced copying and piracy techniques, posing challenges for protection of copyrights.

Digital watermarking of content as earlier discussed coupled with encryption of content treated as a whole is common among DRM systems for protection and verification. Using these methods not only provides ease and moderate security, but it is quick and can be built into the content distribution software with no separate infrastructure.

Apart from the security concern of the usage of this method, watermarking and encryption of software pose other risks such as no protection against unintentional leakage or difficulty in presentation to potential buyers. These problems are the most common in the design industry (Lu et al., 2019).

Proposal for a blockchain-based system to be coupled with DRM is easy in theory as all there is to it is a blockchain with rights information as well as a record of transactions. The actual system though is not as simple to implement. Every other type of digital content like photographs, music, video, etc., will require a complete overhaul of the system.

Talking about methodologies adopted for a blockchain-based DRM system, there has been significant work in the past. DRMChain (Lu et al., 2019), being the most noteworthy, utilizes two separate BAIs or blockchain application interfaces, similar to application program interfaces, that help applications to interact with underlying hardware through a series of calls as instructions to store relevant metadata of the digital content.

DRMChain makes smart use of the BAIs, one to store the direct summary information of the data and the other to store the summary of the cipher produced for the data. As expected, digital content can be huge, so a flexible external storage space for the original and cipher content is also proposed with hash IDs of content automatically linked to the relevant block in the blockchain.

DRMChain comes out to be a very secure and fast system with verifiability and usage control as main priorities. It applies multi–signature–based traceability approaches, ensuring efficiency in retrieval of constraint and consumer transaction lists from the blockchain to gather free or paid consumption record history.

9.2 Scalability in blockchains (Garba et al., 2020)

Another popular model of a blockchain-based DRM system utilizing overlay networks to enhance the scalability and speed of the system has been proposed (Garba et al., 2020).

Decentralization, security, and lastly, scalability have been identified as key essential features of blockchain technology, but achievement of only two out of these three crucial features in modern day blockchain applications is seen. Scalability is clearly neglected in today's first-generation blockchain technology, which suffers from immeasurable transaction costs to high energy consumption both in the computation and power contexts.

High latency with visibly slow throughput also riddles these applications. Overlay networks are used in this type of implementation that are different from the legacy implementations using small, centralized networks to transport blocks over the whole system. An overlay network implements cluster heads that blindly forward the block that is given to them by cluster nodes. There are multiple clusters with innumerable number of nodes each with a cluster head.

Nodes in a cluster can transport their blocks to the cluster heads or to their neighboring nodes and then send them indirectly to the cluster heads, ensuring no discrimination by the cluster heads in transporting blocks. The blocks are encrypted and the key to encryption is only made visible to the network once the block has been received successfully at the destination node.

9.3 Proof of stake consensus methodology (Watanabe et al., 2016)

As the previous methodology discussed some of the scalability issues in blockchain technology, the heavy use of computational power to validate and attach each block to the chain, also known as proof of work, can also prove to be a limitation for some applications of this technology. Proof of work mechanism also wastes a lot of electricity toward unfruitful causes, resulting in the proposal of a newer kind of proof of stake (Watanabe et al., 2016) mechanism for validation of blocks.

A block is mined with a probability proportional to the amount of effort done by a miner under the proof of work validation system. Meanwhile, for a proof of stake type of validation mechanism, to validate a block, the miner has to provide proof of the amount of coins they hold and in which blocks. Once verified by all peers, the block is mined, and no more computational load is to be resolved.

Such a system acts for the removal of two drawbacks of the system. First, it solves the problem of a blockchain implementation of any application being very power hungry. Secondly, it also helps prevent monopolization of the workload by a single peer with the most powerful mining rig. If a peer has the strongest system or the ability to solve the puzzles the fastest, they will be the one getting all the mining tasks, establishing a monopoly over the blockchain.

With a proof of stake mechanism though, a peer in the blockchain will have to hold more than 50% of all the coins in the blockchain to be able to monopolize anyone, and that is already a very high mountain to climb Also a deterrence mechanism is set up where the value of the coins held by the monopolizer will be significantly reduced, so the attack will be stopped.

9.4 Master-slave blockchain architecture (Ma et al., 2018a,b) implementation for diversity in mining rigs

Since the genesis of P2P decentralized currency platforms such as Bitcoin, a common question has been raised regarding the lack of ability of anybody on the planet to participate with their own computing device in the heavy lifting and mining of the coins without a dedicated mining rig. This is also recognized as one of the major flaws of the system. A master-slave blockchain architecture or MSB is proposed (Ma et al., 2018a,b). Such a system is recognized to be suitable for mobile devices, home PCs, and tablets for pervasive computing.

An already decentralized system such as blockchain is proposed to be further split into two layers. A master node is established and tasked with collection of transactions and distribution of computing tasks to the slave agents. Slave agents are established in a star-like topology with their own master nodes and are tasked to compute and commit computational exercises that they are assigned to by their masters. A low-power device such as a personal desktop computer or mobile device such as smartphone or tablet may be the slave machine and a high-power server such as a supercomputer can be the master.

Whenever such a system with a central authority that assigns tasks to dedicated individuals in a network is proposed, a simultaneous system to efficiently assign the said tasks is brought under question. Two approaches, namely, noncomputing model (NCM) and partially computing model, are proposed under the same MSB blockchain architecture. NCM uses equivalent proof of work (PeW) consensus, while proof of contribution is used for partially computing model.

When the master node has dispatched computing tasks partially to each slave, the nonce value found by each slave is verified, and the slave producing the correct nonce is rewarded. For the NCM model, only the master does the heavy computing tasks, as usual, while the slaves have to provide service-related contributions such as visit view and unique visitor, etc., and are given a part of the reward that the master gains according to their contribution in the service-related sector.

9.5 DRM approach based on blockchain with automatic license assignment

Getting back to preexisting DRM technologies implemented using blockchain, Zhang (Zhang and Zhao, 2018) presents an implementation that records license information and copyright transactions, so all records are safer and more transparent. Reliability and integrity of copyright transaction issued is ensured using smart contact and assignment of licenses automatically, thereby eliminating the need for centralized servers.

Of course, the system has the functionality to provide copyright owners the ability to set prices to content as well as the mode and channel of content delivery. An example of such could be seen in streaming services, such as Netflix, that allow, say, content viewing up to 1080p quality and on a single screen at a time for its base subscription pack.

These are known as content usage rules. Customers are also empowered with their own usage rules and flexibility in payment frequency. As with every new technology that solves issues of the past and is commissioned for public consumption, blockchain-powered DRM systems have to abide by standards set in place to ensure fair use of digital content, and the proposed implementation presents an easily promotable license structure designed by closely keeping in mind current DRM standards.

Copyright transactions are recorded in blocks for reliability and transparency. Smart contracts are used for lasting reliability of each transaction. Overall, a credible and authoritarian system for content producers at the individual as well as upper levels is provided that ensures scalability and safety.

We see the proposal of a new consensus mechanism called Tendermint (Zhang and Yin, 2019, Buchman, 2016), which is a consensus engine for blockchain for simplifying implementation of the blockchain.

10. Advantages of integrating blockchain with digital content

10.1 DRM approach based on blockchain with automatic license assignment

There will always remain a demand for digital content, and people will continue to access and use it. New digital media content like songs, movies, videos, compositions, news articles, and photos are the sources of entertainment for the mass users. As the content in the digital media increases, it becomes much more difficult to handle the millions of transactions that take place every second for the consumption of such content. The illegal copying of data causes the increase in the transaction costs and deliberately leads to an inefficient system of distribution.

As the advent of blockchain makes the copyrighting system more efficient, it is hard for people to copy resources and send them illegally, which provides more profit to the content owners and the content creators, thus leading to a change in the pricing schemes for the same. This eventually leads to lost-cost settlement between content owners and buyers. Currencies involving Bitcoin technology like Bitcoin and Ethereum also provide a feature to undergo smaller transactions such as transaction cost of listening to a single track music, watching a single video, or reading a news headline. It can also help in providing more monetized options, which require fewer or no ads. All of this uses blockchain to help in fluid transactions of the content available across the internet and more options for the same.

10.2 Blockchain helps to bypass the middlemen present between the transactions

In a traditional transaction system, where transactions for content take place between creators or producers and the users, there is sometimes an involvement of a middle person or agent, which increases the overall cost of accessing the content when data finally reaches the user.

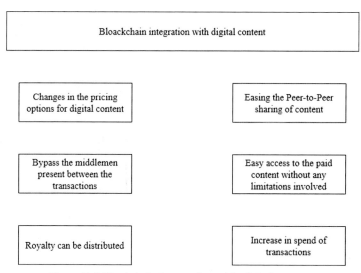

Figure 7.4 Blockchain integration with digital content.

Blockchain technology helps all users present in the market, either the sellers or the buyers, to become their own distributors, as the records of the transactions can be easily tracked and maintained. Nowadays, each person can create content from their homes and can use it to perform transactions. They can also list their sources of advertisement and can directly get involved with the end users without the need of an advertiser or a middle agent with the help of blockchain technology. This will also help in the transparent and proper tracking of revenues, as the artists can generate content on their own and, by using blockchain, can track its distribution across the globe. This will help make the market involving advertisements more liberal and provide options for better opportunities to track advertisement processes (Käll, 2018) (Fig. 7.4).

10.3 Payments including royalty can be easily distributed

Since blockchain eases the way out for content creators to showcase their content, different productions and companies provide contracts to the creators and pay them some fee in return, called a royalty, if they use or show their content in any way. Some of the examples include music productions, show music of independent artists, film productions using video contents in their films, and especially television channels showing advertisements to generate revenue.

However, there are many problems and complexities that can occur while settling the royalty payments. The actual amount depends on the number of times the content is shown by the company or agency, which is not linked in any way with the creator. This leads to generation of royalties that are vaguely generated and are not fully correct in reality. Thus, artists and creators do not get their desirable share of the royalty payments, which acts as a disadvantage.

The usage and distribution of content is controlled by the blockchain technology, also helping with precise and proper analysis of payments with the royalties. This helps in reallocation of these payments. A blockchain system can track the actual usage of the content being used by a company after being associated with the content owner. Credits are accumulated and stored in this system, and the content owners are then paid according to the share they deserve.

10.4 Easing the peer-to-peer sharing of content

The traditional P2P networks that have been used for a long time still possess many flaws and disadvantages. Since the content involved is so vast, it is very difficult to maintain a record of the data that is exchanged from one to another network.

The P2P content usage and sharing can be made transparent using the blockchain system. It helps in digitizing the transactions by producing bills that are automatically generated and easy to maintain. The billing systems are purely automated and are also fully controllable.

This provides a better way of regulating content for which money has to be paid by the users, and it provides an additional way of generating revenue for creators and right owners. This can also be applied to data copy that are shared to the end users, when the physical contents are provided on a blockchain (Fei, 2019).

10.5 Easy access to the paid content without any limitations involved

All the boundary limitations that are set by states or countries to the content providers are limited by the use of blockchain. The DRM complexities of the system are also decreased by the use of blockchain. Blockchain authentication helps in linking the contents that are directly consumed by the individual users.

The blockchain system also has the ability to retire the DRMS and decrease its availability, as all the transactions that are made available are always tracked by the blockchain and fully linked to the owner and copyright holder. The money is generated automatically and processed in accordance with the terms and rights of the content.

11. Limitation of blockchain in DRM

The use of encryption in DRM is secure as long as the key is secure. The encryption keys should be carefully protected and secured and still be accessible to the required users. After the data is decrypted the encryption process can no longer secure the data and prevent its distribution.

DRM systems may cause restrictions on sharing data, so to make DRM systems shareable, the traders or data providers have a little information about the protective schemes that may bring the system into a state of vulnerability.

A leak in the system may compromise the entire system of DRM content. The improper use of the DRM tools such as collecting and reporting data for personal gain may cause serious implications.

The fingerprint scanning process requires the existence of a trustworthy third party responsible for producing fingerprints as well as tracking copyright infringement. In a few other schemes that have avoided the use of such a group, it is computerized and communication levels are very high due to the use of technology like encryption. The use of blockchain in DRM makes the system vulnerable to more attacks, and some nodes may reverse the processes to process double spending and prevent others from accessing the system.

The privacy and security of users' resources may be at risk. The IP addresses can be marked and traced, and other information can be detected to get the real identities of the users through connected nodes.

There are also scalability problems in blockchain. Unauthorized blockchains make data available, allowing its public access to all stakeholders. This could jeopardize data privacy. In addition, in the event that sensitive or confidential data is loaded by mistake into the public blockchain, there is no way to repair the damage.

Though the concept of blockchain is revolutionary and to be used widely in the industry in the future, integrating blockchain with almost all management-based systems will not be fully efficient to perform. The concept of blockchain is often misunderstood as storing and managing data, which is very similar to what a database management system is used for. It is very important to understand that if blockchain is used for the sake of maintaining records of data, it is very much not required and is unnecessary to perform.

The major advantage of using blockchain over a database management system is that it helps in distributing the data instead of centralizing it. Another better feature of blockchain is that it is designed in such a way that it provides a better way to prevent the problem of double spending. However, in case of database systems, similar functions can be performed, but the users should have full trust in the administrator of the database.

Considering the DRMS, the use of blockchain is still less advantageous. This is because a blockchain is useful when the record should not be copied; however, in this case, the record is copyright information and not the actual content. The problem is content can still be copied, whereas it is the copyright information that is actually protected. The only way to protect data is to encode data in the blockchain, but the content can inevitably escape the blockchain.

12. Conclusion and future research

One of the most important ways to curb the issue of piracy on the internet is DRM, which is a process of combining different secure technologies to provide protection to the owners and secure their ownership rights. It provides certain rules and guidelines across all forms of digitized content, mainly depicting the process of distribution and sharing. The data are converted into different formats and are flagged in such a way that they are available only to trustworthy devices and users. This prevents unauthorized users to access content and illegally share precious digital content. These guidelines can also restrict useful processes such as backup maintenance, accessing the content of different devices by the same owner, and so on.

There will always remain a demand for digital content, and people will continue to access and use it. New digital media content like songs, movies, videos, compositions, news articles, and photos are sources of entertainment for the mass users. As the content in the digital media increases, it becomes much more difficult to handle the millions of transactions that take place every second for the consumption of such content. The illegal copying of data causes the increase in the transaction costs and deliberately leads to an inefficient system of distribution.

To make DRM safe and efficient, it is very important to integrate the same with blockchain technology. This new process of using DRM with blockchain is also being introduced by many companies to protect copyrighted content. As bad as videos of unlawful distribution of rights in the blockchain and the loss of record-keeping rights, some new concepts were introduced using the DRM blockchain.

The blockchain technology comprises cryptographic hashing algorithms, consensus protocol, and hash chains. The blockchain can be used in various aspects of DRMS. It can be used to provide irreversible traceability for digital contents; it can be used to provide monitoring of the content being accessed. It provides the capability for DRM in network media. The main characteristics of blockchain are data verifiability and being tamper-proof and decentralized in nature. There are various researches being carried out in this field to improve the governance and technical aspect of blockchain. A well-known research is the Interplanetary File System. From the application of blockchain in the industry, we can be sure that blockchain is not just a buzzword: it is going to impact every aspect of technology in the long run.

As a whole, the thought of using blockchain with DRM may still have loopholes due to the poor understanding of a copyright, blockchain, or both. This is because of the faulty understanding of blockchain solving the double spend problem, which causes the issue of protecting content and not the copyright.

References

Buchman, E., 2016. Tendermint: Byzantine Fault Tolerance in the Age of Blockchains.
Cho, S., Jeong, C., 2019. A blockchain for media: Survey. In: International Conference on Electronics, Information, and Communication (ICEIC). IEEE, pp. 1—2.
Congress, U.S., 1998. Digital millennium copyright act. Publ. Law 105 (304), 112.
Fei, X., 2019. BDRM: a blockchain-based digital rights management platform with fine-grained usage control. Intermt. J. Sci. 54—63.
Finck, M., Moscon, V., 2019. Copyright Law on blockchains: between new forms of rights administration and digital rights management 2.0. IIC-Int. Rev. Intellect. Prop. Compet. Law 50 (1), 77—108.
Garba, A., Dhar Dwivedi, A., Kamal, M., Srivastava, G., Tariq, M., Anwar Hasan, M., Chen, Z., 2020. A digital rights management system based on a scalable blockchain. Peer-to-Peer Network. Appl. 1—16.
Guo, J., Li, C., Zhang, G., Sun, Y., Bie, R., 2019. Blockchain-enabled digital rights management for multimedia resources of online education. Multimed. Tool. Appl. 1—21.
Käll, J., 2018. Blockchain control. Law Critiq. 133—140.
Karuppiah, M., Saravanan, R., 2014. A secure remote user mutual authentication scheme using smart cards. J. Inform. Secur. Appl. 19 (4—5), 282—294.

Karuppiah, M., Saravanan, R., 2015. A secure authentication scheme with user anonymity for roaming service in global mobility networks. Wireless Pers. Commun. 84 (3), 2055–2078.

Karuppiah, M., Kumari, S., Das, A.K., Li, X., Wu, F., Basu, S., 2016. A secure lightweight authentication scheme with user anonymity for roaming service in ubiquitous networks. Secur. Commun. Network. 9 (17), 4192–4209.

Karuppiah, M., Kumari, S., Li, X., Wu, F., Das, A.K., Khan, M.K., Basu, S., 2017. A dynamic id-based generic framework for anonymous authentication scheme for roaming service in global mobility networks. Wireless Pers. Commun. 93 (2), 383–407.

Karuppiah, M., Das, A.K., Li, X., Kumari, S., Wu, F., Chaudhry, S.A., Niranchana, R., 2019. Secure remote user mutual authentication scheme with key agreement for cloud environment. Mob. Network. Appl. 24 (3), 1046–1062.

Kumari, S., Karuppiah, M., Li, X., Wu, F., Das, A.K., Odelu, V., 2016. An enhanced and secure trust-extended authentication mechanism for vehicular ad-hoc networks. Secur. Commun. Network. 9 (17), 4255–4271.

Li, X., Niu, J., Bhuiyan, M.Z.A., Wu, F., Karuppiah, M., Kumari, S., 2017. A robust ECC-based provable secure authentication protocol with privacy preserving for industrial internet of things. IEEE Trans. Ind. Inf. 14 (8), 3599–3609.

Lu, Z., Shi, Y., Tao, R., Zhang, Z., 2019. Blockchain for digital rights management of design works. In: IEEE 10th International Conference on Software Engineering and Service Science (ICSESS), Beijing, China, 2019, pp. 596–603.

Ma, Z., Huang, W., Bi, W., Gao, H., Wang, Z., 2018a. A master-slave blockchain paradigm and application in digital rights management. China Commun. 15 (8), 174–188. Aug.

Ma, Z., Jiang, M., Gao, H., Wang, Z., 2018b. Blockchain for digital rights management. Future Generat. Comput. Syst. 89, 746–764.

Maria, A., Pandi, V., Lazarus, J.D., Karuppiah, M., Christo, M.S., 2021. BBAAS: Blockchain-Based Anonymous Authentication Scheme for Providing Secure Communication in VANETs. Security and Communication Networks, 2021.

Naeem, M., Chaudhry, S.A., Mahmood, K., Karuppiah, M., Kumari, S., 2020. A scalable and secure RFID mutual authentication protocol using ECC for Internet of Things. Int. J. Commun. Syst. 33 (13), e3906.

O'Dwyer, R., 2020. Limited edition: producing artificial scarcity for digital art on the blockchain and its implications for the cultural industries. Convergence 874–894.

Pradhan, A., Karuppiah, M., Niranchana, R., Jerlin, M.A., Rajkumar, S., 2018. Design and analysis of smart card-based authentication scheme for secure transactions. Int. J. Internet Technol. Secur. Trans. 8 (4), 494–515.

Savelyev, A., 2018. Copyright in the blockchain era: promises and challenges. Comput. Law Secur. Rep. 34, 550–561.

Singh, B.P., Kumar Tripathi, A., 2019. Blockchain technology and intellectual property rights. J. Intellect. Prop. Rights 24, 41–44.

Swatman, P.M.C., Krueger, C., Van Der Beek, K., 2006. The changing digital content landscape: An evaluation of e-business model development in European online news and music. Inter. Res. 16 (1), 53–80.

Van Rossum, J., 2018. The blockchain and its potential for science and academic publishing. Inf. Serv. Use 95–98.

Vimal, S., Srivatsa, S.K., 2019. A new cluster p2p file sharing system based on ipfs and blockchain technology. J. Amb. Intell. Human. Comput. 1–7.

Watanabe, H., Fujimura, S., Nakadaira, A., Miyazaki, Y., Akutsu, A., Kishigami, J., 2016. Blockchain contract: securing a blockchain applied to smart contracts. In: 2016 IEEE International Conference on Consumer Electronics (ICCE), Las Vegas, NV, USA, pp. 467–468.

Zhang, X., Yin, Y., 2019. Research on digital copyright management system based on blockchain technology. In: 2019 IEEE 3rd Information Technology, Networking, Electronic and Automation Control Conference (ITNEC), Chengdu, China, pp. 2093–2097.

Zhang, Z., Zhao, L., 2018. A design of digital rights management mechanism based on blockchain technology. In: Chen, S., Wang, H., Zhang, L.J. (Eds.), Blockchain – ICBC 2018. ICBC 2018. Lecture Notes in Computer Science, vol. 10974. Springer, Cham.

CHAPTER 8

Blockchain technology in biomanufacturing: Current perspective and future challenges

Muskan Pandey and Barkha Singhal
School of Biotechnology, Gautam Buddha University, Greater Noida, Uttar Pradesh, India

Abbreviations

ACN	AgreCoin
ACTIV	Accelerating COVID-19 Therapeutic Interventions and Vaccines
AI	Artificial intelligence
CDMO	Contract development and manufacturing company
CFR	Code of Federal Regulation
cGMP	Current good manufacturing practice
CI	Carbon intensity
CMO	Contract manufacturing company
DLT	Distributed ledger technology
DON	Deoxynivalenol
DSCSA	Drug Supply Chain Security Act
EPA	Environmental Protection Agency
FDA	Food and Drug Administration
FHIR	Fast Health Interoperability Records
FMD	Falsified Medicines Directive
GPS	Global positioning system
IBM	International Business Machine
IoMT	Internet of medical things
IoT	Internet of things
ISO	International Organization for Standardization
KPMG	Klynveld Peat Marwick Goerdeler
ML	Machine learning
P2P	Peer to Peer
POC	Proof of concept
RFID	Radio frequency identification
SAP	Systems, applications, and products in data processing
SOP	Standard operating procedure
USDA	United States Department of Agriculture

Blockchain Technology for Emerging Applications
ISBN 978-0-323-90193-2
https://doi.org/10.1016/B978-0-323-90193-2.00007-7

1. Introduction

An inevitable transformation has been envisaged from industry 1.0 to industry 4.0 with inculcation of advanced technologic practices commonly known as digitalized manufacturing (Narayanan et al., 2020). The adoption of industry 4.0 has been visualized in various manufacturing sectors, and biotechnology is no longer an exception (Rinker et al., 2021). The increasing realization of the potential of biobased entities for coping with the challenges related to sustainable development, energy requirements, food security, climate change, and productive agriculture has encouraged the scientific community to hasten the pace of biomanufacturing. The inherent advantages of biomanufacturing such as reduced toxic by-products, less fossil fuel consumption, eco-friendliness, and no greenhouse gas emissions necessitate the intervention by the latest technologic developments (Zobel-Roos et al., 2020; Gargalo et al., 2020). In the past decade, biomanufacturing has become equipped via the latest internet of things (IoT) and internet of medical things (IoMT) that have been successfully implemented by enhancing the research diaspora managing and sharing research data for their wider utilization (Kelly et al., 2020; Koutras et al., 2020). In fact, various chemical companies have adopted biomanufacturing for reducing the burden of pollution into the environment as their preferred method of production. The trend is continuously growing for the massive production of biobased products per day. Therefore, there is a dire need to strengthen the arena of biomanufacturing from low cost to high production speed with flexibility in the production capacities as well as to transform consumer's expectations and enhance business capabilities. However, the complexity and high specificity of the biologic system has caught biomanufacturing into a Sisyphean task, and the business and notions of commerce and trade are still a trap of Victorian grandeur. The execution of all business practices is still relying on the intervention of intermediaries, so the development of technology that embraces the glory of security, transparency, immutability, and auditability will definitely transform the height of biomanufacturing. We are living in the era of technology overhaul where digitalization is intervening in private and public domains with lots of information and innovation. Thus, among various technologies, blockchain technology is being heralded as a major breakthrough in the life science and biotechnology sectors, which directly affects the pace of biomanufacturing (Justinia, 2019; Makridakis and Christodoulou, 2019). This technology mainly comprises a peer-to-peer

(P2P) integrated network platform involving mathematical expressions, advanced statistical algorithms, and cryptography for alleviating the discrepancies of conventional distributed database by replacing consensus algorithms. Blockchain has been hailed as a revolutionary digital architecture constituting a shared and immutable ledger having decentralized, open-source, anonymous, and transparent data for public or private organizations (Kuo et al., 2017). Biomanufacturing involves critical steps of involving biologic cells or enzymes to convert various substrates into commercially important products.

This requires diverse avenues for process development for monitoring and control in which blockchain fits for secure and traceable data, for giving the platform of precision and accuracy, as well as providing predictive control for successful execution. The data produced during upstreaming can be well utilized for framing various downstream processes, providing provenance that further paves the way for various collaborative research and development. From inventory to supply of bioproducts, blockchain technology can be well applied for creating the transparent, auditable, and secure data that leads to development of strong relationships with customers. The implementation of blockchain technology has heightened the framework of various business policies to expand the horizon of biomanufacturing that can be directly correlated with bioeconomy (Weking et al., 2020). Fig. 8.1 summarizes the applications of blockchain technology in various sectors contributing the economic growth. The technology also provides a digital backbone for inculcating other advanced technologies such as artificial intelligence, cloud computing, eHealth, and mHealth applications (Lake et al., 2014; Shi et al., 2020; Ding et al., 2019). This digitalized ledger was introduced first through Bitcoin and various other blockchain architectures consisting of consensus algorithms that were developed depending on the specific applications, which have been well cited in the literature. For diversified applications based on access and permissions, three types of blockchain—public, private, and consortium—have been reported. Though the technology has marvelous credentials, it is still evolving and needs to access its full potential in this arena. Thus, the chapter discusses the current applications of emerging blockchain technology in biomanufacturing, current challenges, and future perspectives. The information given in this chapter should not be considered all inclusive, but rather it serves as a foundation in the attempt to give certain glimpses of the future of biomanufacturing.

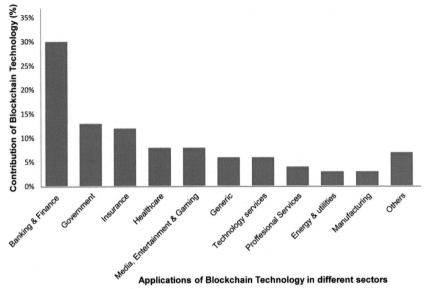

Figure 8.1 Applications of blockchain technology in various sectors and its contribution toward economic growth.

2. Conception and functionality of blockchain

The term blockchain is not clearly defined, but the technology was conceptualized in 2008 under the pseudonym of Satoshi Nakamoto. The technology is designed to facilitate online transfer of money from one party to another without involving the need of any financial organizations or intermediaries. It was introduced as cryptocurrency in the form of Bitcoin (Marella et al., 2020). The timeline diagram in Fig. 8.2 shows the historical development of blockchain technology. The purpose of this technology is to ensure the authenticity and security of data and money transactions, with complete information given to all participants (Ikeda, 2018). It is a kind of integrated P2P networking platform in which each member is designated as a node that can be connected with single or multiple computer systems. After receiving a certain amount of information either in form of data or transaction record or clinical data, patient information, or manufacturing batch number, they become validated and combined to form an immutable "block," and every new bit of information is added in a new block to the existing chain to be continued as a blockchain (Hoy, 2017). Recently, the International Organization for Standardization (ISO) described blockchain technology as a kind of digital platform for storing and verifying the various

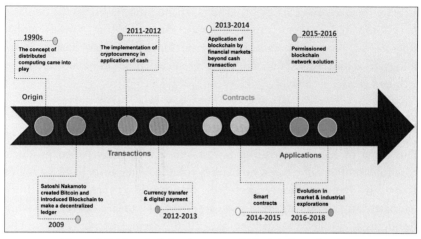

Figure 8.2 Historical development of blockchain technology.

classes of data through a shared, immutable ledger (Tasca and Tessone, 2019). The distributed ledger technology (DLT) is the part of blockchain that opens a door for multiple business operations in various verticals (Kuo et al., 2017). The flexible option for sharing a network among private and public organizations, or the combination of both, enhances its applicability in the wider context. The market size of this technology is expected to grow from USD 3.0 billion in 2020 to USD 39.7 billion by 2025, and the estimated compound annual growth rate is expected to reach 67.3% during 2020−25. The most popular framework of blockchain was launched by Linux foundation in 2016 by the name of Hyperledger. Later on, various other platforms such as Ethereum, R3, BigDB, Ripple, and EOS have been published and applied on various applications per user specifications (Ullah et al., 2020).

A stupendous stride has been seen in the domain of biomanufacturing that is considered the most heterogenous and complex system among the commercialized sectors. However, with the advent of automation, smart equipment, advancements in unit operations of upstream and downstream processes, process engineering tools, and digitalization of batch-to-batch documentation, an enormous amount of data has been generated (Deepa et al., 2020; Yuheng et al., 2020). As biomanufacturing requires stringent regulatory compliances and standardization before market launch, data should be quite secure, authenticated, and reproducible. Therefore, per the specification of US Food and Drug Administration (FDA) the output of the generated data must be attributable, legible, contemporaneous, original, and accurate (Radziwon et al., 2014). The postpandemic era brings the demand for coordinated manufacturing strategies for combating various global issues. Thus, blockchain can be clearly envisioned as a blockbuster technology to achieving such an ambitious project that could never have been executed before its arrival.

3. Why blockchain is needed in biomanufacturing

The arena of biomanufacturing is vast and involves diversified products from low to high value based on market volume. The purity level is a major factor in having bioproducts of therapeutic value. Thus, both manufacturing and purification process comprises critical steps for achieving the desired success (Ahmad et al., 2018; Zhang et al., 2017). The manufacturing involves the fermentation process, culturing of mammalian and higher plant cells, as well as recovery and purification steps that require critical chromatography processes such as gas chromatography, high performance liquid chromatography, gel-exclusion chromatography, affinity chromatography, centrifugation, ultrafiltration, and other advanced purification processes (Aijaz et al., 2018). The diversified layout of bioreactor designs also plays a pivotal role for execution of successful biomanufacturing. Thus, monitoring critical process parameters during the manufacturing is an important step for mitigating the risks of the process. One of the prime challenges to retain the stability and functionality of biologic products depends on the structure of biomolecules and posttranslational modifications in the host. These posttranslational modifications enable the bioproducts to cope with harsh environmental conditions and enabled them in remain in an active state. Therefore, the various aspects mentioned in the arena of biomanufacturing need an automated, transparent, immutable, and digitalized infrastructure to observe and recorded the various process inflows and outflows as well as product distribution in the consumer forum. Thus, by evaluating these requirements, blockchain technology is very fit for this purpose as applied to different facets of biomanufacturing (Zobel-Roos et al., 2020). Though biopharmaceuticals mainly known for their production of biologics are skeptical to imbibe the full potential of this technology, currently, various big names like Bayer, Sun pharma, Pfizer, Sanofi, Johnson & Johnson, and others have adopted this technology in their framework (Xu et al., 2020; Haq and Muselemu, 2018). It is clearly envisioned that though the technology is not the solution for a panacea of problems in biomanufacturing, with the integration of advanced digitalized technologies, it should be a boon for biomanufacturing and provides a more comprehensive and transparent fast-track platform from the manufacturer to consumer perspectives (Gargalo et al., 2020). The key features of blockchain technology used in biomanufacturing are summarized in Table 8.1. This will certainly accelerate the production of biobased commodities and contribute prolifically in the growth of bioeconomy and sustainable development.

4. Key elements of blockchain that are required in biomanufacturing

Blockchain technology offers nonrepudiation of transactions across a distributed P2P network in the absence of intermediary sources. The world of biomanufacturing is also warming up to the innovativeness of blockchain technology. The biomanufacturing industries can share and integrate the data of various capital, operating, and administrative costs for setting up the industry. The immutable information on the purchased cost of equipment and specification of various bioreactors and downstream processing equipment can also provide trusted information for assessing the quality attributes that have been used for manufacturing purpose. This technology offers various features that can be a transformative factor for broadening the horizon of biomanufacturing. The mind map represented in Fig. 8.3 depicts various facets of blockchain in biomanufacturing. The key elements of blockchain that play a crucial role in developing smart manufacturing are described subsequently.

4.1 Data governance and management of records

The domain of biomanufacturing comprises various regulatory issues in terms of ethical and social acceptability (Quaye et al., 2009). The specificity of biobased products and utilization for therapeutic and food purposes posits a stringent level of regulation. Thus, significant burden has been seen among consumers and manufacturers for building trust and developing a long-term relationship by keeping records and making legal documents. Therefore, unimaginable possibility can be conferred by blockchain technology to maintain the data and associated records in a secured and encrypted manner in a digitalized framework. This will facilitate the smart contract between companies and consumers that builds trust and offer more opportunities for the growth of biomanufacturing business (Paliwal et al., 2020).

Table 8.1 Key features of blockchain technology that can be implied in the biomanufacturing arena.

S.No.	Characteristics of blockchain	Functionality description	Its benefits in biomanufacturing
1.	Autonomy	This means that each node of blockchain can access, transfer, store, and update the date securely.	• Data can also be shared with public sectors securely to reap more benefits.
2.	Decentralized	This means that the data can be accessed, monitored, stored and updated on several computers.	• A manufacturer can access the data and monitor the work and if there is any diversion from the given protocol. • It will be easy to trace and track the supply chain.
3.	Transparent	This means that the data is transparent to its user; it helps in preventing data from being altered or stolen.	• Consumer and manufacturers will develop a transparent relationship with more trust. • A quality check can also be possible in every step.
4.	Immutable	This means that the blockchain ledger remains unchanged, and the data stored once is reserved always in the form of a specified hash value.	• Products cannot be counterfeited in the journey. • Any changes in manufacturing conditions can be kept on record.
5.	Open-source	This means that blockchain has open-source access to all of its connected networks.	• Consumers can have access to the manufacturing processes to be assured of the quality of the product.
6.	Anonymity	This means that as the data is being transferred from one node to another node, the identity remain anonymous.	• Stringent conditions required by several bioproducts could be keep in check on a regular basis by various organizations.

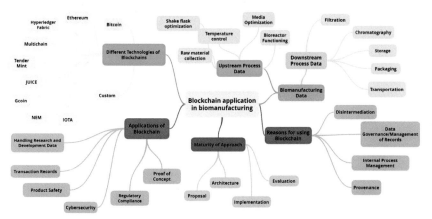

Figure 8.3 A mind map depicting the various avenues of blockchain technology in biomanufacturing.

4.2 Disintermediation

The major strength of blockchain lies with the nonrequirement of intermediaries. This will save cost and time for companies and obviate fake and fraudulent information that can posits risks for business management. The transmission of secured information to all the parties whether in terms of private or public will develop the trust among networking partners and facilitate a collaborative environment (Tan et al., 2021; Giannini and Terenzi, 2020). The trials on assessing the therapeutic efficiency of monoclonal antibodies imparts a successful example in which investigators, regulators, manufacturer and trial sites can be connected with one digitalized platform and all data can be shared in encrypted manner.

4.3 Internal process management

The manufacturing sector has its own internal system to manage the raw materials, factory operations, product processing, waste management, packaging, and labeling of the products. Each domain requires a separate record of transaction among the internal members of the organization (Mendling et al., 2018). The blockchain provides a holistic approach to reconcile all transactions through a single shared ledger. This will enhance the transparency in every domain of the manufacturing followed by the development of trust among employees for making a better environment.

4.4 Provenance

The attribute of tracing the origin and authenticity of the various objects in the manufacturing sector is known as provenance. The manufacturing sector has to face various counterfeit trading objects from supply of raw material to out-of-order equipment. The process modification also affects the batch-to-bath variability. Therefore, for keeping the records in immutable form, blockchain provides a magnificent platform for tracing all the inventory from process manufacturing and product packaging to transportation. Inconsistencies can be traced due to the interconnection of blocks with their predecessors in encrypted code.

4.5 Handling research and development data

The biggest challenge among biomanufacturing is the reproducibility of the process, as the biology has inherent complexity in terms of cellular framework as well as in products profiles. Therefore, rigorous research must be needed periodically to upgrade the system and assess its reproducibly. These tasks require considerable money, which is a major roadblock in small-scale and startup biomanufacturing sectors. Therefore, any malicious access to research and development data will impact the reputation in terms of funding and consumer relationship of an organization (Wang et al., 2019). Thus, blockchain technology provides a wonderful platform for enabling the access of sensitive research data to the real users with the consensus of trusted parties and investigators. Thus, to leverage the growth of biomanufacturing, an ecosystem with generation and sharing of data must be required nowadays to fulfill the rising demands of biobased commodities (Naz et al., 2019; Ozercan et al., 2018).

5. Various avenues of utility of blockchain technology in biomanufacturing

5.1 Infrastructure development

The infrastructure of biomanufacturing has to carefully comply with cGMP practices and other stringent containment regulations. The clean room facilities and stringent regulation of temperature in biologic reactions require careful monitoring of data in secured and nonauditable form to prevent any discrepancies in the biologic process.

The capital cost of running the industry and operation cost for different utilities required to manufacture the products constitute an important segment of infrastructure. Thus, the documentation of cost and maintenance, audits, and regulatory framework requires extensive data management for running a smooth and cost-effective process. All these requirements can be leveraged by blockchain technology where transparent and secure data can be shared to desired parties in immutable form, and modification can only be done by consent from all involved parties (Rui et al., 2019). The technology is flexible enough to work on both privatized and public forums, or combination of both, which adds more dynamism. The past decade has seen tremendous efforts to develop various platforms from recording the data of raw materials to manufacturing and transportation to end users (Darvazeh et al., 2020). In 2017, the joint efforts of 15 pharma and biopharmaceutical companies enabled the development of SAP Pharma blockchain POC (proof of concept) app with collaboration of software giant SAP for tracking the supply chain management of various drugs and biologics, and it currently adds more technology features to upgrade with advanced facilities. The rising popularity of this technology in the biotechnology industry facilitated the development SAP Information Collaboration Hub for Life Sciences in 2019. This blockchain-based platform provides the connection of a customer forum directly complied with the US Drug Supply Chain Security Act (DSCSA). The discrepancies in drug manufacturing can also be tracked by inclusion of this technology.

Recently, Novartis created a blockchain technology-based solution for tracking counterfeit medicines. Along similar lines, Merck also developed its own technology platform for enhancing the security of its supply chain (Jennings, 2021; Morris, 2018). Moreover, Boehringer Ingelheim (Canada) collaborated with IBM for improvements in data sharing and storage of various clinical trials and patient data. In addition to that, the joint efforts of Amgen, Sanofi, and Pfizer developed a trial platform using blockchain technology to optimize the process for cost-effective drug production. The more powerful platform based on this technology was developed by Exochain for allowing patients to control the interaction and usage of their medical data by the research community, which leads to further the trust development among various parties (Mackey et al., 2019). MediLedger developed, by collaborative effort of 20 companies, has been used as an interoperable system constituting multiple parties, including manufacturers, wholesale distributors, hospitals, and pharmacies for verification and transfer of various biologic and chemical drugs with trust and authenticity (MediLedger, 2017). The global supply chain platform was developed by the joint effort of IBM with KPMG, Merck, and Walmart for efficient supply of biologic drugs (Miller, 2019). Though the current examples have been more directed toward supply chain management, which is an essential part of infrastructure development, various blockchain platforms are under development that can be exclusively used for monitoring the manufacture of biobased products. The increasing realization of potential of gene and immunotherapies leads to the development of personalized medicines. Thus, the rising trend of production of very high-value, low-cost, bio-therapeutic products utilizes a single-use bioreactor strategy (Jacquemart et al., 2016; Bandyopadhyay et al., 2017). Monitoring various biologic parameters and recording the data is a secure manner facilitates data sharing and tracking opportunity for customers and other verifiers and regulators, which enhances the visibility and trust of the product and industry. The viral contamination of high-value products manufactured from mammalian cell culture techniques requires extensive column chromatographic techniques, so by integrating the process with blockchain platform, the data can be used for continuous monitoring and shared for its verification and authenticity. Apart from that, this technology has provided a magnificent platform for Contract Research Development Organization (CMO/CDMO) sharing the research and development data in a secured manner. The infrastructure development of 3D printing of personalized drugs requires an advanced manufacturing system that can be integrated with blockchain and machine learning platforms to analyze the secured data for assessing the correct dosage and formulation of drug, depending on the profile of patients, as well as its production.

5.2 Advancing machines as a service

Biomanufacturing involves the complex process of upstream and downstream processing for harnessing the products from living cells. This process requires a different class of machine from production to purification. Currently, the concept of innovative pay-per-use model for machinery has been more prevalent and is known as "machines as a service" (Lillrank and Särkkä, 2011). The model works on the principle of providing the service of equipment or machine use on the basis of the generated output on a charged basis that curtails large investments and gains accesses to upgraded, latest technology. The model also provides flexibility to enhance the production capacity of manufacturers and makes the arduous scale-up process cost-effective. The model can only be used when this process is integrated with a tamper-free, secured, and shared data platform, and blockchain provides feasible option for the implementation (Machine-as-a-Service, 2018).

5.3 Enabling machine-controlled maintenance

An advanced biomanufacturing facility requires automated service agreements and shorter maintenance times. The technologic sophistication and the health of each piece of equipment can be monitored and maintained by appending the installation documentation and service agreements in the device through a blockchain platform for the creation of a digital twin (Zobel-Roos et al., 2020). By integrating with a blockchain platform, an automated execution and payment of scheduled maintenance can be done in a secured way. The equipment that needs maintenance itself can trigger a request for servicing and create a smart contract for the work execution or replacement part. After accomplishment of work, automatic processing of payments happens, and history is appended in nonauditable documents connected with a blockchain platform. This enhances the reliability and reproducibility of the utility of the correct equipment for the manufacturing. Though this concept is in its development phase, it enables the reduction of cost and maximizes profits for manufacturers without compromising credibility or trust (Justinia, 2019; Shi et al., 2020).

5.4 IP and tech transfer

There is considerable gap in technology transfer from academia to industry that confers a strong roadblock for wider dissemination of research among the scientific community. The timely delivery of research is a tedious process due to difficulty in identification of potential opportunities and management of data among collaborating scientists from different institutions and industries. Therefore, the research data generated during research and development of biologic products should be carefully stored and secured to develop a chain, and updated data will be added time to time for attaining transparency. Thus, blockchain-based platforms are well suited for the management of technology information and tracing the research and development work through a decentralized and convoluted platform (Qureshi and Megías Jiménez, 2020). This platform is also well suited for investors for identification of required owners and recording deals, regulations, and payments for future use. This technology paves the way for achieving milestones in protecting intellectual property and license agreements between interested parties in a digitalized form.

5.5 Inventory management

Biologic products can be made from a wide range of raw materials that can be available locally or imported. Natural and waste bioprocessing requires critical inventory management due to fluctuation in the availability of raw materials that further leads to batch-to-batch variation. The stock of raw materials and their maintenance is coming under the umbrella of good practices. The regulatory framework and financial aspects need to be carefully stored and monitored for their stability and storage. Thus, for accomplishing this task, blockchain technology is a sustainable option for maintaining consignment stocks globally, enabling the tracking of the location and custody of materials in a secured and immutable way (Astarita et al., 2019).

5.6 Simplifying and safeguarding quality checks

Currently, biomanufacturing has been recognized as the factory of the future due to highly specificity of bioproducts and an ecofriendly approach toward the environment. The inherent property of blockchain platform for creating the immutable documents for the production and supply chain data of bioproducts can be used for quality checks and verification of these products at different stages of manufacturing. This application can only be feasible when automated quality checks have been done with accurate measurements and their documentation through blockchain. The information can be further utilized by a controlling authority for the timely update of data, reducing the need of auditing by quality control personnel and other manual interventions (How blockchain, 2019).

5.7 Serialization of bioproducts

The arrival of gene therapies has led to a devastating impact on the biomanufacturing sector. In 2020, four gene therapies were approved by the US FDA, and 900 therapies are estimated to be in the pipeline. It is clearly envisioned that there is need of serialization to enhance the business opportunities at a global scale through standardized supply chain management. The process of serialization involves giving a unique identity number of each biologic or drug that is used to decode the batch number, location, date, and its logistic route and manufacturer that can be shared with supply chain trackers as well as with consumers. The objective of this process is to trace the products from their origin.

The security and transparency of blockchain technology is to comply with the industry's standard serialization regulations that can be applicable throughout the globe. Till date, two major governing bodies, US DSCSA and EU Falsified Medicines Directive 2011/62/EU (FMD), have been acknowledged as certified serialization organizations, and blockchain technology readily complies with these organizations to manage the supply chain in an efficient manner (Naughton, 2017, 2018). Currently, serialization process is in great demand to boost the dimensions of business, and recently the company Servier, which has spread in 148 countries and is a major player in serialization and global supply chain, developed a blockchain-based platform that is connecting the biomanufacturing hubs of different countries. Thus, blockchain technology makes the biomanufacturing sector more recognizable through the interconnected industries, opening the door for more collaborative developments in this field.

5.8 Bioproducts expiration and bioproducts recall

The panorama of biobased products is vast and various generalized to specific products are manufactured through either whole cell or immobilized cell and enzymes through fermentation as well as biotransformation. The stringent operations have been more directed toward those bioproducts that can be used for therapeutic purpose. Various cellular products like interferons, interleukins, growth hormones, insulin, monoclonal antibodies, embryonic stem cells, and vaccines have been used for therapeutic interventions. These products require sophisticated control of temperature and humidity and have a shelf life. Though utmost care has been taken for biomanufacturing of these products, sometimes inevitable conditions lead to the deterioration of product, which may lead to life-threatening conditions for the patient. Thus, with the help of blockchain technology the exact identification and tracking of expired bioproducts can be done while applying the principles of reverse logistics for complete disposal of these products based on standard operating procedures (SOPs) (Sahoo and Halder, 2020). In addition, the other side of this coin is that future recalling of bioproducts due to any discrepancy in manufacturing, packaging, or conferring conspicuous side effects can be easily done by implementing this technology. This technology provides the correct location and chain of custody information by tracking product, batch number, and manufacturer information in a legitimate way (Subramanian et al., 2020).

6. Applications of blockchain technology in biomanufacturing (case studies)

6.1 Blockchain in alcohol biomanufacturing: a case study

Alcohol production is one of the most historical processes in the world of biomanufacturing. The consumption of alcohol is as old as humanity itself.

There is a continuous rise in the consumption of alcohol, and in the future, there is no hope for giving up this habit in spite of imposing many prohibitions. The biomanufacturing capacity of alcohols and alcohol-based beverages is growing at an undeniable high pace and is expected to rise to the $2 trillion mark by the year 2025 (Industrial Alcohol, 2020). The contribution of alcohol production and sales contributes high revenue generation for all nations. The pricing of all alcoholic beverages has been determined by the cost of production and the duties levied on those costs. Therefore, developing a smart manufacturing of alcohol is urgently required for meeting the demand of the rising population. Blockchain technology is a boon for marketing and supply chain management of alcoholic beverages. as 30%−60% of alcohol is fake nowadays. To identify counterfeit product and curb the need for traditional advertising formats for promotion of a variety of alcoholic beverages, this technology plays significant role in the global context. Recently, technology was utilized in the smart and shared information known as AgreCoin (ACN) on feed stock (agave biomass) availability for tequila production. ACN comprehensively known as an Agricultural Agreement Coin, based on an Ethereum ERC20 blockchain platform, is a P2P solution for executing the trade and financial management of agricultural alcoholic products and services (Blockchain Benefits, 2019). In the United States, $2.6 billion of agave biomass is produced annually for the commercial manufacturing of tequila, but the slow growth of the plants (approximately 6 years) leads to a supply crisis of agave that confers a dilemmatic situation among farmers when the product is required at high demand (Enescu et al., 2020; Davis et al., 2010). Therefore, this platform has been used to resolve the agave crisis and save a billion-dollar industry from huge losses. The same concept can be well correlated with beer manufacturing from barley and wine from grapes and other feedstocks. Thus, this platform channelizes the transparent flow of information from producers to consumers and various stakeholders. Apart from that, this concept can be proposed for downstream development of alcohol. The distillation process leads to various products from alcohol, so a digitalized platform can be used for tracking this process for getting authentic products from the manufacturer. The story of the other side of this platform is also worth mentioning here: ACN also facilitates a social impact plan that contributes the utilization of funds for providing free education for underprivileged students of the Mexican community and mining operation in Guadalajara, Mexico (Oñiguez et al., 2014).

6.2 Blockchain in the development of COVID-19 vaccine: a case study

The whole world is scourged by the catastrophe of the ongoing COVID-19 pandemic that confers devastating impact on economic, social, and public health at a global level. This situation witnessed a lot of loopholes in current healthcare management systems that lack the transparency, security, and fast tracking of data for efficient management. However, a silver lining growth has been envisaged in the biopharmaceuticals for the development of vaccine in a global context to defeat the outbreak of SARS-CoV-2 (AgreCoin, 2018). The great efforts of vaccine development have been done throughout a global context by a collaborative approach of the scientific community and biotechnology industries, rather than a competitive one. Thus, it would require an unprecedented level of manufacturing and distribution capacity. It is estimated that approximately seven billion vaccine doses will be required to suffice the need of every age group in all continents. In addition to that, it has been also estimated that 20%−30% loss will occur during transport and distribution, so approximately 10 billion doses will be needed, and furthermore, keeping in view of the requirement of two doses of vaccine per individual, 19 billion vaccine doses will be required to stop the further spread of the virus (Calina et al., 2020). Thus, it is doubtless simple to comprehend that there is equitable role of manufacturing as well as supply chain management. Thus, there is strong upsurge in the development of a decentralized, distributed blockchain technology that can provide real-time monitoring of secure and encrypted data without alteration of real information that leads to the development of trust without the involvement of a third party that encumbers the risk as well as fraud and fake information related to vaccine development and distribution. The year 2020 witnessed the prolific development of various blockchain software assisted by artificial intelligence and IoT platforms to overcome the discrepancies in the process of defeating the pandemic. The development of vaccine requires prodigious research on the mechanism of virus replication, attachment, and its binding mechanism. However, the clinical data from the patients and their symptoms provide a broader understanding of the infection outcome. Thus, various research projects at a pilot scale comprising blockchain technology have been implemented for collecting and storing the data on a wider public forum. Recently, a public−private partnership has been reported to develop a framework to accelerate the development of vaccine and drug molecules, streamlined clinical trials, and coordinated regulatory compliances, known as "the Accelerating COVID-19 Therapeutic Interventions and Vaccines (ACTIV)," which is based on blockchain technology. Apart from that, various research projects implemented at a gross scale have been reported, and some of the examples are listed.

6.3 MiPasa platform for preventing false infodemics in the public forum

The management of COVID-19 pandemic needs authentic and verifiable data for creating policies for governments and industrialists. MiPasa is a blockchain technologic platform based on Hyperledger fabric that is connected with authentic sources like WHO, registered health authorities, and organizations for relaying the information of virus spread and their outcome in the public forum (Kim et al., 2021). This authentic and immutable information is further utilized by the government and private authorities to develop various pharmacologic and nonpharmacologic solutions for eradicating the spread of the virus. This platform is also helpful for identifying COVID-19 carriers and infection hotspots. Similarly, Hashlog is a blockchain-based platform that provides data about the COVID-19 outbreak integrated with WHO and ECDC databases.

6.4 VIRI platform for preventing spread of COVID-19

The identification of infection hotspots of the virus through digital contact tracing has proven to be a milestone for limiting the spread of airborne infection of COVID-19. Data privacy as well as authenticity are two key issues that are able to solved by the blockchain-based digitalized VIRI platform. In fact, the wider applicability of this platform for identification of virus carriers across different countries has given the idea of the fast viral emergence and outbreak. This platform fully preserves the user's data and is integrated with artificial intelligence (AI) and machine learning (ML) tools that can be further used for the accurate prediction of COVID-19 pandemic in a global context (Salah et al., 2020).

6.5 WIShelter platform for assurance of privacy of COVID-19 data

WIShelter is smart phone–based application originating from Wisekey's digital identity platform for providing secured data to consumers. The clinical data both from healthy and diseased individuals is stored in a secured and encrypted manner through a blockchain technologic platform. This forum can also be equipped with uploading a COVID-19 testing certificate, which is information can be further used to decide the home quarantine possibilities or hospitalization. This application is also helpful for deciding travel requirements of the public based on their data availability and situation.

6.6 Blockchain in the development of biofuels: a case study

The realization of depletion of fossil fuels in the 1970 and 1980s propelled the scientific community to find out a sustainable alternative to fulfill the rising demand for energy. The development of bioethanol from corn as feedstock led to the groundbreaking step for the development of biofuel in various countries across the globe (VIRI Creates, 2020). Brazil has been in the forefront in this development, but this is not yet highly used because of using land and food crops for the production of biofuel. This approach is called first-generation bioethanol, but later on, biofuel development from waste lignocellulosic biomass laid the foundation for second-generation biofuels (Bušić et al., 2018). The inherent complexity of lignocellulosic biomass is imposing considerable challenges for its commercialization in spite of the technology being ecofriendly and reducing the carbon footprint in the environment. Copious research has been carried for consolidated bioprocessing for the conversion of lignocellulosic biomass by using advanced molecular biology, transcriptomics, proteomics, and system and synthetic biology approaches and has paved the way for establishment of biorefineries for harnessing the maximum possible value-added products (Robak and Balcerek, 2018). Thus, it is a dire need to establish a tracing mechanism and to store the information in secured manner from "feedstock to fuel." Various countries are adopting the technology of biofuel for reducing the burden of pollution and attaining sustainability. The prime challenges in this paradigmatic shift are the stringent regulation, unpredictability of feedstock type and availability, thinner margins, and demand of transparency from the consumers' side. Thus, blockchain technology is indeed a suitable platform for addressing these challenges by developing a "digital passport" for every process of biofuel development (like types of feed stock, availability, storage, process development, sugar content, production information, ignition value, and supply chain) (Pathak et al., 2019; Andoni et al., 2019). The prospective applications of blockchain technology in the biorefinery sector are represented in Fig. 8.4. This information should be stored in separate blocks and added in a chain that can be encrypted with digital code, so information cannot be forged, giving

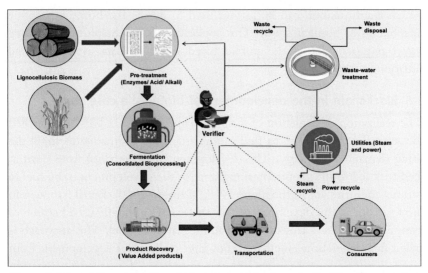

Figure 8.4 Futuristic application of blockchain technology in the biorefinery sector.

transparent and updated information. The most critical parameter for adopting biofuels is carbon intensity (CI). The fuel quality would be good if it achieves lower CI, which is possible only by growing the feed stocks in a reduced amount of nitrogen fertilizers. The farmers should be incentivized for using the lower amount of nitrogen technology for the growth of crops by adopting engineered nitrogen-producing microbes and slow-release nitrogen nanotechnology. These practices reduced the burden of nitrogen fertilizers that further impact the low CI of biofuel. The blockchain platform is also use for tracing the contamination of feedstock with toxins like vomitoxin (DON), which can prevent million-dollar losses in this industry (Wu and Tran, 2018). Recently, Grain Discovery blockchain platform developed in Canada has been used for resolving the problem of DON contamination in the ethanol supply chain. The test data has been added by corn sellers to the crop's "digital passport," which includes the concentration level of DON from testing in labs. If found in critical concertation, their sale will be rejected, further saving manufacturing losses in the industry (Lane, 2019).

7. Blockchain technology as a prospective tool for bioeconomy

The growth of biomanufacturing is directly corelated with bioeconomy. Currently, the bioeconomy is precisely understood by conjuring the images of recombinant products recovered from genetically modified organisms and biorefineries. The development of biofuels like bioethanol, biodiesel, biohydrogen, etc., from waste biomass and diversified value-added products retrieved from waste valorization is the key technology behind the setup of biorefineries (Becker and Whittmann, 2019). The massive utilization of these products in mundane activities can only be accomplished with legislation and intervention of various government policies. Thus, for a sustainable bioeconomy, the marketing of biobased products will have to be done by highlighting their superiority over petroleum-based commodities in terms of carbon footprint. The feed stock that has been utilized for establishment of biorefineries is also independent of direct land use and based on nonedible crops. The stringent regulatory setup of government authorities also imposes a strong check on falsified news and low-quality manufacturing. Thus, to overcome these limitations, blockchain technology can be relied on to maintain a single flow of secured information in digitalized document forms containing all necessary information from emission profiles of biofuels, carbon benefits, water utility, waste disposal regimes, and valorization process and their value-added products and, most importantly, sustainability credentials. This would alleviate the need for authorities to check compliance records and other stakeholders as well as other "black box" sections. Thus, this model holds tremendous potential that can help build biorefineries as factories of the future. Recently, GoodFuels, a leading company in developing sustainable marine fuels, tested the world's first zero-emission marine fuel. The company announced the use of a blockchain model to store carbon footprints and emission savings for capturing the market of cleaner fuels by building trust, transparency, and a financially sustainable platform for zero-carbon shipping.

8. Current progress

The remembrance of an old adage is quite relevant in the current context: "If you have a hammer, everything looks like a nail." This statement highlights the prominent role of technology for addressing every problem, but the hammer needs to be changed based on latest trends and developments. Blockchain should be considered revolutionary technology possessing the credentials of security, transparency, and digitalization (Justinia, 2019; Makridakis and Christodoulou, 2019; Ikeda, 2018). There is plenty of research work that has been translated at a commercialized scale by adopting blockchain technology, but the vertical of biomanufacturing is quite complex and challenging. As the world is moving toward digitalization at a fast pace, many developments have been seen in this sector also. However, the legal, social, and regulatory compliances of exploring and commercializing the biologic world are quite arduous. The technology is not acceptable in the industrial forum unless its credibility has been proven across a national or international context. Thus, for proving the credibility of blockchain technology in the biomanufacturing sector, various technical standards and guidelines should be formulated by government officials, the scientific community, and industrialists that can be considered SOPs for massive utilization. However, the development in this is under progress, and some of the currently published standards are based on the Open Standard for Finance and the Enterprise Ethereum chain alliance (Dewey et al., 2019). For supply chain management, guidelines should be adopted from global supply chain standards (GS1) for attaining uniformity in identity, storage, and sharing of supply chain data. The sharing of clinical data should be channelized through the framework of HL7 (Health Level Seven International) standards for electronic health management systems. The more prolific blockchain-based platform was developed for recording electronic health data in a secured manner that is based on FHIRChain (Fast Health Interoperability Records + blockchain) (Zhang et al., 2018). More emphasis should be laid on the Title 21 Code of Federal Regulations that should be adopted in the biomanufacturing sector. The implementation of blockchain technology for high-value, low-volume products should originate from the guidelines of the US Environmental Protection Agency, the US FDA, and the US Department of Agriculture (Kamilaris et al., 2019). Currently, big pharmaceutical giants Biogen, Pfizer, Merck, AstraZeneca, Deloitte, and GlaxoSmithKline have developed their supply chain framework based on blockchain. Apart from that, the amalgamation of blockchain technology with location-based technologies such as GPS, RFID tags, and Sigfox has been envisaged for the development of automated platforms where manufactured products themselves tell us where they are, what condition they are in, who has received them, and whether they have been paid for. However, blockchain is amenable to be upgraded with technologic frameworks like 5G, AI, and ML for more comprehensive applications at a successful rate.

9. Proposed model of biomanufacturing through "FabRec" platform

Blockchain technology is still too much in its infancy to be comprehensively applied in biomanufacturing through connected machines and their accessories to develop decentralized manufacturing ecosystems. The technology should be equipped with proper authentication for recording the identity of machines and the process flow in a distributed ledger that requires verification of various nodes and their roles and responsibilities. Apart from that, the technology will also assist the design of layouts for interacting networks with their different levels of participants in manufacturing marketplaces. A prototype of a smart manufacturing ecosystem that was developed based on blockchain technology is the FabRec platform (Angrish et al., 2018). It is a framework in which a decentralized network of customers and manufacturers can interact through a laboratory-based setup of nodes and system-on-chip board for visualizing the integrity of data and process workflow for the development of trust. Here, FabRec is proposed for a decentralized framework for the development of a biomanufacturing ecosystem. The overview of the proposed model based on FabRec that can be applied in biomanufacturing sector has been represented in Fig. 8.5. The model depicts the integration of nodes that represent the participants, which can be human or machine, that can be interact with each other through blocks. Each block has all the relevant information of manufacturers that can be located in remote areas or developed areas, and the information can be shared through encrypted codes to the users or customers. The dashed lines represent the information inflow among trusted

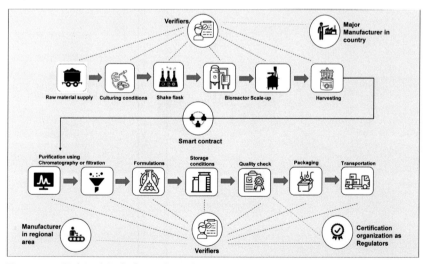

Figure 8.5 "FabRech" platform—based proposed model of blockchain technology in biomanufacturing.

members. Every participant has been allocated with a unique identity, and a diverse arena of people from both private and public sector can join this network. The quality control community such as ISO can join and validate claims conferred by a manufacturer. This platform also provides flexibility of joining the regulators and compliance agents that can help in further verification of biobased products. Thus, this model provides a layout for the development of a smart and digitalized integrated platform for consumer and manufacturers in the biomanufacturing sector. This will certainly play a game-changing role in this sector. However, the true potential needs to be evaluated at a wider scale for its commercialization.

10. Current challenges

Blockchain technology seems promising in the biomanufacturing sector, but it is not a panacea for all the problems, having its own challenges from conception to implementation. As the canopy of blockchain is composed of secured and shared information, it requires the networking of millions of computers at a global level. This networking requires consumption of a huge amount of electricity (terawatt hours) that encumbers the energy consumption of many countries and contributes to a larger carbon footprint. The benefits and challenges of blockchain technology are represented in Fig. 8.6. Another challenge is that although the information will

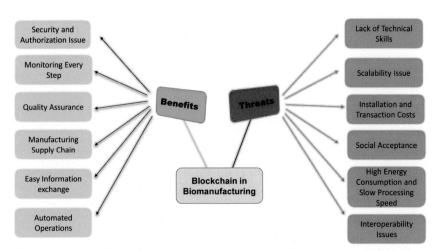

Figure 8.6 Benefits and threats of blockchain technology in the biomanufacturing sector.

be not tampered with after adding to the blockchain platform, the data originator can enter falsified information that is used by other participating members.

Thus, losing the credibility of organization or manufacturer also impacts the wider adoption of this emerging technology. The technology is still lagging behind global usage in the manufacturing sector due to the less attention being paid toward formulating the associated guidelines and regulations. Currently, with the ongoing advancements in bioprocessing 4.0, the research and manufacturing of biologic products create enormous data, but industries are always skeptical to share their data due to security. Therefore, certain commercialized blockchain-based platforms should be developed that can be exclusively utilized in this sector. The technology is new and various applications have been created at a high rate. Proving the credibility of these applications is another daunting task in the biomanufacturing sector. Thus, one can envision that the technology will prove to transformative in the biomanufacturing area, but prodigious research and development should be done prior to implementation of handling sensitive biologic data for global use.

11. Future prospects

The emerging application of blockchain will definitely intervene all facets of life and lead toward the transformation for betterment in the future, the potential in the biomanufacturing sector of this technology still needs to be assessed. Currently, in major enterprises, blockchain projects are in experimentation phase, and the technology faces a "trough of disillusionment." The arrival of the World Wide Web in 1990 faced a similar challenge for global acceptance. So, we can foresee that there will be various interoperable blockchain platforms with easy access, greater scale of operation, and a customer-friendly approach.

The current advantages such as immutability, transparency, and P2P networking in both private and public mode cannot be ignored, but it is the cost of implementation and global acceptance that need to be worked out in a futuristic scenario. It is envisioned that the future of blockchain technology in biomanufacturing will move into a bidirectional mode. The future prospects of blockchain technology in the biomanufacturing arena are represented in Fig. 8.7. One direction of development and improvements lies in developing IoT-based super secured networks for sharing the research and development data in the biomanufacturing sector.

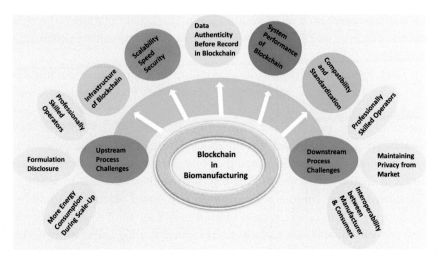

Figure 8.7 Future prospects of blockchain technology in the biomanufacturing sector.

Another direction includes the combination of AI with blockchain technology to upgrade the design of bioprocess, its sustainability, and economic analysis. Furthermore, the cyber security for protecting confidential data of research and development and sensitive data about various pathogenic microorganisms and their process should be also considerable in the future to promote the trust and credibility of this technology in the biomanufacturing sector.

12. Conclusion

Blockchain technology is a revolutionary technology that make the world a smaller place. The applications have started with the financial sector, but its roots are spreading to all business and service sectors. The burst in digitalization and automation accentuates the prolific growth in the development of blockchain technology. The technology has been well embraced in the pharmaceutical sector to maintain effective supply chain management, eradicating the network of counterfeit drugs, but it is nascent in the biomanufacturing sector. As bioprocessing 4.0 is a major technology breakthrough for advanced manufacturing practices, blockchain technology will play an outstanding role in the transformation of this sector. The technology has its own limitations for implementation, but considering its astonishing credentials, it will be an integral part of the bioeconomy in the future. Current advancements in medical devices and diagnostics, tissue engineering and regeneration, biotherapeutics and stem cell therapy, and operative management planning will continue to develop various blockchain platforms that can facilitate biomanufacturing in more secured and transparent way.

Acknowledgment

The authors are really thankful to the support and motivation provided by Gautam Buddha University for accomplishing this work.

References

AgreCoin Will Use the Blockchain to Solve Supply Chain Problems in the Alcohol Industry, 2018. CISION PR Newswire. https://www.prnewswire.com/news-releases/agrecoin-will-use-the-blockchain-to-solve-supply-chain-problems-in-the-alcohol-industry-30060 1987.html (Accessed 31.03.21).

Ahmad, S., Kumar, A., Hafeez, A., 2018. Importance of data integrity & its regulation in pharmaceutical industry. Pharma Innov. 8 (1), 306—313.

Aijaz, A., Li, M., Smith, D., Khong, D., LeBlon, C., Fenton, O.S., et al., 2018. Biomanufacturing for clinically advanced cell therapies. Nat. Biomed. Eng. 2 (6), 362—376.

Andoni, M., Robu, V., Flynn, D., Abram, S., Geach, D., Jenkins, D., Mccallum, P., Peacock, A., 2019. Blockchain technology in the energy sector: a systematic review of challenges and opportunities. Renew. Sustain. Energy Rev. 100, 143—174.

Angrish, A., Craver, B., Hasan, M., Starly, B., 2018. A case study for blockchain in manufacturing: "FabRec": a prototype for peer-to-peer network of manufacturing nodes. Proc. Manuf. 26, 1180—1192.

Astarita, V., Giofrè, V.P., Mirabelli, G., Solina, V., 2019. A review of blockchain-based systems in transportation. Information 11 (1), 1—24.

Bandyopadhyay, A.A., Khetan, A., Malmberg, L.H., et al., 2017. Advancement in bioprocess technology: parallels between microbial natural products and cell culture biologics. J. Ind. Microbiol. Biotechnol. 44, 785—797.

Becker, J., Whittmann, C., 2019. A field of dreams: lignin valorization into chemicals, materials, fuels, and health-care products. Biotechnol. Adv. 37, 1—24.

Blockchain Benefits for the Alcohol and Beverage Industry, September 23, 2019. Alt coin magazine. https://medium.com/the-capital/blockchain-benefits-for-the-alcohol-and-beverage-industry-6c473918d700 (Accessed 31.03.21).

Bušić, A., Marđetko, N., Kundas, S., Morzak, G., Belskaya, H., et al., 2018. Bioethanol production from renewable raw materials and its separation and purification: a review. Food Technol. Biotechnol. 56 (3), 289—311.

Calina, D., Docea, A.O., Petrakis, D., Egorov, A.M., Ishmukhametov, A.A., Gabibov, A.G., et al., 2020. Towards effective COVID-19 vaccines: updates, perspectives and challenges. Int. J. Mol. Med. 46 (1), 3—16.

Darvazeh, S.S., Vanani, I.R., Musolu, F.M., 2020. Big data analytics and its applications in supply chain management. In: New Trends in the Use of Artificial Intelligence for the Industry 4.0, Intechopen, pp. 1—27.

Davis, S.C., Dohleman, F., Long, S.P., 2010. The global potential for Agave as a biofuel feedstock. GCB Bioenergy 3 (1), 68—78.

Deepa, N., Pham, Q., et al., 2020. A Survey on Blockchain for Big Data: Approaches, Opportunities, and Future Directions, ArXiv abs/2009.00858, pp. 1—20.

Dewey, J., Holland, et al., 2019. Global Legal Insights — Blockchain & Cryptocurrency Regulation. Global Legal Group Ltd, London, UK, pp. 1—505.

Ding, M., Nguyen, D.C., Pathirana, P.N., Seneviratne, A., 2019. Blockchain for secure EHRs sharing of mobile cloud based E-Health systems. IEEE Access 7, 66792—66806.

Enescu, F.M., Bizon, N., Onu, A., Răboacă, M.S., Thounthong, P., Mazare, A.G., Şerban, G., 2020. Implementing blockchain technology in irrigation systems that integrate photovoltaic energy generation systems. Sustainability 12 (4), 1—30.

Gargalo, C.L., Udugama, I., Pontius, K., Lopez, P.C., Nielsen, R.F., Hasanzadeh, A., Mansouri, S.S., Bayer, C., Junicke, H., Gernaey, K.V., 2020. Towards smart bio-manufacturing: a perspective on recent developments in industrial measurement and monitoring technologies for bio-based production processes. J. Ind. Microbiol. Biotechnol. 47 (11), 947—964.

Giannini, L., Terenzi, M., 2020. Trust, transparency and disintermediation: an analysis of blockchain implementation in the supply-chain. Mediascapes J. 1—18.

Haq, I., Muselemu, O., 2018. Blockchain technology in pharmaceutical industry to prevent counterfeit drugs. Int. J. Comput. Appl. 180 (25), 8—12.

How Blockchain Technology Will Affect the Audit, 2019. RSM. https://rsmus.com/what-we-do/services/assurance/how-blockchain-technology-will-affect-the-audit.html (Accessed 29.03.21).

Hoy, M.B., 2017. An introduction to the blockchain and its implications for libraries and medicine. Med. Ref. Serv. Q. 36 (3), 273—279.

Ikeda, K., 2018. Security and privacy of blockchain and quantum computation. Adv. Comput. 111, 199—228.

Industrial Alcohol Market Worth $112.0 Billion by 2025 — Exclusive Report by Markets and Markets, 2020. CISION PR Newswire. https://www.prnewswire.com/news-releases/industrial-alcohol-market-worth-112-0-billion-by-2025—exclusive-report-by-marketsandmarkets-301122843.html (Accessed 31.03.21).

Jacquemart, R., Vandersluis, M., Zhao, M., Sukhija, K., Sidhu, N., Stout, J., 2016. A single-use strategy to enable manufacturing of affordable biologics. Comput. Struct. Biotechnol. J. 14, 309—318.

Jennings, K., 2021. Pharma's Blockchain Trials: Novartis, Merck Test the Tech Popularized by Bitcoin. Forbes. https://www.forbes.com/sites/katiejennings/2021/02/02/pharmas-blockchain-trials-novartis-merck-test-the-tech-popularized-by-bitcoin/?sh=537a32337e86 (Accessed 26.03.21).

Justinia, T., 2019. Blockchain technologies: opportunities for solving real-world problems in healthcare and biomedical sciences. Acta Inf. Med. 27 (4), 284—291.

Kamilaris, A., Fonts, A., Prenafeta-Boldú, F.X., 2019. The rise of blockchain technology in agriculture and food supply chains. Trends Food Sci. Technol. 91, 640—652.

Kelly, J.T., Campbell, K.L., Gong, E., Scuffham, P., 2020. The Internet-of-things: impact and implications for health care delivery. J. Med. Internet Res. 22 (11), 1—11.

Kim, J.H., Marks, F., Clemens, J.D., 2021. Looking beyond COVID-19 vaccine phase 3 trials. Nat. Med. 27, 205—211.

Koutras, D., Stergiopoulos, G., Dasaklis, T., Kotzanikolaou, P., Glynos, D., Douligeris, C., 2020. Security in IoMT communications: a survey. Sensors 20 (17), 1—49.

Kuo, T.T., Kim, H.E., Ohno-Machado, L., 2017. Blockchain distributed ledger technologies for biomedical and health care applications. J. Am. Med. Inf. Assoc. 24 (6), 1211—1220.

Lake, D., Milito, R., Morrow, M., et al., 2014. Internet-of-things: architectural framework for ehealth security. J. ICT Stand. 1 (3), 301—328.

Lane, J., 2019. From Feedstock to By-Products: Using Blockchain to Trace Biofuels, the Digest. https://www.biofuelsdigest.com/bdigest/2019/06/04/from-feedstock-to-by-products-using-blockchain-to-trace-biofuels/ (Accessed 03.04.21).

Lillrank, P., Särkkä, M., 2011. The service machine as a service operation framework. Strategic Outsourcing An Int. J. 4 (3), 274−293.

Machine-as-a-Service: New Frontier of Smart Manufacturing, 2018. Birlasoft. https://www.birlasoft.com/articles/machine-as-a-service-new-frontier-of-smart-manufacturing (Accessed 28.03.21).

Mackey, T.K., Kuo, T.T., Gummadi, B., Clauson, K.A., Church, G., Grishin, D., Obbad, K., Barkovich, R., Palombini, M., 2019. 'Fit-for-purpose?' - challenges and opportunities for applications of blockchain technology in the future of healthcare. BMC Med. 17 (1), 1−17.

Makridakis, S., Christodoulou, K., 2019. Blockchain: curent challenges and future prospects/applications. Future Internet 11 (12), 1−16.

Marella, V., Upreti, B., Merikivi, J., Tuunainen, V.K., 2020. Understanding the creation of trust in cryptocurrencies: the case of Bitcoin. Electron. Mark. 30, 259−271.

MediLedger to Explore Use of Blockchain for DSCSA Compliance, 2017. Pharmatech. https://www.pharmtech.com/view/mediledger-explore-use-blockchain-dscsa-compliance (Accessed 27.03.21).

Mendling, J., Weber, I., Aalst, W., Brocke, J.V., Cabanillas, C., et al., 2018. Blockchains for business process management − challenges and opportunities. ACM Trans. Manag. Inf. Syst. 9 (1), 1−16.

Miller, R., 2019. IBM, KPMG, Merck, Walmart Team up for Drug Supply Chain Blockchain Pilot. Techcrunch. https://techcrunch.com/2019/06/13/ibm-kpmg-merck-walmart-team-up-for-drug-supply-chain-blockchain-pilot/ (Accessed 27.03.21).

Morris, N., 2018. Novartis Explores Blockchain's Potential for Pharmaceuticals. Ledger Insights. https://www.ledgerinsights.com/novartis-pharma-blockchain/ (Accessed 26.03.21).

Narayanan, H., Luna, M.F., von Stosch, M., Cruz Bournazou, M.N., Polotti, G., Morbidelli, M., Butté, A., Sokolov, M., 2020. Bioprocessing in the digital age: the role of process models. Biotechnol. J. 15 (1), 1−10.

Naughton, B.D., 2017. The EU falsified medicines directive: key implications for dispensers. Med Access @ Point Care 1, e155−e159.

Naughton, B.D., 2018. Medicine authentication technology: a quantitative study of incorrect quarantine, average response times and offline issues in a hospital setting. BMJ Open 9, 1−6.

Naz, M., Al-zahrani, F.A., Khalid, R., Javaid, N., Qamar, A.M., Afzal, M.K., Shafiq, M., 2019. A secure data sharing platform using blockchain and interplanetary file system. Sustainability 11 (24), 1−24.

Oñiguez, G., Bernal, C., Ramírez, M., Villalvazo, N., 2014. Recycling agave bagasse of the tequila industry. Adv. Chem. Eng. Sci. 4 (2), 135−142.

Ozercan, H.I., Ileri, A.M., Ayday, E., Alkan, C., 2018. Realizing the potential of blockchain technologies in genomics. Genome Res. 28 (9), 1255−1263.

Paliwal, V., Chandra, S., Sharma, S., 2020. Blockchain technology for sustainable supply chain management: a systematic literature review and a classification framework. Sustainability 12 (18), 1−39.

Pathak, P.D., Gedam, V.V., Bhagat, S.L., Chahande, A., 2019. In: Pawar, P., Ronge, B., Balasubramaniam, R., Vibhute, A., Apte, S. (Eds.), Biorefineries: A Sustainable Approach for High Value-Added Products in Rural India. Springer, Cham, pp. 585−593.

Quaye, W., Yawson, I., Yawson, R., Williams, I., Irene, 2009. Acceptance of biotechnology and social-cultural implications in Ghana. Afr. J. Biotechnol. 8 (9), 1997—2003.

Qureshi, A., Megías Jiménez, D.J., 2020. Blockchain-based multimedia content protection: review and open challenges. Appl. Sci. 11 (1), 1—24.

Radziwon, A., Bilberg, A., Bogers, M., Madsen, E., 2014. The smart factory: exploring adaptive and flexible manufacturing solutions. Proc. Eng. 69, 1184—1190.

Rinker, M., Khare, C., Pandhye, S., Fayman, K., 2021. Industry 4.0 digital transformation conference: has the pandemic accelerated digital transformation? J. Adv. Manuf. Proc. 3 (1), 1—5.

Robak, K., Balcerek, M., 2018. Review of second generation bioethanol production from residual biomass. Food Technol. Biotechnol. 56 (2), 174—187.

Rui, Z., Rui, X., Ling, L., 2019. Security and privacy on blockchain. ACM Comput. Surv. 52 (3), 1—34.

Sahoo, S., Halder, R., 2020. Blockchain-based forward and reverse supply chains for e-waste management. In: Future Data and Security Engineering. Springer Nature, Switzerland, pp. 201—220.

Salah, K., Jayaraman, R., Ahmad, R., Yaqoob, I., Ellahham, S., Omar, M., 2020. Mohammed, blockchain and COVID-19 pandemic: applications and challenges. In: Artificial Intelligence and Blockchain in Healthcare, Research Gate, pp. 1—19.

Shi, S., He, D., Li, L., Kumar, N., Khan, M.K., Choo, K.R., 2020. Applications of blockchain in ensuring the security and privacy of electronic health record systems: a survey. Comput. Secur. 97, 1—21.

Subramanian, N., Chaudhuri, A., Kayikci, Y., 2020. Blockchain applications in reverse logistics. In: Blockchain and Supply Chain Logistics. Springer, pp. 67—81.

Tan, T.M., Salo, J., Ahokangas, P., et al., 2021. Revealing the disintermediation concept of blockchain technology: how intermediaries gain from blockchain adoption in a new business model. In: Impact of Globalization and Advanced Technologies on Online Business Models. IGI Global, Germany, pp. 88—102.

Tasca, P., Tessone, C., 2019. A taxonomy of blockchain technologies: principles of identification and classification. Ledger 4, 1—39.

Ullah, A., Shahnewaz Siddiquee, S.M., Akbar Hossain, M., Sayan, K.R., 2020. An ethereum blockchain-based prototype for data security of regulated electricity market. Inventions 5 (4), 1—28.

VIRI Creates Global Anonymous Contact-Tracing Platform to Stop Spread of COVID-19, 2020. CISION PR Newswire. https://www.prnewswire.com/news-releases/viri-creates-global-anonymous-contact-tracing-platform-to-stop-spread-of-covid-19-3010 74918.html (Accessed 02.04.21).

Wang, J., Wang, S., Guo, J., Du, Y., Cheng, S., Li, X., 2019. A summary of research on blockchain in the field of intellectual property. Proc. Comput. Sci. 147, 191—197.

Weking, J., Mandalenakis, M., Hein, A., et al., 2020. The impact of blockchain technology on business models — a taxonomy and archetypal patterns. Electron. Mark. 30 (2), 285—305.

Wu, J., Tran, N., 2018. Application of blockchain technology in sustainable energy systems: an overview. Sustainability 10 (9), 1—22.

Xu, J., Xu, X., Huang, C., Angelo, J., et al., 2020. Biomanufacturing evolution from conventional to intensified processes for productivity improvement: a case study. mAbs 12 (1).

Yuheng, H., Haoyu, W., Lei, W., et al., 2020. Understanding (mis)behavior on the EOSIO blockchain. In: Proceedings of the ACM on Measurements and Analysis of Computing Systems. ACM, New York, pp. 1—29.

Zhang, Y.P., Sun, J., Ma, Y., 2017. Biomanufacturing: history and perspective. J. Ind. Microbiol. Biotechnol. 44 (4—5), 773—784.

Zhang, P., White, J., Schmidt, D.C., Lenz, G., Rosenbloom, S.T., 2018. FHIRChain: applying blockchain to securely and scalably share clinical data. Comput. Struct. Biotechnol. J. 16, 267—278.

Zobel-Roos, S., Schmidt, A., Uhlenbrock, L., Ditz, R., Köster D, D., Strube, J., 2020. Digital twins in biomanufacturing. In: Advances in Biochemical Engineering/ Biotechnology. Springer, Berlin, Heidelberg, pp. 1—82.

CHAPTER 9

Blockchain-based e-voting protocols

Srijanee Mookherji, Odelu Vanga and Rajendra Prasath[a]
Indian Institute of Information Technology, Sri City, Andhra Pradesh, India

1. Introduction

Voting is an act of decision-making that plays an important role in choosing either a leader for a designated position or privileging a contending process or an event to take a lead in a specific situation. It provides a platform to express majority by means of choice in scenarios ranging from small-scale boardroom decisions to large-scale democratic decisions. The concept of elections is said to have been introduced in the Ancient Greek and Roman periods. The conventional method of voting can be classified into five broad classes (Lambrinoudakis et al., 2003):

- hand-counted ballot papers and boxes system
- direct-recording mechanical (lever) voting machines
- punch cards as ballots
- optical mark-sense ballots
- direct-recording electronic voting machines

Talking about the hand-counted ballot paper and boxes system, the Australian Ballot system was embraced by almost every government around the world. Its uniqueness was in the fact that ballots were structured and issued by the government and voters voted in secret (Miller, 1995; Fredman, 1967; Brent, 2006). But, it required innumerous papers, infrastructure, and manpower. In addition, it needed a significant amount of time to count the ballots, and human errors would cause discrepancies in the result. Along with these, many security flaws like lack of voter anonymity, vote integrity, etc., were present. Unethical activities, such as vote manipulation, miscalculation of ballots, biased result declaration, and voter impersonation, took place. This resulted in questioning the accuracy and integrity of such a voting system.

[a] This work was supported by the seed grant funded by IIIT Sri City, Chittoor.

Blockchain Technology for Emerging Applications
ISBN 978-0-323-90193-2
https://doi.org/10.1016/B978-0-323-90193-2.00006-5

To overcome the count bias and delay in result publishing, mechanical lever voting machines were introduced and brought into practice in the 1930s in the United States. These machines counted the votes the moment a voter cast his choice, thus providing the final results minutes after the polls closed. However, the major issue with these machines was that recounting was an impossible task, as no backup of votes was available. There was just an odometer for rechecking, which kept the total vote count for each candidate (Cranor, 2003; Greene et al., 2006).

In 1964, IBM's Portapunch mechanism was used to design Votomatic that used punch cards as ballot papers. The major drawback of the system was that even though recounting was possible, there was no guarantee that the punches would be clean. Also, there was no intuitive system to decipher the vote cast from a mispunched card. After the controversy surrounding the US presidential election in the State of Florida in 2000, in which punch cards were used, governments around the world began scrutinizing and questioning the integrity of the followed voting systems (Saltman et al., 2003; Kohno et al., 2004; Roth, 1998). This has resulted in the rise of the concept of electronic voting.

The optical mark-sense scanner was introduced in 1950s for college grading purposes, and it was applied in the field of electoral systems in 1970s. The voters were required to color the slots next to their desired candidates using a pen or a pencil on a ballot. The scanner would scan the colored area using visible light and note the choices. This system of voting faced a similar problem of human error where a voter does not mark the ballot properly. In the case of the year 2000 US presidential election, many ballots were challenged due to inappropriate marking of the ballots (Awad and Leiss, 2016).

Electronic voting is the process of using computer devices to help in casting and counting votes. Any voting mechanism that uses electronic devices can be categorized into e-voting techniques. Direct-recording electronic voting machines and internet voting are considered the most widely accepted e-voting techniques (Lauer, 2004). Shoup and Microvote had already come up with direct-recording electronic voting systems in 1986. The advantage of the system was it had a better interface, making it easier for people to vote. Everything being done electronically meant that counting was automated and results could be published faster. The only drawback of the system was submission of empty ballots due to improper pressing of buttons on the machine, resulting in wastage of votes. Since the vote was also electronically transmitted, there was no physical existence of the vote, making it impossible to go for a recount. If a machine was tampered with by malicious parties, then the authorities had no option to know whether the votes were authentic (Miller, 1995; Lauer, 2004; Epstein, 2007).

Internet voting is a technique where a voter can vote securely over the internet from any part of the world. In 1997, David Wolf, an American astronaut, became the first person to cast his vote over the internet. The vote was cast via email from Mir Space Station (Lauer, 2004). With the beginning of internet voting, one can now vote in the comfort of their home, and an increase in voter turnaround can be expected as a result. Also the concept of early voting has come into play, where a voter can vote before the election day at satellite polling stations. The only thing that needs to be maintained is the fact that the ballots should be kept uncounted and sealed till the end of the election. With a higher voter turnaround, the frauds that had been occurring due to absentee voting are also expected to decrease (Cranor, 2003; Jones, 2003).

However along with advantages, there are gaps in e-voting that need to be addressed. With most of the e-voting systems being centralized in nature, there is one central trusted authority, and there is a high possibility of a rigged administrator turning the entire voting system into a biased one. This also results in integrity issues and a lack of trust in the voting system from the voter's side. A solution to such a problem can be solved by using a decentralized data management system. The concept of blockchain can provide something similar to the requirement. Blockchain is a decentralized, transparent, and distributed ledger that is immutable in nature.

Blockchain-based e-voting protocol can be implemented in many ways. The main idea is to maintain privacy of votes and voters and integrity of the election. There are currently many researches going on to incorporate blockchain in e-voting. Most of the proposed works are based on permissionless blockchain (Bistarelli et al., 2017), but there are a few issues that arise that are discussed further in the chapter. Again, works (Hjalmarsson et al., 2018; Lee et al., 2016) have used permissioned blockchain. And, there are protocols (McCorry et al., 2017; Liu and Wang, 2017) that function without a trusted third party (TTP). Simultaneously, there are protocols (Lee et al., 2016) that have used the help of TTPs. There are different techniques used by researchers to ensure anonymity and keep votes and information a secret. Others (Hjalmarsson et al., 2018; McCorry et al., 2017) have used the concept of zero-knowledge proof for information hiding purpose. Wang et al. (2018) used ring signature to ensure anonymity. Many different techniques are being combined by researchers around to world to propose a secure blockchain-based protocol. A few of these are summarized in the upcoming sections, and a comparative study for the works is provided.

This book chapter is organized as follows: Section 2 describes the onset of electronic voting and how it evolved over the time. We further discuss the various security properties and performance properties required for a secure electronic voting system. A comparative study of existing research is made based on the aforementioned properties. Finally, issues in electronic voting systems are discussed. Section 3 describes the advances in blockchain-based e-voting systems by going through the significant contributions toward developing such systems. A comparative study of various works is presented, and a discussion on the prevalent issues of blockchain-based systems is provided. Section 4 concludes the book chapter.

2. Electronic voting

An election is an indispensable part of an efficiently functioning modern democracy. An election is a medium to assess the trust of people in their government. As mentioned, after the disruption in the 2000 US presidential election, citizens began questioning different aspects of the electoral system, which gave rise to thoughts about an alternative for conventional voting. Hence, electronic voting was encouraged, as it would ensure higher voter turnout, making the democratic process stronger and more reliable (Lambrinoudakis et al., 2003).

E-voting is cost-effective and easy to implement. The ease of access to voting increases the voter's interest to take part in democratic decision-making. It assures increased voter participation (Raikov, 2018), and it helps in providing accurate decisions. An e-voting system is expected to the overcome the backdrops of a traditional method and provide a secure way of holding an election with the help of devices and infrastructure that use cryptography techniques to secure the voting process.

Fig. 9.1 depicts various phases and functionalities of the actors present in a general e-voting system.

Let us now look at the general structure of an e-voting system. We begin with the actors who are essential for an e-voting system (Baiardi et al.; Joaquim et al., 2003):

- **Voter**: Voters are responsible for casting a vote for their desired candidate.

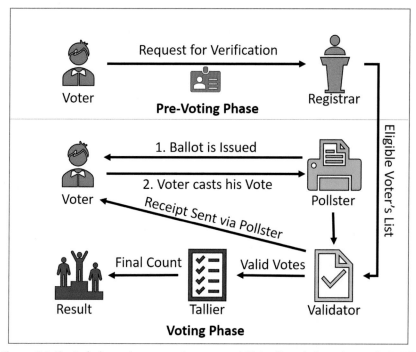

Figure 9.1 Typical phases in an e-voting protocol (Baiardi et al.; Joaquim et al., 2003).

- **Registrar**: The registrar is responsible for the initial setup by registering the voters against a request. In a majority of the systems, only an eligible voter is allowed to register. The registrar holds a list of eligible voters and registered voters. They finally publish a list of verified registered voters, which is used throughout the voting process. The registrar is also responsible for issuing a public key and private key pair to the voters, where henceforth a voter is identified by their identification code and the public key. In many systems, the valid voter list also contains a parameter that is handled by the validator to validate a voter's ballot.
- **Pollster**: After a voter has voted, a pollster is responsible for encrypting the ballot, sending the ballot to the validator, and finally submitting the vote to the ballot box. The voter is required to have trust only in the pollster. The pollster also functions during the time of vote verification by the voter.
- **Validator**: The validator ensures that a voter is valid and has cast their vote only once. Its function is to stop multiple instances of voting.

The validator signs a blind ballot using a validation certificate. The validator uses the valid voters list to check the voter's signature on the ballot using the public key. Once a vote is validated, the parameters on the voter's list are updated. The sequence of vote validation is not recorded. The voter finally unbinds his vote and sends it to the tallier for counting.

- **Tallier**: The tallier verifies the ballot submitted by the voter by checking its uniqueness compared with the other ballots received from other voters. Once the ballot is checked, a receipt is provided to the voter. The tallier is also responsible for counting the votes and publishing the final result.

A voting system is considered secure if it satisfies the following security and performance-related properties:

2.1 Security properties

- **Eligibility**: Only an authorized voter should be allowed to vote. Every voting system should have a fool-proof authentication mechanism.
- **Privacy**: Only a voter should have the knowledge of his choice throughout the voting phase. This property states that the system can keep the voter's choice as a secret even from the concerned authorities.
- **Voter anonymity**: A voter should remain anonymous during the entire time of the election process. It goes hand in hand with privacy, as a vote cast is anonymous and private.
- **Lack of reusability**: A voter can vote only once, and this is used to stop double voting.
- **Verifiability**: This property can be bifurcated into *individual verifiability* and *universal verifiability*. Individual verifiability allows a voter to check if their vote has been counted or not. Universal verifiability ensures that every voter can verify the final result of election at any time after the result has been announced. A more rigid term is end-to-end (E2E) verifiable, which provides a receipt to the voter to ensure that their vote has been noted.
- **Fairness**: This property ensures that the result will be computed only after the end of an election.
- **Lack of coercibility**: This property ensures that vote buying and selling is not possible throughout the process of an election.
- **Receipt-less**: This property entails lack of coercibility, where the voter does not receive any receipt to proving their vote.

2.2 Performance properties

- **Correctness (completeness and soundness)**: Votes should be counted correctly. Correctness can be bifurcated into (1) completeness, which means that all valid votes have to be counted, and (2) soundness, which means that all invalid votes should be excluded from counting.
- **Robustness**: The voting system should function appropriately even when there is a partial failure. It should not be affected by misbehaving voters either.
- **Efficiency**: This is the property that is used to measure the computational complexity of the entire system.
- **Mobility**: This property allows users to vote from mobile devices.

2.3 Significant contributions in e-voting

In 2005, Estonia was the first country to declare that their nationwide election held using a remote internet voting process was successful (Clarke and Martens, 2016). National ID cards issued by the government were used for voter identification. The voters were allowed to vote early over the internet and a chance to vote was open until the election day. To attain the trust of the voters in the system, traditional voting was given a priority, where if a voter chose to go to the polling booth to cast their vote even after casting an e-vote, the e-vote would be deleted and the physical vote would be calculated. The voters were also given an option to re-vote and the old vote would be deleted. If a voter tried to vote twice (which is illegal), only the last vote was considered. An envelope method (Maaten, 2004) was used in the voting system. The voter used their ID card to get into the homepage of the voting website, hosted by the election commission. The ID number was verified against a list of valid IDs. The voter's choice was encrypted, which was the inner envelope. The voter's choice was then confirmed with a digital signature, making it the outer envelope. The outer envelope was removed during counting, and the final tally was done anonymously by the election commission.

The first e-voting scheme as a concept was proposed by Chaum (1981). In the proposed scheme, the votes are transmitted through anonymous channels, utilizing the concept of mixnets (Chaum, 1981). It does not require a centrally trusted authority, and if one authority remains honest throughout the process of mixes, the system remains secured. Voter privacy is ensured using pseudonyms, and a public-key cryptosystem is used. In this scheme, it is assumed that only registered voters are taking part in the election. The details of each voter are masked using the pseudonym. The pseudonym, in turn, decrypts the vote of a voter. In this proposed system, a mix function is introduced to ensure that a voter can vote only once, so in a single mix, voters submit their ballots. For multiple mixes, a group of ballots is generated that is then processed as a single batch. The ballots are finally counted after checking the pseudonyms. This scheme ensures that no voter can vote using two different pseudonyms. The scheme ensures the privacy of voters and vote verifiability.

Cohen and Fischer (1985) proposed an e-voting protocol that uses homomorphic encryption. A time-stamped public bulletin is used for communication between the voters and electoral committee. Beacons are used to generate pseudo-random bits and create one-way location. The issue with the protocol is that the election authorities can read any vote at any time, thus causing privacy and integrity problems. An extension to that work (Cohen and Fischer, 1985) was done by Cohen (1986) where the government is replaced by multiple tellers (mix servers). This distributes the trust to every teller, and if one of the tellers is compromised, then the voting system would be compromised. Also, this paper gave allowance to the government to publish the winner without actually releasing the tally.

In 1994, Benaloh and Tuinstra (1994) proposed a receipt-free election protocol that provided secret verifiable ballots. The voters could not prove the contents of the ballot. This in turn prevented vote coercion. Cramer et al. (1996) showed a multiauthority voting system. A bulletin board is provided for voters to cast, encrypt, and share their votes. Zero-knowledge proofs, being expensive, were eliminated, and instead, a noninteractive proof of validity was proposed, reducing the computation cost from quadratic to linear. Each vote comes with this proof. A threshold system is used to disable a single authority from decrypting the votes. The proposed system is compatible to binary voting. If a different kind of voting is to be implemented, proof numbers will increase.

In Cramer et al. (1997), a multiauthority voting system is proposed that is based on homomorphic characteristics of the ElGamal (1985) crypto-system and proofs of knowledge. The decryption private key is shared to all authorities using a threshold system. Authorities here commit to publicly share their secrets to avoid malicious activities. For decryption, more than half of the authorities are required. In case of binary elections, linear cost is taken with respect to the number of voters. However, a multiway election is computationally a costly affair.

In Juang et al. (2002), a verifiable multiauthority system was proposed that allows nonvoting even if a voter has registered. Also, it supports tallying by providing privacy to voters. To diffuse the power of a single authority, distributed blind signatures (Chaum, 1984) are used. The architecture described consists of seven phases with voters, administrators, scrutineers, and counter. The votes are encrypted, then signed by the administrator using a blind threshold signature. The voters then create the encrypted votes and send them to the counter using an untraceable email system. The final votes are sent to the scrutineer, who then confirms and sends votes back with their secret key. Finally, the decrypted votes are published. Voter privacy is secured in this scheme. The time complexity of the system is linear with respect to the number of voters per administrator.

In Li et al. (2009), the authors present a multiauthority voting system based on blind signatures. Voters cast their vote and the vote is signed by multiple authorities to blind it. The authorities are responsible for an honest and fair election by conforming with government agencies. The protocol has four phases, and four trusted authorities have three pairs of keys. Each voter has two pairs of keys. The main contribution of the paper is that coercion resistance and identification of a voter are not fully dependent on the trusted authorities.

Authors in Porkodi et al. (2011) present a scheme with a bulletin board where the voters post their encrypted votes. The homomorphic properties of encryption allow an anonymous tally of votes from the bulletin board. A threshold scheme is used for key sharing among the administrators. A commitment needs to be posted by each administrator to his/her private key and prove that a voter has a valid, encrypted vote. In the final stage, the tally is decrypted and the results are published. For a smaller key size, elliptic curve cryptosystems (Miller, 1985; Hankerson et al., 2006) are used. Each vote comes with a proof of knowledge, and administrators have to prove the validity of their commitment.

A multiauthority, receipt-free system is proposed by Philip et al. (Adewole et al., 2011) where n authorities are available and a trusted center (TC) is present. The TC is responsible for providing username and password to eligible voters after validating their identities and registering their votes. Each voter has to encrypt their vote, sign it, and craft the proof of correctness. Once that process is over, authorities distribute the shared private key and get the final tally. To provide receipt-less voting, the votes are encrypted again, signed, and have a proof of validity. The computational cost of the protocol is very high.

Cobra by Essex et al. (2012) used the idea of the proof of concept that simultaneously provides ballot authorization. To achieve lack of coercibility, each elector can use a fake credential and cast fake votes, which are finally separated out at the end without revealing any other submission (Schläpfer et al., 2011). Bloom Filter (Bloom, 1970) is used to prevent privacy of the voters. The concurrent ballot authorization is computationally high. Authorities are assumed to be honest and trustworthy. The system also faces scalability issues.

In another work (Nguyen and Dang, 2013), the authors propose a blind signature-based voting scheme using dynamic ballots. The registration of a voter is done using blind signatures and a group of authorities. A dynamic ballot changes for each voter, so it ensures lack of coercibility. Each voter receives a random permutation of the candidates, which is done by the ballot center. Plain-text-equivalence (PET) (Juels et al., 2010) is used for tallying purpose, where invalid and repeated ballots are removed. This protocol satisfies every need for a secured voting system. However, with five different authorities, two sets of bulletin boards, two forms of encryption, and a PET there come scalability issues, and this results in high computation cost.

Aziz (2019) shows an e-voting work with blind signatures that has multiple authorities and is coercion resistant. Freedom from coercion is employed by using a scheme similar to that in Essex et al. (2012). Once the registration process is over, a token authority is responsible for providing tokens to the voters for their anonymous request. It is further used to create a ballot. This ensures receipt-less voting as ballot-making is not in the hands of the voters. The ballots are further signed by a registrar using blind signatures, and these ballots are cast through mixnets. A set of trusted parties is present for decrypting the votes and calculating the final tally. The vote and the proof of validity are delinked by shuffling the ballots, thus preventing the voter from knowing if the vote was tallied or not. This provides resistance to coercion.

Tables 9.1 and 9.2 comprise a comparison of the properties of the various works discussed in the preceding section. The works are compared against the security properties and performance properties required for a secured e-voting system.

2.4 Issues in e-voting

Even though e-voting systems provably increase voter turnout, helping to make the election fair and free from fraud, many gaps remain in the currently used e-voting systems that need to be addressed. Most of the

Table 9.1 Security properties comparison of e-voting systems.

Approaches	Eligibility	Privacy	Voter anonymity	Lack of reusability	Verifiability	Fairness	Lack of coercibility	Receipt-less
Clarke and Martens (2016)	Yes	Yes	Yes	Yes	Yes	Yes	—	—
D.L.Chaum (1981)	No	Yes	Yes	No	Yes	Yes	No	No
Cohen and Fischer (1985)	No	No	Yes	No	No	Yes	No	No
J.D.Cohen (1986)	No	Yes	Yes	No	No	Yes	No	No
Benaloh and Tunistra (1994)	—	Yes	—	—	Yes	Yes	—	Yes
Cramer et al. (1996)	—	Yes	Yes	Yes	Yes	Yes	Yes	Yes
Cramer et al. (1997)	—	Yes	Yes	Yes	Yes	Yes	Yes	Yes
Juang et al. (2002)	—	Yes	Yes	—	Yes	Yes	—	—
Li et al. (2009)	Yes	Yes	Yes	—	—	—	Yes	Yes
Porkodi et al. (2011)	Yes	Yes	Yes	Yes	Yes	—	—	—
Adewole et al. (2011)	Yes	Yes	Yes	—	Yes	Yes	Yes	Yes
Essex et al. (2012)	Yes	Yes	Yes	Yes	Yes	Yes	Yes	Yes
Nguyen and Dang (2013)	Yes	Yes	Yes	Yes	Yes	Yes	Yes	Yes
Aziz (2019)	Yes	Yes	Yes	Yes	Yes	Yes	Yes	Yes

Note: "—", not available; No, property not supported; Yes, property supported.

Table 9.2 Performance properties comparison of e-voting systems.

Approaches	Correctness	Robustness	Efficiency	Mobility
Clarke and Martens (2016)	Yes	Yes	Yes	Yes
Chaum (1981)	Yes	No	Yes	No
Cohen and Fischer (1985)	Yes	Yes	Yes	No
Cohen (1986)	Yes	Yes	Yes	No
Benaloh and Tunistra (1994)	Yes	No	Yes	No
Cramer et al. (1996)	Yes	Yes	Yes	No
Cramer et al. (1997)	Yes	Yes	Yes	No
Juang et al. (2002)	Yes	Yes	Yes	No
Li et al. (2009)	Yes	Yes	Yes	No
Porkodi et al. (2011)	Yes	Yes	Yes	No
Adewole et al. (2011)	Yes	Yes	Yes	No
Essex et al. (2012)	Yes	Yes	Yes	No
Nguyen and Dang (2013)	Yes	Yes	Yes	No
Aziz (2019)	Yes	Yes	Yes	Yes

Note: *No*, property not supported; *Yes*, property supported.

current e-voting systems are centralized in nature, with just one point of trust. Such systems are prone to distributed denial of service (DDoS) attacks, resulting in the stoppage of the server that leads to the failure of the entire system. This leads to authentication issues followed by privacy problems (Bokslag & de Vries). In a majority of the systems, the databases are completely controlled by a single authority, which makes the system vulnerable to biasing, manipulation, and can lead to election fraud.

There have been studies that show online ballots being subjected to vote manipulation and impersonation of votes. When votes are electronically transmitted, it is difficult to detect if a vote is genuine or manipulated (Susskind, 2017). Another major issue is that the voting process, particularly the tallying phase, is not transparent, which entails the trust issue in voters' minds (Bokslag & de Vries; Oo and Aung, 2014). Also, there is no way to recount the ballots in case of any discrepancies. The aforementioned problems instigated researchers to think of alternate methods to secure the voting system.

3. Distributed e-voting

A distributed trust mechanism for the voting system can solve the trust-worthiness issues. The distributed trust model can be established using blockchain to provide transparency and immutability. In 1991, Haber and Stornetta (1991) had introduced the idea of time-stamping digital documents to make them tamper-proof. Something similar, based on the concept of blockchain, was developed in 2008 by Satoshi Nakamoto (Nakamoto). The first application of the concept was seen in Bitcoin, making a mark in the field of cryptocurrency (Homepage). Blockchain can be used in any field that involves any sort of transaction. Blockchains are tamper-resistant distributed ledgers (tamper evident) that are implemented without a central authority. The trust is distributed as each transaction has a joint source and needs to be validated by nodes. The system relies on the concept of asymmetric key cryptography (Nakamoto). A blockchain can be described in simple words as a chain of timestamped blocks that are linked by cryptographic hashes making them immutable and tamper evident. Each block holds the cryptographic hash of the previous block, and once a new block is added, modification of the older block becomes difficult, giving it the property of tamper resistance (Table 9.2).

With the properties that blockchain holds, it can provide the following to the e-voting system:

- Transparency, integrity, verifiability, and confidentiality are possible (Hjalmarsson et al., 2018; Hanifatunnisa and Rahardjo, 2017), as a voter or any independent individual can observe the results of the election without revealing the voter's choice nor identity that are on the blockchain. Blockchains are immutable so establish integrity in the system.
- Consistency is achieved, as the system is distributed in nature, so if any node is disrupted in service, it receives a copy of every transaction once it comes back online (Hjalmarsson et al., 2018; Pathak et al., 2018)
- Availability (Hjalmarsson et al., 2018; Pathak et al., 2018; Akbari et al., 2017) is provided as each node runs separately, so there is no single point of failure.
- Voter confidence is possible since by incorporating blockchain in the e-voting system the process will become noted and results can be published instantly. Moreover with its open-source and transparent nature, it will increase voter confidence and finally increase voter turnaround (Kshetri and Voas, 2018).

Similar to a general e-voting structure, there are various phases in a Blockchain-based e-voting systems. While the actors remain same, the working is a bit different, as depicted in Fig. 9.2. Each voter casts their vote after successfully completing the voter verification phase in a block. If a group of actors mine and verify, a consensus is formed, and the block is

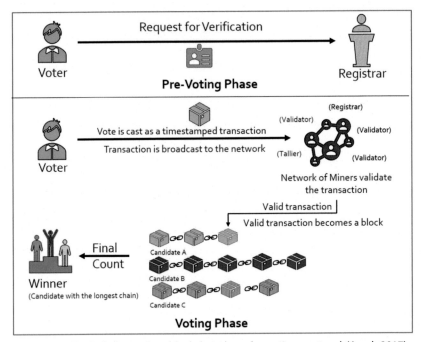

Figure 9.2 Typical phases in a blockchain-based e-voting protocol (Ayed, 2017).

added to the blockchain. Here, each candidate is dedicated to a blockchain, and the candidate with the longest chain length is declared as the winner by the tallier (Ayed, 2017).

3.1 Significant contributions in blockchain-based e-voting

Many researchers have pointed out that blockchain can be incorporated into e-voting to gain accountability and voter's trust in the process (Riemann and Grumbach, 2017; Schiedermeier et al., 2019; Dricot and Pereira, 2018). Riemann and Grumbach (2017) state that building a smart contract can provide an efficient voting protocol based on blockchain by using third-party features, so coercion can be prevented (Sudharsan et al., 2019; Teja et al., 2019; Sadia et al., 2019; Shahzad and Crowcroft, 2019). Many contributions claim that blockchain can produce a solution with respect to security and transparency in a voting system (Zhang et al., 2019; Heiberg et al., 2018; Srivastava et al., 2018b; Bosri et al., 2019).

In 2015, The Blockchain Technologies Corp. proposed a blockchain called VoteUnit (Ruoti et al., 2019) that functioned like BitCoin, except for the fact that it did not require a fee for any transaction. When a voter votes for a candidate, a payment is made to the selected candidate's wallet. The whole system was an offline procedure to safeguard the votes from getting manipulated. The system was able to provide an immutable trail of transactions for the voters and thus establish voter verifiability. But it was dependent on a TTP for voter registration.

In 2017, McCorry et al. (2017) were the first to design a decentralized boardroom voting protocol without using any TTP that supported self-tallying of votes. They used a smart contract that was used on the Open Vote Network (OVN) and ran it on Ethereum. Instead of using blockchain as just a bulletin board, they used it for its power of consensus computing. The system was built with Byzantine fault tolerance consensus. The issues with their systems were that only 50 voters could participate in voting and that there needed to be some trust in the central administration for voter registration and authentication.

Another blockchain-based voting system is FollowMyVote (Anonymous). It is a completely online process that uses Elliptic Curve Cryptography in the creation of votes and uses the blockchain technology as a ballot box. Here a voter has to download the FollowMyVote application on their desired devices and register by submitting his/her picture and government ID along with the Identity Key Pair. The voter then anonymously registers the Voter Key Pair. This ensures the voter's anonymity. Once the verifier approves a voter, the registrar is then responsible for allotting the correct ballot type to the voter. After voting, the ballots are submitted into a blockchain that ensures that the vote is immutable, transparent, and secured. A voter signs the ballot using the Voter Key Pair. The votes are thus anonymous and publicly available and allow any participant of the election to verify and tally the votes. The FollowMyVote application also permits a voter to change his/her vote up to a certain time as decided by the election officials. The system was efficient but not completely secured, as it is dependent on a TTP for voter registration and authentication, which can be compromised.

Lee et al. (2016) proposed the introduction of a TTP along with an authentication organization (AO) that generates the voter's list. This organization determines if a voter has the right to vote and verifies the voter's identity. They stated that an AO can link a vote back to its voter. Also, being the sole institution, it can manipulate the voter's list. In this paper the authors tried to prove that trusting a single organization can result in forgery and malpractice. In their proposed protocol, two different organizations produce their own list, so tallying both can prevent malpractices. Zhao and

Chan used a lottery protocol (Andrychowicz et al., 2014) along with zero-knowledge proof, which is used to distribute random numbers that hide the ballot (Zhao and Chan, 2016). Even though this was one of the first attempts, there were many limitations in this approach. The authors did not speak about voter verification nor authentication. Also it worked only for two candidates, and voter identification was also ignored. Proof of Vote was used by Li et al. (2017) to ensure privacy, accuracy, and reliability of the voting system.

Seifelnasr et al. (2020) tried to improve the OVN and introduced an off-chain administrator. There is no need to trust a single authority, and bulk computations can be performed by the off-chain administrator. Every voting requirement, namely, vote privacy, voter anonymity, etc., was fulfilled by the proposed protocol. Lack of reusability was not ensured in the system. Wang et al. (2018) used homomorphic encryption and ring signature for large-scale voting. They used smart contracts on Ethereum. The system provided anonymity but is neither robust nor resistant to coercion.

Kshetri and Voas (2018) addressed the challenges of fraudulent votes. They were the first to pay the voters for voting. A voter is allowed to vote only once, but is allowed to change his/her vote within the designated time of the voting process. The problem of fraudulent voting is tackled by the blockchain, as every transaction is visible on the ledger so can be detected by the consensus network. To manipulate an already cast vote, one has to hack all the older blocks, which is computationally difficult.

Tarasov andTewari (2017) proposed a payment-based system where the candidate receives payments as votes from a voter using the concept of ZCash (Bowe et al., 2017). They assumed that voter identities can be verified efficiently. The disadvantage of such a system is that a fraudulent voter might not make a payment to the candidate to hold on to their money. Along with this, the system needs a trusted authority that operates in a centralized manner.

Hardwick et al. (2018) used Ethereum blockchain for implementation of their proposed protocol. There was a trusted central authority (CA) that maintained the voter's list. The authors made a consideration that if multiple CAs could be incorporated, with each CA holding only partial voter information, impersonation attack can be handled. They allowed voters to change their votes until the end of the election. Every voting requirement was fulfilled in the proposed system.

Bistarelli et al. (2017) used the Bitcoin system to implement a decentralized voting system. They claim to have created a system that directly allows a voter to cast his vote in the blockchain. Here, a voter has a wallet containing a set of keys. These keys are used for signing transactions. To prevent the voter's public key from revealing a voter's identity, the authors propose the use of anonymous Kerberos, which provides an authentication mechanism without revealing the client's identity. The authors ensured that all the source addresses of the confirmed voters are remembered, thus ensuring that one vote is counted per authorized voter. When asset coins are used, the token can be marked with the attached metadata that is signed by the election commission. This converts a Bitcoin into a vote, so single votes can be counted. To prevent voters from sending asset coins to an unauthorized voter, the authors suggest that one can use a permissioned blockchain where transactions among voters are not permitted.

Ayed (2017) proposed an e-voting system incorporating blockchain. In the proposal, it is assumed that only registered voters participate in voting. A voter's Social Security number is used for authentication and to check if a voter is a valid. Once a voter is authorized, they are allowed to cast a vote. Once the vote is cast from the provided user interface in the voter's device, the system generates a unique input containing the voter's ID number, full name, and the hash of the previous vote. This input is then encrypted using SHA-256 and is stored in the block header of each vote that is cast. This ensures that voter information cannot be obtained from the votes. For each vote, a block gets created. Every time a candidate is voted for, a new block gets added to their corresponding blockchain. The authors have dealt with the problem of concusses that occurs when multiple voters vote at the same time. As a solution to this problem, The longest chain rule (followed by Bitcoin) is used. Each candidate has a different chain. The votes cast in the blockchain are public and verifiable. This protocol fulfills every requirement for secured voting.

Na and Park (2018) proposed a chat-based voting system. The system was implemented using Hyperledger Fabric. It used the idea of taking group decisions for voting purpose. It assured anonymity and fulfilled other voting properties. Bartolucci et al. (2018) proposed SHARVOT protocol that used circle shuffle, which requires a CA to control the whole process, thus bringing a single point of failure. This protocol prevented linking a voter's identity with their ballots. However, their system is vulnerable to multiple vote casting and only a limited number of participants were allowed.

Votereum (Thuy et al., 2019) was built on the Ethereum platform, where the authors tried to reduce trust on any CA. The proposed system provided privacy, robustness, and verifiability to the voters. The system however fails to be receipt-free and resistant to coercion. Also, the application server used for authorization is vulnerable to DDoS attack. In 2018, Hjalamrsson et al. (2018) proposed a scheme using private Ethereum blockchain and used smart contracts for tallying the result. They ensured transparency by allowing the voters to access the blockchain during voting.

Yavuz et al. (2018) developed a voting app on the android platform using Ethereum, but it failed to provide robustness and resistance to coercion. Quantum blockchain (Kiktenko et al., 2018) was used by Sun et al. (2019), which allows a classical channel to not be fully authenticated as the quantum channel is authenticated. They used quantum binding to achieve anonymity and fairness. Another group of authors (Srivastava et al., 2018a,b) used phantom protocol (Sompolinsky & Zohar) that is used to handle large transactions to attain the property of scalability. They also proved that their protocol was a fast one and took little time to produce results.

Lai and Wu (2018) used Ethereum blockchain to provide transparency to voters, who were able to view the results. Liu and Wang (2017) proposed a voting scheme without using any TTP. They use a combination of blind signature and blockchain in their protocol. Blind signature preserves a voter's choice and blockchain provides transparency to the election. A ballot is considered valid if it has the correct message format, has all the signatures, is cast on time, and has not been counted. The authors did not mention any tallying technique. After the tally process is over, the organizer publishes a list of all the valid ballots and the result. This information can be verified by all participants who have the permission to view the blockchain. There were some security issues in this protocol. The IP address of the voter can be obtained, which can expose the connection between the voter and ballot. Also, since the ballots can be viewed during the election process, it can affect the outcomes of the election. They fulfill every secured voting property except robustness, coercion resistance, and fairness.

Shahzad and Crowcroft (2019) proposed a system where the transactions are sealed with another hash function to provide integrity. Chaieb et al. (2019) proposed a system of identity-based encryption techniques ensuring all security features. Gao et al. (2019) designed a small-scale code-based voting protocol using public key cryptography. Luo et al. (2018) proposed a system using ring-based consensus algorithm, ensuring all security features.

On March 7, 2018, Sierra Leone became the first country in the world to conduct a blockchain-based election using the Agora platform (Chohan). Blockchain ensured that the election was transparent. Since a permissioned blockchain was used, votes were visible to all users, but validation was conducted only by authorized personnel. The country also saw a decline in electoral violence, so it can be used as a case study to prove the accountability of blockchain in an electoral process.

Tables 9.3 and 9.4 depict a comparative study of the aforementioned research works with respect to security properties and performance properties.

3.2 Some issues in blockchain-based e-voting

The advantages of blockchain-based e-voting lie in the protocol and how it has been implemented. The main issue arises when there is a possibility of violation of the election rules. These need to be very carefully specified in the smart contracts, so there is a dependency on an administrator or a TTP to incorporate the same.

Another issue arises when a public blockchain is used in a voting protocol. Anyone can access and see the transactions present there, thus creating a biased election. As a solution, a private blockchain can be used, which in turn questions transparency. Furthermore, scalability issues in blockchain are yet to be explored. Along with that the encryption algorithms that are used in such various protocols need to be robust.

Also, an election is an event where a lot of people are involved. They vote around the same time. This requires a system with high throughput. Existing blockchain networks, however, lack in this aspect, with Bitcoin having a throughput as low as 7 transactions per second (TPS) and Hyperledger Fabric having about 500 TPS (Huang et al., 2021).

Since blockchain addresses are generated randomly, a voter can vote anonymously, but it has been shown (Feng et al., 2019) that transactions can be traced back to revealing user identities and that users' pseudo-identities can be linked to their IP addresses (Biryukov et al., 2014), thus questioning the users' privacy and security.

Finally, an eligibility check and authentication process for a voter is mainly dependent on the TTP or a trusted authority, which still remains as a challenge for most of the blockchain-based voting protocols.

Table 9.3 Security properties comparison of blockchain-based e-voting systems.

Approaches	Eligibility	Privacy	Voter anonymity	Lack of reusability	Verifiability	Fairness	Lack of coercibility	Receipt-less
McCorry et al. (2017)	No	Yes	Yes	Yes	No	Yes	No	Yes
Kshetri and Voas (2018)	Yes	Yes	Yes	Yes	No	–	–	–
Hardwick et al. (2018)	Yes	Yes	Yes	No	–	–	–	–
Bistarelli et al. (2017)	No	Yes	Yes	No	–	–	No	–
Na and Park (2018)	Yes	Yes	Yes	Yes	–	–	–	–
Zhao and Chan (2016)	No	Yes	Yes	Yes	Yes	–	–	–
Ahmed Ben Ayed (2017)	Yes	Yes	Yes	Yes	No	Yes	No	Yes
FollowMyVote (Anonymous)	Yes	Yes	Yes	Yes	Yes	Yes	Yes	Yes
Seifelnasr et al. (2020)	Yes	Yes	Yes	No	Yes	Yes	Yes	Yes
Bartolucci et al. (2018)	Yes	Yes	Yes	Yes	Yes	Yes	No	No
L.V.C Thuy et al. (2019)	Yes	Yes	Yes	Yes	Yes	Yes	No	No
Hjalmarsson et al. (2018)	Yes	Yes	Yes	Yes	–	Yes	Yes	Yes
Teja et al. (2019)	Yes	Yes	Yes	Yes	Yes	Yes	Yes	Yes
Yavuz et al. (2018)	Yes	Yes	Yes	Yes	Yes	Yes	Yes	No
Zhang et al. (2019)	Yes	Yes	Yes	Yes	No	No	No	No
Tarasov and Tewari (2017)	Yes	Yes	Yes	Yes	Yes	Yes	No	No
Sun et al. (2019)	Yes	Yes	Yes	Yes	No	Yes	Yes	Yes
Srivastava et al. (2018a)	Yes	Yes	Yes	Yes	Yes	Yes	Yes	Yes
Lai et al. (2018)	Yes	Yes	Yes	Yes	Yes	Yes	Yes	Yes
Wang et al. (2018)	Yes	Yes	Yes	Yes	Yes	Yes	No	No
Liu and Wang (2017)	Yes	Yes	Yes	Yes	Yes	Yes	Yes	Yes

Shahzad and Crowcroft (2019)	Yes	Yes	Yes	Yes	Yes	Yes	Yes	Yes
Murtaza et al. (2019)	Yes	Yes	Yes	Yes	Yes	Yes	Yes	Yes
Chaieb et al. (2019)	Yes	No	Yes	Yes	Yes	Yes	Yes	Yes
Venkatpur et al. (2018)	Yes	Yes	Yes	Yes	Yes	Yes	Yes	Yes
Gao et al. (2019)	Yes	Yes	Yes	Yes	Yes	Yes	Yes	Yes
Luo et al. (2018)	Yes	Yes	Yes	Yes	Yes	Yes	Yes	Yes
Li et al. (2009)	Yes	Yes	Yes	Yes	Yes	Yes	Yes	Yes
Leonardos et al. (2020)	Yes	Yes	Yes	Yes	Yes	Yes	Yes	Yes
Kibin Lee et al. (2016)	Yes	Yes	Yes	Yes	Yes	Yes	No	Yes

Note: "—", not available; *No*, property not supported; *Yes*, property supported.

Table 9.4 Performance properties comparison of blockchain-based e-voting systems.

Approaches	Correctness	Robustness	Efficiency	Mobility
McCorry et al. (2017)	Yes	Yes	Yes	Yes
Kshetri and Voas (2018)	Yes	Yes	Yes	Yes
Hardwick and Gioulis (2018)	Yes	Yes	Yes	Yes
Bistarelli et al. (2017)	Yes	Yes	Yes	Yes
Na and Park (2018)	Yes	Yes	Yes	Yes
Zhao and Chan (2016)	Yes	Yes	Yes	Yes
Ahmed Ben Ayed (2017)	Yes	Yes	Yes	Yes
FollowMyVote (Anonymous)	Yes	Yes	Yes	Yes
Seifelnasr et al. (2020)	Yes	Yes	Yes	Yes
Bartolucci et al. (2018)	Yes	Yes	Yes	Yes
L.V.C Thuy (2019)	Yes	Yes	Yes	Yes
Hjalmarsson et al. (2018)	Yes	Yes	Yes	Yes
Teja et al. (2019)	Yes	Yes	Yes	Yes
Yavuz et al. (2018)	Yes	No	Yes	Yes
Zhang et al. (2019)	Yes	Yes	Yes	Yes
Tarasov and Tewari (2017)	Yes	Yes	Yes	Yes
Sun et al. (2019)	Yes	Yes	Yes	Yes
Srivastava et al. (2018b)	Yes	Yes	Yes	Yes
Lai et al. (2018)	Yes	Yes	Yes	Yes
Wang et al. (2018)	Yes	No	Yes	Yes
Liu and Wang (2017)	Yes	Yes	Yes	Yes
Shahzad and Crowcroft (2019)	Yes	Yes	Yes	Yes
Murtaza et al. (2019)	Yes	Yes	Yes	Yes
Chaieb et al. (2019)	Yes	Yes	Yes	Yes
Venkatpur et al. (2018)	Yes	Yes	Yes	Yes
Gao et al. (2019)	Yes	Yes	Yes	Yes
Luo et al. (2018)	Yes	Yes	Yes	Yes
Li et al. (2009)	Yes	Yes	Yes	Yes
Leonardos et al. (2020)	Yes	Yes	Yes	Yes
Kibin Lee et al. (2016)	Yes	Yes	Yes	Yes

Note: *No*, property not supported; *Yes*, property supported.

Therefore, it can be observed that solutions toward scalability, throughput, authentication, voter privacy, vote and election integrity, and protocol security need to be inspected with respect to blockchain-based e-voting protocols.

4. Conclusion

The concept of voting has been in play for many decades now. With the advancement in technology in the past few years, electronic voting systems have gained popularity. The integrity of elections is subject to debates regarding security issues faced by the systems. We looked into the various conventional voting system and studied their drawbacks. The 2000 US presidential election challenged the integrity of such a voting system. It gave rise to the concept of electronic voting. Internet voting became popular among citizens because it provided them the opportunity to vote from the comfort of their homes. We studied various researches proposing efficient and secured e-voting protocols. However, there were a few drawbacks like a single point of failure and biased voting. With the introduction of the blockchain concept in 2008, researchers found a solution to the problems that were being faced with existing protocols.

Many researchers have been working toward securing such e-voting protocols using the concept of blockchain, a decentralized distributed architecture that provides data consistency, immutability, transparency, and security. In this chapter, we summarized various existing blockchain-based e-voting protocols that researchers have tried to implement to develop tamper-resistant, transparent, secured voting mechanisms and finally presented a comparative study of both e-voting protocols and blockchain-based e-voting protocols.

References

Adewole, A.P., Sodiya, A.S., Arowolo, O.A., 2011. A Receipt-free Multi-Authority E-Voting System.

Akbari, E., Wu, Q., Zhao, W., Arabnia, H.R., Yang, M.Q., 2017. From blockchain to internet-based voting. In: Proceedings of the 2017 International Conference on Computational Science and Computational Intelligence (CSCI), Las Vegas, NV, USA, pp. 218—221, pp. 14—16.

Andrychowicz, M., Dziembowski, S., Malinowski, D., Mazurek, L., 2014. Secure multi-party computations on bitcoin. In: 2014 IEEE Symposium on Security and Privacy, SP 2014, Berkeley, CA, USA, May, 2014, pp. 443—458, pp. 18—21.

https://followmyvote.com/.

Awad, M., Leiss, E.L., 2016. The evolution of voting: analysis of conventional and electronic voting systems. Int. J. Appl. Eng. Res. 11 (12), 7888—7896.

Ayed, A.B., 2017. A conceptual secure blockchain-based electronic voting system. Int. J. Netw. Secur. Appl. 9 (3), 01—09.

Aziz, A., 2019. Coercion-resistant e-voting scheme with blind signatures. In: 2019 Cybersecurity and Cyberforensics Conference (CCC). IEEE, pp. 143—151.

Baiardi F., Falleni A., Granchi R., Martinelli F., Petrocchi M., Vaccarelli A., Seas, a secure e-voting protocol: design and implementation. Comput. Secur. 24 (8), 642.

Bartolucci, S., Bernat, P., Joseph, D., 2018. SHARVOT: secret SHARe-based VOTing on the blockchain. In: Proceedings of the 1st international workshop on emerging trends in software engineering for blockchain, pp. 30—34.

Benaloh, J., Tuinstra, D., 1994. Receipt-free secret-ballot elections. In: Proceedings of the Twenty-Sixth Annual ACM Symposium on Theory of Computing.

Biryukov, A., Khovratovich, D., Pustogarov, I., 2014. Deanonymisation of clients in bitcoin p2p network. In: Proceedings of the 2014 ACM SIGSAC Conference on Computer and Communications Security, pp. 15—29.

Bistarelli, S., Mantilacci, M., Santancini, P., Santini, F., 2017. An end-to-end voting-system based on bitcoin. In: Proceedings of the Symposium on Applied Computing, pp. 1836—1841.

Bloom, B.H., 1970. Space/time trade-offs in hash coding with allowable errors. Commun. ACM 13 (7), 422—426.

Bokslag, W., de Vries, M., Evaluating E-Voting: Theory and Practice, arXiv preprint arXiv:1602.02509.

Bosri, R., Uzzal, A.R., Al Omar, A., Hasan, A.S.M.T., Bhuiyan, M.Z.A., 2019. Towards a privacy-preserving voting system through blockchain technologies. In: 2019 IEEE Intl Conf on Dependable, Autonomic and Secure Computing, Intl Conf on Pervasive Intelligence and Computing, Intl Conf on Cloud and Big Data Computing, Intl Conf on Cyber Science and Technology Congress (DASC/PiCom/CBDCom/Cyber-SciTech), pp. 602—608.

Bowe, S., Hornby, T., Wilcox, N., 2017. Zcash Protocol Specification.

Brent, P., 2006. The australian ballot: not the secret ballot. Aust. J. Polit. Sci. 41 (1), 39—50.

Chaieb, M., Koscina, M., Yousfi, S., Lafourcade, P., Robbana, R.D., 2019. Distributed authorities using blind signature to effect robust security in e-voting. In: Prague, C.R. (Ed.), Proceedings of the 16th International Joint Conference on E-Business and Telecommunications, pp. 228—235, pp. 26—28.

Chaum, D.L., 1981. Untraceable electronic mail, return addresses, and digital pseudonyms. Commun. ACM 24 (2), 84—90.

Chaum, D., 1984. Blind Signature System, Advances in Cryptology. Springer, Boston, MA.

Chohan, U.W., Blockchain Enhancing Political Accountability? Sierra Leone 2018 Case, Sierra Leone.

Clarke, D., Martens, T., 2016. E-voting in estonia, Real-World Electronic Voting: Design, Analysis and Deployment, pp. 129—141.

Cohen, J.D., Fischer, M.J., 1985. A Robust and Verifiable Cryptographically Secure Election Scheme. Yale University. Department of Computer Science.

Cohen, J.D., 1986. Improving Privacy in Cryptographic Elections. Yale University, Department of Computer Science, New Haven, CT.

Cramer, R., Franklin, M., Schoenmakers, B., Yung, M., 1996. Multi-authority secret-ballot elections with linear work. In: International Conference on the Theory and Applications of Cryptographic Techniques. Springer, pp. 72—83.

Cramer, R., Gennaro, R., Schoenmakers, B., 1997. A secure and optimally efficient multi-authority election scheme. Eur. Trans. Telecomm. 8 (5), 481—490.

Cranor, L.F., 2003. In search of the perfect voting technology: No easy answers. In: Secure Electronic Voting. Springer, pp. 17—30.

Dricot, L., Pereira, O.S. U.L.a., 2018. And Their Impact on Voting Systems. arXiv arXiv:180108064.

ElGamal, T., 1985. A public key cryptosystem and a signature scheme based on discrete logarithms. IEEE Trans. Info Theory 31 (4), 469—472.

Epstein, J., 2007. Electronic voting. Computer 40 (8), 92—95.

Essex, A., Clark, J., Hengartner, U., 2012. Cobra: Toward concurrent ballot authorization for internet voting. EVT/WOTE 12.

Feng, Q., He, D., Zeadally, S., Khan, M.K., Kumar, N., 2019. A survey on privacy protection in blockchain system. J. Netw. Comput. Appl. 126, 45−58.

Fredman, L.E., 1967. The introduction of the Australian ballot in the United States. Aust. J. Polit. Hist. 13 (2), 204−220.

Gao, S., Zheng, D., Guo, R., Jing, C., Hu, C., 2019. An anti-quantum e-voting protocol in blockchain with audit function. IEEE Access 7 (16), 15304−11531.

Greene, K.K., Byrne, M.D., Everett, S.P., 2006. A Comparison of Usability between Voting Methods. EVT.

Haber, S., Stornetta, W.S., 1991. How to time-stamp a digital document. J. Cryptol. 3, 99−111.

Hanifatunnisa, R., Rahardjo, B., 2017. Blockchain based e-voting recording system design. In: Proceedings of the 2017 11th International Conference on Telecommunication Systems Services and Applications (TSSA), Lombok, Indonesia, pp. 1−6, pp. 26−27.

Hankerson, D., Menezes, A.J., Vanstone, S., 2006. Guide to Elliptic Curve Cryptography. Springer, Science & Business Media.

Hardwick, F.S., Gioulis, A., Akram, R.N., Markantonakis, K.E.-V.w.B., 2018. An E-Voting Protocol with Decentralisation and Voter Privacy. arXiv arXiv:180510258.

Heiberg, S., Kubjas, I., Siim, J., Willemson, J., 2018. On Trade-Offs of Applying Blockchains for Electronic Voting Bulletin Boards, International Association for Cryptologic Research Available Online. URL. https://eprint.iacr.org/2018/685.pdf.

Hjalmarsson, F.P., Hreioarsson, G.K., Hamdaqa, M., Hjalmtýsson, G., 2018. Blockchain-based e-voting system. In: 11th IEEE International Conference on Cloud Computing, CLOUD 2018, San Francisco, CA, USA, July 2−7, 2018. IEEE Computer Society, pp. 983−986. https://doi.org/10.1109/CLOUD.2018.00151. URL.

Homepage, B., Available online: URL, https://bitcoin.org/.

Huang, J., He, D., Obaidat, M.S., Vijayakumar, P., Luo, M., Choo, K.-K.R., 2021. The application of the blockchain technology in voting systems: a review. ACM Comput. Surv. 54 (3), 1−28.

Joaquim, R., Zúquete, A., Ferreira, P., 2003. Revs−a robust electronic voting system. IADIS Int. J. WWW/Internet 1 (2), 47−63.

Jones, D.W., 2003. The evaluation of voting technology. In: Secure Electronic Voting. Springer, pp. 3−16.

Juang, W.-S., Lei, C.-L., Liaw, H.-T., 2002. A verifiable multi-authority secret election allowing abstention from voting. Comput. J. 45 (6), 672−682.

Juels, A., Catalano, D., Jakobsson, M., 2010. Coercion-resistant electronic elections. In: Towards Trustworthy Elections. Springer, Heidelberg, pp. 37−63. Berlin.

Kiktenko, E.O., Pozhar, N.O., Anufriev, M.N., Trushechkin, A.S., Yunusov, R.R., Kurochkin, Y.V., Lvovsky, A., Fedorov, A.K., 2018. Quantum-secured blockchain. Quant. Sci. Technol. 3 (3), 035004.

Kohno, T., et al., 2004. Analysis of an electronic voting system. In: on Security, I.S. (Ed.), Privacy, 2004, Proceedings. 2004. IEEE.

Kshetri, N., Voas, J.B.-E.E.-V., 2018. IEEE softw 35, 95−99.

Lai, W.-J., Hsieh, Y., Hsueh, C.-W., Wu, J.-L.D.A.D., 2018. Anonymous. In: Proceedings, I. (Ed.), Transparent E-Voting System, of the 2018 1st IEEE International Conference on Hot Information-Centric Networking (HotICN), Shenzhen, China, pp. 24−29, pp. 15−17.

Lambrinoudakis, C., Gritzalis, D., Tsoumas, V., Karyda, M., Ikonomopoulos, S., 2003. Secure electronic voting: the current landscape. In: Secure Electronic Voting. Springer, pp. 101−122.

Lauer, T.W., 2004. The risk of e-voting. Electron. J. eGovernment 2, 177−186.

Lee, K., James, J.I., Ejeta, T.G., Kim, H.J., 2016. Electronic voting service using blockchain. J. Digi. Foren. Secur. Law 11 (2), 8.

Leonardos, S., Reijsbergen, D., Piliouras, G., 2020. Weighted voting on the blockchain: improving consensus in proof of stake protocols. Int. J. Netw. Manag. 30 (5), e2093.

Li, C.-T., Hwang, M.-S., Lai, Y.-C., 2009. A verifiable electronic voting scheme over the internet. In: 2009 Sixth International Conference on Information Technology: New Generations. IEEE, pp. 449–454.

Li, J., Liu, Z., Chen, L., Chen, P., Wu, J., 2017. Blockchain-based security architecture for distributed cloud storage. In: Proceedings of the 2017 IEEE International Symposium on Parallel and Distributed Processing with Applications and 2017 IEEE International Conference on Ubiquitous Computing and Communications. ISPA/IUCC), Guangzhou, China, pp. 408–411, pp. 12–15.

Liu, Y., Wang, Q., 2017. An E-Voting Protocol Based on Blockchain, International Association for Cryptologic Research Available online. URL. https://eprint.iacr.org/2017/1043.pdf.

Luo, Y., Chen, Y., Chen, Q., Liang, Q.A., 2018. New election algorithm for dpos consensus mechanism in blockchain. In: Proceedings of the 2018 7th International Conference on Digital Home (ICDH), Guilin, China, 30 November-1, pp. 116–120.

Maaten, E., 2004. Towards Remote E-Voting: Estonian Case, Electronic Voting in Europe-Technology, Law, Politics and Society, Workshop of the ESF TED Programme Together with GI and OCG. Gesellschaft fur Informatik eV.

McCorry, P., Shahandashti, S.F., Hao, F.A., 2017. Smart contract for boardroom voting with maximum voter privacy. In: Cryptography, F., Security, D. (Eds.), Lecture Notes in Computer Science, Kiayias, A, Cham, Switzerland Volume 10322. -3-319-70971-0. Springer, pp. 357–375.

Miller, V.S., 1985. Use of elliptic curves in cryptography. In: Conference on the Theory and Application of Cryptographic Techniques. Springer, Heidelberg. Berlin.

Miller, W.R.H.C.M., 1995. Election fraud in late 19th century texas. Reg. Local Hist. 7, 111–128. URL. http://history.smsu.edu.

Murtaza, M.H., Alizai, Z.A., Iqbal, Z., 2019. Blockchain based anonymous voting system using zksnarks. In: Proceedings of the 2019 International Conference on Applied and Engineering Mathematics. ICAEM, Taxila, Pakistan, pp. 209–214, pp. 27–29.

Na, S., Park, Y.B., 2018. Web-based nominal group technique decision making tool using blockchain. In: Proceedings of the 2018 International Conference on Platform Technology and Service (PlatCon), Jeju, Korea, pp. 1–6, pp. 29–31.

Nakamoto, S.B.A., Peer-to-Peer Electronic Cash System, Available online. URL, https://bitcoin.org/bitcoin.pdf.

Nguyen, T.A.T., Dang, T.K., 2013. Enhanced security in internet voting protocol using blind signature and dynamic ballots. Electron. Commer. Res. 13 (3), 257–272.

Oo, H.N., Aung, A.M., 2014. A survey of different electronic voting systems. Int. J. Sci. Eng. Technol. Res. 3 (16), 3460–3464.

Pathak, A., Wasay, A., Singh, C., Bhavan, R., Umale, J., 2018. Design anddesign implementation of a secure and robust voting system based on blockchain. Int. J. Advert. 4, 869–875.

Porkodi, C., Arumuganathan, R., Vidya, K., 2011. Multi-authority electronic voting scheme based on elliptic curves. IJ Netw. Secur. 12 (2), 84–91.

Raikov, A., 2018. Accelerating technology for self-organising networked democracy. Futures 103, 17–26. https://doi.org/10.1016/j.futures.2018.03.015. URL.

Riemann, R., Grumbach, S., 2017. Distributed Protocols at the Rescue for Trustworthy Online Voting. arXiv arXiv:170504480.

Roth, S.K., 1998. Disenfranchised by design: voting systems and the election process. Inf. Des. J. 9 (1), 29–38.

Ruoti, S., Kaiser, B., Yerukhimovich, A., Clark, J., Cunningham, R., 2019. Blockchain technology: what is it good for? Commun. ACM 63 (1), 46−53.

Sadia, K., Masuduzzaman, M., Paul, R.K., Islam, A., 2019. Blockchain Based Secured E-Voting by Using the Assistance of Smart Contract. arXiv arXiv:191013635.

Saltman, R.G., et al., 2003. Public confidence and auditability in voting systems. In: Secure Electronic Voting. Springer, pp. 125−137.

Schiedermeier, M., Hasan, O., Mayer, T., Brunie, L., Kosch, H.A., 2019. Transparent Referendum Protocol with Immutable Proceedings and Verifiable Outcome for Trustless Networks. arXiv arXiv: 190906462.

Schläpfer, M., Haenni, R., Koenig, R., Spycher, O., 2011. Efficient vote authorization in coercion-resistant internet voting. In: International Conference on E-Voting and Identity. Springer, pp. 71−88.

Seifelnasr, M., Galal, H.S., Youssef, A.M., 2020. Scalable open-vote network on ethereum. In: International Conference on Financial Cryptography and Data Security. Springer, pp. 436−450.

Shahzad, B., Crowcroft, J., 2019. Trustworthy electronic voting using adjusted blockchain technology. IEEE Access 7, 24477−24488.

Sompolinsky, Y., Zohar, A. Phantom, IACR Cryptology ePrint Archive, Report 2018/104.

Srivastava, G., Dwivedi, A.D., Singh, R., 2018a. Phantom protocol as the new crypto-democracy. In: a. K., H. (Ed.), Computer Information Systems and Industrial Management; Saeed, Cham, Switzerland Volume 11127. -3-319-99953-1; Lecture Notes in Computer Science. Springer, pp. 499−509.

Srivastava, G., Dwivedi, D., Singh, A., 2018b. Crypto-democracy: decentralized voting scheme using blockchain technology. In: Proceedings of the 15th International Joint Conference on E-Business and Telecommunications, Porto, Portugal, pp. 674−679, pp. 26−28.

Sudharsan, B., Nidhish Krishna, M.P., Alagappan, M., et al., 2019. Secured electronic voting system using the concepts of blockchain. In: 2019 IEEE 10th Annual Information Technology, Electronics and Mobile Communication Conference (IEMCON). IEEE, pp. 0675−0681.

Sun, X., Wang, Q., Kulicki, P.A., 2019. Simple voting protocol on quantum blockchain. Int. J. Theor. Phys. 58, 275−281.

Susskind, J.D.D., 2017. Incentivizing blockchain voting technology for an improved election system. San. Diego Law Rev. 54, 785−821.

Tarasov, P., Tewari, H., 2017. Internet voting using zcash. IACR Cryptol. ePrint Arch. 2017, 585.

Teja, K., Shravani, M., Simha, C.Y., Kounte, M.R., 2019. Secured voting through blockchain technology. In: Proceedings of the 2019 3rd International Conference on Trends in Electronics and Informatics (ICOEI), Tirunelveli, India, pp. 1416−1419, pp. 23−25.

Thuy, L.V.-C., Cao-Minh, K., Dang-Le-Bao, C., Nguyen, T.A.V., 2019. An ethereum-based e-voting system. In: Proceedings of the 2019 IEEE-RIVF International Conference on Computing and Communication Technologies (RIVF), Danang, Vietnam, pp. 1−6, pp. 20−22.

Venkatapur, R.B., Prabhu, B., Navya, A., Roopini, R., Niranjan, S.A., 2018. Electronic voting machine based on blockchain technology and aadhar verification. Int. J. Innov. Eng. 3, 12−15.

Wang, B., Sun, J., He, Y., Pang, D., Lu, N., 2018. Large-scale election based on blockchain. Procedia Comput. Sci. 129, 234−237.

Yavuz, E., Koc, A.K., Cabuk, U.C., Dalkilic, G., 2018. Towards secure e-voting using ethereum blockchain. In: Proceedings of the 2018 6th International Symposium on Digital Forensic and Security (ISDFS), Antalya, Turkey, pp. 1–7, pp. 22–25.

Zhang, Q., Xu, B., Jing, H., Zheng, Z.Q.-C., 2019. An Ethereum Based E-Voting System. arXiv arXiv:190505041.

Zhao, Z., Chan, T.-H.H., 2016. How to vote privately using bitcoin. In: O, S., K, E., L, a.K. (Eds.), Information and Communications Security; Qing, Cham, Switzerland Volume 9543, 3-319-29813-9, Lecture Notes in Computer Science. Springer, pp. 82–96.

CHAPTER 10

Influence of blockchain technology in pharmaceutical industries

T. Poongodi[1], S. Sudhakar Ilango[2], Vaishali Gupta[1] and Sanjeev Kumar Prasad[1]
[1]School of Computing Science and Engineering, Galgotias University, Greater Noida, Delhi-NCR, India; [2]School of Computer Science and Engineering, VIT-AP University, Amaravati, Andhra Pradesh, India

1. Introduction

Blockchain technology is a distributed, secured log file or shared ledger with a mechanism to trust all the transactions without any centralized authority (third party). Blockchains are primarily expedited on a platform of databases with some inherent pre-agreed technical and business logical criteria, using peer-to-peer mechanisms and pre-agreed consensus algorithms. Immutable data are being stored in blockchains, meaning that the data or objects cannot be modified after they are created. A few important points about the blockchain technology are described next:

- A shared ledger mechanism permits any participant within the business network to view the established ledger or a record (via distributed consensus).
- All the viable group activities are maintained in the shared public ledger.
- Every peer address is anonymous, and multiple addresses could be assigned to the same transactor.
- All the transactions are placed in blocks, which are connected by a one-way hash function.
- This will work in peer-to-peer mode, based on the Domain Name System and seed nodes.

Electronic health records, drug supply, education, biomedical research, and health insurance are some of the applications in the medical domain. The utilization of this blockchain technology is still immature, with lack of professional expertise, which makes it difficult to have a strong strategic perception to identify its potential. Still, there are several challenging issues with scalability, user adoption, and securing smart contracts. Health

Blockchain Technology for Emerging Applications
ISBN 978-0-323-90193-2
https://doi.org/10.1016/B978-0-323-90193-2.00009-0

practitioners should be aware of using this blockchain technology to achieve more benefits. This chapter describes the role of blockchain technology in the pharmaceutical industry by covering the benefits and challenges
of incorporating this technique.

1.1 Background study of blockchain

The objective of blockchain is to handle digital content by storing and
distributing it as received. This technology was developed by two scholars,
Stuart Haber and W. Scott Stornetta. They had a plan for the deployment
of a secure system to ensure that the timestamps in a document cannot be
altered. Almost 2 decades later, the first blockchain was devised by Satoshi
Nakamoto, which functioned as a public ledger. This was mainly used for
enabling transactions for Bitcoin in 2009. Nakamoto constructed Bitcoin as
a form of money that could be passed among peer-to-peer nodes without a
bank or other centralized authorities, where a ledger is maintained
(Muniandy et al., 2019). Bitcoin uses the technology stack of blockchain to
secure the ledger payment record, and it also achieves the immutable
property of the record (Nakamoto, 2008). The evolution of blockchain is
classified into three phases:

(i) Transaction phase: blockchain 2.0 and Bitcoin emergence (2008−13)

Bitcoin, which hit the airwaves in the form of packages, has cropped out
in such a way to leverage the concepts and abilities of the virtual ledger
technology. Consequently, blockchain records incorporate a prolonged
listing of packages that evolve rapidly.

(ii) Contract phase: blockchain 2.0 and Ethereum development (2013−15)

Vitalik Buterin commenced a malleable blockchain to introduce various
distinct features in a peer-to-peer network. Ethereum was recognized as a
modern-day public blockchain in 2013 with different functionalities in
comparison with Bitcoin, an improvement that emerged in blockchain
history.

(iii) Application phase: blockchain 3.0 and the future (2018)

Blockchain technology is the biggest innovation of the 21st century and
is widely used in various sectors like cryptocurrency exchange, finance and
banking, supply chain, overall resource management and tracking, voting
mechanisms, publicizing sectors, construction of unique and innovative
content, and the educational sector (Astarita et al., 2020). For example,
banking institutions are established to connect different groups of people
together and allow all kinds of commercial activities and trade between

them with centralized controlling authorities. Blockchain also accomplishes the same except it is decentralized and no single entity can own it (Amin, 2020). Figs. 10.1 and 10.2 show banking transactions with and without using blockchain technology.

Blockchain can make trade efficient by removing the manual paper-based process and introducing a trusted, streamlined, automated process. A few benefits are given next:

- faster payment processing
- simplified digital identity verification
- effective peer-to-peer transactions
- hedge fund management
- buying and selling assets
- fund raising, credit, and loans

The need for blockchain technology is described subsequently.

Decentralized: Customers participate in the blockchain network using their devices, and it does not require any governing authority. The participation is granted immediately to carry out further activities.

Immutability: Immutability describes how the blockchain ledger stays unchanged, intact, and ineffaceable. Moreover, records inside the

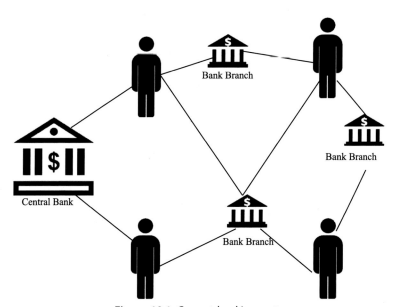

Figure 10.1 Current banking system.

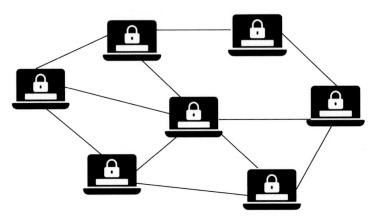

Figure 10.2 Blockchain-based banking system.

blockchain cannot be altered. Each block of information, which includes records or transaction details, continues the use of a cryptographic precept or a hash value.

Security: Information in the blockchain is hashed cryptographically. All the blocks inside the ledger include a unique hash code and the hash code of the preceding block. It will offer a specific identity for each piece of information. It is very hard to modify or tamper with the information, which suggests converting the complete hash IDs, and the hash value is also irreversible, making it more robust.

Distributed ledgers: A public ledger maintains the information regarding the transaction and the participant. These facts are known to the customers because the distributed ledger is maintained among the users who are in the community. This mechanism affords robustness throughout the complete process, which assures a better outcome (Pandey and Litoriya, 2021; Hyperledger).

Consensus: Consensus algorithms highly support the decision–making procedure among the participants. In a distributed environment, a consensus algorithm is a technique that enable all parties in a blockchain network to agree on the shared data state of the distributed ledger and trust unknown peers. Nodes now no longer believe every other node; however, they can believe the consensus algorithms that are executing on them.

Faster processing: Traditional banking structures are less powerful compared with using blockchain technology. This can permit quicker settlements for any type of contract, and it facilitates the consumer to switch cash rapidly, which reduces time consumption (Azzi et al., 2019).

Some of the challenges in blockchain technology are described next.

Complexity of blockchain: Blockchain is constructed using cryptographic mechanisms to offer protection and set up consensus over a disbursed network. Some complicated algorithms have to be executed to authenticate users, which in turn introduces computational overhead. Furthermore, storing a worldwide blockchain with "m" people containing "n" precise blocks as a set of lists, with the worst-case state of affairs, results in O (m.n) memory (Viriyasitavat and Hoonsopon, 2019).

Scalability: It is a primary problem in the overall performance of the system, even with fault-tolerant systems using authorization-based blockchains. The number of transaction nodes is not restricted, and it can be used for large-scale applications, but it will slow down the processing of transactions.

51% attack: In a public blockchain environment, a 51% attack is a malicious miner or a collection of miners taking advantage of greater than 50% of a network's mining strength or hash rate.

Operations are sluggish and cumbersome: Due to the consensus mechanism and extra layers of encryption, the procedure is slower compared with conventional processing. This postponement creates a primary risk in the public blockchain.

Energy consumption: Energy is consumed to perform the complicated mathematical computations to trigger and verify the procedure, which makes the complete network stable. In general, Bitcoin core takes up around 200 GB storage area in each node within the blockchain network. In addition, it requires 5 GB of storage to add and 500 MB to download every day.

The blockchain consists of application, distributed computing, platform, and infrastructure layers, and it is depicted in Fig. 10.3. Each block has a block index, timestamp, previous hash value, current hash value, and data. Each block is secured with a hash code, which is irreversible. The block details are shown in Fig.10.4.

Ever since Satoshi Nakamoto released Bitcoin in 2009, cryptocurrency has reached our footsteps. More recently, people are using blockchain for various real-time applications such as real-time IoT, medical data sharing, digital IDs, digital voting, cloud storage, real estate marketing, advertising insights, and supply chain and logistics monitoring (Hyperledger).

1.2 Blockchain in the pharmaceutical and healthcare industries

The advantage of blockchain technology is its capability to create verifiable trials and launch drug sourcing throughout the supply chain. Pistoia

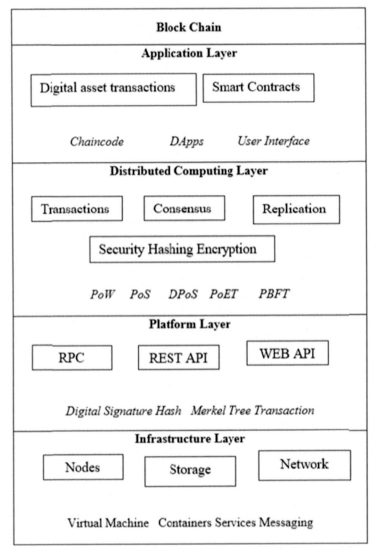

Figure 10.3 Layered architecture of blockchain.

Alliance survey says that around 70% of pharmaceutical and life science leaders trust that blockchain will create a larger impact in the pharmaceutical and healthcare industries. Decentralized blockchain solutions allow manufacturers and their customers to autonomously validate the quality and origin of drugs rapidly and securely (Chen et al., 2018). Transparency and security are the two important factors of blockchain technology for the

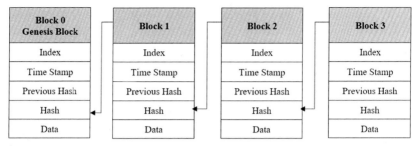

Figure 10.4 Block details.

users in pharmaceutical and healthcare industries. All stakeholders in the supply chain need to share and update data and ensure it is on time. Using this technology, the entire supply chain can be managed with a single software shared among legitimate stakeholders. Pharmaceutical companies and their suppliers, payers, pharmacies, and patients can access the real-time data. With this technology, a single piece of software is shared across the supply chain among legitimate stakeholders. The industry people and their stakeholders can access the data when it is released. Blockchain technology can also help in avoiding diversion, fabricating, and interfering. Medicines for the patients can be traced from manufacturer's end to reaching the market. If any attempt is made in modifying the registry, it would be immediately visible to all involved parties.

1.2.1 Patient data management

Blockchain technology is expected to simplify the process of managing patient data between service providers, including different insurance companies and R&D institutes, using a unique identifier. The data is gathered from portable devices, always where the patient is, including what tests they have undergone, and can be used in other transactions. Perhaps most importantly, the patient can regulate the granting of access. This system considerably reduces the management costs. This requires great cooperation among the parties. A scalable system with standard approval and authentication capabilities could be deployed with limited real-world patient data. The patient management system could be implemented with primary medical records, and accessibility would be managed by the patient (Khatoon, 2020).

1.2.2 Payer data management

The pharmacy benefit manager acts as an intermediary between pharmacies, medicine companies, and paymasters by managing formulas, negotiating concessions and refunds, and processing and paying for drug orders.

Usually, an electronic platform is used, and it reduces waste, price fluctuations, and improves customer understanding. For example, blockchain technology and smart contracts can speed up the life insurance approval process and speed up the processing of claims. Distributed ledger technology (DLT) tracks bills throughout their lifecycle and tracks up to 50 million transactions per day for many patients. For small-scale industry, some insurance companies, providers, and testing service leaders are participating in the Synaptic Health Alliance. Focus is on preserving an exact provider directory. Moreover, it highly focuses on developing a physician license verification system and it is significantly required in healthcare and Medicaid service centers.

1.2.3 Blockchain infrastructure

Blockchain architecture is built by focusing on data sharing and transaction tracking throughout the pharmaceutical industry supply chain. The application-oriented software companies and many startups are focused on evolving solutions that can take advantage of blockchain technology. In addition to developing these physical systems, the acceptance of data exchange is also promoted. This requires participation and practice of the security and privacy features of a blockchain solution (Wu and Lin, 2019).

Meanwhile, several small efforts have started to test the potential of blockchain technology for the benefit of the pharmaceutical industry. A pharmaceutical company worked with SAP to build the SAP Pharma Blockchain POC (proof of concept) application for medicine tracking. Since its release in 2017, it has been repeated many times. In early 2019, SAP declared the readiness of the SAP Information Partnership Center for Life Sciences, a new solution designed to help customers comply with the US Pharmaceutical Supply Chain Security Act.

1.2.4 Problems faced in the pharmaceutical industry

Among the various healthcare applications, the most significant and crucial part is the pharmaceutical industry. The functioning of pharmaceuticals is done in three phases, namely, discovery, development, and finally the distribution process. Various issues that arise in the pharmaceutical industry are described next.

1.2.4.1 Data disparity in pharmaceuticals

It has been observed that this is the most conventional and common issue that has been faced by several pharmaceutical industries. Discrepancy in data arises during the development of the drug. Normally, pharmaceutical data is recorded and placed where it needs a proper accessing methodology across the platforms. Departments that are associated with this business adopt an individual data structure and model. Accessing the sensitive data for further analytics needs more focus, and it is considered a crucial task. There is a necessity for the amalgamation of technologies like blockchain and big data analytics, so efficiency and accuracy can be enhanced (Rabah, 2017). Fig. 10.5 shows the challenges in the pharmaceutical industry.

1.2.4.2 Collection and data handling
Data that is used for analysis comes from diverse sources. Collection and managing the data is a time-consuming process since it might vary in its form. Apart from handling, analyzing the data is also a challenging task due to its nature.

1.2.4.3 Ambiguity and data inaccuracy
Ambiguity exists in the pharmaceutical data. As the data could be accessed through several channels, there is no guarantee for the data to be new and informative. Through the deployment of blockchain in this domain, focus could be more on the data while it is registered and stored for further process (Khan et al., 2020). The implementation of the blockchain enables data to be sorted based on relevance and to be unambiguous.

1.2.4.4 Supply chain
The most significant issue in the pharmaceutical industry is to retain the supply chain, and it is a complex task (Tseng et al., 2018). In the supply

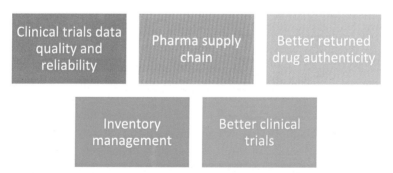

Figure 10.5 Solving pharmaceutical challenges using blockchain.

chain management system, it is found that there are more possibilities for great monetary loss, drug counterfeiting and fraudulent activities (Bryatov and Borodinov, 2019).

1.3 System architecture of blockchain in the pharmaceutical industry

Drug traceability is the process of accessing information that is associated with a drug during its life cycle, so evidences are recorded continuously. In this context, a paper discussed the utilization of the GS1 (General Specifications) standards barcodes that are used in Smart-Track (Al Huraimel and Jenkins, 2020). Bar codes are used to determine the identifier of the product, expiration date, and production number. This information is recorded during the process of several supply chains, so it ensures keeping a record of the transfers of ownership. There is a possibility of the verification of the authenticity by the end user since the repository is maintained globally. This is made possible with a smartphone app also. At the receiving end, the barcode on the product is used for the verification of its features. In Huang (Huang et al., 2018), a data matrix system is maintained for each drug. This denotes the various characteristics such as the identifier of the product, manufacturer identification, package ID, authentication code, and the metadata, which is optional. Through this information, it becomes easy for the patient to check the source of the drug (Lin et al., 2017). Complete transparency and visibility could be ensured with the help of near field communication technology in the supply chain.

Ethereum has been deployed by Figorilli (Figorilli et al., 2018) to perform anticounterfeiting. This solution works based on a smart contract. A drug ledger for a drug traceability system has been suggested (Huang et al., 2018). The proposed solution works similarly to the transaction logic of drugs that happens in the supply chain and thereby results in the privacy and authentication of the stakeholders' information. This work made use of the expanded UTXO (unspent transaction output) data structure. But the usage of UTXO data structure results in huge storage cost, less space utilization, and poor programmability (Wigand et al., 2011). A Hyperledger-based solution has been proposed toward drug traceability. Through this method, the throughput has been increased and latency is minimized. Moreover, the utilization of the resources is comparatively lower.

A detailed journey of a drug is created at each and every phase by scanning the barcodes. Later, these codes are stored on a ledger system that works based on the principle of blockchain. The inclusion of sensors in the supply chain records the humidity, temperature, and other recorded parameters, and these data are stored in the ledger. The objective of the implantation of the sensors is to check the respective drugs that require refrigeration for storage (Caro et al., 2018). As soon as the arrival of the drug in a pharmacy or hospital, one can ascertain whether it has been compromised during its journey from the source. The audit trail reveals distinguishing features, and the checking process could also be recorded on the ledger. Through the implementation of the blockchain, it becomes easy for finding discrepancies. Certain benefits are as follows:

- Due to the drug traceability, the supply chain becomes easier.
- Various information such as expiration date leads to the control of the stock and rotation.
- Authentication and verification of drugs could be performed; thus, it results in the reduction of errors.
- Harm to the patient is reduced since the checking of drugs is enhanced.
- Drug counterfeiting is also reduced (Kumar and Tripathi, 2019).

1.3.1 Smart contract and blockchain tracking for handling drug counterfeiting

Various industries have deployed smart contracts and blockchain protocols for tracking the supply chain in the pharmaceutical industry (Molina et al., 2019). The inclusion of a DLT is also a good choice for handling counterfeiting. It has been observed in various articles that the adoption of the blockchain results in the reduction of fraudulent medical businesses. Fig. 10.6 will give the various application areas of the pharmaceutical industry (Hasan et al., 2019).

The automation of smart contracts is discussed next.

The nature of a smart contract is that it can safeguard funds. Adoption of Ethereum, Bitcoin, a stablecoin, or a Central Bank Digital Currency could also be used. In spite of practicing currencies, smart contracts will lead to several new supply chain practices:

- Escrowing of funds shall be done prior. The retailer makes use of the blockchain to pay in terms of digital funds through the smart contract. When the shipping company identifies the smart contract, then the funds will be released automatically (Lin et al., 2018).
- Shipping companies also utilize the concept of the smart contract so the payment shall be released. This results in huge benefits for the company.

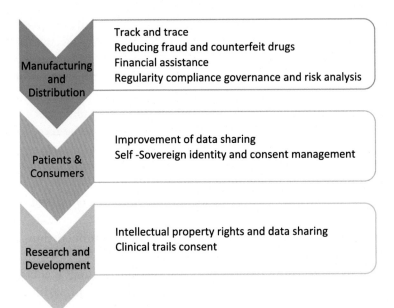

Figure 10.6 Blockchain in the pharmaceutical industry.

Apart from that, remittance done at the international level is found to be rapid and cost effective. Thus, it leads to a drastic improvement in the current financial system.

- Through the deployment of smart contract payments, the administrative costs are decreased and the efficiency is improved. During this process, the expense incurred in administration is greater since more attention is required in managing invoices and payments. Deployment of a smart contract is highly automated, so this results in the reduction of the supply chain costs (Xie et al., 2019).

2. Drug supply chain management in the smart pharmaceutical industry

The distributed and decentralized features of blockchain technology have prolonged the privacy and security of the pharmaceutical industry's drug supply chain. The full drug supply chain is presented as the blockchain network by involving participants where they can manage and update the activities of the entire supply chain. Blockchain-based systems store data relating to users of hospitals, pharmacies, manufacturers, distributors, suppliers, doctors, and patients. The major components in drug supply chain management are drugs, order details, record repository, and raw material. The users in this system receive a client-side, application-based front end where their transaction can be quickly carried out and interact with the blockchain network (Williams and McKnight, 2014). By using the client application, the status of the drug delivery can be monitored by all the concerned participants during the entire process. A stored-off blockchain is a separate data library that acts like a data storage pool. It is an efficient tool used for data analytics and visualization since data visualization can be exploited in the medical-related institutes. In this, a machine learning model can endorse the best medicine to the patients. Furthermore, the participants belonging to this framework obtain permission to search the complete details of medicines, raw material stock, and further relevant information such as manufacture date, expiration date, price, etc.

To achieve the goal of distributed ledger consistency, actively participating peer nodes in the system are responsible for executing the consensus algorithm. The first supplier initiates the process of sending required raw materials to the drug company. With the web application portal, the participants involved in the system can be logged in where the transaction can be carried out by each user. For instance, if a manufacturer places orders for the raw material, every peer node in the blockchain network would be involved in validating the transaction; then the supplier receives the order. Once the order for the raw material is prepared, the supplier proceeds with the order confirmation. Doctors can place an order for medicines in a company using the blockchain system. Initially, a doctor should be authenticated. Proceeding with the transaction proposal submission process, the transaction is validated and confirmed. Then the status is confirmed with the doctor by communicating about the successful transaction (Yue et al., 2008).

The primary and significant purpose of the blockchain network is to accumulate data in a distributed manner, where several transactions are maintained in each block. Such transactions are maintained in an encoded form and hashed manner because of security issues. In the service-oriented architecture, the smart contract and ledger-oriented functionalities are offered as a service to users. End users such as suppliers, manufactures, dealers, pharmacies, clinicians, and patients will use the front-end web application to execute the transaction where they are able to carry out medicine orders, supply raw materials, update medicine details, update orders, and record verification, products supplied, data exchanged, drug monitoring, drug control, managing clients, etc. The primary objective of the scheme is the prevention of counterfeit drugs, and this affords the end users with a secure scheme. With blockchain, each participant in the blockchain system can monitor the conveyance of the medicine.

In addition, it is capable of performing operations such as creating, reading, updating, and deleting among the connected peer nodes. Furthermore, to maintain security among the nodes, a private network can be introduced where data can be directly exchanged among nodes without revealing information to other nodes. For security purposes, every participant can build their own private network. Suppose the patients are not able to proceed with further transactions; they can check that the drug being bought from the pharmaceutical store is original or counterfeit by performing barcode scanning. Patients are provided details related to the drug manufacturing company such as manufacture date, expiration date, price, etc. This is possible because of this blockchain concept, which may also limit suppliers from just performing the raw material transaction with the manufacturer. And, the participants use the system as a private network.

The recommendation system functions to recommend the appropriate drug to pharmaceutical company customers. Sentiment analysis and machine learning techniques can be used on the data set, which contains comments provided by clients on the websites regarding whether the medicine is in good condition or not. The best medicine is recommended to the clients such as pharmacies, physicians, clinics, patients, and hospitals. With permissioned blockchain systems, unique participants are allowed to use this system. Moreover, users on the blockchain network are validated and registered by the administrator by supplying them with confidential credentials and registration certificates. Then, only the users are permitted to access the blockchain network.

In addition, it is the responsibility of the consensus algorithm to connect the registered private network users for executing and handling the transactions and the orders as well. In virtual environments, each participating node has a facility for exploiting smart contracts and a distributed ledger where they can maintain their data and execute transactions. Because of the smart contract, the nodes are capable of validating a transaction once after executing it and then write the transaction block into the distributed ledger. Furthermore, the distributed ledger holds all transaction histories, events, logging details of every transaction, and behavior carried out by the participants.

2.1 Smart contract in drug supply chain

The simple concept of a smart contract is to provide transparency for the parties to exchange properties, money, or shares without the intervention of an agent or broker of a third party. It is considered the best characteristic of blockchain networks. Smart contracts are technically viewed as multiple lines of computer code that implement the agreement among two parties without any extra payment to the third party. This is composed of a predefined set of rules on which the two parties agree. And, the smart contract is activated automatically once the stated condition satisfies the same requirements as the database events. In addition, intelligent contracts make it simpler for users to handle the privileges and their properties between various parties. Smart contracts are maintained in the blockchain platform's distributed ledger, where they are fully secured and protected against illegitimate activities such as deletion or tampering (Huang et al., 2018). Moreover, smart contracts are a safe method to execute business terms and conditions that could be implemented and prompted automatically by the blockchain network consensus algorithm.

Some significant technical challenges that arise with smart contracts are described as follows;

For writing a smart contract, a programming language called Solidity can be utilized. In this the learning rate is low and difficult to maintain. In addition, the rate of execution of all transactions is comparatively low and consumes excessive time to finish, since transactions are performed regularly or in sequence between all peer nodes of the network. This problem is solved by implementing smart contracts only for a specific set of nodes, which is not applicable for all network nodes. Healthcare supply chains are dynamic networks that cover numerous organizational and geographic borders, delivering vital services to daily life. Incorrect details, lack of clarity, and limited provenance of data may result in such systems. One result of such restrictions in the existing supply chains is counterfeit medicines, which not only have a severe adverse effect on human health but can also cause serious economic losses to healthcare industries. Thus, end-to-end monitoring systems for pharmaceutical supply chains have been highlighted in recent studies. To ensure product protection and eradicate counterfeits, an end-to-end monitoring system in the pharmaceutical supply chain is therefore imperative. Many recent tracking systems are centralized, leading to problems in healthcare supply chains with data protection, transparency, and authenticity.

An Ethereum-based blockchain system leverages smart contracts and automated off-chain storage for successful drug traceability in supply chain management. Furthermore, the smart contract assures data provenance, removes the necessity for any intermediary third parties, and offers all stakeholders a secure, immutable transaction background. To assess its efficacy and to increase traceability within pharmaceutical supply chains, testing and validation are performed along with cost and security analysis.

2.2 Transaction procedure in supply chain management

The procedure for executing transactions of drugs in the supply chain management is explained in this section. Initially, users are provided the interface of a client application that permits the user to join using their registered credentials for the blockchain system, and they can complete their requests for transactions. The registration of all users is the administrator's responsibility, and it is essential to carry out the transaction by a customer. To request a proposal for a transaction, initially the user logs in to the client application and exploits registered credentials to send his or her transaction request. After that, all the peer nodes can send the transaction proposal (Iakovou and Shi, 2019).

There are two groups of these peer nodes: committers and endorsers. The endorsers are responsible for enforcing or signing the transfer proposals and accepting the approval if it is legitimate or refusing it if it does not comply with the smart contract requirements. Committer peers are expected to confirm the outcomes of the transactions before loading them into the ledger's transaction block. Simply stated, endorser peers are the particular category of committer peers that hold the smart contract. In addition, in their own simulated environment, these endorser peers execute the smart contract of the demanded transactions before updating them into the distributed ledger while receiving proposals for the transactions.

In a simulated environment, known as the (read/write) RW package, the endorser peers would obtain the read and written data when the transactions are executed. The data that is in read mode contains the world state data, and in reality, written data is the data being written in the world state once the transaction is executed in a simulated environment. Then, the endorser peers with RW sets will transmit the signed transaction to the client. The customer sends the signed transaction to the consensus manager again with all RW sets, and the transaction is sent to the committer nodes, as well as the data being arranged into a block.

Afterward, by matching the present world state, the committer nodes verify the transaction, and then the transaction data is loaded into the distributed ledger. At last, according to the written records, the distributed ledger is updated. Ultimately, peer committers will send the transaction status update to the client either submitted or not submitted. Using REST API and a software development kit, communication between the client and the blockchain network occurs.

2.3 Distributed ledger in supply chain management

In business, the supply chain is a movement of knowledge and products by various suppliers, such as suppliers of raw materials, producers, distributors, retailers, end users, etc. SCM assists multiple users in the seamless tracking of products and data. The current supply chain management systems, however, lack information in transparency, user privacy, on-demand reports, inappropriate information monitoring, quality management, repudiation, user confidence, etc. An architecture for pharmaceutical supply chain management that includes an Ethereum blockchain, with DLT, can be used to solve these problems. This system helps to achieve consumer privacy, drug supply accountability, drug monitoring, quality control, and nonrepudiation with increased confidence among consumers.

3. Blockchain technology to prevent counterfeit drugs

3.1 The problem of counterfeit drugs

At present, the problem of counterfeit drugs is one of the serious problems for the pharmaceutical industry and has created an increasingly acute issue for human health worldwide. The World Health Organization (WHO) reported that nearly 30% of the total drugs sold in developing countries are fake or counterfeit. According to WHO, counterfeit drugs are defined as "drugs that are manufactured fraudulently, low quality, mislabeled, hiding the source detail or identity and do not follow the defined standard" (Al-Jaroodi and Mohamed, 2019). While some counterfeit drugs may contain active ingredients, an improper amount of ingredients or impure production that may contain toxic ingredients can cause serious health problems.

Drug counterfeiting is one of the most lucrative businesses worldwide. One of the main reasons for counterfeit drugs is the pharmaceutical supply chain. Due to advancement in technology, production and distribution of counterfeited drugs has increased, and these drugs can be produced in large quantities in a short amount of time. Due to lack of transparent drug delivery and supply chain process, it is difficult to detect counterfeited drugs. There are number of major gaps in pharmaceutical supply chains:

- fragmented and nontransparent supply chain infrastructure;
- number of intermediaries, making it difficult to trace the counterfeited drug's origin;
- adoption of different systems among the different drug companies that leads to multiple; solutions;
- lack of point-to-point systems infrastructure to keep data in sync across the healthcare supply chain.

To prevent counterfeit drugs, pharmaceutical companies need a secure and transparent drug supply chain management that can trace and track drug supply chains at every phase of the supply chain process, which includes raw material suppliers, drug manufacturing, distribution of drugs, pharmacies, hospitals, and consumers.

3.2 Blockchain: the solution

Blockchain is one of the latest innovations in the field of computing that can be considered an efficient solution for the problem of counterfeit drugs. The blockchain is a perfect solution where data security and privacy protection are major concerns in developing a secure drug supply chain. Blockchain is a decentralized distributed digital system that consists of a chain of blocks containing transaction data that can be shared across a network among the participants connected to the network in an encrypted form. All transactions are stored in a secure ledger with a timestamp and eliminate the need for third parties. A transaction, verified by the network participants using a majority consensus agreement protocol, can be added to blockchain. Any recorded transaction in a ledger cannot be modified or erased and can also be viewed at any point of time. To protect blocks in chains, hashing and digital signature techniques are used. There are a number of reasons to use blockchain technology in the pharmaceutical drug supply chain:

- **Extended security:** Blockchain is designed to provide 21st-century cybersecurity to prevent data and transactions from any illegal or unauthorized access. Using blockchain, trust can be increased among the participants in traditional drug supply chain systems, where they can anonymously exchange their transactions without third party interference.

- **Traceability:** Blockchain can also be used to track transactions on the network at any point of time. Therefore, blockchain is a suitable option to record the drug status throughout the entire drug supply chain process.
- **Transparency:** Blockchain maintains all recorded transaction history in a ledger, which helps to find the actual origin of the transaction in the network. This characteristic of blockchain brings more transparency to the drug supply chain where every drug changes ownership and new transactions take place.
- **Privacy protection:** Blockchain also provides privacy protection where every participant on the network is protected using a key-pair identifier. A transaction can be made from the public key of one participant to the public key of another. Using blockchain in the pharmaceutical supply chain, a patient's private medical data can be kept secret, and medical records can be used anonymously using a public key.

3.3 Drug supply chain

A drug supply chain in the pharmaceutical industry can be defined as a process where prescribed drugs or medicines are delivered to patients from manufactures (Poongodi et al., 2020). The basic entities in the drug chain are supplier, manufacturer, wholesaler distributor, packager, pharmacy, hospital, and also patients. The supplier supplies the raw material or ingredients for drugs sourced from different places to the manufacturer. The manufacturer ensures their inventory of drugs and sends the drugs to the distributor or wholesaler. The wholesaler or distributor delivers drugs to thousands of hospitals and pharmacies using transport agencies. The wholesaler can be categorized in two categories: primary or secondary. Primary wholesalers directly purchase drugs from manufacturers, whereas secondary wholesalers purchase drugs from other parties. Depending on the demand for certain drugs, a primary wholesaler may also purchase drugs from secondary wholesalers. The buying and selling of drugs or medicines between wholesalers and repeatedly repackaging of drugs by wholesaler is very common within the pharmaceutical industry. At last, pharmacies and hospitals sell drugs to the patient or consumer. Fig. 10.7 shows a typical drug supply chain scenario in the pharmaceutical industry.

In the drug supply chain, the drug moves among various entities, and every movement gives the ability for counterfeit drugs to invade the drug

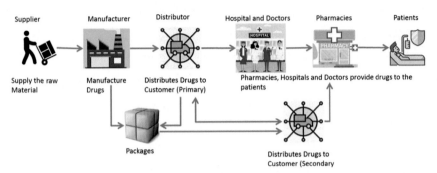

Figure 10.7 A typical drug supply chain.

supply chain. For example, fake drugs or medicines can be merged and be mistaken for legitimate drugs, or at the time of repackaging, false drugs might be given genuine labels at the wholesalers.

Therefore, drug traceability has become an important issue for public health officials, pharmaceutical industries, and government regulators. A reliable drug traceability system can track or follow the drug movement and benefit all stakeholders of the drug supply chain. Blockchain is a promising technology that can bring several useful changes to the drug traceability system in the drug supply chain. Blockchain-based systems could forbid data modification, ensure the authenticity, and enhance the security, flexibility, and durability of the system in peer-to-peer architecture.

3.4 Designing Drugledger

Drugledger is a framework for drug traceability and regulation that incorporates blockchain with drug supply chain (Thangamuthu et al., 2020). In the design of Drugledger, the following three principles are followed:

(i) An expanded version of UTXO-based transaction model is used to construct the whole, true, practical drug supply chain workflow, especially for drug packaging, repackaging, unpackaging, drug order cancellation, drug manufacturing, and drug arrival.

(ii) In the design of Drugledger, the service provider is separated into three independent roles:
- **Certificate service provider (CSP):** A public key infrastructure service provided by the CSP is integrated into Drugledger that allows node participation in Drugledger with only a valid certificate. This property could be utilized to stop Sybil attacks where troublesome nodes could flood the network with several fake names and numbers of pointless or malicious transactions. Since in the

Drugledger the stakeholder's public key is recorded in the certificate, illegal participation of stakeholders could also be banned. Furthermore, the main role of every pharmaceutical stakeholder is also verified and added to the certificate, so Drugledger can deal with fake and meaningless drug production transactions. The CSP also ensures protection of stakeholder identity from the those that are not participating in transactions. The CSP can be the drug supply chain regulator and can be integrated with Drugledger.

- **Query service provider:** Drugledger allows each node in the network to act as a query service provider and enables participants to be free to register and cooperate with any number of query service providers of their choice. Then service providers can correlate participants' public keys with their physical identities in real life, for example, a pharmacy name or distributor name. Whenever a drug transaction happens in the Drugledger network, participants in Drugledger are needed to compute an appropriate one-way cryptographic hash function of the encoded raw information of the drug (barcode or the RFID label attached to drug package) as metadata. This encoded information will be treated as a future index for querying the service provider for tracking the drug information relating to a particular stakeholder. This information will be recorded in the blockchain-based Drugledger as a blockchain transaction across every replica.

- **Antiattack service provider (ASP):** In Drugledger design, the ASP provides supervision for unusual and malicious activities such as abused transactions by suspicious stakeholders in the network to ensure smooth functioning. The ASP works as an antivirus software for a Drugledger system that helps to detect possible attacks on the Drugledger network. Fig. 10.8 shows the Drugledger basic workflow and service architecture.

(iii) In Drugledger design, a scenario-driven, storage-pruning approach is used to solve the problem of continuously increasing storage in the blockchain system. In a real-world scenario of the drug supply chain, the workflow can be optimized by the expiration date of drugs. In Drugledger, the blockchain is pruned based on drug expiration date and executes the corresponding storage-pruning algorithm, so the blockchain can accomplish a stable storage.

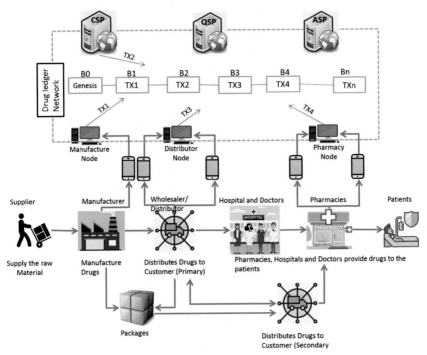

Figure 10.8 Drugledger basic workflow and service architecture.

3.5 Performance measures of Drugledger

(i) Practicality, the first and important performance measure of Drugledger is its practicality in that it can be used to track the drug supply chain in a real scenario. Following are the key concepts that are used in the design of Drugledger to trace and regulate the practical drug supply chain in the pharmaceutical industry.

(ii) Drugledger reconstructs the service provider architecture by dividing it into three different service layers to ensure a practical, sustainable service delivery system and also maintains data privacy protection and authentication.

(iii) As a use of blockchain in the drug supply chain, it records drug transaction data to trace drug status throughout the drug supply chain from manufacturers to patients.

(iv) Drugledger uses a scenario-oriented storage prune approach to decrease blockchain storage with drug expiration date, which enables blockchain to achieve stable and acceptable storage.

- **Security**: The blockchain system is permissioned to counter Sybil attacks in Drugledger design. The CSP and ASP limit the access control of participants to Drugledger by prohibiting network access among commercially ill-reputed or suspicious stakeholders in the network. Due to peer-to-peer architecture, Drugledger is also less prone to denial-of-service attacks in comparison to traditional client-server architectures.
- **Efficiency:** The efficiency of Drugledger is collectively determined by the blockchain protocols and service providers' communication overhead.
- **Transparency:** As blockchain records all drug transaction history in a ledger, Drugledger can easily find out the drug transaction's origin in the network, which makes Drugledger more transparent among the stakeholders on the drug supply chain network.

The main challenge in traditional systems is to provide security for data. The proposed system uses smart contracts and blockchain to provide the security for data over transfer and storage and reduces the chances for entering counterfeit drugs into the supply chain, as well as preventing the data from attacks. By providing encrypted data, smart contracts preventing data loss and make data transfer much more secure. Blockchain in the proposed system holds the potential to enhance the supply chain's security, integrity, data provenance, and functionality. The performance comparison between the existing and the proposed system is detailed in Table 10.1.

The proposed system facilitates all phases of the supply chain. The system enables streamlined visibility of movement and the stakeholders through which drugs transit in the supply chain. The improved traceability facilitates the optimization of flows of goods and an efficient stock

Table 10.1 Performance comparison of the existing system with the proposed system.

Performance measures	Existing system	Proposed system
Central dependency	Yes	No
Security	Low	Moderately high
Smart contract management	No	Ethereum smart contracts
Encryption	No	Public key cryptography
Error rate	Moderate	Low
User privacy	Low	High
Traceability	Low	High

management system. The system also provides decentralization to ensure each node's participation in the data flow. To reduce the error rate, the system focuses on data digitization and eliminates the paper trail used by doctors. Digital prescriptions make admittance of patients easier and simpler.

4. Blockchain use cases and its applications in the pharmaceutical industry

The blockchain is found to be the most useful, efficient, secure, and well-suited technology by all key partners in the pharmaceutical industry. They are actively engaged in exploring several real-world use cases involving tracking drugs in the drug supply chain, medical products provenance, and pharmaceutical supply chain governance rule and regulations (Chilamkurti et al., 2021). There are number of use cases of blockchain in pharmaceuticals discussed subsequently.

4.1 Prevention of counterfeit drugs and medical products

It is difficult to keep track of drugs or medical product status in the pharmaceutical supply chain where products move between many entities including manufacturers, distributors, hospitals, and patients; thereby the supply chain is prone to counterfeiters. Blockchain introduces provenance of data that avoids forgeries in the pharmaceutical supply chain. Block-chain's ability to provide complete traceability of drugs helps to identify the exact origin where the supply chain breaks down. US company Blockverify has introduced a project where a blockchain approach is used into the pharmaceutical supply chain to avoid forgeries. It uses the Bitcoin block-chain together with a private side chain where the private key of every product or drug is stored in a public blockchain. Every product is also given a tracking number to trace the change of ownership, and every change is stored in the private blockchain.

4.2 Compliance and governance in pharmaceutical supply chain

As supply chain drugs and medical products frequently move from one stakeholder to another stakeholder, it becomes necessary to adhere to important logistics rules and regulations by the stakeholders' companies that include guidelines for drug handling, transport, and storage. There are a number of operating constraints that need to be monitored, for example, maintaining temperature range for vaccines, humidity, air quality limits, and other environmental conditions that directly influence quality and efficiency of medicines throughout the supply chain. Blockchain technology enables the consumer to easily check and monitor any event occurrence at any point of time. Smart contracts, programmed within the blockchain, can be executed automatically when compliance conditions are not adhered to by notifying the relevant stakeholders in the supply chain.

Properties like inherent transparency, immutability, decentralization, and distributed nature enable blockchain to add compliance measures and governance guidelines within the supply chain in a better way.

4.3 Improving clinical trial management

Blockchain integration into clinical trial management gives improved and more reliable clinical trial data. There are a number of use cases of blockchain that have significant potential in pharmaceuticals. Blockchain is a decentralized, immutable ledger that ensures transparency and recorded clinical trial data in a more secure, verified, and unfalsified manner. Blockchain prevents clinical trial results from tampering by suspicious or false stakeholders, thus improving the reliability of data. Blockchain can also be used to maximize the number of patients recruited for clinical experiments. In the blockchain system, patients can store and have access to and control of their personal medical records, as well as being able to make them visible to recruiters for clinical trials of their choice. A blockchain pharmaceutical startup called Exochain, based on blockchain, manages secure storage of patient medical data. It also allows individual patients to control the interaction with their private data from clinical trial researchers.

5. Open Challenges related to blockchain in the pharmaceutical industry

The blockchain approach has a number of potential applications in healthcare industries. However, there are many open research challenges and issues with the implementation and adoption of blockchain in the pharmaceutical industry. Following are some of the key challenges:

- **Security:** Blockchain systems have a number of safety vulnerabilities due to their structural design and working process. These blockchain protection vulnerabilities are associated with the traditional consensus system responsible for verifying and confirming transactions in a blockchain. The consensus system is incapable of handling security threats in the shared blockchain mechanism.

- **Privacy:** Using blockchain-based electronic health record (EHR) to provide a cryptographic system architecture to maintain confidentiality and reliability of individual patient medical data is one of the key challenges. Blockchain-based EHR takes a lot of computation power and time to complete all the tasks. Further, to add a new patient to the network requires a number of various verification steps even for a genuine patient.
- **Latency and throughput restrictions:** Bitcoin blockchain takes a lot of time to verify transactions (approximate transaction latency is 10 min) in the network, while the usual database methods take less time (a couple of seconds) to respond to a transaction.
- **Blockchain size:** When all nodes in a network conduct a transaction at same time, then the IoMT mechanism fails to handle the tiny size of blockchains.

Open challenges and issues related to blockchain in the pharmaceutical industry are shown in Fig. 10.9.

- **Scalability:** The requirement for blockchain in the pharmaceutical industry is to manage and process a large number of health-related transactions, which decreases the performance of the system. Hence, blockchain size in the pharmaceutical industry directly affects the speed of the process, which means a bigger blockchain size will result in a

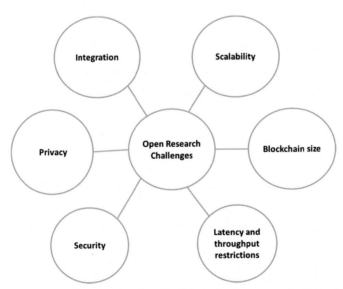

Figure 10.9 Challenges related to blockchain in pharmaceutical industries.

slower process. System scalability becomes a major challenge when the number of transactions performed by different entities increases (Kumar et al., 2021).

- **Integration:** In the pharmaceutical industry, blockchain-based solutions need to incorporate multiple distributed applications and platforms to operate, and this leads to security and interoperability issues.

6. Future direction

First, there is a need to see how the smallest amount of time can be achieved for a transaction to gain consensus. Further, there is also a requirement to check the possibility of reducing the cost of implementation, so the technology can be commercially appropriate for larger enterprise solutions. There also exists a significant need for more education and awareness for adoption of blockchain technology among the stakeholders of the pharmaceutical industry. The development of technical standards that concern the integration of blockchain into existing healthcare systems is also another area where researchers can see further solutions of blockchain technology. As a unifying solution, blockchain offers the potential for managing the supply chain of drugs. The decentralized architecture would promote real end-to-end supply management and encourage multiple stakeholders to participate, rather than being involved in this business at a greater level as unreliable, patchwork database approaches. Interoperability is the biggest problem involved in this project. Scalability, storage, social acceptance, and expectations need to be achieved. Blockchain primarily suffers from the problem of interoperability where, with sufficient need, the communication provider requires careful supply study. This poses many barriers to the success of data sharing.

In the future view of this technology, this industry produces enormous quantities of technology. Initiatives exist on a larger basis. For many sectors to step forward in future years, integrating blockchain with IoT will have a major effect. In addition, many pharmaceutical industry stakeholders are looking at blockchain as a great opportunity for their lives to evolve. The service providers are required on a large scale in the supply chain management for enhancing patient's life quality.

7. Conclusion

Despite the fact that blockchain technology is still in its early stages, already, there is a drastic progression of its application in day-to-day life, especially in the pharmaceutical industry. For blockchain to achieve its complete potential and be used in healthcare, it must address a number of significant challenges, the most significant of which are the data access controls and scalability. Accessibility to a massive pool of anonymized healthcare data could be exploited. Customized drug development, rationalization of health insurance expenses, and advancement of public health policies are some of the most significant benefits that implementation of this technology in healthcare could provide. Furthermore, patients will have access to private health records, giving them control over what information professionals obtain and hold, under what conditions, and for how long. This kind of patient involvement, when combined with the availability of data about healthcare providers, could lead to a new era of healthcare. To summarize, the literature on blockchain applications in healthcare systems is still severely lacking. Health practitioners and decision-makers should be more attentive in terms of practicing medicines by implementing blockchain technologies in order to provide more security.

References

Al Huraimel, K., Jenkins, R., 2020. Smart Track. Accessed: May 26, 2020. [Online]. Available: https://smarttrack.ae/GS1 https://www.gs1.org/docs/healthcare/MC07_GS1_Datamatrix.pdf. DataMatrix: A Tool to Improve Patient Safety Through Visibility in the Supply Chain. Accessed: May 26, 2020. [Online]. Available:

Al-Jaroodi, J., Mohamed, N., 2019. Blockchain in industries: a survey. IEEE Access 7, 36500–36515.

Amin, A.D., 2020. Blockchain technology in banking and finance sector: its effects and challenges. CARE J 31, 349–358.

Astarita, V., Giofrè, V.P., Mirabelli, G., Solina, V., 2020. A review of blockchain-based systems in transportation. Information 11, 21.

Azzi, R., Chamoun, R.K., Sokhn, M., 2019. The power of a blockchain-based supply chain. Comput. Ind. Eng. 135, 582–592.

Bryatov, S., Borodinov, A., 24–27 April 2019. Blockchain technology in the pharmaceutical supply chain: researching a business model based on Hyperledger Fabric. In: Proceedings of the International Conference on Information Technology and Nanotechnology (ITNT), Samara, Russia.

Caro, M.P., Ali, M.S., Vecchio, M., Giaffreda, R., 8–9 May 2018. Blockchain-based traceability in Agri-Food supply chain management: a practical implementation. In: Proceedings of the 2018 IoT Vertical and Topical Summit on Agriculture-Tuscany (IOT Tuscany), Tuscany, Italy, pp. 1–4.

Chen, G., Xu, B., Lu, M., Chen, N.S., 2018. Exploring blockchain technology and its potential applications for education. Smart Learn. Environ. 5, 1.

Chilamkurti, N., Poongodi, T., Balusamy, B. (Eds.), 2021. Blockchain, Internet of Things, and Artificial Intelligence, 1. CRC Press, p. 350.

Figorilli, S., Antonucci, F., Costa, C., Pallottino, F., Raso, L., Castiglione, M., Pinci, E., Del Vecchio, D., Colle, G., Proto, A.R., et al., 2018. A blockchain implementation prototype for the electronic open source traceability of wood along the whole supply chain. Sensors 18, 3133.

Hasan, H., AlHadhrami, E., AlDhaheri, A., Salah, K., Jayaraman, R., 2019. Smart contract-based approach for efficient shipment management. Comput. Ind. Eng. 136, 149−159.

Huang, Y., Wu, J., Long, C., Jul./Aug. 2018. Drugledger: a practical blockchain system for drug traceability and regulation. In: Proc. IEEE Conf. Internet Things, pp. 1137−1144.

Huang, Y., Wu, J., Long, C., 2018. Drugledger: a practical blockchain system for drug traceability and regulation. In: 2018 IEEE International Conference Internet of Things (iThings) and IEEE Green Computing and Communications (GreenCom) and IEEE Cyber, Physical and Social Computing (CPSCom) and IEEE Smart Data (SmartData).

Hyperledger. Hyperledger Blockchain. Available online: https://www.hyperledger.org/ (accessed on 10 January 2020).

Iakovou, E, Y., Shi, W., 2019. Blockchain in global supply chains and cross border trade: a critical synthesis of the state-of-the-art, challenges and opportunities. Int. J. Prod. Res. 1−18.

Khan, P.W., Byun, Y., Namje, P., 2020. A data verification system for CCTV surveillance cameras using blockchain technology in smart cities. Electronics 9, 484.

Khatoon, A., 2020. A blockchain-based smart contract system for healthcare management. Electronics 9, 94.

Kumar, R., Tripathi, R., 7−11 January 2019. Traceability of counterfeit medicine supply chain through Blockchain. In: Proceedings of the 2019 11th International Conference on Communication Systems & Networks (COMSNETS), Bengaluru, India, pp. 568−570.

Kumar, R.L., Wang, Y., Poongodi, T., Imoize, A.L., 2021. Internet of Things, Artificial Intelligence and Blockchain Technology, 1, p. 341.

Lin, Y.P., Petway, J.R., Anthony, J., Mukhtar, H., Liao, S.W., Chou, C.F., Ho, Y.F., 2017. Blockchain: the evolutionary next step for ICT e-agriculture. Environments 4, 50.

Lin, J., Shen, Z., Zhang, A., Chai, Y., 28−31 July 2018. Blockchain and IoT based food traceability for smart agriculture. In: Proceedings of the 3rd International Conference on Crowd Science and Engineering, Singapore, pp. 1−6.

Molina, J.C., Delgado, D.T., Tarazona, G., 2019. Using blockchain for traceability in the drug supply chain. In: Proceedings of the International Conference on Knowledge Management in Organizations, Zamora, Spain, 15−18 July 2019. Springer, Berlin, Germany, pp. 536−548.

Muniandy, M., Gabriel, O., Ern, T., Jun. 2019. Implementation of pharmaceutical drug traceability using blockchain technology. Int. J. 2019, 35.

Nakamoto, S., 2008. Bitcoin: A Peer-To-Peer Electronic Cash System. Available online. https://bitcoin.org/bitcoin.pdf (accessed on 12 September 2019).

Pandey, P., Litoriya, R., 2021. Securing E-health networks from counterfeit medicine penetration using blockchain. Wireless Pers. Commun. 117 (1), 7−25.

Poongodi, T., Agnesbeena, T.L., Janarthanan, S., Balusamy, B., 2020. Accelerating data acquisition process in the pharmaceutical industry using Internet of Things. In: An Industrial IoT Approach for Pharmaceutical Industry Growth. Academic Press, pp. 117−152.

Rabah, K., 2017. Challenges & opportunities for blockchain powered healthcare systems: a review. Mara Res. J. Med. Health Sci. 1, 45−52.

Thangamuthu, P., Ranganathan, I., Mani, K., Shanmugam, S., Palanimuthu, S., 2020. Blockchain technology and its relevance in healthcare. Blockchain and Machine Learning for e-Healthcare Systems, p. 1.

Tseng, J.H., Liao, Y.C., Chong, B., Liao, S.W., 2018. Governance on the drug supply chain via gcoin blockchain. Int. J. Environ. Res. Publ. Health 15, 1055.

Viriyasitavat, W., Hoonsopon, D., 2019. Blockchain characteristics and consensus in modern business processes. J. Ind. Inf. Integr. 13, 32–39.

Wigand, R.T., Mande, D.M., Wood, J.D., 11–13 April 2011. Information management and tracking of drugs in supply chains within the pharmaceutical industry. In: Proceedings of the 2011 Eighth International Conference on Information Technology: New Generations, Las Vegas, NV, USA, pp. 500–507.

Williams, L., McKnight, E., 2014. The real impact of counterfeit medications. U.S. Pharm. 39, 44–46.

Wu, X., Lin, Y., 2019. Blockchain recall management in pharmaceutical industry. Procedia CIRP 83, 590–595.

Xie, W., Wang, B., Ye, Z., Wu, W., You, J., Zhou, Q., 8–11 December 2019. Simulation-based blockchain design to secure biopharmaceutical supply chain. In: Proceedings of the 2019 Winter Simulation Conference (WSC), National Harbor, MD, USA, pp. 797–808.

Yue, D., Wu, X., Bai, J., 2008. RFID Application Frame- Work for Pharmaceutical Supply Chain. IEEE Interna- tional Conference on Service Operations and Logistics, and Informatics, Beijing, pp. 1125–1130.

CHAPTER 11

A forefront insight into the integration of AI and blockchain technologies

Muralidhar Kurni[1], K. Saritha[2], D. Nagadevi[3] and K. Somasena Reddy[4]

[1]Department of Computer Science, School of Science, GITAM (Deemed to be Univerity), Hyderabad, Telangana, India; [2]Sri Venkateswara Degree & PG College, Anantapur, Andhra Pradesh, India; [3]Department of ECE, CBIT, Hyderabad, Telangana, India; [4]Department of CSE, JNTUACEA, Anantapur, Andhra Pradesh, India

1. The rise of blockchain technology

Blockchain, which is expected to store 10% of the world's GDP by 2025, is no more just a concept. If 2016 was the era of blockchain prototypes, 2017 saw the mass adoption of blockchain globally across all business and government fields (Rahul, n.d.). A viable case that any tech expert knows about regarding blockchain technology is the digital Bitcoin cryptocurrency.

Today, it is a multibillion-dollar industry where businesses that range from technology giants to manufacturers spend heavily to develop their environments (Brodersen et al., 2019).

While blockchains were initially viewed as a financial innovation, i.e., introducing cryptocurrencies such as Bitcoin, they have proven to be far more useful in other industrial contexts as well as institutional, legal, and government cases.

1.1 Why is blockchain so popular?

Inherently, blockchain has three main features (Rahul, n.d., Fig. 11.1) that make it a rosy option for private and public actors.

- **Decentralized control:** The blockchain runs on a mutual control system, providing various players with a common mechanism to agree on a common cause. There are no exclusive rights given to any entity in a blockchain network, which allows for the smooth creation of consortia or decentralized networks for various transactional services. It is highly prominent wherever the most competent practices must be accessible to

Blockchain Technology for Emerging Applications
ISBN 978-0-323-90193-2
https://doi.org/10.1016/B978-0-323-90193-2.00005-3

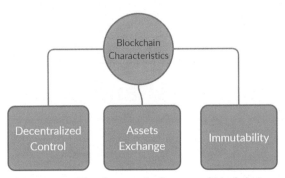

Figure 11.1 The three main features of blockchain.

all sectors to strengthen the system and promote better enforcement of and compliance by all key players.

- **Asset exchange:** This could be the most extensive feature of blockchain because all transactions are registered, and no person has complete authority over what is going on in the network, allowing the transparent interchange of value objects, i.e., value units such as digital money, energy unit data, storage unit data, etc. A trusted network for essential data sharing with blockchains becomes easier to manage. This will dramatically revolutionize how blockchain technology transactions are carried out compared to today's conventional system. More reliability, protection, and straightforward monitoring will ensure that transactions are feasible and that ethical policies are in place.

- **Immutability:** Once registered, the transaction is irreversible and cannot be removed from the network. It is like carving the information in stone. A robust digital audit trace helps everyone in the network identify who carries out activities in that network and provides smart contract management data in which contractual obligations become easier for all parties involved to verify. Ideally, this means the total exclusion of illegal activities and verification of all transactions on such networks. No person nor group would be able to manipulate the whole network in a flawed transaction, and whatever the size of the network, all previous operations will be subject to public monitoring and review by all concerned participants and stakeholders.

These three key features lay the groundwork for a new technology infrastructure planned to trigger dramatic changes in the global economy on a scale seen when the internet achieved renown 2 decades ago.

2. Artificial intelligence

Artificial intelligence (AI) has become a part of everyday life today. For instance, taking an Uber to the airport is not at all uncommon for someone, enabling them to use the time in the car to catch up on email and do some online shopping, appearing at their destination after a productive, smooth experience.

Less than a decade ago, it would have been unusual to contemplate an experience like this. This sort of experience is possible due to AI breakthrough technologies nowadays. AI empowers people to engage with one another, locate an optimal route through traffic, and discover the correct route. It prioritizes email and screens bogus messages while providing consumers with product and service ratings. Finally, it delivers a tailored music profile to the rider. Even more than that, autonomous vehicles aided by AI are about to be licensed for wide-scale implementation on public roads, which means that vehicles can be driverless.

Intelligent machines form a broad ecosystem of technologies, including advanced process automation, predictive analytics, mechanical automation, and robotics. The proliferation of AI has accelerated in the personal and business-to-consumer (B2C) settings in recent years, and it will soon have a substantial impact on the corporate sector.

AI will interrupt company operations by helping companies:

- make educated choices
- use current data better
- create new perspectives from vast volumes of human data
- improve learning
- automate routine, transactional, judgmental tasks
- minimize human physical presence
- develop new programs and services

Two recent events provide evidence of how far AI capabilities have advanced. According to recent reports, an institution of higher learning created "Jill Watson," an AI-based teaching assistant that answered emails (a system that goes by the name of "Google Duplex") (Korn, 2016) and an application that booked a restaurant table over the phone (Hyken, 2018). In both cases, individuals interacting with the systems failed to recognize that they were talking to a robot.

Despite various conditions and feelings that must be considered, AI is utilized to handle routine scheduling, rule-based operations, and steadily more sophisticated duties, such as stock market investment management. More than fifty percent of hedge funds utilize AI to make investment choices, and over a quarter use it to perform deals without human input (Mcdowell, 2020). Overall, today's AI appears to emulate the human brain to perform basic tasks and make conventional digitization and automation more futuristic, allowing the human workforce to be more productive, efficient, and innovative.

For example, AI enhances the human workforce by capturing and using existing information in automated algorithms and generating new perceptions through machine learning. Consequently, AI can play an essential role in maintaining and driving productivity and development in places where there is a shrinking workforce.

AI can disrupt any part of today's business model (administration, customer engagement, logistics, etc.) and open the door to new services and products. For instance, it might allow companies to do the following (Elser et al., 2018):

- perform highly focused, proactive sales with AI-based customer-estimating and demand sensing, which could deliver products before ordering;
- minimize price leakage by improving product quality and innovation cycles, using data-driven R&D;
- improve consumer awareness and better define potential applications or markets for current and new goods;
- improve production throughput by ensuring correct first-time performance, targeting reaction output, streamlining changeover, and advancing maintenance that eliminates unplanned downtime;
- minimize consumer churn rates by 24/7 customer support, with higher data quality levels;
- Use on-site, natural language-enabled, virtual sales agents that are available to communicate often with customers on issues and remind them of the latest offers.

AI can dramatically impact individual job profiles and the overall workforce by allowing new modern productivity levels and adequate effectiveness in all business functions and operations. AI would perform several transactional, necessary tasks, allowing people to concentrate on more value-added work requiring nuanced imagination and judgment.

3. The arrival of AI in blockchain

While blockchain technology is a revolutionary step within itself, the incorporation of AI opens an overabundance of never-before-seen opportunities that can be drawn into by private and public sector stakeholders (Rahul, n.d.). AI networks are today constituent of many large-scale technology structures. Around you, in all digital technology, there is a bit of AI. While searching to buy a dress from Amazon, your decisions are being influenced by algorithms that have been developed to accommodate every kind of person.

Integrating these two leads to solutions for problems that have been troubling entrepreneurs for a long time. Blockchain offers a way to share value-embedded data without friction. AI allows routing data into action to generate value without the effort of humans. To preserve immutability in a blockchain network, AI can be used as the governing factor, thus building one of the world's most stable ecosystems for data exchange and transactions.

3.1 Integration of artificial intelligence and the blockchain

Intriguingly, AI and blockchain vary in various ways philosophically (Pinto, 2018):

- In contrast to the open, distributed nature of blockchain, AI has a more centralized infrastructure.
- While many AI technologies are owned and run by centralized vendors, most blockchain players on the market publish open-source code, publicly accessible for anyone to search.
- AI is more of a black box approach, while blockchain is more open in all the processed transactions.
- AI is based on probabilistic formulas, while blockchain in nature is more deterministic.

AI start-ups, including IBM, Apple, Amazon, Alibaba, Facebook, Google, and Intel, acquire customers for themselves rather than other companies (Bass and Brustein, 2020). Data give these organizations an insurmountable advantage in training their AI agents. Since data and capabilities are mutually exclusive, the data and capabilities are entirely inaccessible to the rest of the world.

Because of the centralized artificial intelligence, such as massive surveillance with facial recognition and computer-based technology, people have room to do things they should not (Feldstein, 2019). At the same time, organizations relinquish control of their data security and hand it over to third parties.

3.2 Merging AI and blockchain

Because it can help overcome several AI challenges, blockchain is relevant here. We deploy numerous AI and machine learning (ML) tools to recognize and authenticate users' blockchain identities.

Experts are currently researching ways in which blockchain can be used to build a decentralized AI marketplace. This enables people to freely share their PII (personally identifiable information), ensuring that it will stay safe and private through decentralization and secure computing provided by the blockchain. In reality, users can easily exchange sensitive information such as financial and health data, and only the intended service provider will be able to decode and decrypt user PII with the user's express consent. We assume that massive data will accumulate and keep large corporations competitive through the use of AI algorithms.

An article on Hackernoon lists some new ventures integrating block-chain and AI to build state-of-the-art solutions (Pinto, 2018). One of the most remarkable is SingularityNET, an AI marketplace where companies can acquire AI capacity globally to increase storage growth. Namahe AI is also a platform designed to enhance supply chain productivity through the combination of AI and blockchain to ensure that processes are tracked seamlessly in real time, helping to catch irregularities and fraud in real-time as well. Numerai, an AI-based hedge fund, supports competitions to create and apply prediction models and solutions for industry enthusiasts.

3.3 Why is there great potential for AI-integrated blockchain?

AI's passion for consuming as much data as possible makes it a blockbuster for all stakeholders and improves blockchain's reputation providing the data. The following ecosystems can be generated by combining the two (Rahul, n.d.).

1. *Improved business data models:* While current businesses powered by AI models depend on the information provided by organizations and their ecosystem partners, open data sharing has its problems like privacy concerns, fraudulent contracts, and misuse of data, thereby prohibiting the implementation of entirely accessible data systems. AI requires practically no barriers to access knowledge from the market environment to

make the most accurate decisions. Blockchain systems will have this frictionless access to information as all stakeholders exchange information, and no single individual owns the network. All key players can easily integrate data sources when AI is driving analytics or insight mining. The way the information is used will be specified in the blockchain directory for the entire transaction, so data holders are unable to be exposed to situations where the integrity and value of their data are lost. When data is continuously supplied from many stakeholders, AI systems can immerse themselves and investigate patterns, attitudes, and other aspects to reveal insights never seen before. More players will allow more opportunities to gain reliable insights. The practices will prepare them to adapt more efficiently to the situations based upon how every player responds by assessing best practices and finding the best solutions for a complex scenario.

2. *Newer insights and discovery:* With open access, data caches are combined efficiently, which will help handle new AI data combinations and uncover new data trends and behavior. It is easier to remove false statements and practices with blockchain, and AI can also generate new trustworthy classifiers and filters for scientific data information. This is especially important for retail and predictive customer involvement scenarios in which more data sets will allow companies to gain more traction in sales. A lot of marketing automation can also be accomplished by the integration of blockchain-centric customer data acquisition. Smart business systems may feed professional and unstructured leaders into comparing data to information gathered from other forms of conversation and interaction, including social media, email campaigns, etc., to arrive at more accurate sales opportunities. This will allow quicker sales cycles, provide more meaningful filters to classify the desired product for end customers, and generate more effective shopping stories. This will lead to higher expectations of satisfaction and rising loyalty. Branding support from ordinary people would reinforce retail brands more than any other way.

3. *Smart forecasts:* AI has done a lot to predict results based on operational ecosystem data. However, such forecasts may often be inaccurate because of faulty device data generation, dishonest data source manipulation, or flawed analytical methods used in AI-driven systems. With blockchain, data generators and analytical methods would easily be authenticated since they must accept existing best practices and contracts. Those criteria will be continuously checked in a decentralized

framework. This helps AI systems operate only on genuine and authentic data sets, leading to accurate predictions. More genuine data will make AI systems work more effectively. These observations will then be used to arrive at accurate decisions through deep learning algorithms more factually, which boosts the estimation of end–user behavior for organizational or governance-related means. As forecasts become wise, it undoubtedly aligns marketing and awareness strategies in the right direction, thus ensuring that companies have substantial returns on these fronts. Given that almost 40% of marketers in a recent Hubspot survey have pointed out that providing return on investment in marketing is a significant challenge, the use of blockchain AI-driven systems for smart predictions is critical under current market conditions.

4. *Digital intellectual property rights:* Models have helped AI build exceptional success stories that motivate others. However, more frequently, such model designers refuse to disclose their critical data model information for lack of copyright and security policies. Although copyright policies exist, data models intelligently reveal entirely distinct architectures so even original data models cannot be identified. With the integration of blockchain technology, developers can easily allow others to share their data models without losing exclusive rights and patents. Data and related models can be stored with the owner's cryptographic digital signature, for a tamper-resistant global registry. What makes it nearly impossible for someone to assert authorship of creations using these publicly available data is that the integrated AI tools allow study of these data models' patterns and behaviors and discovery of robust insights. Also, companies and data owners are authorized for an interim duration to assert their rightful privileges and intellectual property rights. This provides an engaging way of monetizing innovative knowledge or content in varied streams for professionals.

5. *Self-governing organizations:* The dream scenario of AI is a world in which computers carry out tasks without human action. All that is needed to set up an AI-enabled training and learning environment that is globally validated is a working policy and instructions to be secure, tamper-resistant, and not owned by a single entity. This system is simpler than blockchain, and AI systems can read data and process and execute professional assignments quickly. Smart contracts on decentralized blockchain networks control chances of failure or malfunctioning and adverse operational effects for the entire system. The network nodes store the entire operations system for the states, parameters, behavior,

performance, etc., and enable AI systems to behave in compliance with predetermined intelligent policies. Such an autonomous level of service has never been seen before except in science fiction films from the past. However, this autonomous operating mode is very feasible with AI that enables protected blockchain systems with data. Variations from planned actions occur when the system is needed to regulate nodes supervised by all actors. Secure and transparent control mechanisms ensure that things don't go haywire at any time, and human intervention is kept to a minimum or eliminated in ideal circumstances. Entire bureaus supporting back-office operations can be run as autonomous units with scalable AI-enabled blockchain systems without human resources.

4. The possibilities of AI integrated with blockchain

Notwithstanding all the advantages of new technologies, they are not without drawbacks. Though blockchain suffers from scalability, performance, and safety deficiencies, AI has a share of concerns about data protection, description, and confidentiality. The integration of these two capable technologies will help each other complement and revolutionize the next digital generation. AI will help build a ML framework on the blockchain network through its integration, enhancing scalability, security, efficient governance, and personalization. On the other hand, blockchain technology can contribute to the privacy, clarification, and trust of AI (Dinh and Thai, 2018). Fig. 11.2 shows the resulting features of the integration of AI and blockchain.

4.1 Artificial intelligence for blockchain

A blockchain platform's functioning implies various parameters and compensations between efficiency, decentralization, safety, and many characteristics. Incorporating AI will help make these decisions simpler by optimizing and automating blockchains to boost performance. All data on the blockchain openly allows AI to play a prominent role in maintaining user privacy and confidentiality (Dinh and Thai, 2018).

1. *AI for security and scalability:* Blockchains are considered immutable and virtually impossible to hack. However, the same cannot be said for the applications developed on the framework, as shown in Decentralized Autonomous Organization (DAO) hacking. With the unbelievable advancement of ML, an AI-run blockchain can detect the possibility of an attack and use the proper defense to handle it. AI can

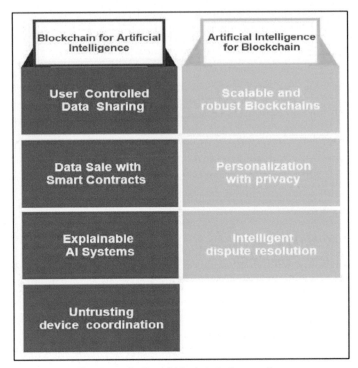

Figure 11.2 AI and blockchain integration.

also be used for the scalability and robustness of the blockchain framework. For instance, the platform may incorporate intelligence to
increase the block development rate when transactions spike. This
would help to improve the system's efficiency.

2. *AI for privacy:* Today, we collect information about our users through
   apps to customize content on the site. Enabling blockchain ML information can help to provide privacy while personalizing content. Instead
   of moving it as conventional centralized systems, the system would pull,
   view, and display the information. It conducts all local calculations,
   removing the need to pass data to an external source while protecting
   user privacy.

3. *AI for smart contracts:* Smart contracts are central to the management of
   blockchain transactions. However, they are not smart enough to settle
   conflicts at present. The progress of ML enables AI to solve such
   complex situations. By incorporating AI into blockchain, users can settle
   both   off-chain   and   on-chain   litigations   without   third-party

intervention. An AI-backed blockchain platform would execute automated arbitrations in a manipulative and impartial way. The decisions made are guided by data, making them more justified and consistent.

4.2 Blockchain for artificial intelligence

Blockchain can manage coordination mechanisms and decentralized markets for various AI components, including computing power, algorithms, and data. This will promote AI's adoption, creativity, and openness to an unparalleled degree (Dinh and Thai, 2018).

1. ***Blockchain for user-controlled data sharing:*** Data in the present data-driven economy is regarded as the new gold. Huge data availability is one of the guiding forces of AI systems. However, extracting data from training models is difficult even as a significant player, primarily because of current privacy issues. Blockchain incorporation, with its inherent accountability and transparency, can promote data sharing. Users should also be aware of all data information, such as who downloaded or accessed the data. Blockchain helps to give the consumer more trust in the management of data for sharing. The future effect of such data sharing would be immense.

2. ***Blockchain for data sales with smart contracts:*** Blockchain integrations with AI will allow data sales using smart contracts. This sets the platform for a safe, private data market without intermediaries. These markets are the foundation for all players, reducing price barriers and promoting creativity.

3. ***Blockchain for explainable AI systems:*** While ML has succeeded in developing autonomous systems, users are reluctant to implement them. This is because many of the actions taken by these processes cannot be demonstrated to people. An immutable trail must be developed to improve adaptability that tracks the data flow in these complex systems. By monitoring decision-making and data treatment at any stage, blockchain technology allows this. This understanding of a straightforward direction will allow people to grasp the whole process better.

4. ***Blockchain for untrustworthy devices:*** Coordinating and making decisions together, devices such as mobile phones, internet of things (IoT) devices, or swarm robotics have bright potential for AI in the future. These systems can be used from teamwork robots on tactical missions

to software upgrades for devices such as refrigerators. Integrating such platforms with blockchain would boost safety and defend networks against future hacks.

They still have a long way to go for all the innovations and advances in the blockchain and AI space. Technologic developments in algorithms, protocols, computational resources, and data management are inadequate to solve the challenges of the human environment. However, AI and blockchain's integration provides infinite opportunities that further research and development will realize on the future path.

5. Applications of AI and blockchain

The following are the common AI and blockchain applications (Banafa, 2019). Fig. 11.3 shows a list of AI and blockchain applications.

1. *Smart computing power:* You would need a considerable amount of processing power to run a blockchain on a device with its whole encrypted data. AI helps us to step beyond this and to handle tasks more smartly and productively. An example of the hack algorithms used to mine Bitcoin blocks follows a "brutal force" strategy, which systematically lists all possible solution candidates and tests whether all candidates meet the problem assertion to verify a transaction (Pollock, 2018). Guess a learning-based computer algorithm that can glint its real-time ability if sufficient training information is provided (Pollock, 2018).

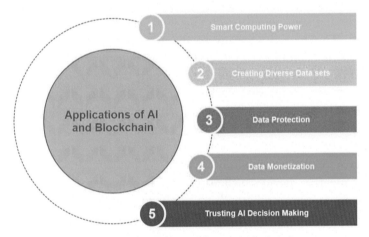

Figure 11.3 Applications of AI and blockchain.

2. *Creating diverse data sets:* Blockchain technology produces decentralized, open networks accessible worldwide in public blockchain networks, unlike AI-based initiatives. However, blockchain network technology is used for decentralization in various industries to supply cryptocurrencies. SinguarlityNET, for example, is explicitly designed to use blockchain technology to facilitate disseminating algorithms and data, help ensure future AI, and to create decentralized AI. SingularityNET combines AI with blockchain and creates decentralized smarter AI networks that host different data sets. By building an API on the blockchain, an AI intercommunication will be possible. Various algorithms can be developed for data sets (Wolfson, 2018).

3. *Data protection:* AI's success solely depends on the data input. Via data, AI receives valid information and events about the planet. Data feeds AI, which will continue to develop itself through the data. On the other hand, blockchain technology enables secure data storage in a distributed directory. It facilitates the development of entire protected databases to be reviewed by approved parties. By integrating blockchain with AI, a backup mechanism for beneficial and essential personal data is adopted. Financial and health knowledge is too sensitive to be passed to a single entity and its algorithms. The storage of this data on a blockchain accessible by an AI will give us the immense advantage of personalized advice when storing sensitive data securely once we have undergone the proper procedures.

4. *Data monetization:* Monetization of data is another disruptive breakthrough possible by integrating the two technologies. Monetizing collected data is a significant income source for major firms like Google and Facebook (Wolfson, 2018). It reveals that data is being armed against us when others determine how data is sold to profit corporations. Blockchain helps us encrypt our data and use it in the way we think it is appropriate without sacrificing our details and allows us to monetize personal data if we choose. To combat prejudicial algorithms and create a wide variety of data sets in the future, this is necessary to understand (Wolfson, 2018). To learn and improve AI algorithms, AI networks are expected to directly buy data from data markets through their creators and make the whole process even more precise than today without technology firms taking advantage of their users (Wolfson, 2018). Such a data market will also open up AI for small businesses.

For firms that do not produce their data, AI production and feeding are incredibly costly. Using decentralized data markets, they may access costly and privately held data.

5. *Trusting AI decision-making:* As AI algorithms get smarter through learning, data scientists gradually find it increasingly difficult to interpret these programs' implications. This is because AI algorithms can process unbelievably large quantities of variables and data. To ensure that they nevertheless represent the truth, we must continue to audit AI findings. The variables, data, and processes used by AIs for decision-making are stored immutably using blockchain variables. This makes auditing the whole process much more straightforward. All steps are observed using acceptable blockchain programming from data entry to conclusions, and the observer can ensure that these data have not been changed. It builds trust in the AI program's conclusions. It is crucial because using AI apps by firms and individuals will start when they understand how to operate using their knowledge decisions.

The fusion of AI and blockchain technology remains mostly unknown. While there has been a fair amount of wisdom in integrating the two technologies, initiatives dedicated to this innovative alliance are still constrained. These technologies can be combined to use data in ways never before thought possible.

Data are the main component for creating and enhancing AI algorithms, and blockchain means that this data can be audited, any intermediate measures taken by AI to conclude the data can be taken, and the individuals can monetize their data. AI can be unbelievably innovative, but it needs to be planned with the utmost precautions: blockchain can significantly assist in this. The success of the interaction between the two technologies is anyone's guess. However, there is a strong and rapidly developing potential for real disruption.

6. Challenges of merging AI and blockchain

AI solutions vary from legacy solutions because they adopt probabilistic models. The standard program, in other words, follows "If A happens, THEN follow B." AI, in comparison, uses probabilistic responses to make a good move. This feature makes AI the perfect technology for versatile solutions. The concession, however, is that such AI systems make errors (Pinto, 2018).

To date, AI agents often appear to go wrong, and it remains difficult for users to know whether they are mistaken. Some unforgettable examples include a rogue Microsoft chatbot, Wikipedia edit bots feuding with each other, Uber's self-driving cars ignoring red lights, and Promobot IR77, the Russian robot that escaped from the laboratory (Pinto, 2018).

Compliance is another concern (Pinto, 2018). Regulation of AI solutions to prevent causing harm continues to be a significant concern. AI and blockchain solutions need a real challenge for data aggregation. The IoT is nevertheless essential in providing the data necessary for AI training. In reality, the protection and privacy of data in this field will be crucial.

Talent is another obstacle to face when connecting blockchains and AI (Pinto, 2018). While IoT devices can collect data, training AI models is secondary, and it is necessary for AI models to run in a decentralized or distributed form. Fortunately, like Deep Brain Chain and SingularityNET, other businesses are still looking for ways to improve their algorithms.

Computing resources remain a challenge when AI and blockchain are combined. Fortunately, it is possible to utilize global idle computing resources to conduct resource-intensive blockchain AI training.

7. The integration of AI and blockchain for industry 4.0

Over time, blockchain and AI have formed their pathways with a slight overlap. There is a direct, coordinated link between the two technologies in the form of data. However, according to a survey, the future of banks and insurance companies is primarily ordered to shift from blockchain to distributed AI. The loss of significant consumers would then be just one of the possible disruptive situations, and industry 4.0 would be affected by the same situation.

In comparison, AI has sliced through the embryonic stage of advanced technology development, a distinct but related path. Its usage and acceptance have increased, and its implementation has reached a critical stage of organization. Interfacing one or more blockchains to banks and insurance undertakings will speed transactions, improve protection and accountability, and optimize data control (Kumar, 2019).

1. *Integrating AI and blockchain in rising performance:* AI and blockchain can gain and endorse each other to move into the fourth industrial revolution. For example, a chatbot can handle customer service if a client wants clarification on a specific subject or has a particular request.

As ML and algorithms push chatbots, the solution is certainly more rewarding and quicker. Here, the AI approach will evolve, and a channel is needed to achieve this purpose, where those customers who have a direct interest can share information and communicate in complete protection.

2. *Integration offers a strategic advantage for businesses:* The reason behind the AI revolution is big data progress. It helps organizations organize a massive dataset of organized components that can be processed very quickly by computers. Simultaneously, this data value has encouraged blockchain development because its distributed directory is a revolutionary way for data to be stored alternatively and effectively. The integration of AI and blockchain impacts various areas, including the following.

   a. *Security*: AI and blockchain can provide a double shield against cyberattacks. Finding suspicious incidents is one of the most significant obstacles for prospective companies.

   b. *Speed*: Using both technologies will increase information processing and data transfer speed and allow consumer experiences with companies to be more comfortable and quicker.

   c. *Usability*: Services can be more personalized in the coming years and be the framework for large companies' suggestions.

3. *What incorporation implies for industry 4.0:* It has been seen that blockchain solves a variety of inefficiencies in existing technology and AI efficiency due to the value of data currently available. The prevalent delivery of AI and the introduction of blockchain will also be significant for industry 4.0. At present, companies address software, algorithms, automation, robotics, and hardware and discuss more complicated topics such as on-demand design and development of goods, dematerialization, and disintermediation. Industry 4.0 will be the first big transition to switch from one technologically centered state to another, possibly being more advanced, emphasizing various cornerstones like information transparency, assistance, and interconnection.

8. How the app development industry is using blockchain and AI integration to innovate

The application development industry combines AI and blockchain into its newly developed applications. The advantages can be seen in the following points (Laura, 2020):

1. ***Encrypted security:*** The data held in the blockchain would be protected with inherent encryption. If anyone wants to encrypt highly sensitive information, like their bank accounts and other confidential records, blockchain is what any developer should think of as the best technology. In the meantime, using AI would be easier to find documents with a single click, because it collects a high volume of data. Researchers worldwide are now working on ways of using AI to prevent security from being encrypted.

2. ***Unengaging the AI thinking process:*** The user will only benefit from AI if he knows using and understands machine language. However, with blockchain, every change and every click is registered, making it easier to use the software or system.

3. ***Managing and accessing data market:*** Market players such as Google and Facebook have access to a lot of data, which will be very useful in AI processing. However, smaller industries continue to search for AI. When designing applications, incorporating problems with the blockchain would help record all changes and data entered and facilitate users in imitating the behavior using AI.

4. ***Energy optimization and smart contracts:*** For energy use optimization, AI requires training on historical data from data centers, and technology must be incorporated into organizations. The same idea also applies to the mining industry and would further slash mining hardware costs. Any glitches must be treated carefully, and immediate action should be taken.

Integration of these two technologies supports both the Android and iOS app developers. For example, blockchain's incorporation has turned the payment portal into a smooth channel, and AI defines payments. Security is a serious problem that has hit mobile applications but can be solved using blockchain and AI.

9. Blockchain and AI building a powerful match

Various companies merge blockchain and AI with excellent results (Daley, 2019; Choudhury, 2020).

AI and blockchain are two of the most popular and elegant techniques. When combined, the two common techniques can deliver robust results and can be used for several purposes, including supply chain management, financial security, and various data sets. Following are the top projects where companies have merged blockchain and AI.

1. **FINALIZE:** The software platform Finalize creates applications to enhance civil infrastructure using blockchain and ML. It automates and speeds up workflow, verification procedures, and the construction industry's management, integrating with wearables to satisfy safety regulations.
2. **BLACKBOX AI**: Blackbox AI designs new AI tools. The organization's engineers build a custom information infrastructure that facilitates computer training and language processing for blockchain tools. Further building blockchain technology, the company also provides consulting services for its products to unlock blockchain potential.
3. **CORE SCIENTIFIC:** Core Scientific combines customized AI and blockchain infrastructure among existing business networks to update the business's servers, infrastructure, and apps that get real-time data reporting from supply chain management.
4. **BEXT360:** Bext360 uses AI and blockchain to increase accountability and productivity in the coffee, wood, seafood, and mineral industries' supply chains. AI analyses crops and forecasts growing trends, whereas blockchain ensures that from the seed to the finished product, the supply chain is documented.
5. **BURSTIQ:** BurstIQ developed a "Health Wallet" incorporating blockchain, AI, and big data for comprehensive patient data handling. BurstIQ wallet provides a patient healthcare team entry to their insurance history and health plans. Health professionals may then purchase, exchange, or sell patient data for various clinical experiments or to learn about a particular disease. Conversely, the blockchain helps patients keep personal identity details secret, even exchanging only large-scale health data.
6. **VIA:** VIA integrates blockchain and AI to enable some of the biggest potential firms worldwide to design and use data more efficiently. The Trusted Analytics Chain secures data of a power utility, secretly collects from various locations and firms, and uses smart contracts to give businesses more profound insights into the potential market as a whole.
7. **COINGENIUS:** CoinGenius is an AI-driven cryptocurrency trading platform that offers AI-based scoring, high-quality data feeds, and advanced projections for cryptocurrency traders to increase their potential by tailoring news and trading features.
8. **ALPHANETWORKS:** A new entertainment platform that utilizes AI and blockchain to increase user insights and viewership algorithms is AlphaNetworks. This company's proof-of-engagement tools use AI and blockchain to enable automatic payments to content creators.

9. **NETOBJEX:** NetObjex is a smart urban technology network using AI, IoT, and blockchain to power connected devices and cloud-based goods. These technologies are allegedly combined to enhance logistics monitoring, data and system authentication, and real-time failure detection.

10. **FIGURE:** Figure incorporates blockchain and AI into the home loan system to accommodate new entry points for consumer credit products. These solutions include home equity lines of credit, home remodeling loans, and even home buy-lease offers. According to the organization, loans can be made available to customers as soon as they have filled out a loan application.

11. **WEALTHBLOCK.AI:** Wealthblock.AI is a SaaS (software as a service) platform that enables organizations seeking financing to handle automated marketing and messaging. Firms will monitor and operate their suitability checking method using a blockchain to ensure their business partners are of excellent quality. More than that, Wealthblock's AI assists with content creation, keeping investors in the loop at all times.

12. **CYWARE LABS:** Cyware Labs integrates AI and blockchain-based threat intelligence solutions. One example of supporting mobile threat intelligence, safe messaging, and suspicious incident reporting is the Cyware Situational Awareness Platform. With this approach, users may inspect their current real-time mobile security protocols in great detail.

13. **CHAINHAUS:** Blockchain and AI consultancy education and marketing firm Chainhaus offers everything from training and software expansion to research, and capital raising is covered in a full spectrum of services provided by the firm.

14. **VERISART:** Using AI and blockchain, Verisart can identify and authenticate fine art in real time. Artists can establish tamper-proof certificates of work that ensure credit and immutability using the company's blockchain. By using blockchain technology and time-stamping, these certificates do not allow fakes to be sold as originals.

15. **BOXSPRING MEDIA:** Boxspring Media claims to generate original programming for new-starting careers, which is interactive, on-demand, and is made to be viewed while employed. To help employees stay current on industry developments, each Boxspring Media platform features a specific subject (such as networking, new technology, etc.) to supply employees with relevant and consumable material.

16. **VYTALYX:** To give healthcare professionals blockchain-based access to medical knowledge and insights, Vytalyx, a health technology company, uses AI. By storing medical information on a blockchain, a patient's medical staff may instantly use AI to search for clinically relevant medical studies, personalize medications and diet plans, and enhance patient and doctor contact.

17. **WORKDONE:** Workdone automates processes between SaaS platforms. The "work heuristics management" company uses ML and smart contracts to gather work-related, customer-specific features from entire SaaS platforms in a business ecosystem to lessen the time spent on repetitive tasks such as customer retention and analysis processes.

18. **STOWK:** A blockchain-based platform by Stowk aims to speed up data access, IT governance, and procurement by using AI.

19. **MOBS:** Mobs is a blockchain-based video marketplace where mobile videos are sold and purchased. When a consumer sells his video, potential customers—claim advertisers who need to have convincing footage—can click through the application to find their needs. Mob's blockchain then produces a smart contract that allocates money directly to the producer of content based on interaction rates and views.

20. **HANNAH SYSTEMS:** Hannah Systems is creating AI and blockchain technology for self-driving automobiles. A car equipped with ML may rapidly access, examine, and securely store data using the company's data-sharing network, an analytics dashboard, real-time mapping tool, and a blockchain.

21. **LIVEEDU:** LiveEdu is an online learning platform where students learn how to create authentic goods by getting training with the developers who make them. The platform offers classes on all elements, including the implementation of AI and the fabrication of Bitcoin development instructions. It delivers on what it promises as LiveEdu incorporates blockchain and smart contracts to benefit authors of the content.

22. **OBEN:** ObEN built a technology that enables intelligent virtual avatars in Augmented reality (AR) and virtual reality (VR). Anyone can build their virtual avatars for communication on the platform. To provide a more personal and social experience, AI, blockchain, and VR all work together.

23. **NEUREAL:** Neureal is a prediction engine that incorporates AI, blockchain, and cloud computing to forecast various things, including stock market movements and Google search data. In predicting past events, the company's AI scans past projections to anticipate possible future events. In addition, the blockchain database keeps account of every outcome, and the computer networks may search for patterns to see if their predictions are correct.

24. **NUMERAI:** This is a decentralized hedge fund where over a hundred data scientists worldwide collaborate on AI and blockchain matters. As part of the ongoing NUMERAI ML competition, Ethereum and ML data are made available to the researchers, creating ML models based on the data. Only the most sophisticated scientists receive Numeraire (NMR) crypto.

25. **COMPUTABLE:** Computable Labs dedicates itself to building blockchain-based solutions for AI marketplaces. By facilitating the sharing of data and algorithms on the decentralized AI marketplaces, the company empowers individuals to have more access to a larger range of information.

26. **SYNAPSE AI:** The Synapse AI network gives participants tokens (SYN Tokens) to exchange data when users share it. Users who use the Synapse Marketplace to exchange data may also acquire Bitcoin, Ethereum, or US dollars in return for their SYN Tokens. By leveraging the ability to share data as part of the reward system, Synapse AI's data-sharing marketplace provides users with the opportunity to contribute their data to a larger pool of available data. This makes data purchasers in the advertisement, education, entertainment, and pharmaceutical industries better able to access a more comprehensive data supply.

27. **DOPAMINE:** The market for AI and data providers' intellectual property is driven by Dopamine. The company's blockchain records each data provider's reputation and allocates incentives based on this information. By sharing insights, databases, and AI and blockchain technology, data providers can make money by solving problems and becoming important collaborators to the Dopamine community.

28. **BOTCHAIN:** BotChain facilitates uniform software registration, assessment, audit, and collaboration of AI agents. AI-enabled bots are certified on the blockchain BotChain ecosystem to log all data and get "BotCoin" by running apps on the distributed network.

29. **AI BLOCKCHAIN:** The AI blockchain uses intelligent digital agents to maintain the network. The blockchain company's platform and ledger are used to maintain the security of all the major businesses, from real estate to media to healthcare and the financial sector. Next, the firm uses AI to handle everything from developing and administering blockchains to expanding and maintaining the network.

30. **BLACKBIRD.AI:** Blackbird.AI, with its usage of AI and blockchain, rates the authenticity of news content. When confronted with "fake news," the organization relies on AI to analyze content and identify potentially false, hateful, or satirical content. Blackbird.AI blockchain acts as a database where the verified results of AI and crowdsourced reports are recorded.

31. **GAINFY:** The Gainfy healthcare platform combines AI, IoT devices, and blockchain technology to improve the healthcare business experience. As with other industries, there are various ways that this business incorporates new healthcare technology developments, including a digital urgent care network, an identity verification system, a data encryption tool, a crypto payment system, and a clinical trials database.

32. **AICOIN:** AICoin is a financial term that combines AI modeling advantages with a token. In this project, developers have developed AI models to define trading trends in about 20 liquid cryptocurrency markets. According to the developers, AICoin aims at enabling investors to create wealth through AI and blockchain.

33. **DEEPBRAIN CHAIN:** A decentralized, low-cost AI computer network that uses blockchain technology and privacy-preserving technology is called DeepBrain Chain. It is a decentralized neural network in essence. The purpose of this network is to provide a decentralized AI development cloud network. It is also a value-maximizing data network that provides data ownership and consumption as separate entities. NEP-5 chains will be replaced with a native substratum token with decentralized governance.

34. **MATRIX AI:** AI-based technologies such as natural language processing are used to fulfill the blockchain pledge. Matrix AI utilizes autonomous AI contracts, state-of-the-art cybersecurity, dynamic blockchains, and more. A protected virtual machine is driven by AI that commonly finds prospective vulnerabilities and hostile intentions, helping to keep the system robust during a large-scale attack.

35. **NAMAHE:** Namahe is a blockchain-based supply chain solution. It combines AI with blockchain technology to create a safe ecosystem

that saves on expensive audits and increases supply chain performance. Namahe improves supply chain productivity by allowing AI layers to seamlessly track the supply chain, seeking trend anomalies for detecting fraud, delays, irregular events, and flagging the analysis data.

36. **PECULIUM:** Peculium is an entirely open, decentralized AI and ML savings management platform. It seeks to help its users overcome the risks of the current investment market. Peculium also provides users with cryptocurrency asset tracking and control. The goal of the project is to optimize profits and savings based on ML. This is done by the financial advisor AIEVE of Peculium, i.e., AI, ethics, principles, and balance.

37. **SINGULARITY NET:** The whole-stack AI solution Singularity-NET is a decentralized protocol-driven solution. It is the only decentralized forum for AI to collaborate and organize on a scale. The SingularityNET network is the central framework for interacting and transacting AI services. SingularityNET helps everybody to benefit from an international network of AI algorithms, resources, and agents.

10. Conclusion

The emergence of blockchain and integrating AI into conventional services and products has created an entirely new range of possibilities for any of these powers to join hands and collaborate. The convergence of AI and blockchain produces possibly the world's most secure technology-driven decision-making systems that are practically tamper-proof and offer reliable insights and decisions. Over the years, businesses have spent heavily on AI-driven automation software, and today, with the advent of blockchain, it is possible to trust the interaction of machines with the system. Soon, we will witness the widespread acceptance of stable and intelligent business and governance environments aided by AI-integrated blockchain networks.

References

Banafa, A., 2019. Blockchain and AI: a Perfect Match? OpenMindBBVA. https://medium.com/the-capital/blockchain-and-ai-a-perfect-match-e9e9b7317455.

Bass, D., Brustein, J., 2020. Big Tech Swallows Most of the Hot AI Startups. Bloomberg. https://www.bloomberg.com/news/articles/2020-03-16/big-tech-swallows-most-of-the-hot-ai-startups.

Brodersen, C., Tanco, C.C.T., Chang, J., 2019. Deloitte'S 2019 Global Blockchain Survey - Blockchain Gets Down to Business. Deloitte Insights, pp. 2—48. https://www2.deloitte.com/content/dam/insights/us/articles/2019-global-blockchain-survey/DI_2019-global-blockchain-survey.pdf.

Choudhury, A., 2020. Top 8 AI-Blockchain Projects One Must Know. AnalyticsIndiaMag. https://analyticsindiamag.com/top-8-ai-blockchain-projects-one-must-know/.

Daley, S., 2019. 31 Ways Blockchain & AI Make a Powerful Pair. Builtin. https://builtin.com/artificial-intelligence/blockchain-ai-examples.

Dinh, T.N., Thai, M.T., 2018. AI and blockchain. IEEE Comput. 48—53. https://doi.org/10.1007/978-3-030-04468-8_11.

Elser, B., Ulbrich, M., Fasshauer, P., Aggarwal, V., 2018. Artificial intelligence and blockchain. In: Accenture. https://www.forbes.com/sites/bernardmarr/2018/03/02/artificial-intelligence-and-blockchain-3-major-benefits-of-combining-these-two-mega-trends/#9649ae44b44b.

Feldstein, S., 2019. The Global Expansion of AI Surveillance the G. https://carnegieendowment.org/2019/09/17/global-expansion-of-ai-surveillance-pub-79847.

Hyken, S., 2018. Google Introduces Lifelike AI Experience with Google Duplex. Www.Forbes.Com. https://www.forbes.com/sites/shephyken/2018/05/13/google-introduces-lifelike-ai-experience-with-google-duplex/?sh=25d509194dcf.

Korn, M., 2016. Imagine discovering that your teaching assistant really is a robot. Wall St. J. http://www.wsj.com/articles/if-your-teacher-sounds-like-a-robot-you-might-be-on-to-something-1462546621.

Kumar, V., 2019. The Integration of AI and Blockchain for Industry 4.0. Analytics Insight. https://www.analyticsinsight.net/the-integration-of-ai-and-blockchain-for-industry-4-0/.

Laura, A., 2020. How Is Blockchain & AI Integration Changing the App Development Industry ? Yourstory. https://yourstory.com/mystory/blockchain-ai-integration-changing-app-devlopment-industry.

Mcdowell, B.H., 2020. More than Half of Hedge Funds Now Using AI Technology. https://www.thetradenews.com/half-hedge-funds-now-using-ai-technology/.

Pinto, R., 2018. Artificial Intelligence and the Humanities. Forbes. https://doi.org/10.1007/BF02259633.

Pollock, D., 2018. The Fourth Industrial Revolution Built on Blockchain and Advanced with AI. Forbes. https://www.forbes.com/sites/darrynpollock/2018/11/30/the-fourth-industrial-revolution-built-on-blockchain-and-advanced-with-ai/?sh=3cca14b24242.

n.d. Rahul, A.R., n.d. Blockchain-in-Ai.Pdf, pp. 1—17.

Wolfson, R., 2018. Diversifying Data with Artificial Intelligence and Blockchain Technology. Forbes. https://www.forbes.com/sites/rachelwolfson/2018/11/20/diversifying-data-with-artificial-intelligence-and-blockchain-technology/?sh=591dc4694dad.

Index

Note: 'Page numbers followed by "f" indicate figures and "t" indicate tables.'

A

Agri-food sector, 62
AICoin, 318
Alcohol biomanufacturing, 221—222
Alert generating, 109—110
AlphaNetworks, 314
Ambiguity, 275
Anomaly-based IDS, 108
Antiattack service provider (ASP), 287
Application protocol-based intrusion
    detection system, 112
Artificial intelligence (AI)
  AICoin, 318
  AlphaNetworks, 314
  asset exchange, 298
  Bext360, 314
  Blackbird.AI, 318
  Blackbox AI designs, 314
  blockchain, 305—308, 318
    explainable AI systems, 307
    privacy, 306
    security and scalability, 305—306
    smart contracts, 306—307
    untrustworthy devices, 307—308
    user-controlled data sharing, 307
  BotChain, 317
  Boxspring Media, 315
  BurstIQ, 314
  business data models, 302—303
  Chainhaus, 315
  challenges of, 310—311
  CoinGenius, 314
  computable labs, 317
  Core Scientific, 314
  Cyware Labs, 315
  data monetization, 309—310
  data protection, 309
  decentralized control, 297—298
  decision-making, 310
  deepbrain chain, 318
  digital intellectual property rights, 304

  diverse data sets, 309
  Dopamine, 317
  encrypted security, 313
  energy optimization, 313
  Figure, 315
  Finalize, 314
  Gainfy healthcare platform, 318
  Hannah Systems, 316
  immutability, 298
  industry 4.0, 311—312
  integration of, 301—302
  LiveEdu, 316
  managing and accessing data market,
    313
  matrix ai, 318
  merging, 302
  Mobs, 316
  Namahe, 318—319
  NetObjex, 315
  Neureal, 317
  newer insights and discovery, 303
  NUMERAI, 317
  ObEN, 316
  Peculium, 319
  self-governing organizations, 304—305
  SingularityNET, 319
  smart computing power, 308
  smart contracts, 313
  smart forecasts, 303—304
  Stowk, 316
  Synapse AI network, 317
  thinking process, 313
  Verisart, 315
  VIA, 314
  Vytalyx, 316
  Wealthblock.AI, 315
  Workdone, 316
Asset exchange, 298
Attack modeling, 129
Automatic license assignment,
    blockchain with, 198

B

Bext360, 314
Beyond 5G (B5G) technology, 142
Big data analytics, 64
Bioeconomy, 226–227
Biofuels development, 225–226
Biomanufacturing
  advancing machines as a service,
    218
  alcohol biomanufacturing,
    221–222
  bioeconomy, 226–227
  biofuels development, 225–226
  biomanufacturing proposed model,
    228–230
  bioproducts
    expiration, 221
    recall, 221
    serialization, 220–221
  blockchain, 212–213, 214t
    conception and functionality of,
      210–212
    data governance, 213
    disintermediation, 215
    elements of, 213–216, 215f
    infrastructure development, 216–218
    internal process management, 215
    provenance, 215–216
    records management, 213
    research and development data, 216
  COVID-19 vaccine, 223–224
  current challenges, 230–231
  current progress, 227–228
  distributed ledger technology (DLT),
    209–211
  Fabrec platform, 228–230
  future prospects, 231–232, 232f
  International Organization for
    Standardization (ISO), 210–211
  internet of medical things (IoMT),
    208–209
  inventory management, 219–220
  IP, 219
  machine-controlled maintenance, 219
  MiPasa platform, 224
  peer-to-peer (P2P) integrated network,
    208–209

  proposed model, 228–230
  simplifying and safeguarding quality
    checks, 220
  tech transfer, 219
  VIRI platform, 224
  WIShelter platform for assurance of
    privacy, 224–225
Bitcoin, 3–6, 16
Blackbird.AI, 318
Blackbox AI designs, 314
Block body, 36–38
Blockchain, 192–194, 198–199,
    212–213, 305–308, 318
  agri-food sector, 62
  analogy, 3
  applications of, 22–28, 23f
  architecture, 8–18
    consensus mechanisms, 9–10
    delegated proof of stake, 11
    proof of authority (PoA), 11–12
    proof of stake, 11
    proof of weight, 12
    proof of work, 10–11
    understanding, 8–9
  attacks, 51–52
  attacks against, 21–22
    Eclipse attack, 21
    fifty-one percent attack, 22
    Sybil attack, 21
    time-jacking attack, 21
  Bitcoin, 3–6, 16
  challenges of, 19–22
  characteristics of, 3
  consortium blockchain, 13
  Corda, 18
  cross-border payments, 24
  cryptocurrency, 18–19
  cyber technology. See Cyber
    technology
  data governance, 213
  decentralized protocols, 14
  digital signatures, 4–5
  disintermediation, 215
  ecosystem
    blockchain developers, 15
    blockchain exchanges, 15
    blockchain miners, 14–15

blockchain users, 15
elements of, 213–216, 215f
energy consumption, 20
EOS, 17–18
Ethereum, 6, 17
explainable AI systems, 307
history of, 5–6
Hyperledger, 17
infrastructure development, 216–218
internal process management, 215
limitations
    awareness and adoption, 132
    complexity and latency, 132
    cost and energy, 132
    management and regulations, 132
    security and privacy, 132
    size and organization, 132
liquidating real estate assets, 28
mortgages and loans, 22–24
motivation, 2–3
Multichain, 17
NEO, 18
online identity management, 25
overlay networks, 13
pharmaceutical industry, 268–271,
    269f–270f, 284–285
    clinical trial management, 284
    compliance and governance, 284
    counterfeit drugs and medical
        products prevention, 284
    integration, 293
    latency and throughput restrictions,
        292
    privacy, 292
    scalability, 292–293
    security, 291
    size, 292
privacy, 13, 306
property records, 27
protocols, 4–5
provenance, 215–216
public blockchain, 12, 12f
public health security, 25–26
public perception, 20
quorum, 18
real estate regulations, 28
records management, 213

rental property, 26–27
research and development data, 216
scalability, 20
security and scalability, 305–306
smart contracts, 6, 306–307
    data sales with, 307
standards and regulations, 20
stock trading, 24–25
summarizing, 3
support system, 14
system architecture of, 276–278
technology, 33–35
testing, 65
tracing of medicine, 26
traditional technologies, benefits over,
    6–8
    confidentiality, 7–8
    decentralized control, 6–7
    enhanced security, 8
    faster processing, 8
    integrity, 7
    transparency, 7
untrustworthy devices, 307–308
user-controlled data sharing, 307
user interface, 14
validity, 50–51
wallets, 4–5
Blockchain-based intrusion detection,
    120–122
Blockchain-based solution, 121–122
Blockchain-enabled cyber-physical
    systems
    healthcare sector, 76–78
    industrial control systems, 78–79
    nontechnical challenges, 83
    security attacks, 84–85
    smart cities, 79–80
    supply chain management,
        75–76, 77f
    technical challenges, 84
Blockchain-IoT aware drone-based
    medical delivery, 149–162
    collaborative and multiagent delivery,
        155–156, 157f
    epidemic support delivery, 156–159,
        158f
    forensic delivery, 159, 159f

Blockchain-IoT aware drone-based
  medical delivery (*Continued*)
  5G- and AI-assisted delivery, 161—162,
    162f, 163t—164t
  last mile delivery, 155, 156f
  smart city delivery, 159—161, 160f
Block header, 36
BotChain, 317
Boxspring Media, 315
BurstIQ, 314
Business data models, 302—303

C

Certificate service provider (CSP),
  286—287
Chainhaus, 315
Cloud-based centralized server, 122
CoinGenius, 314
Collaborative intrusion detection system
  (CIDN), 122—125, 123f
  data sharing, 124—125
  trust computation, 125
  trust management, 124
  working model of, 123—124
Combating counterfeit goods, 93
Communication, generator and server,
  96
Consensus, 186, 270
  algorithms, 43—49
    definition, 43
    delegated proof of stake (DPoS), 48
    forking, 43—46
    practical byzantine fault tolerance
      (PBFT), 48—49, 49f
    proof of stake (PoS), 46—48
    proof of work (PoW), 43—46, 45f
Consortium blockchain, 13, 113—114
Containers, 184
Content access, protecting, 182
Content control, 182
Content distribution, 180
Content recognizer, 183
Copyrights
  discoverability, 190
  law, 192—194
  multimedia works, 191—192
  trading fairness, 190

Corda, 18
Core Scientific, 314
Counterfeit drugs problem, 283—284
Cross-border payments, 24
Cryptocurrency, 18—19, 179
Cyber-physical system (CPS)
  background of, 69—73
  blockchain-enabled cyber-physical
    systems, 75—83, 81t—82t
  healthcare sector, 76—78
  industrial control systems, 78—79
  nontechnical challenges, 83
  security attacks, 84—85
  smart cities, 79—80
  supply chain management, 75—76,
    77f
  technical challenges, 84
defense systems, 72—73
  blockchain, 73—75
  consensus algorithms, 74
healthcare systems, 69, 70f
sniffing attack, 84
transportation, 69—70
urban infrastructure, 71, 72f
vehicular ad-hoc networks, 69—70
Cybersecurity, 62—63
Cyber technology
  architecture, 35—38
  big data analytics, 64
  block body, 36—38
  blockchain
    agri-food sector, 62
    attacks, 51—52
    cybersecurity, 62—63
    education, 58—59
    future scope, 64—65
    healthcare, 59—60
    identity management, 63—64
    logistics, 61—62
    supply chains, 61—62
    technology, 33—35
    testing, 65
    transportation, 61—62
    validity, 50—51
  block header, 36
  challenges, 54—56
  consensus algorithms, 43—49

definition, 43
delegated proof of stake (DPoS), 48
forking, 43—46
practical byzantine fault tolerance
(PBFT), 48—49, 49f
proof of stake (PoS), 46—48
proof of work (PoW), 43—46, 45f
decentralization, 65
emerging applications of, 56—64
Hash functions, 38—39
history, 33—35
Internet-of-Things (IoT), 56—57
merkle trees, 52—53
privacy leakage, 55—56
recent advances, 54—56
scalability, 54
secure, 53—54
selfish mining, 55
smart contracts, 57—58
timestamp, 39—43, 40f—41f
Cyware Labs, 315

D
Data governance, 213
Data handling, 275
Data monetization, 309—310
Data protection, 309
Decentralization, 65
Decentralized protocols, 14
Decision-making, 310
Deepbrain chain, 318
Deep learning (DL) technique, 143
Defense systems, 72—73
blockchain, 73—75
consensus algorithms, 74
Delegated proof of stake, 11
Design industry, blockchain
implementation in, 194—195
Designing drugledger, 286—287
Digital content
integrating blockchain with, 198—201
privacy of identity for, 182
Digital rights management (DRM)
automatic license assignment, 197—198
blockchain, 192—194, 198—199
limitation, 201—202
consensus, 186

containers, 184
content access, protecting, 182
content control, 182
content distribution, 180
content recognizer, 183
copyrights
discoverability, 190
law, 192—194
multimedia works, 191—192
trading fairness, 190
cryptocurrencies, 179
decentralized, 185
design industry, blockchain
implementation in, 194—195
digital content
integrating blockchain with,
198—201
privacy of identity for, 182
distributed ledger, 186
diversity in mining rigs, 196—197
educational learning passports, 191
educational resources, multimedia
community of, 191
efficient method, 190
end user player (EUP), 184—185
enhanced security, 185
faster responses, 186
fingerprints, 184
future research, 202—203
immutability, 185
licensing, 182
master-slave blockchain architecture,
196—197
MD5 algorithm, 186—187
meta data, 183
methodologies, 188—190
music industry, 192
noncomputing model (NCM), 197
peer-to-peer sharing, 200
privacy, 190
reception default, 191
repetitive registrations, protection from,
190—191
requirement, 180—182
research data, storing, 180
royalty, 199—200
scalability, 195

Digital rights management (DRM)
    (*Continued*)
  security
    licenses, 184
    maintenance, 190
    SHA-0 algorithm, 187—188
    SHA-1 algorithm, 188
    SHA-2 algorithm, 188
    SHA-256 algorithm, 188
    stake consensus methodolog, proof of,
      195—196
    tamper proofness, content verifiability
      along with, 181—182
    technology in use, 188—190
    trademarking, 182
    violation detection, 182
    watermark, 183—184
Digital signatures, 4—5
Disintermediation, 215
Distributed ledgers, 186, 270
Dopamine, 317
Drone-based medical delivery
    architecture, 141f
Drugledger, performance measures of,
    284
Drug supply chain, 285—286
  management, 278—283
  smart contract in, 281—282

E
Eclipse attack, 21
Ecologic condition, 165
Ecosystem
  blockchain developers, 15
  blockchain exchanges, 15
  blockchain miners, 14—15
  blockchain users, 15
Educational learning passports, 191
Educational resources, multimedia
    community of, 191
Electronic voting
  distributed e-voting, 250—260
    blockchain-based e-voting, 252—257,
      258t—260t
    some issues in, 257—260
  internet voting, 241

  issues in, 248—250
  optical mark-sense scanner, 240
  pollster, 243
  registrar, 243
  security properties
    eligibility, 244
    fairness, 244
    lack of coercibility, 244
    lack of reusability, 244
    privacy, 244
    receipt-less, 244
    verifiability, 244
    voter anonymity, 244
  significant contributions in, 245—248
  tallier, 244
  trusted third party (TTP), 241—242
  validator, 243—244
  voter, 242
Encrypted security, 313
End user player (EUP), 184—185
Energy
  consumption, 20, 271
  management, 165
  optimization, 313
Enhanced security, 185
Epidemic support delivery, 156—159,
    158f
Ethereum, 6, 17
Extended security, 284

F
Fabrec platform, 228—230
Faster processing, 270
Faster responses, 186
Fifty-one percent attack, 22
Finalize, 314
Fingerprints, 184
Forensic delivery, 159, 159f
Forking, 43—46

G
Gainfy healthcare platform, 318
5G- and AI-assisted delivery, 161—162,
    162f, 163t—164t
Generator module, functional units of,
    97—98

H

Handling drug counterfeiting, smart
  contract and blockchain tracking
  for, 277–278
Hannah Systems, 316
Hash functions, 38–39
Healthcare, 59–60
  industries, 271–276
    blockchain infrastructure, 274
    patient data management, 273
    payer data management, 273–274
  systems, 69, 70f
Health record storage cost, 162–165
Hyperledger, 17

I

Immutability, 185, 269–270, 298
Industrial control systems, 78–79
Industry 4.0, 311–312
Infrastructure development, 216–218
Internal process management, 215
International Organization for
  Standardization (ISO), 210–211
Internet of medical things (IoMT),
  208–209
Internet-of-Things (IoT), 56–57
Internet of things (IoT)-based medical
  delivery drones
  beyond 5G (B5G) technology, 142
  blockchain-IoT aware drone-based
    medical delivery, 149–162
  collaborative and multiagent delivery,
    155–156, 157f
  epidemic support delivery, 156–159,
    158f
  forensic delivery, 159, 159f
  5G- and AI-assisted delivery,
    161–162, 162f, 163t–164t
  last mile delivery, 155, 156f
  smart city delivery, 159–161, 160f
  deep learning (DL) technique, 143
  drone-based medical delivery
    architecture, 141f
  ecologic condition, 165
  energy management, 165
  future direction, 167–168
  health record storage cost, 162–165

latency and throughput, 165
legal disputes, 165
medical delivery, drone suppliers for,
  145–149, 150f–151f, 152t–154t
participation incentive, 166
regulatory constraints, 167
research gap, 144
resource utilization, 166
standard architecture, 166
technology adoption, 167
trust management, 143
unmanned aerial system (UAS), 143
vulnerability, 166
Internet voting, 241
Intrusion detection systems
  alert generating, 109–110
  anomaly-based IDS, 108
  application protocol-based intrusion
    detection system, 112
  applications, 125–130
    NIDS mode, 126
    Packet logger mode, 126
    Sniffer mode, 126
    snort-based CID with blockchain,
      126–128
  attack modeling, 129
  block, 116
  blockchain, 118–119
  blockchain-based intrusion detection,
    120–122
  blockchain-based solution,
    121–122
  blockchain limitations
    awareness and adoption, 132
    complexity and latency, 132
    cost and energy, 132
    management and regulations, 132
    security and privacy, 132
    size and organization, 132
  cloud-based centralized server, 122
  collaborative intrusion detection system
    (CIDN), 122–125, 123f
    data sharing, 124–125
    trust computation, 125
    trust management, 124
    working model of, 123–124
  consensus algorithms, 117–118, 120

Intrusion detection systems (*Continued*)
  consortium blockchain, 113—114
  design evaluation, 128—130
  false negative (FN), 129
  false positive (FP), 129
  firewalls, comparison with, 134
  future scope, 134
  host-based intrusion detection system,
    119—120
    working of, 119—120
  host intrusion detection system, 111,
    111f
  hybrid blockchain, 114
  hybrid intrusion detection system, 112
  information gathering, 109
  integrity, 120
  limitations, 130—131, 133
    handling capability limited, traffic
      overhead with, 130
    incorrect profile establishment,
      130—131
    limited range, signature coverage in,
      130
    major false warnings, 131
  miners, 116
  network intrusion detection
    system, 110
  nodes, 116—117
  organization of the paper, 108—109
  practical byzantine fault tolerance
    (PBFT), 117
  privacy, 120
  private blockchain, 113
  proof of burn (PoB), 117—118
  proof of capacity (PoC), 118
  proof of elapsed time (PoET), 118
  proof of stake (PoS), 117
  proof of work (PoW), 117
  protocol-based intrusion detection
    system, 112
  public blockchain, 113
  scalability, 120
  security, blockchain, 114—117
  signature-based IDS, 108
  true negative (TN), 129
  true positive (TP), 129
Inventory management, 219—220

L

Last mile delivery, 155, 156f
Latency, 165
Legal disputes, 165
Licensing, 182
Liquidating real estate assets, 28
LiveEdu, 316
Loans, 22—24
Logistics, 61—62

M

Machine-controlled maintenance, 219
Master-slave blockchain architecture,
  196—197
Matrix ai, 318
MD5 algorithm, 186—187
Medical delivery, drone suppliers for,
  145—149, 150f—151f, 152t—154t
Merkle trees, 52—53
Meta data, 183
Mining rigs diversity, 196—197
MiPasa platform, 224
Mobility, 245
Mobs, 316
Mortgages, 22—24
Motivation, 2—3
Multichain, 17
Music industry, 192

N

Namahe, 318—319
NEO, 18
NetObjex, 315
Neureal, 317
NIDS mode, 126
Noncomputing model (NCM), 197
Nontrusted module communication, 97
NUMERAI, 317

O

ObEN, 316
Optical mark-sense scanner, 240

P

Packet logger mode, 126
Participation incentive, 166
Peculium, 319

Peer-to-peer (P2P) integrated network, 208–209
Peer-to-peer sharing, 200
Pharmaceutical industry
  ambiguity, 275
  antiattack service provider (ASP), 287
  blockchain, 268–271, 269f–270f, 284–285
    blockchain size, 292
    clinical trial management, 284
    complexity, 271
    compliance and governance, 284
    counterfeit drugs and medical products prevention, 284
    integration, 293
    latency and throughput restrictions, 292
    privacy, 292
    scalability, 292–293
    security, 291
    system architecture of, 276–278
  certificate service provider (CSP), 286–287
  collection, 275
  consensus, 270
  counterfeit drugs problem, 283–284
  data handling, 275
  decentralized, 269
  designing drugledger, 286–287
  distributed ledgers, 270
  drugledger, performance measures of, 284
  drug supply chain, 285–286
    management, 278–283
    smart contract in, 281–282
  energy consumption, 271
  extended security, 284
  faster processing, 270
  handling drug counterfeiting, smart contract and blockchain tracking for, 277–278
  healthcare industries, 271–276
    blockchain infrastructure, 274
    patient data management, 273
    payer data management, 273–274
  immutability, 269–270

  pharmaceuticals, data disparity in, 274–275
  privacy protection, 285
  query service provider, 287
  scalability, 271
  security, 270
  sluggish and cumbersome operations, 271
  supply chain, 275–276
    distributed ledger in, 283
    transaction procedure in, 282–283
  system architecture of blockchain, 276–278
  traceability, 285
  transparency, 285
Pollster, 243
Practical byzantine fault tolerance (PBFT), 48–49, 49f
Privacy, 190
  leakage, 55–56
  protection, 285
Proof of stake (PoS), 11, 46–48
Proof of weight, 12
Proof of work (PoW), 10–11, 43–46, 45f
Proposed model, 228–230

Q
Query service provider, 287

R
Real-time transactions, novel secured ledger platform for
  combating counterfeit goods, 93
  generator and server communication, 96
  generator module, functional units of, 97–98
  nontrusted module communication, 97
  server module, functional units of, 98–100
  use cases, 100–103
  validator and server communication, 96–97
  validator module, functional units of, 98
Reception default, 191

Records management, 213
Registrar, 243
Regulatory constraints, 167
Repetitive registrations, protection from, 190–191
Research and development data, 216
Research data, storing, 180
Resource utilization, 166
Robustness, 245
Royalty, 199–200

S

Scalability, 54, 195, 271
Security, 270
  attacks, 84–85
  licenses, 184
  maintenance, 190
  properties
    eligibility, 244
    fairness, 244
    lack of coercibility, 244
    lack of reusability, 244
    privacy, 244
    receipt-less, 244
    verifiability, 244
    voter anonymity, 244
Self-governing organizations, 304–305
Selfish mining, 55
Server module, functional units of, 98–100
SHA-0 algorithm, 187–188
SHA-1 algorithm, 188
SHA-2 algorithm, 188
SHA-256 algorithm, 188
Simplifying and safeguarding quality checks, 220
SingularityNET, 319
Sluggish and cumbersome operations, 271
Smart cities, 79–80
  delivery, 159–161, 160f
Smart computing power, 308
Smart contracts, 57–58, 313
Smart forecasts, 303–304
Sniffer mode, 126
Snort-based CID with blockchain, 126–128

Stake consensus methodolog, proof of, 195–196
Standard architecture, 166
Stowk, 316
Supply chain, 61–62, 275–276
  distributed ledger in, 283
  management, 75–76, 77f
    transaction procedure in, 282–283
  transaction procedure in, 282–283
Sybil attack, 21
Synapse AI network, 317

T

Tamper proofness, content verifiability along with, 181–182
Technology in use, 188–190
Time-jacking attack, 21
Timestamp, 39–43, 40f–41f
Traceability, 285
Trademarking, 182
Transparency, 285
Transportation, 61–62, 69–70
Trusted third party (TTP), 241–242
Trust management, 143

U

Unmanned aerial system (UAS), 143
Urban infrastructure, 71, 72f

V

Validator, 243–244
  server communication, 96–97
Vehicular ad-hoc networks, 69–70
Verisart, 315
VIA, 314
Violation detection, 182
VIRI platform, 224
Voter, 242
Vulnerability, 166
Vytalyx, 316

W

Watermark, 183–184
Wealthblock.AI, 315
WIShelter platform for assurance of privacy, 224–225
Workdone, 316

Printed in the United States
by Baker & Taylor Publisher Services